FRAGMENTED FATHERLAND

Monographs in German History

FRAGMENTED FATHERLAND

Immigration and Cold War Conflict
in the Federal Republic of Germany,
1945–1980

Alexander Clarkson

berghahn
NEW YORK · OXFORD
www.berghahnbooks.com

Published in 2013 by

Berghahn Books

www.berghahnbooks.com

© 2013 Alexander Clarkson

Library of Congress Cataloging-in-Publication Data

Clarkson, Alexander, 1977-
    Fragmented fatherland : immigration and Cold War conflict in the Federal
    Republic of Germany, 1945-1980 / Alexander Clarkson. -- First edition.
      pages cm
    Includes bibliographical references.
    ISBN 978-0-85745-958-9 (hardback : acid-free paper) -- ISBN (invalid)
978-0-85745-959-6 (ebook)
1. Minorities--Germany (West)--History--20th century. 2.
Immigrants--Germany (West)--History--20th century. 3. Immigrants--Germany
(West)--Politics and government--20th century. 4. Immigrants--Government
policy--Germany (West)--History--20th century. 5. Cold War--Social aspects-
-Germany (West)--History. 6. Ethnic conflict--Germany (West)--History--
20th century. 7. Cultural pluralism--Germany (West)--History--20th century.
8. Germany (West)--Ethnic relations--History--20th century. 9. Germany
(West)--Emigration and immigration--Social aspects--History--20th century. 10.
Germany (West)--Politics and government--1945-1990. I. Title.
    DD258.5.C55 2013
    305.9'06912094309045--dc23
                                                                2012032940

British Library Cataloguing in Publication Data
A catalogue record for this book is available from the
British Library

Printed in the United States on acid-free paper

ISBN 978-0-85745-958-9 (hardback)

ISBN 978-0-85745-959-6 (institutional ebook)

To Διdo and Pompa

Contents

ACKNOWLEDGEMENTS

For all the kindness they have shown in the course of this project I would like to thank Christoph Bachmann and Otto-Karl Tröger at the Bavarian State Archives, Knud Piening at the Politisches Archiv des Auswärtigen Amtes and Christian Schwack at the BStU in Berlin. I am also indebted to Father Josip Klaric at the Croatian Catholic Mission in Offenbach as well as Volodymyr Lenyk and Iwanna Rebet at the Ukrainian Free University for the many insights they offered into the life of their communities.

For their help and advice I would like to thank Rainer Ohliger, Michael Masepow and Tetyana Cherevko at the Humboldt Universität, Karen Schönwälder at the WZB and Roberto Sala at the Freie Universität in Berlin. I would also like to thank David Parrott and Ruth Harris at New College, Dominik Zaum at Reading, Oliver Zimmer and Hartmut Pogge von Strandmann at University College and Martin Conway at Balliol for the support they have given. A big thank you to my supervisor Nick Stargardt at Magdalen, whose patience, guidance and enthusiasm was invaluable throughout this project.

I would like to thank my mother, Irene, my father, Harold, and my sister, Claudia, for always being there for me as well as my little sister, Emma, for showing up along the way. Finally, I would like to thank my wife, Heather, for being my anchor in a stormy sea.

ABBREVIATIONS AND ACRONYMS

Countries

BRD/FRG   Bundesrepublik Deutschland/Federal Republic of Germany.
DDR/GDR   Deutsche Demokratische Republik/German Democratic Republic.
USSR   Union of Soviet Socialist Republics.

Political Parties

CDU   Christian Democratic Union/Christlich Demokratische Union (FRG).
CSU   Christian Social Union/Christlich-Soziale Union (FRG).
DKP   German Communist Party/Deutsche Kommunistische Partei (FRG).
EDA   United Democratic Left/Eniaa Dimokratiki Aristera (Greece).
ETA   Basque Homeland and Freedom/Euskadi Ta Askatasuna (Spain/Basque Country).
FDP   Free Democratic Party/Freie Demokratische Partei (FRG).
FLN   National Liberation Front/Front de Libération Nationale (Algeria).
GDP   Pan-German Party/Gesamtdeutsche Partei (FRG).
HDO   Croatian Liberation Movement/Hrvatski Domobrani Odbor (Croatia).
HNO   Croat People's Resistance/Hrvatski Narodni Otpor (Croatia).
HOP   Croatian Liberation Movement/Hrvatski Oslobilacki Pokret (Croatia).
IMRO   Internal Macedonian Revolutionary Organization/ Vnatrešna Makedonska Revolucionerna Organizacija (Macedonia).
KKE   Greek Communist Party/Kommunistiko Komma Elladas (Greece).
KPD   Communist Party of Germany/Kommunistische Partei Deutschlands (FRG).

MHP	Nationalist Movement Party/Milliyetçi Hareket Partisi (Turkey).
NPD	National Democratic Party/Nationaldemokratische Partei Deutschlands (FRG).
OUN	Organization of Ukrainian Nationalists/Orhanizatsiya Ukrayins'kykh Natsionalistiv (Ukraine).
OUN-B	Organization of Ukrainian Nationalists-Bandera (Ukraine).
OUN-M	Organization of Ukrainian Nationalists-Melnyk (Ukraine).
PAE	Panhellenic Antidictatorial Union (Greece).
PAK	Panhellenic Liberation Movement/PanellinioApeleftherotiko Kinima (Greece).
PAM	Patriotic Antidictatorial Front (Greece).
PCE	Communist Party of Spain/Partido Comunista de España (Spain).
PKK	Kurdistan Workers Party/Partiya Karkerên Kurdistan (Turkey/Kurdistan).
PSOE	Socialist Party of Spain/Partido Socialista Obrero Español (Spain).
NTS	National Alliance of Russian Solidarists/Narudno-Trudovoy Soyuz (Russia).
RAF	Red Army Faction/Rote Armee Fraktion (FRG).
SED	Socialist Unity Party of Germany/Sozialistische Einheitspartei Deutschlands (GDR).
SPD	Social Democratic Party of Germany/Sozialdemokratische Partei Deutschlands (FRG).

Organizations and Groups

ABN	Anti-Bolshevik Bloc of Nations (International).
ALN	Armée de Libération Nationale/National Liberation Army (Algeria).
ACLI	Association of Catholic Workers of Italy/Associazioni Cristiane Lavoratori Italiani (Italy).
CISNU	Confederation of Iranian Students/National Union (Iran).
DGB	German Trade Union Federation/Deutscher Gewerkschaftbund (FRG).
DPs	Displaced Persons (International).
FDJ	Freie Deutsche Jugend/Free German Youth (GDR).
OAS	Secret Armed Organisation/Organisation Armeé Secrete (France).
SDS	Socialist German Student Union/Sozialistischer Deutscher Studentenbund (GDR).
UFU	Ukrainian Free University (Ukraine).
VDS	Confederation of German Student Unions/Verband Deutscher Studentenschaften (FRG).

| VVN | Association of Victims of the Nazi Regime/Vereinigung der Verfolgten des Naziregimes (FRG). |
| VW | Volkswagen (International). |

Security and Intelligence Organizations

BfV	Federal Office for the Protection of the Constitution/ Bundesamt für Verfassungsschutz (FRG).
BGS	Federal Border Protection Agency/Bundesgrenzschutz (FRG).
BKA	Federal Criminal Police Office of Germany/ Bundeskriminalamt (FRG).
BND	Federal Intelligence Service/Bundesnachrichtendienst (FRG).
CIA	Central Intelligence Agency (United States).
CIC	Counter Intelligence Corps (United States).
KGB	Committee for State Security/Komitet Gosudarstvennoy Bezopasnosti (Soviet Union).
KYP	Central Intelligence Service/Kentralii Ypiresia Pliroforion (Greece).
LfV	State Office for the Protection of the Constitution/ Landesamt für Verfassungsschutz (FRG).
LKA	State Criminal Police Agency/Landeskriminalamt (FRG).
MAD	Military Intelligence Service/Militärischer Abschirmdienst (FRG).
NATO	North Atlantic Treaty Organization (International).
NKVD	People's Commisariat for Internal Affairs/Naro'dnõi Komissariat Vnutrennih Del (Soviet Union).
OG	Organization Gehlen (FRG).
OZNA	Department for Protection of the People/Organ Zaštite Naroda (Armije) (Yugoslavia).
SAVAK	Organization for Intelligence and National Security/ Sazeman-e Ettelaat va Amniyat-e Keshvar (Iran).
SD	Security Service/Sicherheitsdienst (Germany).
SIS (MI6)	Secret Intelligence Service (UK).
SS	Protection Squad/Schutzstaffel (Germany).
Stasi	State Security Service/Staatssicherheitsdienst (GDR).
UdBA	Yugoslav Internal Security Services/Uprava državne Bezbednosti (Yugoslavia).
UPA	Ukrainian Patriotic (Insurgent) Army/Ukrayins'ka Povstans'ka Armia (Ukraine).

Archives

Bay. HstA. Mun.	Bayerisches Hauptstaatsarchiv Munich.
B.K.	Bundesarchiv Koblenz.
BStU	Berlin Bundesbeauftragte für Staatsicherheitsunterlagen.
HstA. H.W.	Hauptstaatsarchiv Hessen Wiesbaden.
HstA. NRW	Hauptstaatsarchiv Nordrhein Westfalen.
L.B.	Landesarchiv Berlin.
NHstA. Hann.	Niedersächsisches Hauptstaatsarchiv Hannover.
Pol. A.A.Ber.	Politisches Archiv des Auswärtigen Amtes Berlin.

Newspapers and Magazines

Bild	*Bild Zeitung.*
B.G.	*Bonner Generalanzeiger.*
B.R.	*Bonner Rundschau.*
F.A.Z.	*Frankfurter Allgemeine Zeitung.*
F.R.	*Frankfurter Rundschau.*
H.A.Z.	*Hannoversche Allgemeine Zeitung.*
H.P.	*Hannoversche Neue Presse.*
M.M.	*Münchener Merkur.*
D.S.	*Der Spiegel.*
S.Z.	*Süddeutsche Zeitung.*
D.W.	*Die Welt.*

Introduction

NEW NEIGHBOURS, NEW CHALLENGES
RECOGNIZING DIVERSITY

On a cold winter's day in 1995, the war for Kurdish independence claimed another victim. Activists belonging to the PKK and other Kurdish nationalist organizations fighting the Turkish Army in Eastern Anatolia had decided to go ahead with a demonstration in a large industrial city, despite a ban on such protests imposed by the local police. With scores of Kurds facing off against a similar number of Turkish nationalists in a volatile neighbourhood, the police decided to send in riot squads to break up the demonstration. This only managed to enflame the situation, leading to running battles between Kurds, the police and Turks that spread into the city centre. In the chaos, a policeman surrounded by PKK supporters pulled his gun and fired several shots, hitting and mortally wounding a sixteen-year-old Kurdish activist. As with thousands of similar cases across Turkey, his subsequent funeral was transformed into yet another violent demonstration for Kurdish independence.[1]

This incident did not take place in Turkey, Iran or Syria. Rather, it marked the climax of a wave of protests organized by Kurdish immigrants in the north German city of Hanover. These demonstrations were part of a wider political campaign waged by the PKK against the Turkish government across the Federal Republic. It included blockades of key Autobahns by Kurdish women and children and public acts of self-immolation by Kurdish activists in several German cities. Losing the guerrilla war in Turkey itself, the PKK hoped that these measures could force the German government to break off diplomatic relations with the Turkish state. In many cities and towns, Germans suddenly saw neighbours, who they had lived next to for years, arrested or questioned by the police as a state crackdown on the PKK widened to include every kind of Kurdish organization.[2] Though these measures proved counterproductive, they did manage to raise the profile of the Kurdish war among German journalists and politicians. Together with the growth of Islamic fundamentalist organizations in Muslim immigrant communities, the PKK campaign drew the attention of the German state and public towards the political life of its immigrant population.[3]

These communities were not the first to engage in widespread and often violent political action in the Federal Republic. Long before Kurdish nationalist or Islamic fundamentalist organizations took centre stage in the 1990s, immigrant political movements were doing their best to attract the attention and support of West German citizens and governments. Rather than being a post-Cold War phenomenon, protest and violence organized by immigrant activists has been an established part of West German political life since the first days of the Federal Republic. By 1989, West German government officials and politicians had developed forty years of experience in dealing with many different kinds of immigrant political organizations. As a consequence, the activity of these movements not only shaped the political and social environment of West Germany's immigrant population, it also had a major impact on the political development of the Federal Republic.

The political parties (SPD, CDU/CSU and FDP), trade union and business federations, security services and bureaucratic institutions, which collectively defined the West German political establishment by 1989, were confronted with immigrant communities that had emerged as a result of several different forms of migration. In the immediate aftermath of the Second World War, millions of refugees from Eastern Europe found themselves in displaced persons (DPs) camps in the Federal Republic. Though most moved on to North America, some stayed in West Germany in order to live as close as possible to their homelands.[4] The second and more numerically significant wave of migration was triggered by a state-backed guest worker programme to ameliorate labour shortages in the late 1950s and early 1960s. By 1988, over 5.2 million of these economic migrants, who mostly came from Southern Europe and Turkey, had settled permanently in the Federal Republic.[5] Along with the guest worker programme, thousands of other migrants settled in West Germany for many other reasons during this period. Causes as diverse as refugees seeking asylum, North Atlantic Treaty Organization (NATO) soldiers stationed in West Germany settling there after leaving the army or non-German students staying on after receiving their degrees lay behind the expansion of immigrant communities.[6] The successive waves of immigration between the end of the Second World War in 1945 and the termination of the guest worker programme in 1975 laid the groundwork for the ethnic and religious diversity that has become such an important aspect of contemporary German society.

Despite the rapid growth in the number of immigrants and refugees, the centre-right Christian Democratic and Christian Social Unions (CDU/CSU) as well as many members of the centre-left Social Democratic Party of Germany (SPD) remained unwilling to accept that Germany was no longer an ethnically homogeneous society. Though by the early 1990s the liberal Free Democratic Party (FDP) and the Green Party acknowledged the new social and ethnic realities created by mass immigration, the CDU/CSU continued to claim that Germany was not a 'country of immigration' until Helmut Kohl was voted out of office in 1998.[7] This fixation on ethnic homogeneity was fostered by a national narrative based on shared guilt and suffering during the Second World War as well as assertions of solidarity with ethnic German minorities living in the Soviet bloc.[8]

The unwillingness of the two largest political parties to grapple with the social implications of mass immigration had a direct impact on policy making throughout the Cold War. In the early 1970s, a backlash among working-class voters against what they perceived to be increasing competition for a decreasing number of jobs forced an SPD-led government to end the officially sanctioned recruitment of guest workers in 1973.[9] In order to mollify their working class electoral base, SPD politicians repeatedly claimed that they would 'get tough' on guest workers and other economic migrants whose work visas or employment contracts had expired. This even included bans on further work permits for non-Germans in cities in which the guest worker population was considered to be too large.[10] At the same time, the centre-right CDU/CSU responded to popular malaise about immigration by promising to encourage the repatriation of immigrants to their native countries through a (unsuccessful) system of resettlement grants.[11]

These measures were the product of a kind of institutional schizophrenia towards immigrant communities that had already begun to take shape in the early years of the Federal Republic. On the one hand, claims made by West German politicians and senior officials that the large-scale presence of non-Germans was temporary ensured that, on both the federal ('Bund') and regional ('Land') levels of government, very few efforts were made to prepare state institutions and the West German public for the social changes caused by mass immigration. On the other hand, local police, education and welfare authorities were forced to cope with the challenge of integrating large numbers of immigrants and assuaging the concerns of Germans who were learning to live together with new neighbours who possessed very different religious and ethnic backgrounds. The abject failure of SPD and CDU/CSU policies to decrease immigrant numbers before 1989 demonstrated that a remarkably diverse range of ethnic communities had become a permanent part of the German social landscape.

Many of these newcomers did not necessarily conform to the stereotype, held by many Germans to this day, of the immigrant as an impoverished economic migrant. Each immigrant community had its own complex social structure depending on the educational and class background of its members. Though the majority of DPs, guest workers or refugees found work in industrial or menial occupations, many better educated immigrants were academics and professionals, while a number of entrepreneurs also emerged in some of the largest immigrant communities.[12]

The social diversity of the immigrant population helped foster its politicization. By the late 1960s, many non-German students and academics were heavily involved in radical left-wing movements hostile to both the social democrats and pro-Soviet communists. Moreover, conservative and fervently anti-communist immigrant academics and businessmen openly supported the West German Right.[13] Though politicized students often helped less educated compatriots in their dealings with West German authorities, immigrants working in low paying occupations were also able to play a leading role in political organizations. The existence of vigorous workers' movements in several immigrant homelands also meant that a significant number of guest workers were prepared to join West German trade unions. In the early 1970s, a series of strikes in Cologne led by Turkish and Greek guest workers in defiance of local union functionaries demonstrated the ability of working-class immigrants to organize themselves independently.[14] As immigrants of all social backgrounds began to settle more permanently in major cities, many set up local community organizations that were involved in a variety of national and local issues from the improvement of local schools to environmental conservation projects.[15]

Despite such considerable ethnic and social diversity, there was one factor that most of these immigrant communities had in common. With the exception of Italy, the countries involved in the West German labour importation programme were governed by authoritarian regimes: Spain and Portugal were ruled by right-wing dictatorships until the mid 1970s; a military junta controlled the Greek government between 1967 and 1974; Turkey experienced three military coups between 1961 and 1985; Algeria, Tunisia, Egypt and Jordan all experienced colonial domination and, after decolonization, authoritarian government; Yugoslavia was governed by a communist regime whose ambivalent relationship with the West was only ameliorated by its hostility to the Soviet Union. Moreover, East European émigrés had fled from either the USSR or countries under Soviet control in which communist parties were prepared to use force against their internal opponents. Thus, many organizations and parties opposed to the social status quo of these countries did their best to recruit guest workers and refugees to their cause in the relatively open political spaces of the Federal Republic.[16]

As a result, the majority of immigrant political movements in Cold War West Germany were, like Kurdish nationalist movements, preoccupied with the political development of their homelands, rather than the integration of their members into West German society. The East European émigré communities that had emerged from the displaced persons camps were particularly well organized. DPs and other refugees from the Soviet bloc remained fixated upon achieving regime change in their homelands, in the hope that they could return after the fall of the communist governments that had forced them into exile. Succeeding waves of refugees and students from Third World countries such as Iran were similarly dominated by political organizations affiliated with opposition or insurgent groups in their homelands.[17]

The transient nature of the guest worker population, a key element of the labour importation programme, strengthened the homeland orientation of most economic migrants. Both West German policy makers and many guest workers themselves believed that the presence of imported labour was only temporary. The former hoped that guest workers could be replaced by Germans once the labour shortages of the early 1960s had been overcome, while the latter hoped to eventually return to their homelands after a few years of work in West Germany. Until the recruitment was stopped by the Brandt government in 1973, forcing many to make a permanent choice, guest workers regularly moved back and forth between West Germany and their country of origin. Even after many economic migrants brought their families over to the Federal Republic, most still aimed to return to their old homelands once they had saved up enough money.[18] Such a strong fixation on the 'myth of return' encouraged many guest workers to continue to take a deep interest in the political fate of their homelands long after they had first arrived in Germany.

These tendencies were aggravated by the many legal and social obstacles that confronted immigrants who wanted to take a direct part in the West German political process. West German state institutions and political parties actively encouraged senior émigrés living in the Federal Republic to concentrate on their own community infrastructure in order to channel them away from German politics.[19] Because West German citizenship law made it extremely difficult for anyone without German ancestry to acquire a West German passport, the immigrant workers arriving after 1954 were excluded from the mainstream political process in an even more fundamental fashion. Consequently, most guest workers interested in politics were more likely to participate in organizations focused on the countries of which they were still citizens rather than the country in which they lived and worked.[20]

This book will examine the responses of West German state and party-political institutions towards such immigrant political movements during the Cold War. Based primarily on written sources from German state archives, the aim of this study is to explore how diaspora politics has affected the position of immigrants in West German society. On a wider level, it will also try to develop a better understanding of how immigration was intertwined with other major social and political trends, which shaped the Federal Republic. Over five chapters, this study will particularly focus on the Ukrainian, Croatian, Algerian, Spanish, Greek and Iranian communities. It will cover the period from the late 1940s, when the state and party-political institutions that confronted immigrants were created, to the aftermath of the termination of the guest worker programme in the mid and late 1970s, which marked a shift in West German attitudes towards immigration.[21]

The first chapter will examine the relationship of anti-communist émigré activists in the Ukrainian community, one of the largest ethnic groups in the displaced persons camps of the 1940s, with West German state institutions and politicians. Though it contained several political groups, the Ukrainian community managed to maintain a minimum of cohesion, enabling its leaders to use good relations with a variety of senior figures in West German federal and provincial governments to their own advantage. This chapter will consequently show how interaction between the historical legacy of the Nazi era and ideological polarization fostered by the Cold War had a crucial impact on relations between East European émigrés and their German counterparts.

The second chapter will explore the fate of Croatian nationalists in the Federal Republic. After the introduction of the guest worker programme in 1954, community institutions set up by the small group of Croatian émigrés who had settled in Germany after the Second World War were quickly overwhelmed by a growing number of Croatian guest workers. The Croatian community was therefore the only immigrant group that was made up of both postwar émigrés and guest workers. After 1962, relations between Croatian émigrés and their allies in the CDU/CSU came under increasing strain as militant Croatian nationalists and the Yugoslav state began to fight a proxy war on German territory. This chapter will look at how the willingness of senior Croatian activists to use violence against their opponents affected West German attitudes towards the wider Croatian community. In particular, it will examine the reasons why the use of violent tactics by Croatian activists increased pressure on West German conservatives to distance themselves from militantly anti-communist Croatian groups.

By focusing on Algerian and Spanish communities in the Federal Republic, the third chapter will scrutinize two immigrant groups in which left-wing organizations dominated political life. The first part of this chapter will examine the activity of Algerian nationalists, while the second part will take a look at the extensive links between Spanish opposition groups and the mainstream West German Left. In both cases, the international political context and specific nature of the immigrant communities in which these opposition movements operated imposed certain constraints on mainstream West German politicians who wished to help them. Though Algerian nationalists enjoyed the backing of many individual German liberals and social democrats, they did not acquire the kind of direct institutional support that the SPD or trade union organizations were willing to provide to Spanish socialists.

The fourth chapter will explore the different approaches taken by West German political parties and state institutions towards the activity of militant political organizations within the Greek community. The internal political and social diversity of the Greek community meant that various kinds of left-wing community organizations had to actively compete with each other as well as right-wing groups for the support of their fellow countrymen. The reaction of West German state officials and politicians towards acts of protest and terror committed by members of such an ideologically heterogeneous community were not conditioned by any deep abhorrence of violent action within the West German political establishment. Rather, this chapter will show how the response of West German political and state institutions towards the actions of politicized Greek immigrants was shaped by a combination of strategic ideological concerns on the national level and tactical considerations on a local level.

The fifth chapter will scrutinize the impact of Cold War conflict upon Iranians in the Federal Republic. By transcending cultural and religious differences, the common language of Cold War conflict provided a means with which Iranian political groups opposed to their homeland government could position themselves in the political framework of the Federal Republic. At the same time, allusions to the Nazi regime were used by both supporters and opponents of the Iranian opposition to either glorify or discredit the actions of

Iranian activists. This final chapter will illustrate how the ideological language of the Cold War shaped the way Iranian activists used such historical comparisons, exacerbating political pressures, which forced Iranians opposed to their homeland regime to work with German organizations outside the parliamentary mainstream of the Federal Republic.

By focusing on ethnic communities with very different social structures, this study will examine the interaction between immigrant networks and West German state institutions as well as the ways in which such patterns of cooperation and conflict differ. In focusing on groups from Italy and the Turkish Republic, the great bulk of academic research on the effect of immigration on the Federal Republic has tended to gloss over the extent to which this extensive period of mass migration drew in students, refugees, ex-soldiers and workers from an extraordinarily wide range of countries. Though it will regularly use Turkish, Kurdish and Italian groups as points of comparison, this study looks at communities that have attracted less academic attention, asking whether assumptions made about immigrant communities in Germany based on studies of groups from Italy and Turkey necessarily reflect the experience of individuals with other ethnic origins.

One of the key issues examined in each chapter of this book is the approach taken by West German security services towards immigrant political movements. While several other state institutions played a significant role in dealing with immigrant activists, the security services had the most regular contact with guest worker and émigré organizations. Thus, the expansion of police and intelligence agencies between 1949 and 1975 had a direct impact on the immigrant population as a whole.[22] New bureaucracies quickly engaged in turf battles over spheres of jurisdiction made more complex by the federal structure of the West German state. A whole network of *Bundestag* (the federal parliament) and *Landtag* (the regional assemblies) committees had to be set up in order to maintain legislative oversight of this increasingly elaborate security apparatus.[23]

As in other Western states, there were considerable rivalries between different intelligence services. Conflict over jurisdiction and financial resources undermined relations between the four main West German intelligence services: the *Bundesnachrichtendienst* (BND) responsible for external espionage, the *Bundesamt für Verfassungsschutz* (BfV), which dealt with counter-intelligence and political extremism, the *Bundeskriminalamt* (BKA), which focused on criminal intelligence and the armed forces' intelligence unit, the *Militärischer Abschirmdienst* (MAD). While the BND had no equivalent on the provincial (*Land*) level, the federal (*Bund*) Interior and Justice Ministries along with the criminal and counter-intelligence services had to compete with their *Länder* equivalents, the *Landeskriminalamt* (LKA) and *Landesamt für Verfassungsschutz* (LfV).[24] Although the expansion of the *Bundesgrenzschutz* (BGS) in the 1970s transformed the border guard into a kind of uniformed national police force, approaches to frontline policing often diverged radically from *Bundesland* to *Bundesland*, since basic policing remained under regional control.[25] The amount of space immigrants and émigrés had to express their own views depended as much on the political constellation of regional and city governments as it did on developments at the national level.

As the internal structure of the radical Right and Left evolved, new measures to protect the constitutional order of the Federal Republic were introduced by *Land* and *Bund* governments, which often had unintended consequences. Rigid legal limitations on the right to protest in the 1950s and the 1960s, as well as a law in the 1970s banning anyone suspected of hostility to the constitutional order from state employment, helped to tarnish the image abroad of the Federal Republic of Germany (FRG) as a modern democracy, without effectively bringing the radical Right or Left under control at home.[26] Each new wave of internal political conflict led to an increase in resources for police and intelligence services at all levels of government. In the late 1940s, social instability after the collapse of the Third Reich enabled local police services to use extremely aggressive tactics, despite attempts by British and American occupation officials to strengthen civil liberties.[27] In the 1950s, the *Bundesnachrichtendienst* and the *Bundesamt für Verfassungsschutz* were provided with considerable resources as the covert operations run by the *Stasi* and other East German intelligence agencies fuelled fears that extreme left-wing movements could destabilize the West German state.[28] Finally, the street violence of the 1960s and the urban terrorism of the 1970s led to a massive expansion of the *Bundeskriminalamt.*[29]

The behaviour of the security services and the other West German state institutions directly or indirectly involved in immigration policy was shaped by the ideological environment in which they operated. The continuing existence of an East German state aligned to the Soviet bloc presented a lasting challenge to the political legitimacy of the Federal Republic. Any West German involved with East German or communist organizations was treated as a potential security threat by the security services and by state institutions such as the *Auswärtiges Amt,* the Bonn Foreign Ministry. The extensive and often successful efforts undertaken by the *Stasi* and KGB to place their agents in major West German institutions, including political parties, nongovernmental organizations and even intelligence agencies, indicate that such concerns were well grounded.[30] Such an environment also put immense pressure on the SPD and other left-wing groups loyal to the constitution to prove that they were not tainted by association with the kind of socialist ideology propagated by the Soviet bloc.[31]

Intertwined with this inter-German ideological rivalry was the necessity to reassure West Germany's American, British and French allies that the democratic experiment in the Federal Republic could resist pressure from the extreme Right.[32] Yet the effort to keep nationalist or neo-Nazi groups under control took up considerably less state resources than the underground war against the East German regime. After the *Sozialistische Reichspartei* was banned in 1952, the campaign to keep the extreme Right under control lost momentum as many Germans tried to put the wartime past behind them.[33] For figures such as the head of Adenauer's secretariat, Hans Globke, the founder of the BND, Reinhard Gehlen, or even one of the most powerful officers in the BKA, Paul Dickopf, more than questionable careers under the Nazi regime did not hinder their rise to senior positions in government. In the many turf wars between ministries and agencies on both the *Land* and federal levels, such contacts often proved useful, although they also provided the *Stasi* with a means with which to discredit the West German political establishment.[34]

Similar continuities in personnel could also be found in other state institutions that exerted influence over immigration policy. In the 1950s and 1960s, the senior echelons of the *Auswärtiges Amt* were largely made up of officials who had worked in similar positions during the 1930s and 1940s. With the small policy units responsible for international relations in *Land* governments also run by members of this 'old guard', most officials formulating foreign policy during the Adenauer era had been heavily involved in the expansionist projects of the Nazi regime. Émigrés or immigrants lobbying the *Auswärtiges Amt* in order to influence West German policy towards their homelands had to regularly deal with such holdovers from the pre-1945 era. Confronted with immigrants from across Europe and the Third World, other ministries on both the *Land* and federal levels consulted heavily with *Auswärtiges Amt* officials who were considered to be the main repositories of information on the culture and attitudes of non-Germans.[35] The ideological outlook of the *Auswärtiges Amt* and its personnel was therefore another key factor shaping West German responses to immigrant political movements.

State welfare agencies and social services also played a significant role. As Albrecht Funk has pointed out, the expansion of the social welfare system in the 1960s and 1970s encouraged state institutions to develop methods or technologies that could help gather information on those who needed state aid and track its social impact.[36] At a local level, immigration offices, known as *Ausländerämter*, controlled by city governments, had the power to intervene in almost every aspect of an immigrant's life. In Bonn, the Federal Interior Ministry (or *Bundesministerium des Innern*), which was responsible for immigration issues, remained fixated upon differentiating between 'legitimate' migrants with the legal right to reside in Germany and 'illegitimate' migrants who had either overstayed their visas or had entered the country illegally. Immigration officials on every level of government were therefore accustomed to cooperating with the police and other security services.

Such West German state institutions helped their political masters to set up the labour importation programme without anticipating the far-reaching political consequences of allowing hundreds of thousands of economic migrants to enter the Federal Republic on an annual basis. As we have seen, the CDU/CSU and significant elements within the SPD continued to claim that the Federal Republic was not a 'country of immigration' until the mid 1990s, long after guest workers had started settling permanently.[37] Yet, beyond general worries among most West German voters over the economic and cultural consequences of the guest worker programme, attitudes towards immigration and immigrant communities varied across the political spectrum.

Many supporters of the centre-right parties feared that the guest worker population might become a dangerous potential recruiting ground for communist movements. The establishment of the *Kampfverband zur Schutz ausländischer Arbeiter in der Bundesrepublik Deutschland* by the East German trade unions, an organization designed to coordinate the actions of communist parties from labour exporting countries, hardened suspicions within the CDU/CSU that the guest worker population contained communist infiltrators.[38] A surprisingly large number of grass-roots members of the SPD and West German trade unions believed that a permanent immigrant population would only benefit the 'capitalist class' and might lead to a rise in support for the radical Right.[39] Conversely, business circles that supported the guest worker system claimed that by increasing the wealth of their home countries, guest workers would keep them from succumbing to Soviet communism.[40] For many in the left-liberal social milieu from which the Green Party emerged, the successful integration of immigrants could prove that Germany had truly broken with its Nazi past.[41] The fierce debates over immigration between these different sociopolitical groups, fuelled as they were by divergent perceptions over its impact on German society, have had a major impact on most academic studies dealing with these issues.

Once historical research exploring the national socialist system began to widen in scope during the 1960s and 1970s, some historians started to examine the Nazi regime's use of foreign labourers to compensate for labour shortages in Germany during the Second World War. Forcibly deported to the Third Reich, living and often dying in terrible conditions, by 1944 over seven million foreign workers could be found in German factories.[42] Some historians saw parallels between this wartime importation of labour and the guest worker programme of the late 1950s. With the first guest workers subject to curfew and housed in barracks, Ulrich Herbert and Joachim Lehmann began to look at the role of migrant labourers in twentieth-century Germany in this wider historical context.[43] The mass expulsion of Germans from Eastern Europe also inspired several major studies on German emigration throughout the nineteenth and twentieth centuries, which gradually shifted towards broader work on the migration process itself. Through this route, migration specialists such as Barbara Dietz and Klaus Bade began to examine the impact of immigration on the Federal Republic.[44]

As these initial migration specialists shifted their attention towards the guest worker programme, the main focus of their research remained remarkably uniform. This was largely because the aim of most immigration scholars in the 1970s was to prove to Germans who still wanted to believe that Germany was an ethnically homogeneous society that economic migrants were settling permanently in the Federal Republic. The fraught nature of the immigration debate in the 1970s and 1980s, along with the fact that until 1990 many politicians and government officials did not accept the fact that immigrants had become a permanent presence, makes this tendency to concentrate on the immigrant population as a whole rather than on individual ethnic groups entirely understandable.[45] Moreover, sociologists such as Stephen Castles became particularly disturbed by the manner in which disparities in economic growth between Northern and Southern Europe were adversely affecting the socio-economic position of immigrants.[46] As a result, the considerable numbers of immigrants at the lower end of the social hierarchy and their growing economic marginalization after the recession of the late 1970s and early 1980s reinforced a tendency among those working on immigration issues to frame their arguments in class terms.[47] By contrast, most studies on guest worker immigration have ignored the DPs, despite the considerable amount of research conducted on displaced persons and émigrés in postwar Europe by historians and political scientists such as Wolfgang Jacobmeyer.[48]

Though the impact of immigrant political activity on the development of guest worker communities was not entirely neglected, these first academics conducting research on immigration focused on other issues that they believed to be of greater significance to the fate of immigrants in the Federal Republic. For Stephen Castles, the ability (or inability) of the West German education system to cope with an influx of newly arrived children who did not speak German was one of the crucial factors shaping the internal development of immigrant communities.[49] The many legal obstacles to the acquisition of West German citizenship that immigrants had to face was of central importance to the research of immigration scholars such as Reinhard Lohmann,[50] while the work of academics such as Hartmut Esser focused on the high levels of unemployment and lack of social mobility in certain immigrant communities.[51] Many of these studies examined the fate of individual guest workers in certain city neighbourhoods (often ignoring their particular regional or ethnic backgrounds) in order to underline statistical conclusions made about the immigrant population as a whole. At the same time, immigration historians such as Klaus J. Bade[52] and Ulrich Herbert[53] examined the relationship between mainstream German society and successive waves of immigrants and migrant workers rather than exploring the considerable political and social divisions that existed between and within immigrant communities.

Parallel to this research on the socio-economic position of immigrants, West German political activists following the lead of lawyers including Hans Heinz Heldmann[54] and academics such as Albrecht Funk,[55] who were examining structural changes in the judiciary and executive, began to scrutinize the treatment of immigrants by the police and in the courts. These studies drew attention to the manner in which the civil rights of the immigrant population were curtailed by the extensive powers conferred upon the police and social services by West German immigration law.[56] Though it does focus upon the individual experiences of immigrants, much of this work does not investigate how the political life of their communities may have shaped the attitude of the West German state institutions they were confronted with. These studies also overestimate the ability of the West German state to control the movement of guest workers and the internal development of immigrant communities. In fact, documents that have recently emerged in German state archives demonstrate that the security services often knew very little about developments within the immigrant communities they were trying to keep under control.[57]

These initial academic approaches towards immigration issues tended to treat immigrants as a uniform bloc, glossing over the possibility that each ethnic community might develop its own individual relationship with its host society. They also reflected a mistaken underlying assumption that Germans did not differentiate between various ethnic minorities.[58] Though they played a vital role in making immigration a serious topic of historical research in Germany, these first guest worker studies are problematic in four ways:

1. When looking at immigration, researchers in the 1970s and early 1980s were usually preoccupied with migration-related social problems in labour-importing countries and their impact on the attitude of the indigenous population rather than the internal social and political structures of immigrant communities.
2. Because of their visibility and size, those communities whose origins lay in Italy and the Turkish Republic attracted the greatest attention from researchers. Yet to see the impact of migration entirely through the filter of Turkish or Italian communities is to underestimate the level of ethnic and religious heterogeneity that has emerged in the Federal Republic over the last half century.
3. Though this first wave of immigration scholarship made a perfunctory nod to the potential relevance of different historical or political traditions within the immigrant population, few have made any attempt to take a closer look at how these traditions could have influenced the integration of these communities into West German society.
4. Most of this work tends to look at the immigration process in isolation, focusing upon its specific economic and social effects rather than looking at how it related to other major developments in West German politics.

This neglect of diversity within the immigrant population was mirrored by a tendency towards overgeneralization when it came to theoretical analyses of the impact of mass migration in the work of political scientists such as Rogers Brubaker and Yasemin Soysal. Brubaker[59] insisted that the entire German political class was culpable in the propagation of the myth that Germany was 'not a country of immigration'. Yet this overlooked major shifts in the attitude of many social democrats over the course of the 1980s as the parliamentary Left began to accept the possibility that immigrant communities had become a permanent presence.[60] In the mid 1990s Soysal claimed that immigrants in

Germany were developing a form of postnational identity that would foster their integration into West German society despite the lack of easy access to German citizenship. Yet this theoretical model does not take into account the possibility that, rather than conforming to some standard pattern, the relationship between immigrants and their wider social environment might be shaped by their own individual ethnic and political backgrounds.

Partly in reaction to the generalizing tendencies of much of the initial academic work on immigrants in Germany, in the late 1980s and early 1990s an increasing amount of research was conducted on individual immigrant communities in the Federal Republic. With the fall of the Berlin Wall, a gradual shift in emphasis in the state's approach to immigrant communities has been mirrored by a more differentiated approach towards the immigrant experience among a wide variety of historians and sociologists. Heavily influenced by the work of Pierre Bourdieu, many of these studies focus on specific cultural symbols in order to develop a more nuanced sense of social relationships within ethnic groups. Sociologists such as Ayse Caglar[61] have scrutinized such key cultural issues as the wearing of headscarves or the construction of mosques,[62] or analysed social hierarchies within individual neighbourhoods.[63]

More concerted efforts were also made to examine the political and cultural development of individual ethnic communities, particularly those from Turkey and the Kurdish regions.[64] One of the most detailed studies of Turkish and Kurdish organizations in Germany and their influence on political conflict in Turkey is a study by Ertekin Özcan. Özcan's comprehensive analysis is both a sociological study of the Turkish community and a look at how the Turkish experience in Germany may have affected Turkey itself.[65] More recently, Eva Østergaard-Nielsen,[66] Vera Eccarius-Kelly[67] and Martin Sökefeld[68] have built on this work by analysing the impact of certain homeland-oriented left- and right-wing political groups in the 1980s and 1990s on social structures within the Turkish community. As the collapse of the Soviet bloc led to a new influx of economic migrants from Eastern Europe along with ethnic Germans and Jews from the former Soviet Union, researchers used a similar approach when trying to gauge how this form of migration was going to affect a reunified Germany. The research work of Barbara Dietz, among others, helped to renew academic interest in the postwar expellee generation and pointed out some of the parallels between the integration of expellees and that of guest workers. It also drew attention to the fact that the generosity of West German state institutions towards ethnic Germans from the Soviet Union when it came to the acquisition of citizenship had increased tension between this new community and more established Turkish or Italian immigrants.[69]

There have also been several historical studies of West German immigration policy in the last decade. With almost forty years having elapsed between the fall of the Berlin Wall and the signing of the first guest worker treaties in 1954, the guest worker programme itself was increasingly seen as a historical phenomenon. One of the most significant historical studies of the 1990s was produced by Karen Schönwälder, who has looked at how popular images of immigrants shaped political discourse over immigration issues in the 1960s in both the Federal Republic and the U.K.[70] At the same time, there was also a growth in interest in the internal culture of the DP camps among historians specializing in diaspora studies, such as Wsewolod Isajiw[71] and Wolodymyr Kulyk.[72] These studies have contributed towards a more complex understanding of the political and social impact of migration in the first decades of the Federal Republic.

Yet neither this historical research nor the sociological work of Özcan and Østergaard-Nielsen have really grappled with the effects that ethnic, social and political diversity *within* the immigrant population had on the relationship that guest workers and émigrés had with the West German state. By largely focusing upon immigrants of Turkish and Kurdish origin, these studies do not explore whether ethnic communities with other political or cultural traditions were treated differently by West German state institutions and political parties. This compounded the tendency among historians and sociologists such as Soysal and Caglar to conflate the experience of the Turks in Germany, who were one of the largest immigrant communities, with that of other Muslim or even non-Muslim groups. As a result, many studies that were partly designed to increase academic and public awareness of the effects of immigration on Germany did not engage with many of the political and social implications of ethnic diversity.

These underlying problems with sociological studies of immigrant communities often reflect an unwillingness to construct any kind of historical narrative. While the older generation of immigration specialists do construct a narrative of sorts, their abiding interest is in the migration process, rather than the immigrants themselves, creating an image of the average guest worker as distortedly uniform as any to be found in the press or popular stereotypes. Sociological studies covering the new ethnic minorities may have helped to counteract these distortions, but they neglect any sense of how these communities may have developed over time. By looking at immigration-related issues in isolation, both approaches fail to develop an understanding of how immigration may have become intertwined with other important social or political issues in West German public discourse.

More recently, another factor that has distorted aspects of academic research on migrants and migration policy in the Federal Republic has been an emphasis on radicalization and political violence shaped by the aftermath of the 11 September 2001 attack on the World Trade Centre in New York. On a theoretical level, however much many of them have developed a more differentiated approach towards structures of political violence, scholars such as Alexander Straßner[73] or Kai Hirschmann[74] have compared and contrasted the impact of Islamist as well as other radical immigrant networks with 'indigenous' political movements such as the Red Army Faction, which had focused on a coordinated assault on state institutions. Yet not all of the migrant networks that were prepared to use violent tactics during the Cold War period saw the West

German state as their primary target. In several of the case studies explored in the following chapters, migrant movements either only confronted the German security services when they got in the way, or even saw themselves as covert allies of the West German state. At least in the Cold War period, this kind of immigrant political violence was not automatically a product of discrimination and marginalization by an ethnic German majority.

Moreover, the specific focus on violent Islamist groups in the past decade, particularly in influential studies by David Kilcullen[75] and Peter Neumann,[76] has led to an emphasis on the transnational nature of terrorist networks, which becomes increasingly fixated on violence as an end in itself regardless of whether they are based on, secular, religious or ethno-nationalist ideologies. However, such an approach is problematic because, for several immigrant political movements examined in the course of this study, forms of violence were just one of a variety of different tactics, the use of which did not necessarily inevitably have to lead to organized terror. Moreover, though the immigrant political movements explored in this study were heavily tied into wider transnational diasporic networks, their methods of operation and strategic alliances were often heavily influenced by the specific national or regional political spaces in which they interacted with their German counterparts. Rather than providing a more nuanced understanding of how the emergence of immigrant political networks has reshaped the political landscape in Germany and beyond, this stronger focus on political violence after 2001 has only proven as reductivist as preceding theoretical approaches towards immigrant political life in the Federal Republic.

Only very recently have historians and political scientists such as Roberto Sala, Vera Eccarius-Kelly, Karen Schönwälder, Martin Sökefeld and Simon Green acknowledged the ethnic complexity of the immigrant population in the Federal Republic in their research. Green in particular has emphasized the unwillingness of West German politicians and academics to come to terms with the fact that immigrants might not all respond to state measures designed to foster their integration or assimilation into West German society in quite the same way.[77] In turn, Schönwälder has pointed to some of the continuities in the way in which DPs or East European émigrés and guest workers were perceived by the West German public while underlining the different social and political status these various types of immigrant had in the Federal Republic.[78] Of the three, Roberto Sala's work on radio and television programmes for guest workers in the 1960s takes the most direct look at how the different political and ethnic backgrounds of those involved in this project shaped their relationships with West German broadcasters and government officials. Yet this focus on guest worker communities in Sala's work as well as that of Eccarius-Kelly and Sökefeld does not grapple with the quite distinct experiences and internal divisions within other immigrant groups.[79] Moreover, since both Green and Schönwälder are primarily interested in the approach taken by the German policy makers towards the immigrant population as a whole, the implications of political and ethnic diversity within immigrant communities have not been the central focus of their work.

By concentrating on the experience of immigrant political movements in a variety of ethnic communities, this study addresses some of the challenges that ethnic diversity posed for West German governments. For the ethnic diversity of the immigrant population in the Federal Republic was not articulated in a political vacuum. There were two major sociopolitical trends in particular that affected the relationship of the Ukrainian, Polish, Croatian, Algerian, Spanish, Greek and Iranian communities with West German state institutions and political parties. One common factor that managed to cut across differences in national culture and religious tradition in an increasingly ethnically diverse society was the political language of Cold War conflict. The ideological polarization between the American and Soviet blocs, which found its most extreme manifestation in German division, could be found in every state exporting labour to the Federal Republic. Another major sociopolitical issue that affected the relationship of West German political institutions with immigrants and their homeland states was the historical legacy of the Nazi regime.

Through the exploration of the impact of these and other political factors upon immigrant political movements, each chapter will show how West Germans have dealt with the challenge of ethnic diversity from the very first days of the Federal Republic. In every year of the West German state's existence, debates, demonstrations and disturbances involving politicized immigrants have openly, and at times violently, contradicted the myth that Germany is a culturally homogeneous society. The West German response to immigrant political and ethnic diversity examined in the following chapters will therefore shed new light on how immigration as a social phenomenon fits into the wider context of German history in the Cold War period.

Notes

1.   S. Falk. 1998. *Dimensionen Kurdischer Ethnizität und Politisierung: Eine Fallstudie Ethnischer Gruppenbildung in der Bundesrepublik Deutschland*, Baden-Baden: Nomos, 71.
2.   G. Stein. 1994. *Endkampf um Kurdistan?: Die PKK, die Türkei und Deutschland*, Munich: Aktuell, 114–18.
3.   Falk, *Dimensionen Kurdischer Ethnizität und Politisierung*, 79–80.
4.   P. Panayi. 2000. *Ethnic Minorities in Nineteenth and Twentieth Century Germany: Jews, Gypsies, Poles, Turks and Others: Themes in Modern German History*, Harlow: Longman, 201–3.
5.   K.J. Bade. 1994. *Ausländer, Aussiedler, Asyl: Eine Bestandsaufnahme*, Munich: Beck'sche Reihe, 34.
6.   C. Leggewie. 1990. *Multikulti. Spielregeln für die Vielvölkerrepublik*, Berlin: Rotbuch.
7.   Panayi, *Ethnic Minorities*, 258–61.
8.   R.G. Moeller. 2001. 'Remembering the War in a Nation of Victims: West German Pasts in the 1950s', in H. Schissler (ed.), *The Miracle Years: a Cultural History of West Germany 1949–1968*, Princeton: Princeton University Press, 2–8.

9.   D.L. Bark and D.R. Gress. 1993. *A History of West Germany (Part 2): Democracy and its Discontents 1963–1991*, Oxford: Blackwell, 47–52.

10. H. Esser. 1983. 'Gastarbeiter', W. Benz (ed.), *Die Bundesrepublik Deutschland: Band 2 – Gesellschaft*, Frankfurt a.m.: Fischer Verl., 138–39.

11. T. Faist. 1994. 'How to Define a Foreigner? The Symbolic Politics of Immigration in German Partisan Discourse 1978–1992', in M. Baldwin-Edwards and M. Schain (eds), *The Politics of Immigration in Western Europe*, Newbury-Portland: Frank Cass, 50–71.

12. D. Adineh and M. Schuckar. 1992. 'Iraner in Deutschland', in Berliner Institut für Vergleichende Sozialforschung (ed.), *Ethnische Minderheiten in Deutschland: Arbeitsmigranten, Asylbewerber, Ausländer, Flüchtlinge, regional und religiöse Minderheiten, Vertriebene, Zwangsarbeiter*, Berlin: Parabolis Verlag, 3.1.5.-1–3.1.5.28.

13. R. Lohmann. 1974. 'Politische Auswirkungen auf die Bundesrepublik Deutschland', in R. Lohmann and K. Manfrass (eds), *Ausländerbeschäftigung und Internationale Politik*, Munich: Oldenbourg, 125–29.

14. M.J. Miller. 1981. *Foreign Workers in Western Europe: an Emerging Socio-political Force*, New York: Praeger, 106–11.

15. U. Schöneberg. 1985. 'Participation in Ethnic Associations: the Case of Immigrants in West Germany', *International Migration Review* 19(3), 426–31.

16. D. Reynolds. 2001. *One World Divisible: a Global History since 1945*, London: Penguin, 30–36, 96–97, 339–47.

17. M. Ghaseminia. 1996. *Zur Lebenssituation und Integration Iranischer Staatsangehöriger in Niedersachsen*, Hanover: Universität Hannover, 36–39.

18. U. Herbert and K. Hunn. 2001. 'Guest Workers and Policy on Guest Workers in the Federal Republic', in H. Schissler (ed.), *The Miracle Years – a Cultural History of West Germany*, Princeton: Princeton University Press, 187–98.

19. Bundesarchiv Koblenz (B.K.), B 106, Nr. 63084, *Loseblattsammlung des Bundesministerium des Inneren*, Re.: 'Vorwort', Bonn, 1960.

20. R. Brubaker. 2001. 'The Return of Assimilation? Changing Perspectives on Immigration and its Sequels in France, Germany and the United States', *Ethnic and Racial Studies* 24(4), 535–39.

21. Herbert and Hunn, 'Guest Workers and Policy on Guest Workers in the Federal Republic', 187–89.

22. U. Wölker. 1987. *Zur Freiheit und Grenzen der politischen Betätigung von Ausländern*, Berlin: Springer Verl., 6–7.

23. J. Katzenstein. 1990. *West Germany's Internal Security Policy: State and Violence in the 1970s and 1980s*, Cornell: Western Societies Program (Cornell Centre for International Studies nr. 28), 27–29.

24. H. Prantl. 2002. *Verdächtig: Der starke Staat und die Politik der inneren Unsicherheit*, Hamburg: Europa Verl., 53–4.

25. M. Winter. 1998. *Politikum Polizei – Macht und Funktion der Polizei in der Bundesrepublik Deutschland*, Münster: LIT (Politische Soziologie, Band 10), 21–26.

26. A. Funk and W.-D. Narr. 1984. *Verrechtlichung und Verdrängung: Die Bürokratie und Ihre Klientel*, Opladen: Westdeutscher Verl., 250–51.

27. R.J. Evans. 1996. *Rituals of Retribution: Capital Punishment in Germany 1600–1987*, Oxford: Penguin, 752.

28. Katzenstein, *West Germany's Internal Security Policy*, 18–31.

29. B. Rabert. 1995. *Links- und Rechtsterrorismus in der Bundesrepublik Deutschland von 1970 bis Heute*, Berlin: Bernard & Graefe Verl., 214–18.

30. M. Mueller and P.F. Müller. 2002. *Gegen Freund und Feind – Der BND: Geheime Politik und Schmutzige Geschäfte*, Hamburg: Rowohlt Verl., 254–60.

31. C. von Braunmühl. 1973. *Kalter Krieg und Friedliche Koexistenz: Die Außenpolitik der SPD in der Großen Koalition*, Frankfurt, a.M.: Suhrkamp Verl., 38–42.

32. T. Naftali. 2004. 'Berlin to Baghdad: the Perils of Hiring Enemy Intelligence', *Foreign Affairs* 83(4), 127.

33. D. Schenk. 2003. *Die Braunen Wurzeln des BKA*, Frankfurt a.M.: Fischer Verl., 304.

34. Ibid., 286–93.

35. See, for example, Politisches Archiv des Auswärtigen Amtes Berlin (Pol. A.A.Ber.), B 40, Nr. 111, *Aufzeichnung*, Re.: 'Interministerielle Besprechung im Bundesministerium für Vertriebene über Förderungsmassnahmen für osteuropäische Emigranten, am 12. Dezember 1962', Bonn, 14 December 1962.

36. Funk and Narr, *Verrechtlichung und Verdrängung*, 167–74.

37. Panayi, *Ethnic Minorities*, 258–61.

38. *Bonner Rundschau*, 'Trick mit Fremdarbeitern', 2 December 1963.

39. K. Schönwälder. 2001. *Einwanderung und Ethnische Pluralität: Politische Entscheidungen und öffentliche Debatten in Großbritannien und der Bundesrepublik von den 1950er bis zu den 1970er Jahren*, Essen: Klartext, 174–77.

40. This sentiment was reflected in a succession of press articles in the early 1960s expounding on the benefits and dangers of the guest worker system, such as, *Süddeutsche Zeitung* (*S.Z.*), 'Vier Ausländer in der Bundesrepublik: Lob und Tadel im deutschen Gästebuch', 24/25/26 December 1962; or *Die Welt* (*D.W.*), 'Pablos Freunde ließen nicht locker – Das rote Netz der Dolores Ibarruri – Kommunistische Agenten beeinflussen spanische Gastarbeiter', 8 July 1962.

41. B. Winkler. 1994. *Was Heißt denn Hier Fremd?: Thema Ausländerfeindlichkeit und Verantwortung*, Munich: Humboldt Verl., 122–23.

42. U. Herbert. 1986. *Geschichte der Ausländerbeschäftigung in Deutschland: 1880–1980*, Berlin: J.H.W. Dietz, 154–56.

43. J. Lehmann. 1988. 'Die Hypothek der Vergangenheit: Das Verhältnis der Bundesrepublik zu Spanien', *Hispanorama*, 50; or Herbert, *Geschichte der Ausländerbeschäftigung in Deutschland*.

44. K.J. Bade. 1984. 'Die Ausländerbeschäftigung in der Bundesrepublik zwischen Arbeitswanderung und Einwanderung', in K.J. Bade (ed.), *Auswanderer – Wanderarbeiter – Gastarbeiter*, Ostfildern: Scripta Mercaturae Verlag, 11 – 15 and B. Dietz. 1997. *Jugendliche Aussiedler: Ausreise, Aufnahme, Integration*, Berlin: Spitz.

45. Lohmann, 'Politische Auswirkungen auf die Bundesrepublik Deutschland', 130–33.

46. S. Castles. 2000. *Ethnicity and Globalisation*, London: SAGE Publications, 46–51.

47. H. Korte. 1984. *Die etablierten Deutschen und ihre ausländischen Aussenseiter – Macht undZivilisation (Materialien zu Norbert Elias' Zivilizationstheorie 2)*, Frankfurt a.M.: Suhrkamp, 261–79.

48. W. Jacobmeyer. 1985. *Vom Zwangsarbeiter zum Heimatlosen Ausländer: Die Displaced Persons in Westdeutschland 1945–1951*, Göttingen: Vandenhoeck & Ruprecht.

49. Castles, *Ethnicity and Globalisation*, 52–60.

50. Lohmann, 'Politische Auswirkungen auf die Bundesrepublik Deutschland', 134–35.

51. H. Esser. 1980. *Aspekte der Wanderungssoziologie: Eine Handlungstheoretische Analyse*, Darmstadt: Luchterhand.

52. Bade, *Ausländer, Aussiedler, Asyl*, 53–89.

53. Herbert, *Geschichte der Ausländerbeschäftigung in Deutschland*.

54. H.-H. Heldmann. 1972. 'Araber-Hatz in der BRD: Schlimme Neuigkeiten aus unserer Fremdenrechtspraxis', *Vorgänge* 10(11), 298–303.

55. Funk and Narr, *Verrechtlichung und Verdrängung*.

56. A good example is H.-E. Schultz. 1990. 'Politische Justiz gegen eine "Auslandsvereinigung" und die Rolle des "Kronzeugen" als zentrales Beweismittel in schauprozeßartigen Mammutverfahren: Der PKK-Prozeß in Düsseldorf', in H. Janssen and M. Schubert (eds), *Staatssicherheit: Die Bekämpfung des politischen Feindes im Inneren*, Bielefeld: AJZ Verl., 158–69.

57. Pol. A.A.Ber., B 42, Nr. 1007, *Konsularische Angelegenheiten*, Re.: 'Berichte des Konsulates Zagreb über Arbeitnehmer aus Jugoslawien, Gastarbeiter und Studiengruppen', 23 September 1963-8 February 1968.

58. R. Münz, *Zuwanderung nach Deutschland. Strukturen, Wirkungen, Perspektiven*, Frankfurt a.M.: Campus, 187-190.

59. R. Brubaker, 2001. 'The Return of Assimilation? Changing Perspectives on Immigration and its Sequels in France, Germany and the United States', *Ethnic and Racial Studies* 24(4), 537-539

60. Y. Soysal. 2000. 'Citizenship and Identity: Living in Diasporas in Postwar Europe?', *Ethnic and Racial Studies* 23(1), 1-15.

61. A. Caglar. 1991. 'Das Kultur-Konzept als Zwangsjacke in Studien zur Arbeitsmigration', *Zeitschrift für Türkeistudien* (31), 93-105.

62. R. Mandel. 1989. 'Turkish Headscarves and the "Foreigner Problem": Constructing Difference through Emblems of Identity', *New German Critique* 46, 27-46.

63. A. Pitsela. 1986. *Straffälligkeit und Viktimisierung ausländischer Minderheiten - Dargestellt am Beispiel der Griechischen Volksgruppe*, Freiburg: Max-Planck Institut für Strafrecht, 119-28.

64. H. Beste. 2000. 'Feindbildkonstruktionen und Bedrohungsszenarien - Die Kurden', in H. Beste (ed.), *Morphologie der Macht*, Opladen: Lesle und Budrich, 415-20.

65. E. Özcan. 1989. *Türkische Immigrantenorganisationen in der Bundesrepublik Deutschland*, Berlin: Hitit Verl.

66. E.K. Østergaard-Nielsen. 1998. *Diaspora Politics: the Case of Immigrants and Refugees from Turkey Residing in Germany since 1980*, Thesis (D.Phil.), Oxford: University of Oxford, 11-27.

67. V. Eccarius-Kelly. 2008. 'The Kurdish Conundrum in Europe: Political Opportunities and Transnational Activism', in W. Pojmann (ed.), *Migration and Activism in Europe since 1945*, New York: Palgrave Macmillan, 57-80.

68. Martin Sökefeld. 2008. *Struggling for Recognition: the Alevi Movement in Germany and in Transnational Space*, Oxford: Berghahn Books.

69. Dietz, *Jugendliche Aussiedler*, 24-37.

70. Schönwälder, *Einwanderung und Ethnische Pluralität*.

71. W.I. Wsewolod (ed.). 1992. *The Refugee Experience: Ukrainian Displaced Persons after World War II*, Edmonton: Canadian Institute of Ukrainian Studies Press.

72. V. Kulyk. 2003. 'The Role of Discourse in the Construction of an Émigré Community: Ukrainian Displaced Persons in Germany and Austria after the Second World War', in R. Ohliger and K. Schönwälder (eds), *European Encounters: Migrants, Migration and European Societies since 1945*, Aldershot: Ashgate, 214-18.

73. A. Straßner. 2004. 'Terrorismus und Generalisierung - Gibt es einen Lebenslauf Terroristischer Gruppierungen?', *Zeitschrift für Politik* 4(51), 368-71.

74. K. Hirschmann. 2001. 'Terrorismus in neuen Dimensionen: Hintergründe und Schlussfolgerungen', *Aus Politik und Zeitgeschichte* 51, 8.

75. D. Kilcullen. 2005. 'Countering Global Insurgency', *Journal of Strategic Studies* 28(4), 599.

76. P.R. Neumann. 2009. *Old and New Terrorism*, London: Polity Press, 47-49.

77. See S. Green. 2004. *The Politics of Exclusion: Institutions and Immigration Policy in Contemporary Germany*, Manchester: Manchester University Press.

78. Schönwälder, *Einwanderung und Ethnische Pluralität*, 217-30.

79. R. Sala. 2005. '"Gastarbeitersendungen" und "Gastarbeiterzeitschriften" in der Bundesrepublik (1960-1975) - ein Spiegel internationaler Spannungen', *Zeithistorische Forschungen* 3, 366-371.

Chapter 1

OLD ALLIES IN A NEW WORLD

THE RELATIONSHIP BETWEEN ÉMIGRÉS AND THE GERMAN POLITICAL ESTABLISHMENT

Though most Germans accepted that national socialist rule had had disastrous consequences, the postwar debate over recent history remained selective. When discussing recent history, many West Germans concentrated on their own suffering during the 1940s, emphasizing the depredation and division visited upon Germany by the Soviets.[1] The focus upon collective victimhood rather than collective responsibility, explored by Robert Moeller in his groundbreaking study, War Stories, had a significant impact upon many aspects of West German society.[2] Widespread attitudes among West Germans towards the historical legacy of the Hitler regime were therefore bound to have a major impact upon immigrant communities. This focus on German suffering strengthened the hand of organizations representing the interests of ethnic Germans who were expelled from Poland, Czechoslovakia and other Eastern European states after 1944. The close relationship between the CDU/CSU alliance and these expellee organizations was part of a concerted attempt by CDU strategists to bind expellees to the centre-right. But it was made possible by a shared conviction that the expellees had suffered an injustice at the hands of the Soviets that needed to be rectified. With considerable sway over key factions in the CDU/CSU, the representatives of the Landsmannschaften (as the expellee associations were called) had substantial influence over West German foreign policy until the mid 1960s.[3]

The special status enjoyed by German expellee organizations in the 1950s and 1960s helped several East European émigré groups gain support from the West German centre-right. Both expellee and émigré leaders in the 1950s aimed to bring about the collapse of the communist bloc. Many expellees believed that the defeat of Soviet communism could lead to the return of ethnic Germans to Eastern European territories from which they had been forced to flee. Anti-communist émigrés hoped that the end of Soviet dominance would lead to regime change in their homelands and, in some cases, independence for those ethnic groups who did not have their own nation state. Émigré groups with a political agenda compatible with that of associations representing expellees from the same part of Eastern Europe could often depend upon expellee support when dealing with the West German state. Conversely, bad relations with an expellee association could severely damage an émigré group's ability to attract public or state support.[4] Continuity in personnel between the prewar German state and state institutions in the Federal Republic affected the development of immigrant communities and émigré organizations as well. Though some on the Left did display scepticism about these institutional continuities, reluctance in the wider population to engage in a searching debate over the legacy of the Hitler regime enabled many civil servants, academics and politicians to emerge from the denazification process with their careers intact.[5]

Such continuities were mirrored in the leadership of émigré groups. Most émigré organizations operating in postwar Germany had been established by exiles, who before 1945 had worked closely with German bureaucrats and academics who went on to serve the Federal Republic. These links went back to efforts by political movements from Eastern European states to obtain the support of influential Germans in the 1920s and 1930s and intensified during the Second World War. As a result, German bureaucrats and academics who served the national socialist regime met local political leaders who later fled to the Federal Republic.[6]

During the 1950s, such old contacts in the Bonn political establishment could provide émigré organizations with financial or logistical support from the West German state. In some cases, a ministerial official who supported the aims of a certain émigré movement was also a senior member of an expellee organization. East European political exiles, expellees and their partners in the West German political establishment were operating in a kind of political grey zone, where state and academic institutions shored up the position of émigré and expellee leaders. By helping to determine which émigré organizations were best positioned to gain the attention of the wider public, this process strengthened those groups with the best access to the West German political establishment.[7] Yet the majority of East Europeans resident in the FRG had not belonged to the political elites of their homeland states before 1945. After the Germans surrendered in May 1945, older political exiles worked together with DPs to turn underground political networks into a functioning community infrastructure. Refugees who worked as interpreters, security guards or administrators for the British and American armies quickly became mediators between their DP communities and the Allied or German authorities. Often attaining West German citizenship before most other DPs, such East European activists generally remained in refugee issues or reconstruction programmes, providing their ethnic communities with access to state institutions on a local and regional level. With the help of officers and soldiers in the Allied armies who shared the same ethnic background, DPs working for Allied or West German authorities were also able to get in touch with East European immigrant organizations in North America.[8] Apart from a small trickle of defectors from the Soviet bloc in the 1960s and 1970s, this war generation made up the bulk of the membership of East European political organizations in the Federal Republic.

This chapter will focus on the Ukrainians, whose experience was in many ways typical of East European émigré groups as a whole. They experienced a serious decline in numbers in the early 1950s, as the bulk of DPs were either repatriated or left for Australia, North America and Britain. By the early 1960s, of the millions of refugees stranded in Germany after 1945, there were only 220,000 DPs and political exiles still living in West Germany. This émigré population contained approximately 50,000 Poles, 20,000 Ukrainians, 18,000 Russians, 23,000 DPs from Yugoslavia (of whom 13,000 were from Croatia) and under 19,000 from Lithuania, Estonia and Latvia.[9] Of these, only 15,000 émigrés were official members of over 180–200 émigré political organizations. However, officials in the West German state institutions remained convinced that this organized minority exerted considerable influence over the life of their communities.[10] This chapter will therefore investigate how the historical legacy of the Nazi era combined with the political imperatives of the Cold War to shape the relationship that Ukrainian and other East European groups had with their German allies.

****

As a community, the Ukrainians were perhaps the most heterogeneous of all the émigré groups. Both the Autocephalous Orthodox and the Greek Catholic churches (the two largest religious groups in the Ukraine) maintained their own separate institutions throughout the Ukrainian diaspora. The existence of such deep confessional divisions became a potential source of conflict between Ukrainians living in Europe and North America. Equally divisive were the major sociohistorical differences between western and eastern Ukrainians. The social structure of those regions in the Carpathians, Volhynia and Bukovina had been heavily influenced by Austro-Hungarian rule before being partitioned between Czechoslovakia, Poland and Romania after 1918. While western Ukraine only came under permanent Soviet control in 1945, the central and eastern regions had been ruled by Moscow for over 500 years. Exposed to the Soviet regime for a prolonged period, most émigré politicians and intellectuals from eastern Ukraine either had been members of the Communist Party or had served in the Soviet Army. The fact that left-wing Ukrainian organizations tended to have a disproportionately high number of eastern Ukrainian members only heightened uncertainty among western Ukrainians, who often tended to equate any form of left-wing ideology with communism.[11]

The movement with the most widespread support was the organization of Ukrainian Nationalists (OUN). Founded at a clandestine nationalist congress in Vienna, the OUN initially consisted of an alliance of two distinct factions. The first was made up of veterans of the nationalist armies who had fought for Ukrainian independence between 1917 and 1920. Many of these old soldiers had worked together with German intelligence officers who hoped to draw Ukraine into Germany's sphere of influence; hopes that were dashed after the Red Army suppressed the short-lived Ukrainian Republic in 1918.[12] The second group was largely made up of students and intellectuals who had been too young to fight in the First World War or the wars of the early 1920s. While the war veterans split between those who wanted a Ukrainian monarchy (preferably led by a German prince) and those who supported the idea of an independent socialist republic, the younger OUN leaders who emerged in the mid 1920s were more interested in Italian fascism.

After 1922, the fact that most of the older OUN leaders decided to move to Prague, Berlin or Paris rather than remain in the Ukraine exacerbated these ideological differences, since the younger generation of OUN members had to bear the brunt of the Polish and Romanian retaliation against Ukrainian nationalist activity. A campaign of repression conducted by the Polish security services in the mid 1930s ultimately forced many of these student activists to flee to Berlin or Prague as well. This carried ideological infighting over to Ukrainian émigré associations in Berlin where (with the tolerance of the Gestapo) the local *Ukrainische Nationale Vereinigung* became a mouthpiece for younger nationalists.[13] The OUN finally split into two rival organizations after the assassination of its first chairman, Colonel Ievhan Konovalets, by an NKVD (People's Commisariat for Internal Affairs) agent in 1938. The leadership promptly installed another old veteran called Andrii Melnyk as Konovalets's successor without consulting the OUN activists who had remained in their homeland.

Younger activists took advantage of the chaos that enveloped Poland after the outbreak of the Second World War to establish a breakaway movement in February 1940.[14] Following the German invasion of the Soviet Union in 1941, this faction, called OUN-B after its leader Stjepan Bandera, declared Ukrainian independence in Lviv. The rival OUN-M (for Melnyk) tried to set up a Ukrainian National Council in Kiev. Both organizations initially believed that they could draw upon German support for their schemes. They received particular encouragement from *Wehrmacht* officers and academics who wanted to take advantage of the hostility felt by non-Russian peoples in the USSR towards the Soviet state. Yet once the SS and *Wehrmacht* had shored up control over the Ukraine in late 1941, the Nazi leadership speedily ordered the arrest of all Ukrainian nationalist leaders. The increasingly oppressive nature of German rule led to the formation of a nationalist resistance organization that called itself the Ukrainian Patriotic Army (UPA). By 1942, the UPA was both engaged in active combat against the Germans as well as being involved in sporadic fighting against units of the Polish Home Army. In the course of this conflict, the UPA itself quickly split into two autonomous forces; one pledging its loyalty to Bandera and the other aligning itself to Melnyk.[15]

During the interwar period, many German academics working on Eastern European affairs, such as Michael Brackman, Paul Rohrbach or Theodor Oberländer took a great interest in the fate of these rival Ukrainian nationalist organizations. These specialists, who became known as *Ostforscher,* shared the OUN's hatred of Poland and the USSR. Some of the most fervent German nationalists in the academic community envisioned a strategic alliance between the German state and Ukrainian leaders when it came to any future regional conflict. Equally intrigued by the Ukrainian option were *Reichswehr* officers and intelligence officials who had administered the Ukraine during the First World War. This interest among government circles was reflected in significant pension payments to leading members of Simon Petliura's short-lived Ukrainian Republic out of secret *Reichswehr* funds. Nevertheless, even the most pro-Ukrainian *Ostforscher* envisioned a subordinate role for their Ukrainian allies. In the 1920s, figures such as Rohrbach assumed that any future Ukrainian government would thankfully accept the 'guidance' of German officials.[16]

The *Ostforschung* network's approach towards Ukrainian affairs exerted considerable influence over the *Auswärtiges Amt* and German intelligence agencies (particularly the SD [*Sicherheitsdienst*] and *Abwehr*). Although any contact between such agencies remained at a relatively low level, they did encourage both wings of the OUN to believe that Ukrainian nationalism enjoyed the tacit support of the German state. Yet, the SD, *Abwehr* and *Auswärtiges Amt* avoided making any firm commitments when it came to Ukrainian independence. In the 1930s, the Gestapo even ordered Ukrainian associations in Germany to tone down their rhetoric in order to avoid provoking the Soviet or Polish governments.[17] Despite these unpromising circumstances, OUN activists continued to put their trust in conservative academics and bureaucrats whose plans for Eastern Europe were far less radical than Hitler's programme of conquest and racial extermination. Throughout, Ukrainian nationalists failed to recognize the central role played by anti-Slav racism in Nazi ideology. After 1941, academics such as Rohrbach and the sovietologists in Admiral Canaris's *Abwehr* still believed that an alliance with non-Russians in the USSR would ensure the success of any anti-Bolshevik 'crusade'. The confidence that this circle of conservative officials and academics would determine German policy encouraged OUN activists as well as other Ukrainian nationalists to take an active part in the initial invasion of the Soviet Union. After the first months of the war Hitler and the SS administrators who really controlled the conquered territories put paid to these illusions.[18]

Yet, following the example of the nationalist leadership, thousands of Ukrainians joined *Wehrmacht* and SS auxiliary units in the months following the German invasion in June 1941. The brutality of the Soviet security services in western Ukraine and the Great Famine of the 1930s in eastern Ukraine had engendered lasting hatred for the Stalinist state among most Ukrainians.[19] A series of anti-Jewish pogroms in the first days of German occupation also indicated the strength of anti-Semitism in the region. As the underlying racial agenda of the Hitler regime became clear, those Ukrainian nationalists who had avoided initial arrest by the SS fled to the forests. The forced conscription of Ukrainians to work in appalling conditions in Germany only worsened relations between the local population and the occupiers.[20] While those who had joined the *Wehrmacht* and SS in 1941 remained loyal to their units because they feared reprisals from the Red Army, Ukrainians who had initially been neutral began to organize systematic resistance against the Germans. This ultimately shaped the strategic direction of the Ukrainian Patriotic Army. By fighting the *Wehrmacht* during the war and the Soviet Union until the early 1950s, the UPA set itself out as a force beholden to no outside power.[21]

Along with UPA veterans and exiled political figures, former soldiers and officers of such battlefield units as the Ukrainian *Waffen* SS division played a key role in émigré organizations after 1945. Activists with this kind of background often remained in touch with their former German comrades in arms, a link that greatly benefited the postwar émigré lobbying effort. Senior members of the Lithuanian, Latvian and Estonian communities (that the *Auswärtiges Amt* grouped together as 'Balts') who worked closely together with Ukrainian émigré organizations emulated their Ukrainian partners in this respect. Thus Baltic SS veterans' associations and individual exiled Baltic academics that had been trained by German *Ostforscher* before 1939 did their best to reactivate links with conservative West German officials and academics after the war.[22] One future patron of the Ukrainian and Baltic causes was Theodor Oberländer, who had arrived in Lviv in the first days of the war as an officer of a *Wehrmacht* battalion that used Ukrainians as translators. An *Ostforscher* who played a prominent role in the academic circles that backed German expansion during the interwar period, Oberländer became Minister for Refugees and Expellees under Adenauer in the 1950s.[23]

The breakdown in relations between Ukrainians and Germans during the war did not stop the OUN and other nationalist organizations from renewing their relationship with old German contacts in the Federal Republic. To a certain extent, the revival of cooperation between Ukrainian nationalists and influential German academics was strengthened by the inability of the *Ostforschung* network to exert any influence over occupation policy during the war. While the *Ostforschung* circle must bear considerable responsibility for encouraging Hitler's dreams of empire, the fact that few of its members had been directly involved in atrocities during the invasion of the Soviet Union enabled them to avoid responsibility for their support of the national socialist regime. At the mercy of ambivalent Western occupying powers, Ukrainian nationalist leaders with problematic war records of their own were unlikely to pose any difficult questions to their partners in the West German state. Both sides found it more convenient to unite against their common Soviet enemy.[24]

For opponents of Ukrainian nationalism both inside and outside the Iron Curtain, the initial enthusiasm of Ukrainian politicians for the German invasion and the participation of a number of Ukrainians in the Nazi machinery of terror provided enough material with which to discredit Ukrainian émigrés in the 1950s. East German propagandists used this relationship for their own ends, releasing information that implicated prominent West Germans such as Theodor Oberländer in some of the worst atrocities committed by the Germans in Ukraine.[25] Soviet officials or their sympathizers in Germany were not the only groups interested in damaging influential émigrés and their West German patrons either. Russian and Polish political exiles hostile to Ukrainian nationalism also used such information in order to embarrass an émigré political movement with which they were competing for the patronage of Western intelligence agencies.[26]

Such material did not even have to be made public. As reports by the BND and *Auswärtiges Amt* from early 1960s Washington indicate, even when only circulated in government circles such information could seriously dent the support of Western governments for Ukrainian independence.[27] Despite the political influence of the Ukrainian diaspora in the United States and Canada, there were enough suspicions concerning the past of many émigré leaders for such material to do considerable damage to their cause, which was also not helped by the tendency of some political exiles to indulge in anti-Semitic rhetoric. Community leaders' unthinking defence of Ukrainians accused of war crimes, whatever their individual culpability might have been, exacerbated this problem. Such ethnic solidarity did not improve Ukrainian nationalism's image among left-liberal circles in Europe and North America.[28]

Many left-wing members of the prewar diaspora were also suspicious of compatriots who had collaborated with the Nazi regime.[29] These concerns were particularly strong among DPs who had been forced labourers in Germany, even if many refused to return to their homeland because they feared arrest by the Soviet intelligence service (NKVD). Local staff working for elite German SS units often facilitated the initial process of selection and transport of young Ukrainian forced labourers to Germany. After 1945, those who had collaborated either out of conviction or under duress belonged to the same refugee population as the many Ukrainians who had suffered in prisoner of war (POW), concentration or slave labour camps. Nowhere did perpetrators and victims live in greater proximity to one another than in the DP barracks of West Germany.[30]

In the late 1940s, this conflict within the Ukrainian community in the refugee camps was exacerbated by tension between rival political organizations such as the OUN-B and OUN-M.[31] Both movements were heavily involved in widespread disturbances surrounding the repatriation programme designed to return refugees, former concentration camp inmates and POWs to homelands that were now under Soviet control. Although many did return home despite the risks, enough feared retribution from the NKVD to keep the DP camps full despite the best efforts of Allied authorities. The inhabitants of DP camps participated in violent protests when United Nations commissions containing Soviet military personnel arrived to encourage Ukrainians, Russians or Balts to return to the USSR. This initial reaction may have been spontaneous, yet activists who had already been involved in ethnic nationalist causes before and during the war quickly joined these acts of resistance. This activity was helped by the fact that the camps were organized along ethnic lines. As a result, camp infrastructure quickly became synonymous with ethnic infrastructure.[32]

The success of émigré leaders in warding off repatriation through direct action helped to cement the loyalty of DPs to their cause. Even after most DPs had left Germany, this provided larger émigré groups with a basis to mobilize a respectable number of their compatriots for street demonstrations and other forms of protest designed to attract attention to the fate of their various homelands in the 1940s and 1950s. For émigré leaders regular demonstrations served as a means with which to both maintain the fervour of their supporters and grab the attention of the wider public. Long before the first guest workers arrived, many West Germans had already witnessed large numbers of noncitizens protesting against the political order of their homelands. Though Allied occupation authorities retained oversight of security matters until 1950, West German authorities were responsible for bringing such incidents under control in cooperation with British and American troops.[33]

This initially brought West German police officers into conflict with DPs and émigré leaders rather than foster any underlying sense of solidarity. In the immediate postwar years, West German police and civil servants saw DPs as the main cause of black market activity, despite the fact that most of the German population was involved in illegal trading. As Richard Evans has pointed out, the methods used by German police under Allied guidance to crack down upon the black market bore the hallmarks of some of the tactics used by the *Wehrmacht* and SS. So-called 'razzias', in which police surrounded DP camps and then searched them for black market goods, were seen as a legitimate method of law enforcement by German officials, though some Allied officials felt uncomfortable with the practice.[34] This approach to ostensible 'foreigner criminality' (*Ausländerkriminalität*) influenced the methods used by West German authorities to control political demonstrations organized by DPs. When ordered by Allied administrators to break up such events, police commanders therefore felt no qualms when it came to using force.[35]

An example of an aggressive state response to DP unrest was a demonstration organized by Ukrainian émigrés in Munich on 10 April 1949. This incident was described extensively in reports by US intelligence officials based at the Munich station of the Counter Intelligence Corps (CIC). The Americans had hoped that a demonstration at the *Königsplatz*, which had been registered as a religious expression of solidarity with the Hungarian Cardinal Mindeszenty (who had been recently arrested by the NKVD), could be overseen by the Munich police alone. Organized by an émigré organization called the Anti-Bolshevik Bloc of Nations (ABN), émigré activists hoped to use the ostensibly religious background to Mindiszenty's arrest as a pretext for a political demonstration. CIC officers only found out that this ostensible prayer meeting was going to turn into a protest march to the Soviet Mission at *Herkomerplatz* led by members of the Ukrainian Patriotic Army two days before the event. Despite this advance knowledge, American authorities took no pre-emptive action and decided that,

> The Munich MG Field office ruled that it was still a civil police matter and that since it was Sunday and there was little traffic, there was no reason why the German police could not cope with any situation which might arise.[36]

In fact, this small contingent of German police had to deal with a gathering of up to 4,000 Ukrainians.

After the licensed religious meeting at the *Königsplatz* came to end in an orderly fashion, the crowd started moving towards the Soviet Mission, breaking through a small cordon of German police in the process. Once it became clear that the fifteen German policemen on the spot were unable to cope with this incident, units from the U.S. Military Police (MP) were fed into the area in order to avoid the diplomatic incident with the USSR that was likely to result from a successful storming of Soviet diplomatic property by irate DPs. A breakdown in coordination between German police and U.S. MPs meant that some protestors were able to break through the first line of police and troops at *Immaninger Straße,* only a few blocks down from *Herkomerplatz.* Another provisional line of U.S. MPs drawn up further down at *Herkomerstraße* then panicked, opening fire with tear gas before charging the remaining protestors (who were throwing stones by this point) with fixed bayonets. This assault finally managed to break up this demonstration, though minor scuffles between police and DPs continued throughout the evening.[37]

A dozen German policemen had to be hospitalized while hundreds of DPs suffered the after effects of tear gas in the days following the demonstration.[38] Though ambulances had taken several protestors to hospital, information on the extent of their injuries was not collected by either U.S. or German authorities. In one report to the Deputy Governor of the American zone, a Major Murray van Wagoner (who was the Army Land Director on duty) did his best to play down the riot at *Herkomerplatz.* A section in an early outline of this report that described the use of rifle butts and bayonets to control protestors was missing in the final draft. The injuries of German police were written off as minor while attempts were made to emphasize that van Wagoner and his American colleagues had followed proper procedures. When finally forced to deal with the issue of DP casualties, van Wagoner tried to assuage headquarters by stating:

> One DP is reported hospitalized, the result of a bayonet wound in the leg. In the majority, so far as known, bayonets were only used *for prodding and keeping the crowd moving* (author's own italics).[39]

Although press reports in the *Süddeutsche Zeitung, Münchener Merkur* and *Abendzeitung* contained extensive descriptions of the fighting at *Herkomerplatz,* the police only produced some brief situation reports.[40]

Nonetheless, the press sources and the American reports dealing with this incident shed light on some of the tensions that existed between émigré leaders, German bureaucrats and Allied military authorities. For Major van Wagoner and other middle-ranking figures in the U.S. military administration, there were clear reasons why it was necessary to prevent a religious ceremony from turning into a political demonstration. The military government had issued a permit allowing a religious event, but had explicitly forbidden any political protests at *Königsplatz* in order to avoid provoking the Soviets at a time when they were still blockading West Berlin. Although a prayer meeting on behalf of a Cardinal arrested by the Soviets was in itself a manifestation of political opinion, U.S. authorities hoped that an event run by clergymen would take place without attracting much attention. Van Wagoner and other American officials therefore presented the decision by ABN and UPA men to turn this religious meeting into a noisy protest march as an act of disrespect towards the U.S. military government that had to be countered.[41]

Yet some of the émigré activists teargassed and clubbed by U.S. military police at *Herkomerplatz* were also working for American intelligence services such as the CIC or their German subcontractors in the *organization Gehlen* (OG: the future BND). With the Cold War fully underway by 1949, several senior figures in the Ukrainian community were even on the American or OG payroll, as the burgeoning relationship between émigré activists and the Western intelligence community in Munich began to take shape.[42] Thus, while some CIC officers were coordinating the MPs and German policemen who were trying to bring the Ukrainian DPs under control in order to prevent trouble with the Soviets, other members of the same CIC office were working together with the same set of anti-communist DPs in the covert war against Soviet bloc intelligence services.

Certain passages in the CIC report illustrate the importance of shared anti-communism in shaping Allied attitudes towards DP political activity. One of the most extensive sections was filed under 'Subversive Activity'. Here van Wagoner takes an extensive look at the possibility that communists may have infiltrated this demonstration. Although there seems to have been little evidence of a communist operation, van Wagoner was still prepared to accept that communists had intervened, suggesting that:

> There is a suspicion that a communist may have cut a wire connected with the speaking amplifier during the meeting. This cut wire came after two speeches were concluded and hindered the speaking until repaired.[43]

With the exception of this (possibly imaginary) act of 'communist aggression', van Wagoner ultimately concluded that an attack on the Soviet Mission did not serve the interests of world communism.[44] Yet this search for a hidden communist hand indicates that one of the primary concerns for American authorities was the possibility that DPs might wittingly or unwittingly help the Soviets spread communism among similarly disaffected elements of the German population. Providing U.S. support for anti-Soviet organizations within the DP camps such as the ABN was therefore seen as an essential means with which to stabilize liberal democratic institutions in West Germany. Such sentiment reinforced the position of anti-communist émigré leaders who sought the support of the British and Americans.[45]

It was not a coincidence that the instigators of the protests on 10 April 1949 did not have to face any consequences for crossing the boundary from peaceful protest to illegal action. In the days after the demonstration, senior Ukrainian leaders did their best to patch up relations with military authorities in order to keep this incident from endangering their lucrative contacts with the CIA. Conversely, the Americans were happy to sweep the whole matter under the carpet in order to mollify anti-Soviet émigré movements, who could count on strong support from their diaspora communities in the United States and Great Britain. Faced with the murky world of exile politics in Munich, West Berlin and Hamburg, West German authorities therefore had to deal with a powerful third party in American and British intelligence officials. Reflecting the precarious position of a state still dependent on the protection of outside powers, members of federal police and intelligence agencies had to be particularly careful when dealing with exiles from other states on the frontline of the Cold War. Any decisions that West German security services made about either tolerating or suppressing émigré groups therefore had to take the wishes of their possible American, British or French patrons into account until 1990.[46]

At the time of the *Herkomerplatz* incident, however, West German officials and politicians close to the émigré milieu were not yet in a position to give it autonomous support. Old intelligence contacts from before 1945 were mostly working for the OG or the embryonic diplomatic service in Bonn. Moreover, with the impending formation of an autonomous West German state, many of the figures who came to play a key role in the first years of the Federal Republic were still trying to secure jobs in new state institutions and political parties.[47] With such a speedy turnover in departments and parties, it often became difficult for activists to keep track of their German allies. As long as the OG was still a subcontractor of the CIA rather than a department of the Chancellery and other future members of the police and security services remained subordinated to Allied commanders, most German officials remained focused on ensuring the survival of their future state.[48] Only when the German political establishment felt more secure in its own position in the mid 1950s was it able to provide an alternative source of patronage that could compete with American or British forces stationed on German soil.

If Germans played any role between 1945 and 1955, it was often that of intermediary between émigré organizations searching for Western patronage and British or American services looking for East Europeans who could help them infiltrate the Soviet sphere of influence.[49] The large-scale demonstrations that were needed to mobilize the support of the compatriots in the DP camps and the diaspora could often get in the way of this kind of covert manoeuvring. Open demonstrations not only attracted the attention of a wider public, they also drew the anger of Soviet and other homeland states towards West German authorities who permitted such activity. Resulting Soviet diplomatic pressure could turn even the most emollient émigré groups into a liability for their German allies. In the case of immigrant or émigré groups on the right-wing end of the political spectrum, the contacts that existed between their predecessors and the Nazi regime were often publicized with much fanfare by the East German press in order to discredit the Federal Republic and its Western allies.[50]

During this period, Ukrainian leaders in West Germany tried to guarantee that their internal political differences did not lead to any deeper divisions in the community as a whole. In the late 1940s, several rival political movements, often with no more than two dozen members, were established with the aim of giving a voice to political points of view suppressed within the OUN-B. Political discussions between OUN stalwarts and such dissidents as Leo Rebet or Professor Anton Mirtschuk often disintegrated into noisy rows, as in exile even minute ideological differences seemed to acquire vast significance. Religious tension between Ukrainian Orthodox and Greek Catholic clergy only exacerbated these problems. This intolerant atmosphere had its origins in the authoritarianism of 1920s Central and Eastern Europe, which had shaped the world view of many older émigrés. Even the more democratically minded Ukrainian intellectuals of the 1950s still struggled with the legacy of their formative years in which fascist, rather than liberal, ideals were considered to be the wave of the future.[51]

Yet those involved in these ideological disputes often worked side by side for Ukrainian language publications or at the Ukrainian Free University in Munich. Demonstrations in front of Soviet diplomatic buildings, petitions to Western governments or the lobbying of German politicians were all organized along bipartisan lines. Rather than becoming an additional source of conflict, cross-party organizations such as the Ukrainian Central Association or the *Zentralverband der Ukrainer in Deutschland* actually managed to function with relative efficiency.[52] In other East European communities such institutions were hijacked by political organizations and used to promulgate a specific ideological agenda. By preventing any individual organization from playing too dominant a role within its community, Ukrainian émigré leaders managed to make sure that each political group had a stake in common institutions.

Nevertheless, the OUN-B remained the most prominent Ukrainian nationalist organization in postwar West Germany. Its close links with the UPA, which continued to resist the Red Army and NKVD until the early 1950s, strengthened the OUN-B's credibility within the wider community. Of equal significance were the contacts the OUN-B had with Western intelligence agencies eager for information over internal developments in the USSR that UPA operatives could provide. Though these sources dried up after the UPA was finally defeated, intelligence services only severed links with the OUN-B in the 1960s, after it had become clear that émigré groups had lost touch with events in the Soviet Union.[53] Capitalizing on such links, the OUN-B established the Anti-Bolshevik Bloc of Nations (ABN), whose membership consisted of prominent émigrés along with anti-communists from the FRG and other Western nations. Not surprisingly, Theodor Oberländer was one of the leading members of an organization that enabled the OUN-B to portray itself as part of a wider anti-communist coalition. The postwar activities of Bandera and his supporters worried the KGB enough for it to target the OUN-B in a campaign of intimidation waged against anti-Soviet émigrés. Stjepan Bandera himself was to pay a fatal price for his organization's attempts to revive Ukrainian resistance against Soviet rule. His assassination in Munich in 1958 demonstrated how vulnerable émigrés on West German soil were to retribution from the KGB and other Warsaw Pact security services.[54]

Despite the OUN-B's prominence within the community, officials from the *Auswärtiges Amt* and the *Bundesministerium des Inneren* also stayed in touch with Ukrainian exiles involved in rival political organizations. These broad links existed between members of the southern *Land* governments and politically active émigrés as well, some of whom even went on to acquire West German citizenship and join the CDU/CSU. On a wider level, émigrés with an academic background could influence the decision-making process of federal ministries through their participation in research institutes and think tanks such as the *Forschungsgruppe Ost* in Munich or the *Südost Institut* in Düsseldorf. These institutions were established in the early 1950s by academics that had begun successful careers under the Hitler regime. The *Auswärtiges Amt* regularly requested reports from such institutes on events in the Soviet sphere of influence while other ministries relied on their specialist knowledge when dealing with domestic issues involving the communist bloc.[55]

This kind of work enabled Ukrainian activists in the FRG to enjoy some material comfort without having to find employment outside academic or political circles. For similar reasons, a high quotient of German academics working in these organizations had themselves been expellees, strengthening the hand of another set of interest groups who supported an aggressive approach towards the communist world.[56] Thus, a number of key émigré or expellee academics possessed considerable access to the West German policy-making process during the Adenauer era. Though the ethnic background of émigrés who wrote and worked in such institutes was quite diverse, those non-Germans who acquired senior positions in these institutes and the wider academic scene were often of Ukrainian origin. The prevalence of these political exiles created an academic environment with a considerable overlap between political analysis and political activism.[57]

This research activity was fostered by the presence of organizations in West Germany designed to combat Soviet influence funded by the United States as well as other NATO intelligence agencies. Many were established during the Berlin Blockade, a period when many believed that some sort of conflict with the Soviet Union was imminent.[58] Moreover, with a considerable amount of information to sort through and not enough Americans proficient in Eastern European languages, the BND, CIA and MI6 contracted translation work and political analysis out to such reliable émigrés.[59] However, the most prominent employers of émigré staff were American-run radio services. Based in Munich, both 'Voice of America' and 'Radio Liberty' broadcast entertainment and information from an American perspective to the communist bloc. As with the

BBC World Service, these stations provided both established states and the subject nationalities of the Soviet Union with programming in their own languages. Needing native speakers, international radio stations or intelligence services encouraged East European intellectuals to settle in Munich, leading to a concentration of émigré political activity in that city. Intensifying this trend, the CIA had a heavy presence in Bavaria, while the headquarters of the *Bundesnachrichtendienst* (BND), the West German secret service, was set up in the Munich suburb of Pullach.[60]

Ukrainian émigrés were as heavily involved in this international milieu as they were in the local German academic and political scene. Academics such as Leo Rebet managed to find work at 'Radio Free Europe', which could amply augment anything they earned as employees of Ukrainian organizations. Community activists loyal to movements such as the OUN-B, who suddenly found themselves compiling reports for the BND or working for U.S.-backed radio stations, tried to use their positions in order to influence official attitudes or programme content in favour of their own ideological beliefs. By the late 1950s, the radio networks and the intelligence agencies (there was considerable overlap between the two) had to impose strict vetting procedures in order to control the quality and relative impartiality of their reporting. Occasionally, internal lobbying efforts by Ukrainian exiles were also cancelled out by the efforts of Russian conservatives or other émigrés working for organizations that promulgated an agenda that was incompatible with Ukrainian nationalism.[61]

The extent to which an émigré group could influence the output of these organizations depended on the ideological proclivities of their individual Western colleagues. Those who conflated anti-communism with Russophobia backed the promotion of separatism within the Soviet Union. Officials more in sympathy with the Russian point of view might prove deaf to the arguments of non-Russian émigrés such as the Ukrainians. Ultimately, it was the financial security provided by the proliferation of these institutions in the FRG rather than any influence over greater Western policy making, which made them so crucial to the further development of the émigré scene in West Germany. It also helped to strengthen the anti-communist image of Ukrainian activists with their contacts in the West German establishment. Pro-Ukrainian members of the *Ostforschung* network as well as more conventional West German anti-communists could present their support for the Ukrainian diaspora as an important part of the greater Cold War struggle with the USSR.[62] The activities of the CIA and the State Department in 1950s Munich therefore helped to legitimize the close relationship between influential former *Ostforscher* and Ukrainian exiles.

These links manifested themselves most clearly in the Bavarian *Land* government's sponsorship of the Ukrainian Free University (UFU) in Munich. Founded by Ukrainian exiles in 1919, the UFU had originally been a research institute based in Prague during the interwar period designed to provide a base free from Polish or Soviet interference for those who wished to conduct academic work on Ukrainian affairs. With the advance of the Red Army into Czechoslovakia in April 1945, the remaining Ukrainian members of the UFU fled to Augsburg. By the late 1940s, Ukrainian leaders were able to rebuild the UFU in Munich, where it provided the Ukrainian diaspora with a Ukrainian language institute of higher education. Crucial to the further survival of the UFU during the Cold War were the considerable subsidies paid to it by the Bavarian and federal governments who also granted state recognition to the degrees it conferred upon its students. Until the early 2000s, not only did the Bavarian state fund the UFU, it was also directly involved in its administration. By funding the careers of many exiled Ukrainian academics, the Bavarian state was therefore effectively subsidizing political activists from the OUN-B and other nationalist organizations.[63]

The state-sponsored revival of the UFU enjoyed strong support from several members of the *Ostforschung* network. Using his position as a senior official and then minister at the ministry responsible for refugees and expellees, the *Bundesministerium für Flüchtlinge und Vertriebene*, Theodor Oberländer ensured that this ministry provided the UFU with further financial aid. He also used his influence as a member of the CDU in order to lobby ministers in the Adenauer government for the acceptance of the UFU as an institution of higher education rather than as an émigré think tank. In Munich, similar efforts to lobby the Bavarian government were coordinated by former *Ostforscher* close to the Ukrainian community, such as Paul Rohrbach and Hans Koch. Ukrainian academics repaid this favour by providing support for the pet projects of German *Ostforscher* associated with the revival of the UFU. In the early 1950s, some of the most fervent supporters of Hans Koch's move to establish an institute for Eastern European studies in Munich were respected Ukrainian academics such as Anton Mirtschuk. As a consultant for the Bavarian Ministry of Education, Mirtschuk gave Koch strong support during committee meetings in which this project was heavily attacked by officials who thought the institute would be too expensive to run. Ukrainian academics also defended Koch from searching questions about his war record at the Eastern Front.[64]

The close connections between faculty members of the UFU and the wider academic scene in Munich even helped to make Ukrainian community festivals an accepted part of the Bavarian social scene. By the early 1960s, Ukrainian festivals and receptions organized at the UFU were regularly visited by senior members of the CSU, including the Bavarian *Ministerpräsident*. It is difficult to ascertain whether this kind of activity provided Ukrainian activists with any direct influence on policy making, but it does indicate that the CDU/CSU establishment believed that Ukrainian nationalism was a worthy cause.[65]

Other Ukrainian organizations also enjoyed the benefits of West German state funding. The *Auswärtiges Amt* and the *Bundesministerium für Flüchtlinge und Vertriebene* were particularly active in providing Ukrainian associations and political groups with subsidies that enabled them to continue their anti-Soviet activity. While some of this money was intended to help émigré leaders who had fallen on hard times, internal memoranda related to these allocations indicate that the West German officials who controlled these handouts hoped to strengthen anti-communist groups who supported the foreign policy aims of the Adenauer government. Beyond this clear agenda, both West German bureaucrats and émigré activists believed that non-German refugees should be provided with an autonomous ethnic infrastructure in order to prevent their total assimilation into a 'Germanic' culture inimical to their 'Slavic' character.[66] Thus, a continuing obsession with German cultural distinctiveness among the West German centre-right, which was to prove such an obstacle to the integration of immigrant groups after 1965, was of considerable advantage to émigré groups in the 1950s. Not surprisingly, this sort of borderline racist sentiment was particularly strong among members of an *Ostforschung* network whose approach towards Eastern European culture was shaped by racist assumptions.

With the ABN providing it with a strong lobby across Western Europe, the OUN-B was one of the main beneficiaries of the funding provided by the West German government to East European émigré organizations. Yet other Ukrainian organizations also enjoyed grant subsidies of up to 110,000 Deutschmarks a year, sometimes to keep the publishing efforts of smaller splinter groups afloat, but also for cultural events organized by the *Zentralverband der Ukrainer in Deutschland*. In comparison, most other émigré groups did not receive more than 20,000 Deutschmarks.[67] Although these groups obtained considerable donations from Ukrainian organizations in Britain and North America, without the cash provided by the West German government, they would not have been able to either establish such a wide set of programmes and publications or provide so many members of their community with paid positions.[68]

Throughout the Cold War period, Ukrainian organizations exclusively focused their lobbying efforts on politicians and intellectuals affiliated with the CDU/CSU. The authoritarian background of the OUN-B as well as other prominent émigrés marginalized left-wing community organizations, while *Ostforscher* such as Koch or Oberländer had generally supported the persecution of the German Left after the Nazi seizure of power. With the foundation of the FRG, the *Ostforschung* network of academics and bureaucrats had not abandoned either their ideological conservatism or their dislike of social democrats. With its vigorously anti-communist stance and reluctance to accept the Oder/Neisse border with Poland, the West German centre-right proved equally attractive for a German expellee community to which so many former *Ostforscher* belonged. Whereas this network had once put ethnic German activists from across Eastern Europe in touch with the Weimar and Nazi ministerial bureaucracy in the interwar period, after 1945 its surviving members were now in a position to connect the dominant CDU/CSU with expellee and émigré leaders.[69]

Yet the *Herkomerplatz* incident and other cases of DP protest against homeland governments and the repatriation programme were a first indication of the tensions that existed between émigrés campaigning for changes in their homeland and the political priorities of the West German political establishment. It also encapsulates many of the contradictory factors faced by security services when they tried to determine which forms of immigrant political activity could be tolerated and which could not. Even a peaceful protest by émigrés could lead to conflict once contradictions between the political needs of exile movements and those of their German or American backers began to emerge. Anxieties concerning the attitude of both friendly and hostile homeland states, the desire to ensure that nothing undermined the authority of vulnerable police and intelligence agencies, as well as the need to accommodate the interests of more powerful players such as expellee leaders or American officials, could all negate the émigré lobbying efforts.[70]

In this context, the ideological framework of the Cold War remained crucial. For émigré groups hostile to Soviet communism, the strategic implications of German division in the late 1940s and early 1950s provided the basis for a potential alliance with the West German centre-right. In order to attract whatever support they could in preparation for the superpower conflict that many believed to be imminent, East European movements with anti-communist or irredentist agendas emphasized their solidarity with the foreign policy stance of the *Auswärtiges Amt* and the security services. For these émigré activists, support for the systematic diplomatic isolation of the GDR mapped out by the Adenauer government's *Hallstein* doctrine did not pose any problems.[71] Similarly, support for the revision of the Potsdam settlement came easily to émigrés whose nation state ambitions were not affected by the territorial or financial demands of expellee organizations.

The foreign policy doctrine of the Adenauer governments therefore complemented the political goals of most émigré movements. Groups that did not have to cope with expellee hostility went to great lengths to emphasize their anti-communist credentials to the CDU or *Auswärtiges Amt*.[72] The territorial agenda of organizations representing émigré communities such as the Slovaks, Lithuanians or Ukrainians complemented the stated aims of expellee organizations, which included the restoration of Silesia and East Prussia to a united Germany. This combination of irredentist particularism and anti-communism among many émigré activists operating in the Federal Republic was therefore quite compatible with the foreign policy aims of the West German state in the first years of the Federal Republic.

The fervent anti-communism and expellee irredentism of many CDU/CSU supporters in the period between 1949 and 1955 was exacerbated by deep uncertainties over the future of the Federal Republic. Current historiography often portrays the early 1950s as the beginning of a period in which widespread prosperity and full employment quickly overcame the privations and anxieties that had dominated the 1940s.[73] Yet if one examines popular and press opinion in the first years of the Federal Republic, one gains the impression of a society that was still deeply uncertain about the future. Fuelling this malaise were concerns about the long-term viability of an impoverished West German state whose economic reconstruction had only just begun.[74] Adenauer's emphasis on binding the Federal Republic ever closer to the United States, France and the rest of the Western Alliance before improving relations with the Soviet bloc remained controversial until the mid 1950s. Though the integration of the Federal Republic into economic and military institutions such as NATO had already begun, serious doubts existed across the Bonn political establishment about the ability of West German society to withstand the political pressure put upon it by East Germany and the USSR.[75]

Such anxieties were heightened by the release of the so-called 'Stalin Note', a document presented by Soviet diplomats to the United Nations in 1952, which proposed that Germany should be permitted to reunite under the condition that it became a neutral state.[76] Whether or not Soviet intentions were sincere, many on the West German Left found this offer attractive, increasing pressure upon the first Adenauer government for a more conciliatory approach towards the communist bloc and heightening left-wing opposition to plans (implemented in 1955) to create a West German army. Supporters of compromise with the GDR only became marginalized from mainstream political discourse after Soviet troops suppressed the East German workers' uprising in 1953. With memories of the brutal treatment of German refugees by Soviet units in 1945 still fresh, the crushing of East German demonstrations by the Red Army convinced many in the West German centre-left that the USSR could not be trusted.[77]

As long as parliamentary democracy and market capitalism had not taken root in the Federal Republic, political leaders such as Konrad Adenauer or Ernst Reuter believed that the institutional foundations of the West German state were not strong enough to survive a political settlement with its eastern rival.[78] Fearful that American or French politicians might not accept the Federal Republic as an equal partner, the early Adenauer cabinets as well as the SPD-led government of West Berlin appealed for the support of the United States and other NATO members with anti-communist rhetoric similar to that used by East European émigré groups. For example, where Hallstein or Willy Brandt appealed for a 'united western front against Soviet communism' when speaking to British Foreign Secretary Anthony Eden or United States Senators in the summer of 1952, leaders of the Ukrainian community such as Jaroslaw Stetzko or Stjepan Bandera used almost identical language in discussions with West German diplomats or American Congressmen.[79] These similarities in the political language used by West German politicians and anti-communist émigrés led many senior émigré leaders to believe that the political fate of their ethnic homelands had become intertwined with that of the Federal Republic.[80]

Émigré communities also did their best to emphasize their anti-communist credentials. For Ukrainian nationalists, as well as their counterparts in other émigré communities, the political position of a West German state that felt itself to be under siege by its communist rival was identical to that of émigré communities living under the constant fear of retaliation from their communist homeland regimes. The burgeoning relationship between émigré leaders and their old prewar contacts in the *Auswärtiges Amt* and security services seemed to confirm these sentiments. This world view is set out in an angry letter of complaint to the Interior Minister and other senior figures in the *Bundesinnenministerium* written by Jaroslaw Benzal in 1962, a leading figure in the OUN. Denying accusations made in *Das Parlament* (the *Bundestag's* newsletter) that the OUN was an extreme right-wing organization, Benzal went on to claim that:

> Even more surprising is the injustice that has been inflicted upon us, which can only be accounted for by an inexplicable tendency, which will neither serve to bring about German reunification nor the liberation of our homeland.[81]

This belief in shared goals together with the extensive involvement of émigrés with the BND and other NATO intelligence services led many political exiles to overestimate their level of influence over West German diplomats and security officials. Assurances made by *Auswärtiges Amt* or *Bundesministerium für Vertriebene* officials that the West German government remained supportive of émigré agendas only strengthened this impression. Statements such as this one made in a document about the assassination of Stjepan Bandera by the KGB compiled by the federal government's press office, reinforced émigré leaders' belief in their own self-importance:

> the horrifying fact [the assassination of Bandera and Rebet], that one of the highest state agencies of the Soviet Union order – with the knowledge and at the behest of the Soviet government – political murders, whose implementation recklessly infringe upon the sovereignty of other countries as much as they break accepted principles of international law and human rights.[82]

Nevertheless, the influence émigrés claimed to have over the West German government was based more on wishful thinking than political reality. As long as the position of the Federal Republic seemed precarious, a rigid anti-communist policy complementing émigré agendas seemed to be the only option for the Adenauer administration. Once West Germany had anchored itself in the Western Alliance, however, a more flexible approach towards the USSR became possible. The strength of the expellee lobby was still significant enough to limit any kind of permanent settlement with Poland or Czechoslavakia.[83] However, the presence of the Red Army on the West German border together with the large number of German POWs still in Soviet hands necessitated a different approach towards the USSR. This led to negotiations with the Soviets ending in the repatriation of the last German POWs in Soviet camps in 1955. This agreement was one of Adenauer's great political successes and led to the establishment of diplomatic relations with the USSR. Within a year, the Adenauer government had moved from a rigidly anti-Soviet stance akin to that of its émigré allies to a more pragmatic approach towards the Warsaw Pact states.[84]

Though it only represented an incremental shift in policy, without this initial formalization of relations the more far-reaching steps initiated by the SPD after 1969 towards stable coexistence with the Soviet bloc would not have been possible. On the other hand, the anti-communist stance of the CDU/CSU in domestic politics and the limits, which the expellee lobby set upon further compromise with Eastern European states, ensured that compromise with the Soviet Union did not permanently alienate émigré groups.[85] Yet this stabilization of relations with the USSR also revealed how limited the influence on the West German state was of exile groups who wanted to perpetuate the diplomatic isolation of the Soviet Union.

The contradictory nature of West German support for émigré causes can be seen in the response of West German security services to anti-communist émigré activism in the course of the 1950s and 1960s. Some aspects of the relationship between émigrés and their conservative German supporters still seemed to confirm the confidence émigré leaders had in their allies in the Bonn political establishment. Beyond the usual street demonstrations, émigré journalists continued to use their publications as platforms to attack opponents in both their homelands and the Federal Republic, while social events such as concerts or charity balls were still attended by German or other NATO contacts. Events such as the annual UFU ball in Munich were occasionally visited by senior members of the Bavarian CSU, such as Max Streibl, Alfons Goppel or Franz Josef Strauß.[86] This not only provided émigré leaders with access to influential Germans, but it also gave them a chance to demonstrate the ostensible success of their efforts to their own community, enhancing their own standing in the process. Similarly, saint's days or national holidays enabled émigré communities, which were often deeply politically divided, to come together and present a united front to their Western backers.[87]

As long as the work of émigré organizations helped West German officials gather intelligence and find support in the United States, the *Auswärtiges Amt* and the BND were prepared to pay attention to the policy proposals drafted by their activists. Once the interests of émigré organizations diverged even slightly from those of the government, they were quickly marginalized in Bonn, despite the continuing access and funding they received from their contacts in Federal ministries. If a more conciliatory approach towards the Soviet Union could enhance the international position of the Federal Republic, then centre-right politicians pursued such policy even if they contradicted previous assurances given to Ukrainian or Baltic organizations.[88] The restoration of relations with the USSR had a direct effect on policy towards Yugoslavia as well, enabling CDU politicians to adopt a more pragmatic attitude towards the Tito regime. By the late 1950s, a policy of economic cooperation designed to loosen Yugoslavia's bonds with the Warsaw Pact began to drive a wedge between West German state officials and their erstwhile anti-communist friends in the

Croatian community.[89] This need to abandon émigré contacts if they proved inconvenient was quite openly discussed by West German officials at occasions such as this internal meeting over state financial aid to émigré organizations:

> The representatives of the Federal Interior Ministry (Foreigner's Office) expressed their doubts over the suitability of such subsidies, if émigrés on the other hand engage in political activity directed against countries that possess diplomatic relations with the Federal Republic, which is illegal under international law and could have a negative impact upon relations with these countries.[90]

Even though the marginalization of émigré leaders was becoming increasingly evident, many political exiles still maintained to their supporters that they had influence over policy decisions. With any further deepening of ties with the communist bloc unlikely as long as Adenauer was Chancellor, émigré groups from Warsaw Pact countries convinced themselves that the 1955 agreement with the USSR was a one-off.[91] By contrast, as the West Germans joined the general Western effort to detach Yugoslavia from the communist bloc, frustration in the Croatian community with the foreign policy of the Federal Republic fostered growing militancy among younger Croatians as the failure of the leadership's strategy became increasingly evident. In a sense this growing alienation with the West German state among Croatian nationalists foreshadowed the disappointment that would spread to other émigré communities after the social democrats and CDU/CSU formed the Grand Coalition of 1966.[92]

From that point onwards, the *Auswärtiges Amt* under Willy Brandt pursued a policy of détente with the GDR and other Warsaw Pact states. Designed to foster peaceful coexistence with Soviet bloc states, this policy of dialogue with the Soviet bloc in general and GDR in particular came to be known as *Ostpolitik*. As expellees saw their irredentist territorial demands abandoned by the West German state, a sense that the SPD had somehow betrayed the German nation grew among many conservative supporters of the CDU/CSU.[93] Leading to the collapse of the Grand Coalition and with a CDU/CSU unwilling to abandon the *Hallstein* doctrine or offend the expellee lobby, *Ostpolitik* also marked the failure of émigré attempts to garner support from West German state institutions for their own anti-communist or anti-Soviet agendas. A statement by one Ukrainian émigré leader in a leaflet published by the ABN reflects this sense of abandonment and frustration:

> In particular, at this time the Russian and Communist regime uses every thinkable measure to suppress the nationally-oriented ... engaged intellectuals, authors, artists and scientists, in, for example, the Ukraine, White Russia, Turkestan, Georgia, Romania, Bohemia, Slovakia and all other oppressed nations. The behaviour of the Communist leadership makes a mockery of fraudulent claims [made by the German Left] that the system is 'liberalising'. Has the Eastern Europe policy of the Third Reich not damaged German-Ukrainian relations enough? Must old mistakes be repeated?[94]

Having secured their position in the FRG by backing the foreign policy objectives of the Adenauer government, the transformation of West German foreign policy put émigrés in a complex position. East European exiles found it impossible to support *Ostpolitik* as it forced them to abandon any hope of achieving their political goals. In opposition, the CDU/CSU maintained rhetorical support for émigré causes until the late 1970s, reflecting a wider rejection of *Ostpolitik* among members of the CDU/CSU and expellee activists. Yet the foreign policy implications of *Ostpolitik* in the 1970s ultimately crippled émigré movements.[95] The eventual failure of émigré leaders to exert influence over West German foreign policy therefore was one of the factors diminishing their ability to motivate their ageing grass roots to take an active part in exile politics.

The merger of the once influential *Bundesministerium für Flüchtlinge und Vertriebene* with the *Bundesministerium des Innern* immediately after the first Brandt administration took power was symbolic not only of the eclipse of expellee influence, but also of the extent to which East European émigrés' hopes in their West German allies had been misplaced. As SPD and FDP ministers gradually forced the retirement of conservative officials who had at least paid attention to their old émigré contacts, frustration and a sense of betrayal began to take hold of the political rump of émigré communities. By the late 1960s, the dwindling band of émigrés willing or able to take part in demonstrations were protesting as much against an SPD and New Left that they considered to be appeasers of communism as against the communist bloc itself. The slogans painted on placards by Ukrainians and German expellees at one demonstration in Munich reflect this anger:

'GERMANS ARE DEMONSTRATING HERE, NOT THE SDS', '163 [BERLIN] WALL DEAD ACCUSE', 'BUDAPEST AND 17 JUNE ALREADY FORGOTTEN', 'WHERE IS MOSCOW'S ATONEMENT FOR KATYN AND WORKUTA', 'WE HATE EVERY DICTATORSHIP', or 'SMASH KREMLIN IMPERIALISM'.[96]

This rhetoric shows that East European émigrés and their expellee partners felt left behind. The gradual alienation of émigrés from the German political mainstream was the result of shifts in the criteria used by the West German state to judge whether these immigrants were a help or hindrance to government policy, rather than of any ideological shifts within these communities.

A peaceful demonstration, which challenged West German foreign policy, could therefore undermine the more discreet lobbying efforts of senior émigrés. As long as the CDU/CSU dominated West German politics under Adenauer, this did not present such a great problem. The occasional protests that got out of hand, such as those that followed the assassination of Stjepan Bandera, often received the sympathy of politicians who felt equally threatened by Warsaw Pact intelligence agencies. After a symbolic act of punishment, CSU or CDU politicians could quietly pass on expressions of solidarity.[97] But anti-communist East Europeans, to whom the wider German population had at best an ambivalent attitude, had to ensure that they did not embarrass their friends in the West German political establishment. The demonstrations that émigré leaders organized to keep a dwindling band of anti-communist East Europeans in West Germany actively involved in their political battle with the Soviet Union ultimately undermined their position in this respect. While many West Germans outside of the CDU/CSU may have shared the anti-communist beliefs of most East European émigrés, they were only prepared to tolerate émigré activism as long as it did not seem to threaten the interests of the Federal Republic and the safety of individual Germans. If an émigré group engaged in such activity once too often, it could quickly lose the backing of essential local support.

After the late 1950s, West German conservatives tried to avoid any possible accusations by the SPD of supporting foreigners who were endangering public security. An example of how émigré activists could embarrass their German allies in this way was a Ukrainian demonstration against a visit by Soviet delegates to the Dachau memorial during the build-up to the 1972 Olympics. Here former DPs and émigré activists encountered a smaller counter-demonstration organized by the West German Communist Party (DKP). A brawl quickly erupted between infuriated Ukrainians and DKP activists handing out pro-Soviet leaflets. After the police had brought the situation under control, fifteen German communists had to be taken to hospital, representing a small victory for the émigrés in their 'war against world communism' (the main slogan of this demonstration).[98] While the police officer who compiled the official case report showed some sympathy for the Ukrainians' behaviour, the Munich press criticized this demonstration (and the DKP response to it) as an embarrassment to the city in such a vital Olympic year. For West German journalists this incident proved that the émigrés represented a right-wing world view as extreme as the left-wing ideology of the DKP.[99] Ten years earlier the émigrés might have received a more sympathetic hearing from press and politicians, but in an environment now dominated by social democrats, unsympathetic to what they considered to be anti-Soviet particularism, such incidents provided a pretext for further cuts in federal funds to East European community institutions.[100]

Occasionally, the participation of friendly German organizations in anti-Soviet demonstrations could also cause trouble for émigré organizations. While the involvement of expellee groups was uncontroversial during the Adenauer era, expellee fears that the social democrats might abandon their cause led to growing hostility between expellee organizations and the parliamentary Left.[101] Having associated themselves so openly with expellee organizations in the 1950s, most East European émigré movements were dragged into this conflict after 1965. Marches honouring the victims of Stalinism in which expellees took part could often turn into angry protests against SPD policies. As signs emerged that the *Auswärtiges Amt* was preparing the ground for West German recognition of the boundaries determined by the Yalta and Potsdam accords, such frustration became palpable. In October 1969, a point where an SPD takeover of power was imminent, this expellee anger came to the fore in an anti-Soviet march organized by Ukrainian and Baltic organizations. Among a mixed crowd of expellees and émigrés the usual anti-communist and anti-Russian slogans were suddenly accompanied by cries of '*Brandt an die Wand!*' ('Brandt to the execution wall').[102] Such aggressive slogans directed against West German politicians led moderate newspapers such as the *Süddeutsche Zeitung* or the *Abendzeitung* to portray the émigrés and expellees involved as anachronistic extremists. Even the CSU-dominated Munich police force felt moved to charge several participants with 'incitement to violence'.[103]

Yet Ukrainian community leaders continued to emphasize good relations with a diminishing number of contacts in the West German state because they did not have many other factors working for them. Unable to move back and forth from their homeland like the later *Gastarbeiter* communities, they remained cut off from developments in the Ukraine. Though the community grew more united over time, at least in comparison with other émigré groups such as the Russian community, it could still fracture on occasion. Political rivalries between individual leaders continued to trigger extensive debates over ideological minutiae that paralysed meetings. Occasional anti-Semitic statements by Ukrainian activists also repeatedly reminded the Jewish community and left-wing West Germans of the role played by some Ukrainians in the Holocaust.[104]

In the 1950s, the fact that West Germans who were friendly to Ukrainian nationalism encouraged state authorities to be as helpful, or at least as unobtrusive, as possible, meant that such difficulties could ultimately be overcome. A neutral stance on the part of the state would have given the KGB much greater scope to subvert and destroy Ukrainian organizations on West German soil. Yet this dependence upon the support of the West German establishment came to have serious drawbacks. Mired in a belief that the centre-right would remain in power indefinitely, Ukrainian activists were unable to adjust when the shift in the political balance led to the gradual eclipse of the old Adenauer establishment. Once the SPD took power, Ukrainian activists proved ill-equipped to deal with a new political establishment less hostile to the Soviet Union. The continuities in personnel and approach between the bureaucracy of the Hitler regime and the state institutions of the early Federal Republic (that had proved so helpful during the Adenauer era) only accentuated the problematic public image of émigrés in the course of the 1960s. As the liberal press, the student left and, to a lesser extent, the SPD and FDP began to promote various social and administrative reforms, such holdovers from the pre-1945 era were portrayed as an obstacle to change.[105]

Such a shift in attitudes meant that émigré organizations were tarred with the same brush. More liberal media outlets now focused on the authoritarian pre-1945 background of émigré leaders. The *Stasi* did not shy away from publicizing the questionable backgrounds of political exiles and their German contacts either. Such information was either quietly passed on to receptive West German journalists or openly published in East German newspapers and anti-Nazi tracts such as the so-called 'Brown Book', an ostensible record of the Nazi past of prominent West Germans.[106] Though the East European exile infrastructure was established enough to survive hostility from SPD governments, its dependence on state funds meant that West German governments obtained considerable leverage over émigré leaders. In an increasingly hostile environment, any activity considered to represent opposition to the official government line could quickly be brought under control through threats to cut back state subsidies.[107]

The much smaller Baltic organizations succumbed to the demands of their new paymasters more quickly, withdrawing from political activism entirely by the early 1970s, while some Ukrainian émigré leaders did their best to moderate the kind of intemperate anti-left rhetoric with which they had so often offended SPD leaders in the past.[108] Under pressure itself, the West German centre-right did little to help its émigré allies. The *Ostforscher* and their postwar acolytes were ultimately not interested in the Ukrainian cause as an end in itself. Rather, their support for Ukrainian nationalists was based on the assumption that by weakening Poland and the Soviet Union, émigré activity might lead to a revision of the Oder/Neisse border and the demise of communism. If the Ukrainian nationalist movement had at any point stood in the way of ethnic German interests, then it is quite likely that its allies in the West German political establishment would have swiftly distanced themselves from it.[109]

In the postwar period, anti-communist émigrés had boxed themselves into a corner. As long as the CDU/CSU and conservative lobbies such as expellee groups determined the public debate, then such a one-sided approach seemed logical. Throughout the 1950s and 1960s, émigrés did their best to engage in political activities, which they believed would be acceptable to the government of the moment. The fact that they shared the general anti-communist assumptions and social outlook of the Adenauer and Eisenhower administrations made such an approach easier. Yet the assumption that the political order of the Adenauer era was permanent proved to be flawed. By emphasizing their loyalty to that order, they made themselves vulnerable to any sudden change in the Western political consensus. The ultimate fate of most East European émigré organizations therefore demonstrates how being too closely identified with a specific political milieu can damage the long-term prospects of an immigrant movement despite all the short-term advantages it may accrue through such a relationship.

These wider social shifts hit East European exile communities at a time when their own internal development began to hamper their ability to act as an effective political lobby. Only ethnic groups from Yugoslavia were able to benefit from the new wave of immigration triggered by the guest worker programme.[110] The great majority of such émigré groups' membership continued to be former DPs and other refugees who had fled to the Federal

Republic in 1945. As this group aged and the Third World War that many émigrés had predicted in the 1950s entered the realms of science fiction, émigré organizations began to lose their vigour. While former DPs still took part in community events and tried to maintain and finance their community infrastructure, political activism gradually became the exclusive preoccupation of a small number of full-time exile journalists or political functionaries. With infighting fostered by KGB *agents provocateurs* taking its toll, the older and more well established these professional exiles became, the less effective they were.[111] Together with the leftward shift of the West German political consensus, these factors ultimately diminished whatever influence East European exiles had over West German policy making. Playing by the rules and having friends in high places may have helped them to build a community infrastructure and enabled their leaders to establish themselves as middle-class professionals, but when it came to their wider political goals, it brought them nothing.

In comparison to the Ukrainians, there was remarkably little Polish political activity in postwar Germany, even though this community was the largest non-German group within the DP population after the war. In 1960, five years after most of the camps were closed down and most Poles had moved on to Britain or North America, there were still approximately 52,000 former Polish DPs in the Federal Republic. Combined with the remnants of the prewar Polish minority in the Ruhr region, which numbered over 80,000, the Polish community had the potential to become a serious political force.[112] The DP component contained former forced labourers, concentration camp inmates or POWs as well as refugees who had fled the Soviet onslaught in the final stages of the war. These groups tried to avoid repatriation, either because they had supported non-communist resistance movements or risked accusations of collaboration with the Germans.[113]

In the first two years after 1945, Polish DPs received privileged treatment from the Western Allies because of Poland's wartime role. In North Germany, 20,000 Polish soldiers under British command were given administrative control over the Emsland, turning it into a haven for Polish refugees who wished to avoid being repatriated to communist Poland.[114] As relations between the United States and the USSR deteriorated, Polish exiles found employment in Radio Free Europe or in American intelligence agencies based in Munich. Rather than shoring up their position, the backing the British and Americans gave Poles in the late 1940s only seemed to exacerbate German distrust of Polish intentions. West German politicians and security service officials disliked Polish émigrés because of their commitment to the permanent incorporation of East Prussia, Silesia and other territories allotted to Poland in the Potsdam settlement. As long as the West German government did not accept the Oder/Neisse border as permanent, the dangers of lobbying for an agenda that contradicted the doctrines of the Adenauer era were felt by the Polish community.[115] Despite the strength of anti-communist sentiment in the Polish community, the obstacles created by the influence of expellee leaders and the

Ostfrschung network prevented any significant dialogue between Polish émigrés and the German centre-right.[116] The fate of Polish political exiles in the FRG demonstrates that the influence of an ethnic community in 1950s West Germany was not exclusively determined by its size.

Émigré movements did not have to come into direct conflict with the expellees in order to face many of the difficulties that undercut the position of Polish political exiles. Many Russian DPs and exiles in West Germany had fought against the Red Army with the SS and *Wehrmacht* during the war, complicating the relationship of Russian nationalist and monarchist organizations with West German and Allied authorities. Though the CIA did cooperate with Russian groups such as the radical nationalist NTS (National Alliance of Russian Solidarists), this was largely limited to infiltration and disinformation operations directed against the Red Army in the GDR, which occasionally led to bomb attacks organized by the KGB against Russian exiles in Germany.[117]

While Russian émigrés were fervently anti-communist, most also believed that any post-communist regime should keep the borders of the old USSR and ought to be able to exert 'natural' Muscovite influence over Central and Eastern Europe.[118] This stance both led to conflict with Poles, Ukrainians and other émigré groups and alienated West German security officials and diplomats who were not interested in a strong Russia. Rather, leading figures in the intelligence community, such as Reinhard Gehlen, preferred to work with groups such as the Ukrainians and Balts who would weaken both Poland and Russia at the same time, enabling a putative united Germany to dominate Eastern Europe after a Soviet collapse.[119] Thus, while Russian nationalists and German conservatives were at times brought together by a shared fear and loathing of modern Poland, when it came to their actual political position in the Federal Republic, Russian exiles had much in common with their Polish rivals.

Forced to operate in such a difficult atmosphere, Polish or Russian émigrés interested in a political career left Germany. For a political exile, London remained attractive because of the presence of many former members of exile government, while Paris contained a high concentration of émigré intellectuals who could rely upon established contacts with the French elite. With its vast population of East European immigrants, the United States was another destination of choice for many of the more ambitious exiles. Deferring to more senior émigrés in Britain or America, forced to deal with a hostile West German bureaucracy and the reluctance of their own community to get involved, the handful of activists from these communities remained at the periphery of German political life.[120]

∗∗∗∗

Several factors played an important role in shaping the development of émigré communities in the first decade of the Federal Republic. The relative unity of a community could be crucial to its efforts to be taken seriously by West German authorities. Those émigré groups whose community leaders were most prepared to cooperate with one another tended to have the most effective and well connected political organizations. Though it did contain over a dozen political splinter groups, the Ukrainian community managed to maintain a minimum level of political cohesion, enabling its leaders to avoid the kind of infighting that paralysed other communities. This unity was maintained despite a set of factors that would have been more conducive to the kind of internal wrangling that crippled more culturally homogeneous groups.

However much unity and other important factors such as size or support from the broader diaspora may have been significant, the experience of Polish, Czech and Russian organizations demonstrates the crucial nature of the historical relationship between an immigrant homeland and Germany before 1945. Bad relations between Polish exiles and influential West German state officials who had taken part in conflicts with Poland in the interwar period were always going to make it difficult for proponents of the Polish cause in the Federal Republic. The reluctance of Polish leaders to accommodate the political illusions of the Adenauer era (particularly when contrasted with the germanophilia of Ukrainians or Croatians) led to the marginalization of Polish exiles in the Federal Republic.

Yet shared history did not just influence the approach taken by the West German centre-right when it came to émigré and immigrant communities. When dealing with immigrant organizations, recent history was of equal importance to the SPD and other left-wing movements. As we shall see in the next chapter, this awareness of recent history caused serious problems for the Croatians, who remained dominated by right-wing organizations in which activists that had collaborated with the Nazis played a prominent role.

Notes

1. Biess. 2001. 'Survivors of Totalitarianism', in H. Schissler (ed.), *The Miracle Years: a Cultural History of West Germany 1949–1968,* Princeton: Princeton University Press, 58–59.
2. R.G. Moeller. 2001. *War Stories: the Search for a Usable Past in the Federal Republic of Germany,* Berkeley: University of California Press, 2–8.
3. B. Dietz. 1997. *Jugendliche Aussiedler: Ausreise, Aufnahme, Integration,* Berlin: Spitz, 10–12.
4. M. Broszat. 1972. *Zweihundert Jahre Deutsche Polenpolitik,* 2nd ed., Frankfurt a.M.: Suhrkamp, 217.
5. M. Roseman. 1997. 'The Federal Republic of Germany', in M. Fulbrook (ed.), *German History since 1800,* London: Arnold, 375.
6. M. Burleigh. 2002. *Germany Turns Eastwards – a Study of Ostforschung in the Third Reich,* London: Pan, 224–27.
7. W. Jacobmeyer. 1985. *Vom Zwangsarbeiter zum Heimatlosen Ausländer: Die Displaced Persons in Westdeutschland 1945–1951,* Göttingen: Vandenhoeck & Ruprecht, 246–52.

8.   L. Luciuk. 2000. *Searching for Place: Ukrainian Displaced Persons, Canada and the Migration of Memory*, Toronto: University of Toronto Press, 79–82.

9.   Bundesarchiv Koblenz, B 106, Nr. 63084, *Loseblattsammlung Bundesministerium des Innern*, Re.: 'Vorwort', Bonn, 1960; and Bundesarchiv Koblenz, B 106, Nr.63088, *Bundesamt für Verfassungsschutz Bericht*, Re.: 'Die Ostemigration in der BRD', Cologne, 11 March 1963.

10. Bundesarchiv Koblenz, B 106, Nr.63088, *Bundesamt für Verfassungsschutz Bericht*, Re.: 'Die Ostemigration in der BRD', Cologne, 11 March 1963.

11. O. Subtelny. 1989. *Ukraine: A History*, Toronto: University of Toronto Press.

12. O.S. Fedyshyn. 1971. *Germany's Drive to the East and the Ukrainian Revolution 1917–1918*, New Brunswick: Rutgers University Press, 251–53.

13. Landesarchiv Berlin, B Rep. 042, Nr. 27159, *Vereinsakte: Ukrainische Nationale Vereinigung*, Re.: 'Protokoll der Jahresversammlung der Mitglieder der Ukrainischen Nationalen Vereinigung e.V. vom 20. November 1937', Berlin, 23 November 1937.

14. M. Yurkevich. 1992. 'Ukrainian Nationalists and DP Politics', in W.I. Wsewolod (ed.), *The Refugee Experience: Ukrainian Displaced Persons after World War II*, Edmonton: Canadian Institute of Ukrainian Studies Press, 125–28.

15. J.A. Armstrong. 1990. *Ukrainian Nationalism*, 3rd ed., Englewood: Ukrainian Academic Press, 227–28.

16. P. Rohrbach. 1918. 'Ukrainische Eindrücke', *Deutsche Politik 3*.

17. Landesarchiv Berlin, B Rep. 042, Nr. 27159, *Bericht Ukrainische Nationale Vereinigung an Amtsgericht Berlin*, Re.: 'Vereinsakte 'Ukrainische Nationale Vereinigung', Berlin, 23 January 1940.

18. Y. Boshyk (ed.). 1986. *Ukraine during World War II: History and its Aftermath*, Edmonton Canadian Institute of Ukrainian Studies; and Burleigh, *Germany Turns Eastwards*, 244–45.

19. R. Conquest. 1986. *The Harvest of Sorrow: Soviet Collectivization and the Terror-Famine*, London: Hutchinson, 333–39.

20. Burleigh, *Germany Turns Eastwards*, 222–23.

21. Armstrong, *Ukrainian Nationalism*, 213–15.

22. Bay. HstA. Mun., Landesflüchtlingsverwaltung, Nr. 2242, *Niederschrift*, Re.: 'Über die gemeinsame Sitzung des Stiftungsrates und des Kuratoriums des Ost-Europa-Instituts in München am 12.11.1951', Munich, 13 November 1951. Several of the academics involved in these academic funding discussions were Ukrainian political exiles.

23. *Der Spiegel*, 'Oberländer: Drittes Reich im Kleinen', 2 December 1959, 37–39.

24. G. Prokoptschuk. 1963. *Deutsch-Ukrainische Gesellschaft 1918–1963*, Munich: Deutsch-Ukrainische Ges. Verl., 31–40.

25. H. Raschhofer. 1964. *Political Assassination: the Legal Background of the Oberländer and Staschinsky Cases*, Tübingen: Fritz Schlichtumage Verl., 11–15.

26. Bundesarchiv Koblenz, B 106, Nr. 63085, *Brief OUN-B to Bundesministerium des Inneren*, Re.: 'Stellungsnahme zu der Unrichtigen Beurteilung des Politische Charakters der Organisation Ukrainischer Nationalisten (OUN)', Munich, 16 May 1962.

27. Pol. A.A. Ber., B 40, Nr. 37, *Mitteilung – Botschaft der Bundesrepublik Deutschland in Washington DC an Auswärtiges Amt Bonn*, Re.: Besuch – Ehemaliger ukrainischer Premierminister Yaroslav Stetzko', Washington, 7 March 1963.

28. A. Reid. 1997. *Borderland: a Journey through the History of the Ukraine*, London: Phoenix, 165–68.

29. Boshyk, *Ukraine during World War II*, 68–71.

30. V. Markus. 1992. 'Political Parties in the DP Camps', in W.I. Wsewolod (ed.), *The Refugee Experience: Ukrainian Displaced Persons after World War II*, Edmonton: Canadian Institute of Ukrainian Studies Press, 115–17.

31. Yurkevich, 'Ukrainian Nationalists and DP Politics', 129–39; and Jacobmeyer, *Vom Zwangsartbeiter zum Heimatlosen Ausländer*, 76–82.

32. V. Kulyk. 2003. 'The Role of Discourse in the Construction of an Émigré Community: Ukrainian Displaced Persons in Germany and Austria after the Second World War', in R.

Ohliger and K. Schönwälder (eds), *European Encounters: Migrants, Migration and European Societies since 1945*, Aldershot: Ashgate, 214–18.

33. Bay. HstA. Mun., Findbuch OMGBY (Amerikanische Militärregierung Bayern): *Nr. 10/109-1/10, Reports/German Staff*, Re.: 'DP Camps and Security: Report by Alfred Kiss, German Investigator ICD Augsburg', Augsburg, 25 November 1947.

34. R.J. Evans. 1996. *Rituals of Retribution: Capital Punishment in Germany 1600-1987*, Oxford: Penguin, 752.

35. Jacobmeyer, *Vom Zwangsarbeiter zum Heimatlosen Ausländer*, 210–18.

36. Bay. HstA. Mun., Findbuch OMGBY (Amerikanische Militärregierung Bayern): *Nr. 10/89-1/33, CIC Reports/Intelligence Staff*, Re.: 'Ukrainian DP Meeting and Demonstration in Munich on 10 April 1949', Munich, 11 April 1949.

37. *Münchener Merkur*, 'Ukrainische Demonstration am Herkomerplatz', 11 April 1949.

38. *Süddeutsche Zeitung*, 'Schwere Zusammenstöße in München', 11 April 1949; and Bay. HstA. Mun., Findbuch OMGBY (Amerikanische Militärregierung Bayern): *Nr. 10/89-1/33, CIC Reports/Intelligence Staff*,Re.: 'Ukrainian DP meeting and Demonstration in Munich on 10 April 1949', 11 April 1949.

39. Bay. HstA. Mun., Findbuch OMGBY (Amerikanische Militärregierung Bayern): *Nr. 10/89-1/33, CIC Reports/Intelligence Staff*, Re.: 'Ukrainian DP meeting and Demonstration in Munich on 10 April 1949', 11 April 1949.

40. *Münchener Merkur*, 'Ukrainische Demonstration am Herkomerplatz'; *Abendzeitung*, 'Ein Augenzeugenbericht der Münchener Demonstrationen', 11 April 1949; *Abendzeitung*, 'Was die Kommunisten Sagen', 11 April 1949; *Süddeutsche Zeitung*, 'Schwere Zusammenstöße in München'.

41. Bay. HstA. Mun., Findbuch OMGBY (Amerikanische Militärregierung Bayern): *Nr. 10/89-1/33, CIC Reports/Intelligence Staff*, Re.: 'Ukrainian DP meeting and Demonstration in Munich on 10 April 1949', Munich, 11 April 1949.

42. O. Goebel. 1997. 'Gladio in der Bundesrepublik', in J. Mecklenburg (ed.), *GLADIO: Die Geheime Terrororganisation der NATO*, Berlin: Elefanten Press, 70.

43. Bay. HstA. Mun., Findbuch OMGBY (Amerikanische Militärregierung Bayern): *Nr. 10/89-1/33, CIC Reports/Intelligence Staff*, Re.: 'Ukrainian DP meeting and Demonstration in Munich on 10 April 1949', Munich, 11 April 1949.

44. Ibid.

45. Pol. A.A. Ber., B 42, Nr. 981A, *Bericht des Bundesministeriums für Flüchtlinge und Vertriebene*, Re.: 'Förderung von Osteuropäischen Exilorganisationen seit 1948', Bonn, 6 March 1968.

46. L.O. Michaelis. 1999. *Politische Parteien unter der Beobachtung des Verfassungsschutzes – Die Streitbare zwischen Toleranz und Abwehrbereitschaft*, Baden Baden: Nomos Verlag. (Schriften zum Parteinrecht Nr. 26), 67.

47. D. Schenk. 2003. *Die Braunen Wurzeln des BKA*, Frankfurt a.M.: Fischer Verl, 154–60.

48. T. Naftali. 2004. 'Berlin to Baghdad: the Perils of Hiring Enemy Intelligence', *Foreign Affairs* 83(4), 129.

49. Pol. A.A. Ber., B 12, Nr. 455, *Bericht Ref. LR. Scholl/LR. von Staden*, Re.: 'Die Emigration aus der Sowjetunion und den von ihr beherrschten Gebieten', Bonn, 19 November 1956.

50. Bay. HstA. Mun., Präs. D. Bayer. Landpolizei Nr. 3, *Bericht des Bayerischen Staatsministerium des Innern*, Re.: 'Abdruck einer Übersicht der im Bundesgebiet hauptsächlich verbreiteten Agitations und Propagandaschriften' , Munich, 23 February 1967; Bay. HStA. Mun., Landesflüchtlingsverwaltung Nr. 702, *Bericht an das Bayer. Staatsm. d. Innern Abteilung I C 2*, Re.: 'Propagandamaterial östlicher Herkunft', Munich, 24 October 1950.

51. K.C. Farmer. 1980. *Ukrainian Nationalism in the Post-Stalin Era: Myths, Symbols and Ideologies in Soviet Nationalities Policy*, Boston: Martinus Nijhoff Publishers, 165.

52. W. Maruniak. 1994. 'Ukrainians in the Federal Republic of Germany', in A.L. Pawliczko (ed.), *Ukrainians throughout the World*, Toronto: University of Toronto Press, 263–65.

53. Bundesarchiv Koblenz, B 106, Nr. 28187, *Bericht des Bundesamt für Verfassungsschutz*, Re.: 'Die Ostemigration in der Bundesrepublik', Cologne, 11 March 1963.

54. Raschhofer, *Political Assassination*, 186–87.
55. Pol. A.A. Ber., B 12, Nr. 455, *Bericht des Auswärtiges Amtes*, Re.: 'Die Emigration aus der Sowjetunion und den von ihr beherrschten Gebieten', Bonn, 19 November 1956. This document contains a description of this sort of interaction.
56. Bay. HstA. Mun., Landesflüchtlingsverwaltung, Nr. 2242, *Brief Prof. Dr. März and Staatssekretät Prof. Dr. Oberländer*, Re.: 'Ostinstitut und die Zukunft von Dr. Hans Koch', Munich, 11 June 1962.
57. Bay. HstA. Mun., Präsidium der Bereitschaftspolizei, Nr. 127, *Bericht vom Bayerischen Landesamt für Verfassungsschutz*, Re.: 'Die Politische Struktur der Ostemigration', Munich, 1 April 1960.
58. Pol. A.A. Ber., B 12, Nr. 455, *Bericht Ref. LR. Scholl/LR. von Staden*, Re.: 'Die Emigration aus der Sowjetunion und den von ihr beherrschten Gebieten', Bonn, 19 November 1956.
59. *Frankfurter Allgemeine Zeitung*, 'München: das Dorado der Emigranten', 4 March 1963; and P. Mueller and M. Müller. 2002. *Gegen Freund und Feind – Der BND: Geheime Politik und Schmutzige Geschäfte*, Hamburg: Rowohlt Verl, 112–15.
60. *Frankfurter Allgemeine Zeitung*, 'München: das Dorado der Emigranten'.
61. Pol. A.A. Ber., B 40, Nr. 111, *Aufzeichnung des Auswärtigen Amtes*: Re.: 'Interministerielle Besprechung im Bundesministerium für Vertriebene über Förderungsmassnahmen für osteuropäische Emigranten am 12. Dezember 1962', Bonn, 14 December 1962.
62. Bundesarchiv Koblenz, B 106, Nr. 28187, *Dr. Hans Neuwirth (Vorstandsmitglied der Union der Vertriebenen in der CSU) an persönlicher Referent des Bundesinnenministers Dr. Fröhlich*: Re.: 'Verfehlte Behandlung des Ukrainerproblems', Munich, 12 July 1962.
63. Ukrainische Freie Universität. 1962. *Satzung der Arbeits und Förderungsgemeinschaft der Ukrainischen Wissenschaften e.V.*, Munich, Ukrainische Freie Universität, 9–11.
64. Bay. HstA. Mun., Landesflüchtlingsverwaltung Nr. 2242, *Niederschrift des Bildungsministeriums*, Re.: 'Niederschrift über die gemeinsame Sitzung des Stiftungsrates und des Kuratoriums des Ost-Europa-Institutes am 12.11.1951', Munich, 13 November 1962.
65. Prokoptschuk, *Deutsch-Ukrainische Gesellschaft 1918–1963*, 71–79; and B. Scharko. 1988. *Na Hromadsky Nivy*, Munich: Zentralverwaltung der Ukrainer in der Bundesrepublik Deutschland, 45.
66. NHstA. Hann., Nds. 120 Lün.: Nr. 37, *Aufzeichnungen Niedersächsisches Ministerium des Inneren zu Probleme nichtdeutscher Flüchtlinge*, Re.: 'Bericht über eine Tagung des Evangelischen Hilfswerks in der Ostdeutschen Akademie Lüneburg vom 3. Bis 5. April 1957', Hanover, 8 March 1957.
67. Pol. A.A. Ber., B 40, Nr. 111, *Aufzeichnung des Auswärtigen Amtes*: Re.: 'Interministerielle Besprechung im Bundesministerium für Vertriebene über Förderungsmassnahmen für osteuropäische Emigranten am 12. Dezember 1962', Bonn, 14 December 1962.
68. Ibid.
69. Burleigh, *Germany turns Eastwards*, 314–18.
70. Bundesarchiv Koblenz, B 106, Nr. 63088, *Bericht des Bundesamtes für Verfassungsschutz am Bundesministerium des Innern*, Re.: 'Agitation und Terrorakte des Sowjetischen Geheimdienstes gegen die Ostemigration in der Bundesrepublik', Köln, 21 November 1961.
71. For further information on the *Hallstein* doctrine see M. Balfour. 1982. *West Germany: a Contemporary History*, London: Croom Helm, 196–98.
72. Pol. A.A. Ber., B 12, Nr. 450, *Aufzeichnung des DG 31 an MD Freiherr von Welck*, Re.: 'Die Problematik der aus dem Machtbereich der Sowjetunion stammenden Emigration', Bonn, 18 December 1956; and Pol. A.A. Ber., B 40, Nr. 111, *Aufzeichnung LR Pallasch*, Re.: 'Interministerielle Besprechung im Bundesministerium für Vertriebene über Förderungsmassnahmen für osteuropäische Emigranten', Bonn, 14 December 1962. German original: 'Der Vertreter des Bundesinninministeriums (Ausländeraufsicht) zog die Zweckmässigkeit solcher Unterstützungen überhaupt in Zweifel, wenn Emigranten hier andererseits eine völkerrechtlich unzulässige politische Tätigkeit entfalteten, die sich gegen

Länder richtet, mit denen die Bundesrepublik diplomatische Beziehungen unterhält und die vielfach geeignet sein könnten, diese Beziehungen negativ zu beeinträchtigen.'

73. D. Wierling. 2001. 'Mission to Happiness: the Cohort of 1949 and the Making of East and West Germans', in H. Schissler (ed.), *The Miracle Years: a Cultural History of West Germany 1949–1968*, Princeton: Princeton University Press, 119–23.

74. I. Connor. 2000. 'German Refugees and the Bonn Government's Resettlement Program: the Role of the Trek Association in Schleswig-Holstein 1951–3', *German History* 18(3), 337–41.

75. R. Irving. 2002. *Adenauer: Profiles in Power*, London: Longman, 94–103.

76. C. Ross. 2002. *The East German Dictatorship: Problems and Perspectives in the Interpretation of the GDR*, London: Arnold, 152–53.

77. P. Conradt. 2001. *The German Polity*, 7th ed., New York: Longman Press, 19–20.

78. R.G. Moeller. 2001. 'Remembering the War in a Nation of Victims: West German Pasts in the 1950s', in H. Schissler (ed.), *The Miracle Years: a Cultural History of West Germany 1949–1968*, Princeton: Princeton University Press, 100–1.

79. Pol. A.A. Ber., B 40, Nr. 37, *Mitteilung – Botschaft der Bundesrepublik Deutschland in Washington DC an Auswärtiges Amt Bonn*, Re.: Besuch – Ehemaliger ukrainischer Premierminister Yaroslav Stetzko', Washington, 7 March 1963.

80. Prokoptschuk, *Deutsch-Ukrainische Gesellschaft 1918–1963*, 30–32.

81. Bundesarchiv Koblenz, B 105, Nr. 63085, *Brief des Vorsitzenden der OUN J. Benzal and die Wochenzeitschrift 'Das Parlament' und das Bundesinnenministerium*, Re.: 'Politik und Zeitgeschichte – Beilage B20/62', München, 6 June 1962, German original: 'Umso mehr erstaunt das uns zugefügte Unrecht, das wir uns nur mit einer unverständlichen Tendenz erklären können, die weder der deutschen Wiedervereinigung noch der Befreiung unseres Heimatlandes dienlich zu sein scheint.'

82. Pol. A.A. Ber., B 40, Nr. 111, *Bundespresseamt*, Re.: 'Sonderdienst – Mord auf Befehl: Der Hintergrund des Prozesses gegen den politischen Doppelmörder Bogdan N. Staschynskij', Bonn, October 1962, German original: 'Die erschreckende Tatsache [the assassination of Bandera and Rebet], daß von einer obersten staatlichen Dienststelle der Sowjetunion – mit Wissen und im Auftrag der Sowjetregierung – politische Morde befohlen werden, deren Durchführung die Souveränität eines fremden Staates ebenso rücksichtslos verletzt wie die anerkannten Regeln des Völkerrechts und der Menschenrechte.'

83. W.F. Hanrieder and G. Auton. 1980. *The Foreign Policies of West Germany, France, and Britain*, New Jersey: Prentice-Hall Inc., 51–52.

84. Balfour, *West Germany: A Contemporary History*, 196–97.

85. Pol. A.A. Ber., B 12, Nr. 455, *Bericht Ref. LR. Scholl/LR. von Staden*, Re.: Die Emigration aus der Sowjetunion und den von ihr beherrschten Gebieten', Bonn, 19 November 1956.

86. Prokoptschuk , *Deutsch-Ukrainische Gesellschaft 1918–1963*, 69.

87. Pol. A.A. Ber., B 12, Nr. 450, *Referat 508 – Aufzeichnung des DG 31 an MD Freiherr von Welck*, Re.: 'Die Problematik der aus dem Machtbereich der Sowjetunion stammenden Emigration', Bonn, 18 September 1956.

88. Pol. A.A. Ber., B 12, Nr. 451, *Bericht – Ostlektorat*, Re.: 'Bandera, Stepan – ukrainischer Emigrant und Politiker', Bonn, 19 October 1959.

89. Pol. A.A. Ber., B12, Nr. 451 *Bericht des Bayerischen Landesamts für Verfassungsschutz*, Re.: 'Die nationalistischen Organisationen der Ostemigranten (Jugoslawische Emigration – Stand: 15. Januar 1963) ', Munich, 28 March 1963.

90. Pol. A.A. Ber., B 40, Nr. 111, *Aufzeichnung LR Pallasch*, Re.: 'Interministerielle Besprechung im Bundesministerium für Vertrieben über Förderungsmassnahmen für osteuropäische Emigranten am 12. Dezember 1962', Bonn, 14 December 1962, German original: 'Der Vertreter des Bundesinninministeriums (Ausländeraufsicht) zog die Zweckmässigkeit solcher Unterstützungen überhaupt in Zweifel, wenn Emigranten hier andererseits eine völkerrechtlich unzulässige politische Tätigkeit entfalteten, die sich gegen Länder richtet, mit

denen die Bundesrepublik diplomatische Beziehungen unterhält und die vielfach geeignet sein könnten, diese Beziehungen negativ zu beeinträchtigen.'

91. Pol. A.A. Ber., B 12, Nr. 455, *Bericht Ref. LR. Scholl/LR. von Staden*, Re.: 'Die Emigration aus der Sowjetunion und den von ihr beherrschten Gebieten', Bonn, 19 November 1956.

92. Contrast the anger against the West German government expressed by Croatian émigrés in Bundesarchiv Koblenz, B 106, Nr. 63088, *Dossier des Bundesinnenministeriums*, Re.: 'Dokumente des Verfassungsschutzes Kroatischer Organisationen in der BRD betreffend', 24 November 1960 with the largely supportive stance of their Ukrainian counterparts in Pol. A.A. Ber., B 12, Nr. 451, *Bericht LR Ruete an Referat 991*, Re.: 'Erklärung des ZK des ABN im Zusammenhang mit dem Tode von Stefan Bandera', Bonn, 29 January 1960.

93. K. Hirsch. 1979. *Die Heimatlose Rechte: Die Konservativen und Franz Josef Strauß*, Munich, Wilhelm Goldmann Verl, 64–67.

94. Bay. HstA. Mun., Polizei Direktion München: Nr. 9280, *ABN – Propagandamaterial*, Re.: 'Freiheit den Menschen, Unabhängigkeit den Völkern – Die Sowjetrussische Ausstellung – Eine Provokation', Munich, 18 January 1968, German original: 'Insbesondere unterdrückt das russische und kommunistische Regime z.Z. mit allen erdenklichen Mitteln die nationalgesinnten ... sich einsetzenden Intellektuellen, Schriftsteller, Künstler und Wissenschaftler, wie z.b in der Ukraine in Weißruthenien, Turkestan, Georgien, Rumänien, Böhmen, in der Slowakei und in anderen unterjochten Ländern. Dieses Verhalten der kommunistischen Machthaber spottet den betrügerischen Behauptungen (der deutschen Linke) über die "Liberalisierung" des Systems Hohn' and 'Hat die osteuropäische Politik des Dritten Reiches nicht schon genug Unheil in den deutsch-ukrainischen Beziehungen angerichtet? Müssen alte Fehler wiederholt werden?'

95. Bundesarchiv Koblenz, B 106, Nr. 28217, *Bundesamt für Verfassungsschutz – Bericht am Bundesinnenministerium*, Re.: 'Emigration – Kroatische Emigration u.A.', Bonn, 25 May 1970.

96. Bay. HstA. Mun., Polizei Direktion München: Nr. 9280, *Bericht KK III über eine öffentliche Veranstaltung*, Re.: 'Veranstaltung – Zentralvertretung der Ukrainischen Emigration in Deutschland e.v.', Munich, 11 January 1968, German original: 'HIER DEMONSTRIEREN DEUTSCHE, NICHT DER SDS', '163 MAUERTOTEN KLAGEN AN', 'BUDAPEST UND 17. JUNI SCHON VERGESSEN?', 'WO BLEIBT MOSKAUS SÜHNE FÜR KATYN UND WORKUTA', 'WIR HASSEN JEDE DIKTATUR' or 'ZERSCHLAGT DEN KREML-IMPERIALISMUS'.

97. Pol. A.A. Ber., B 40, Nr. 37, *Forschungsdienst Osteuropa – Bericht an das Auswärtige Amt-Legationsrat Dr. Dirnecker*, Re.: 'Bevorstehender Prozeß gegen der Ukrainer Staschinskyj/ Aussage des MdL (CSU-Bayern) Herbert Prochazka u.a. an der Jahresversammlung der Deutsch-Slowakischen Gesellschaft', Düsseldorf, 27 April 1962.

98. Bay. HstA. Mun., Stk. Nr. 13616, *Lageberichte Innere Sicherheit 1968–1972*, Re.: 'Fernschreiberbericht – Exil-Ukrainische Kundgebung anlässlich des Besuches einer sowjetischen Delegation am KZ. Dachau', Munich, 3 September 1972.

99. *Süddeutsche Zeitung*, 'In Kurze: Sowjetische Delegation in Dachau', 4 September 1972.

100. Bundesarchiv Koblenz, B 106, Nr. 28191, *Bundesministerium des Innern – Bericht*, Re.: 'Ukrainischer Schulverein "Ridna Schkola"', Bonn, 27 February 1970. This is typical of many documents where funding for a community institution is made conditional on 'good behaviour', i.e., no open criticism of the SPD's *Ostpolitik*.

101. P. Merseburger. 2002. *Willy Brandt: Visionär und Realist 1913– 1992*, Stuttgart, Deutsche Verlags-Anstalt, 613–16.

102. Bay. HstA. Mun., Stk. Nr. 13613, *Lageberichte zur Inneren Sicherheit 1969*, Re.: 'Gedenkfeier zum Tode Stepan Banderas', Munich, 11 October 1969.

103. *Süddeutsche Zeitung*, 'Gedenkfeier am Grab Banderas', 13 October 1969.

104. Reid, *Borderland: a Journey through the History of the Ukraine*, 165–68.

105. N. Thomas. 2003. *Protest Movements in 1960s West Germany*, Oxford: Berg, 40–45.

106. Schenk, *Die Braunen Wurzeln des BKA*, 286.

107. Bundesarchiv Koblenz, B 106, Nr. 28187, *Bundesministerium des Innern – Vermerk an Ministerialrat Dr. Wolfrum*, Re.: 'Unterredung zwischen Rechtsanwalt Becher und MR Dr. Wolfrum', Bonn, 8 July 1970.

108. Bundesarchiv Koblenz, B 106, Nr. 28191, *Brief Bundesministerium für Flüchtlinge und Vertriebene an das Bundespräsidialamt*, Re.: 'Empfang seiner Exzellenz des Kardinals Slipyi durch Herrn Bundespräsidenten', Bonn, 25 August 1969.

109. O. Anweiler. 1977. '25 Jahre Osteuropaforschung – Wissenschaft und Zeitgeschichte', *Osteuropa* 27, 177.

110. P. Panayi, 2000. *Ethnic Minorities in Nineteenth and Twentieth Century Germany: Jews, Gypsies, Poles, Turks and Others: Themes in Modern German History*, Harlow: Longman, 216–18.

111. Pol. A.A. Ber., B 40, Nr. 111, *Aufzeichnung Auswärtiges Amt*, Re.: 'Interministerielle Besprechung im Bundesministerium für Vertriebene über Förderungsmaßnahmen für osteuropäische Emigranten – 12. Dezember 1962', Bonn, 14 December 1962.

112. Bay. HstA. Mun., Präsidium der Bereitschaftspolizei Nr. 127, *Bericht vom Bayerisches Landesamt für Verfassungsschutz*, Re.: 'Die Politische Struktur der Ostemigration', Munich, 1 April 1960.

113. *Der Spiegel Nr. 15*, 'Nach Hause: Dafür sind wir Polen', 10 April 1948.

114. J. Rydel. 2003. *Die polnische Besatzung im Emsland 1945–1948*, Osnabrück: Fibre Verl., 9–15 and 130–37.

115. Pol. A.A. Ber., B 40, Nr. 111, *Ministerkonferenz – Bundesministerium für Vertriebene*, Re.: 'Förderungsmaßnahmen für osteuropäische Emigranten', Bonn, 14 December 1962; and D. Bingen. 1998. *Die Polenpolitik der Bonner Republik von Adenauer bis Kohl 1949–1991*, Köln: Nomos, 32–34.

116. Bundesarchiv Koblenz, B 106, Nr. 28187, *Katholisches Büro (Bonn) an Bundesministerium für Inneres*, Re.: 'Schreiben des Kommissariats der Deutschen Bischöfe', Bonn, 8 July 1970.

117. Bay. HstA. Mun., Ministerium des Innern: Nr. 91890, *Ministerium des Innern, Clipping from Bild*, 'Bomben-Attentat bei Frankfurt –Auf Geheimsender der Exilrussen', Munich, 27 June 1957.

118. Pol. A.A. Ber., B 12, Nr. 455, *Report from LR. I Scholl/LR. von Staden*, Re.: 'Die Emigration aus der Sowjetunion und den von ihr beherrschten Gebieten – I. Die russische Emigration', Bonn, 19 November 1956.

119. Pol. A.A. Ber., B 12, Nr. 455, *Interner Bericht Bundesministerium des Innern – Allgemeine politische Angelegenheiten der Sowjetunion*, Re.: 'Russische Emigration, Politische Parteien: Die Solidaristen (NTS)', Bonn, 1956.

120. Bundesarchiv Koblenz, B 106, Nr. 63084, *Loseblattsammlung Bundesministerium des Inneren zur Ostemigration*, Re.: 'Die Polen', Bonn, 1960.

Chapter 2

SUPPORT OR SUPPRESS?
CROATIAN NATIONALISTS AND THE WEST GERMAN
SECURITY SERVICES

Throughout the Cold War period, police and security services designed to maintain public order and prevent communist infiltration from the Soviet bloc played a crucial role in the development of immigrant movements in the Federal Republic. Immigrant activists willing to use violence to achieve their goals often provoked a drastic response from West German security services, which in turn could further alienate wider immigrant communities from the West German state.[1] A closer examination of the role of political violence in the development of immigrant groups in Germany therefore has to grapple with two key questions. First, at what point did security officials and politicians begin to believe that certain immigrant communities bore collective responsibility for acts of political violence, rather than focusing on the individual members who had perpetrated them? And second, how did criteria such as ideological allegiance or ethnic background shape the relationship between West German security services and immigrant political movements? Exploring these issues can shed some light on how cooperation between immigrant activists and their German supporters was shaped by the actions of the West German security state.

From the late 1950s onwards, police and intelligence agencies developed complex technological methods with which to monitor criminals and dissident political groups.[2] As local *Ausländerämter* and immigration officials in the *Bundesministerium des Innern* became preoccupied with differentiating between 'legitimate' and 'illegitimate' migrants, cooperation between these agencies and the security services became the norm. The asylum process, labour rotation and integration programmes created a paper trail that provided intelligence agencies with information on the groups and individuals they had decided to target.[3] As a consequence, local police directorates became dependent on information gathered by *Land* and federal agencies by the late 1970s.[4]

Despite all Allied attempts at denazification, many senior members of the BKA, BND and *Verfassungsschutz* had served in the SS or *Wehrmacht*. Paul Dickopf, the first head of the BKA, had accepted an SS rank while working for the German criminal intelligence service in the 1930s.[5] Reinhard Gehlen, whose own American backed *Organization Gehlen* became the *Bundesnachrichtendienst,* had been head of the *Wehrmacht*'s military intelligence operation on the Eastern Front ('*Fremde Heere Ost*'). In the 1950s, Gehlen recruited fiercely anti-communist former SS and *Wehrmacht* officers whose experience he thought was essential to the covert war against the Soviets. By contrast, both the BND and the BKA avoided recruiting anyone who its leadership believed to be 'tainted' by association with the unsuccessful *Wehrmacht* officers' revolt against Hitler in 1944.[6] A partial exception to this rule could be found in the *Bundes-* and *Landesamt für Verfassungsschutz*, which focused on domestic threats to the constitutional order of the FRG. Though there were several senior officials in the *Verfassungsschutz* who sympathized with Dickopf and Gehlen, these agencies also attracted younger individuals who either had an anti-Nazi background or had resolutely broken with their national socialist past.[7]

These continuities were typical of the security services and the judiciary after 1945. Several LKAs contained officials who had been involved in wartime atrocities, while most local police services retained large numbers of staff who had been trained in the national socialist period.[8] In the courts, over 80 per cent of prosecutors and judges who had served under the Nazis continued their careers after 1945.[9] As long as the networks fostered by Gehlen and Dickopf dominated all levels of the security hierarchy, the attitude of many police and intelligence officers towards certain social and ethnic groups was shaped by a fierce conservatism rooted in pre-1945 attitudes and techniques. Only when this older generation began to fade from the scene in the early 1970s did the security services begin to reassess their approach towards immigrant communities.[10]

One group of émigrés that had a particularly complex relationship with the West German security services were Croatian activists. As the importation of foreign labour gained momentum, what had initially been a small émigré community was transformed by Croatian migrant workers who began arriving in large numbers by the early 1960s.[11] As this community expanded, the cordial relationship its leadership had managed to establish with parts of the CDU/CSU came under increasing strain as nationalist Croatians and the Yugoslav state fought a proxy war on German territory. Worsening the position of Croatian nationalist organizations was a major shift in the West German approach towards the Yugoslav state, as investment from West German banks and corporations started to flow into Yugoslavia despite the *Hallstein* doctrine.[12] In conjunction with the strengthening of economic links, after 1965 West German governments tried to improve diplomatic relations with the Tito regime in order to help draw Yugoslavia away from the communist bloc. As we shall see, the resulting upsurge of Croatian nationalist violence after 1962 was to catch both West German officials and their Yugoslav counterparts completely unprepared.

****

The relationship between Croatian émigrés and the West German political establishment after 1945 was shaped by the strong ties between the German-speaking world and Croatia that had intensified in the preceding century. Though Croatia was ruled by the Hungarian part of the Habsburg Empire, Vienna still remained the cultural centre of choice for most members of the Croatian elite. The growing popularity of union with Serbia in the run up to the First World War had more to do with anti-Hungarian sentiment than any hatred for distant German imperial rulers in Vienna. Indeed, in 1918 most Croatian units on the Italian and Russian fronts had continued to fight loyally for the Austro-Hungarian cause until the collapse of the Habsburg monarchy, despite growing nationalist agitation in Croatia itself.[13]

Once the initial enthusiasm for the Yugoslav option began to wane, tensions between Croatian politicians and Serb administrators who wanted to concentrate power in Belgrade undermined the stability of this new state. The final breakdown of relations between the dominant Croatian Peasant Party and the royalist faction in Belgrade led to the replacement of constitutional democracy with an authoritarian system of government, by King Peter in 1928. The resulting purge of moderate Croatian leaders from positions of power drove an entire generation of Croatians into nationalist politics. The most extreme proponents of this nationalist revival founded the *Ustascha* movement in the early 1930s. This was originally a loose network of Croatian intellectuals who aimed to overthrow the Yugoslav monarchy and replace it with an independent Croatian state.[14]

Ustascha ideology combined extreme nationalism with the teachings of the conservative wing of the Catholic Church. The leadership was also heavily influenced by Italian fascism and German national socialism. In the early 1930s, Croatian nationalists gained the backing of the Italian state, which supported secessionist movements such as the *Ustascha* or the Macedonian IMRO (Internal Macedonian Revolutionary Organization) in order to weaken Yugoslavia, a potential rival for control of the Adriatic. By contrast, the *Ustascha* movement had no contact with the Nazi regime in the interwar period because of repeated German attempts to forge an alliance with the Yugoslav government during the 1930s. The involvement of senior IMRO and *Ustascha* members in the assassination of King Alexander in 1934 forced Mussolini to imprison members of both organizations, reducing the ability of Croatian exiles to influence events in their homeland. Despite the continuing popularity of the *Ustascha* movement in Croatian universities, the Peasant Party (led by Vladko Macek) continued to dominate interwar Croatian politics. The electoral strength of the Croatian Peasant Party enabled it to reassert its influence over policy making in the last years before the war despite the wave of repression that followed the assassination of King Alexander. Ignored by the Germans because of Hitler's disinterest in Balkan affairs, the *Ustascha* movement had almost no contact with the German academics and bureaucrats involved in the *Ostforschung* network.[15]

Leading members of the *Ustascha* movement only contacted Nazi party officials after the German invasion of Yugoslavia in April 1941. Immediately after the first German troops entered Croatian territory, *Ustascha* cadres who had even managed to infiltrate military units stationed in Zagreb quickly established their own fascist state with the help of the Axis powers. The leader of this state (known as the *Poglavnik* in direct emulation of the German *Führer*) was Ante Pavelic, one of the founders of the *Ustascha* movement. The *Ustascha* regime's armed units, which mostly consisted of the *Domobrani* militia, and its wider administrative infrastructure remained completely dependent on German help. Though it initially enjoyed some popular support for achieving Croatian independence, a set of miscalculations by the *Ustascha* leadership helped to increase the popularity of its communist and Serb *Chetnik* opponents. In particular, the *Ustascha* regime's enthusiastic collaboration with *Wehrmacht* and SS persecution of Jews, Serbs or leftist Croatians alienated a significant proportion of the Croatian population. The arrest of Macek and other Peasant Party leaders further damaged the *Ustascha*'s position by turning moderate nationalists into embittered enemies of the regime. However much Pavelic was able to instil loyalty in the small circle of extreme nationalists who governed wartime Croatia, his regime was unable to generate any lasting enthusiasm among the broader population for the *Ustascha* project.

As the *Ustascha* became ever more dependent on German support, its activists worked together with SS or *Wehrmacht* officers on a day-to-day basis, cooperation that was symbolized by Ante Pavelic's regular meetings with Hitler. At the same time, the Nazi Party organization responsible for organizing ethnic German communities did its best to take control of the 250,000 strong German minority known as the *Donauschwaben*, which had lived along the Danube valley in Slavonia and Voijvodina for centuries. Yet the communal divide between ethnic Germans and Croatians was so great that Nazi activists within the *Donauschwaben* community did not have any significant encounters with leading members of the *Ustascha* until both were evacuated to the Austrian border in the last months of the war.[16]

Despite troop strength of 110,000, the *Domobrani* were unable to put up any concerted resistance against the communist partisans. In the final stages of the war the *Wehrmacht* and the *Domobrani* lost control of the countryside, triggering the abandonment of Zagreb by the *Ustascha* leadership and its supporters who mostly tried to flee the country. While Pavelic escaped to Italy, tens of thousands of the NDH's soldiers and supporters who fell into the hands of British troops in southern Austria were handed over to advancing partisan units. The great majority of these *Ustascha* supporters were executed at Bleiburg in Slovenia, while those who survived were interned with thousands of *Wehrmacht* prisoners and ethnic Germans in appalling conditions.[17] Leading members of the German occupation regime in Yugoslavia, such as General Glaise-Horstenau, were also imprisoned for a considerable period of time after their capture in 1945. Those German POWs who survived Yugoslav captivity were only allowed to return to the Federal Republic in the early 1950s.[18]

Since most *Wehrmacht* commanders in Croatia had ended up in Yugoslav captivity, the senior German officers who had participated in the Balkan campaigns returned to West Germany when it was too late for them to find a place in the new West German bureaucracy. Apart from a few middle-ranking Balkan specialists in the *Auswärtiges Amt* who had been to Yugoslavia during the war, the small group of diplomats and academics specialized in Yugoslav affairs were either resettled *Donauschwaben* or inexperienced young officials. In any case, the prewar *Ostforschung* network of academics that shaped the research agenda in the FRG on Eastern Europe had not contained many specialists in Balkan affairs. The fact that the Balkans were not originally earmarked for conquest by the Hitler regime meant that the fate of the *Donauschwaben* in Yugoslavia or the *Siebenburger Sachsen* in Romania remained a secondary issue for academics such as Brackmann, Koch and Oberländer. When dealing with south-eastern Europe, until the 1960s the *Auswärtiges Amt* depended on an eclectic group of Balkan 'experts' who often stemmed from the *Donauschwaben* community.[19]

Consequently, Croatian DPs and émigrés trickling into the Federal Republic after 1945 did not have the established relationship with members of the West German academic and bureaucratic elites that their Ukrainian counterparts could build on. West German and Croatian leaders did repeatedly refer to what Branimir Jelic, a prominent political exile, typically called 'the tradition of German-Croatian friendship'.[20] But such cooperation with both moderate nationalists as well as former members of the *Ustascha* on German soil could leave the FRG open to accusations of fascist sympathies by the Yugoslav government, since political discontent in Croatia posed a significant threat to the stability of the Tito regime. Whereas the equally difficult war record of many Ukrainian leaders was ignored because of a shared hostility towards the Soviet Union, Tito's decision to break with the USSR in 1948 made some kind of anti-Soviet alliance with Yugoslavia possible from a relatively early point in the Cold War. It therefore remained imperative for West German officials to keep an émigré community with such a difficult war history at arm's length, even if many fervent anti-communists may have sympathized with the Croatian cause.

Despite their occasional attempts to obtain funding from government in the 1950s, Croatian groups and their German sympathizers did not have the numbers or institutional contacts to attract any significant attention from the West German state. The *Ustascha* background of many Croatian leaders also worried local police officials, who did their best to impose limits on the size and location of Croatian nationalist events in order to avoid trouble with Yugoslav representatives.[21] Yet the security services remained remarkably ignorant of how strong extremist sentiment was among Croatians in Germany until a sudden flurry of attacks on Yugoslav targets in 1962. Reports produced by intelligence services, the *Südost Institut* and the *Forschungsdienst Osteuropa* in the aftermath of the bombing of the Yugoslav trade mission in Bonn-Mehlem in November 1962 demonstrated how little West German officials actually knew about the Croatian nationalist movement in the Federal Republic.[22]

Between 1949 and 1962, the *Auswärtiges Amt* only commissioned one examination of the internal structure of émigré groups from Yugoslavia. Compiled by an academic closely associated with *Donauschwaben* expellees, this report shaped the approach taken by federal ministries towards Croatian nationalist groups. As a consequence, though federal officials remained suspicious of émigré groups in which former *Ustascha* members played a prominent role, the positive gloss that this report put on anti-Tito organizations reinforced sympathy for opponents of a communist regime. The ruthless treatment of German POWs in the late 1940s together with the Yugoslav government's recognition of East Germany as a sovereign state in 1957 (that led to a diplomatic break with the FRG), further reduced West German willingness to accommodate Yugoslav demands for a crackdown on hostile émigré groups. Although they did occasionally rein in Croatian groups in cases where anti-Yugoslav demonstrations ran out of control, the small-scale nature of this activity in the 1950s contradicted the Tito regime's claims that *Ustascha* in the Federal Republic were secretly recruiting a guerrilla army for an invasion of Yugoslavia.[23]

Significant divisions within the Croatian community were another factor behind the complacent attitude of the West German security services. Most DPs who refused to return to Yugoslavia joined the postwar exodus of refugees to North America after 1949. The 13,000 Croatian DPs who decided to stay in West Germany for personal or political reasons were concentrated in Munich, Stuttgart and the Ruhr region. Although political exiles were in as precarious a social position as other minorities in the FRG of the early 1950s, in each of these regions they were still able to set up organizations designed to promote their political aims. These groups ostensibly claimed to be open to Croatian exiles of all political stripes, yet the bulk of their members had been involved with the *Ustascha* regime. The one exception was a Croatian Peasant Party club in Munich set up by Berisav Dezelic, who had been a prominent Peasant Party politician in the 1930s and was also active in Düsseldorf. Yet since the bulk of Peasant Party activists fled to the United States in the late 1940s, most politically active Croatian émigrés based in Western Europe had a more right-wing background.[24]

While a semi-autonomous Croatian Catholic mission in Germany ensured that the Croatian community was not divided by religious conflict, considerable rivalry still existed between these different political groups.[25] The more moderate Peasant Party loyalists remained compromised in the eyes of many Croat nationalists because of Macek's initial cooperation with the Serb royal family in the 1920s.[26] Compounding these difficulties, splits developed between extreme nationalists who had become disillusioned with the NDH state and those still loyal to Ante Pavelic. Quite often low-ranking members of the *Ustascha* saw exile as an opportunity to attain a more prominent position in the nationalist movement, as a proliferation of committee positions helped provide otherwise undistinguished individuals with an ostensibly important role in the diaspora. Leadership squabbles and ideological disagreements often ended with nationalist activists leaving a larger group in order to found their own splinter organizations.[27]

The organization with the heaviest involvement of the wartime *Ustascha* leadership was the Croatian Liberation Organization (HOP). Founded in June 1956 by Ante Pavelic and other *Ustascha* exiles living in Madrid, the HOP quickly found adherents among Croatian émigrés who had been involved with the NDH government. While the main party organization and its so-called military arm, the 'Armed Croatian Forces' (HOS), had relatively few members, it acquired considerable influence over the diaspora through its control of the 'Central Committee of Croatian Clubs in Europe' (SOHDE) along with the 'United Croatians in Germany'(UHNJ). Also established in 1956, these groups claimed to be cultural clubs rather than political organizations. It was through such networks that Croatian activists who would cause trouble for the West German and Yugoslav governments in the 1960s such as Nahid Kulmenovic, Mile Rukavina or Mirolav Peran first came to prominence.[28]

Demoralized by Pavelic's inability to provide inspiring leadership, other former *Ustascha* activists established political alternatives to the HOP. Its most prominent rival was the Croatian National Committee (HNO), which was founded in 1951 by Dr Branimir Jelic and Dr Stjepan Buc, along with a variety of other Croatian intellectuals who had made their way to the Federal Republic. Jelic had been a founder member of the *Ustascha* movement as a student and had fled Croatia in 1929. Interned by the British in the wake of the German invasion before he could return from London to Yugoslavia, Jelic had managed to avoid becoming implicated in the war crimes committed by the Pavelic regime. After his release in 1945, Jelic joined Croatian activists in the Federal Republic such as Buc or General Ivo Brozovic, whose formative political experiences had taken place during the interwar period. The establishment of the HNO at a relatively early point in time gave it an advantage over the HOP in its efforts to garner support among Croatians in Germany. The HNO managed to secure enough funds from private donors (usually right-wing German sympathizers and diaspora Croatians) and the *Ministerium für Flüchtlinge und Vertriebene* to set up Croatian language publications such as *Hrvatska Drzava* and recruit wider grass-roots support before the HOP arrived on the scene.[29]

By the late 1950s, disgruntled members of both the HOP and HNO were leaving these organizations in order to set up semi-autonomous groups of their own. These splits were caused by petty jealousies between individual leaders as well as a desire to take more 'decisive' action against the Yugoslav state among grass-roots members who thought their leaders were being too passive. Prominent activists such as Berisav Dezelic, Ivica Boras or Father Raphael Medic Skoko (Ante Pavelic's former chaplain) had to join several different émigré nationalist groups in order to maintain their influence over the wider community. These ideological spats also helped to radicalize the Croatian nationalist movement in the FRG as a whole, as competition for recruits between different organizations impelled them to reinforce their ideological credentials through the use of extreme rhetoric.

The key turning point for these organizations was the influx of workers from Yugoslavia in the early 1960s. Suddenly, a splinter group with charismatic or at least well connected leaders could recruit hundreds of supporters and gain a foothold in every major West German city.[30] In the early 1960s there were only rough estimates of the numbers of people from Yugoslavia living in West Germany. The usual figures provided by government and press sources at the time were 30,000 migrants from Yugoslavia as a whole, of which 13,000 were believed to be ethnic Croatians.[31] In 1973 the number of Yugoslavs in the Federal Republic had grown to approximately 280,000,[32] and by 1989 there were over 600,000 people from Yugoslavia resident in West Germany, with the proportion of ethnic Croatians making up a third of the Yugoslav population in the Federal Republic.[33]

At first few West German officials were prepared to take a community prone to such political fragmentation seriously. Faced with organizations that were as preoccupied with fighting one another as the Yugoslav state, the Interior Ministry dossier on émigré groups in the Federal Republic dismissed Croatian nationalists as politically irrelevant.[34] Compiled in 1956, this report on the Croatian community only examined the HNO and HOP, while subsequent ministerial and police documents dealing with the Croatian community continued to focus on the two largest organizations. Only when members of these Croatian nationalist groups began to translate their extremist rhetoric into action did West German ministries and security services begin to take a more systematic look at the Croatian community. Once they had begun to pay more attention in the 1960s, both local investigators and officials in the *Auswärtiges Amt* expressed astonishment at the extent to which Croatian extremists had been able to openly recruit and advocate the use of violence to destroy the Yugoslav state.[35]

With few high-level contacts in West German academia or state institutions, Croatian exiles had to use a different approach to that of better connected émigré groups when lobbying the West German political establishment. Here mistreatment of German POWs and *Donauschwaben* by communist partisans in Yugoslavia was of considerable importance to Croatian nationalists because ethnic Germans with a grudge against the Yugoslav state were an obvious partner for any group opposed to the Tito regime. The brutality with which Yugoslav partisans treated Germans helped to lend credibility to émigré claims that Croatians were experiencing similar repression at the hands of Serbian communists.[36] By contrast, West German centre-right politicians or journalists rarely mentioned the atrocities committed by the *Wehrmacht* and SS in Yugoslavia. By pointing to the ideological similarities between 1950s Yugoslavia and the GDR, Croatian exiles could also claim that their political campaign against the Tito regime was part of the broader conflict with the communist bloc. Such rhetoric attracted the attention of the conservative wing of the CDU/CSU (particularly the circle around Franz Josef Strauß), which enjoyed considerable support among police officials in most *Länder*, along with more direct backing from extreme right-wing activists such as Wilhelm Schöttler.[37] The impeccably anti-communist credentials of the Croatian nationalist movement together with the compatibility of its aims with those of expellee organizations enabled Croatian émigrés to initially avoid any interference from the West German state. This gave nationalists the confidence they needed to extend their dominance over their own community and openly propagate the break up of Yugoslavia. So long as the ideological basis of an émigré group remained compatible with that of the government of the day, such a group could therefore organize and agitate with relative impunity.

Yet such toleration does not necessarily mean that these groups had significant influence over the policy-making process of the West German state. While the Ukrainian community's access did not necessarily shape the general direction of West German policy, exiles such as Mirtschuk or Rebet could at least ensure that decision makers were aware of the émigré point of view. By contrast, the Croatian leaders only had a few comparatively low-level contacts. Moreover, the funding Croatian organizations received from the *Auswärtiges Amt* and *Bundesministerium für Vertriebene* was only a fraction of the financial aid provided to such better connected communities as the Ukrainians or Latvians.[38] Since Yugoslavia did not experience the widespread popular resistance to communist regimes that shook Hungary and Poland in 1956, Croatian nationalists were also unable to benefit from the kind of solidarity experienced by Hungarian émigrés and refugees in the FRG after the Red Army stormed Budapest.[39] Though CDU regional officials with a *Donauschwaben* background may have disliked Tito, they were not able to provide access to state funds that could have enabled Croatian émigrés to make a living out of their political convictions. Yet anti-Yugoslav statements made by German conservatives helped to convince exiles that they enjoyed the support of the CDU leadership. In the 1950s the tendency among Croatian activists to confuse the support of individual figures with that of the entire political establishment kept this community broadly supportive of the Adenauer government. However, this attitude was to have quite adverse consequences for Croatian nationalist organizations in the long term.

The willingness of the Catholic Church to maintain a separate pastoral infrastructure for Croatians in Germany was also of great significance for the political development of this community. Although most clergymen were reluctant to make political statements, their churches became spaces in which Croatian political groups could contact and recruit newly arrived compatriots. Such Catholic missions therefore inadvertently enabled nationalists to dominate the Croatian community by giving them regular access to newly arrived immigrants. A small group of openly political clergymen even used their pastoral authority to promote a nationalist agenda.[40] Community meetings commemorating important dates on the Croatian national calendar would usually begin with a church service, before moving to a venue where political demonstrations and speeches could be held. Along with the activism of some priests, the close cooperation between German and Croatian priests encouraged many senior clergy in the Federal Republic to lobby on behalf of fellow Catholics who they believed were suffering from communist oppression. With the close relationship between the CDU, the Catholic Church and expellee groups such as the *Donauschwaben,* these confessional links helped Croatian activists to gain the support of leading members of the CDU/CSU's conservative wing, such as Franz Josef Strauß[41] and leading Christian democrats in Hessen.[42]

As a consequence Croatian émigrés felt able to use radical rhetoric in rallies and demonstrations without having to worry about state intervention. In the 1950s these rallies usually had no more than two or three hundred participants and commemorated events such as the declaration of Croatian independence during the Second World War. They often began with a Catholic mass conducted by a Croatian priest, which was then followed by a protest march that would end at a beer hall or restaurant where local Croatian notables and their German supporters would make a few speeches before everyone dug into their meal. Police officials monitoring these meetings made sure that participants stuck to an agreed route and obeyed legal restrictions imposed by municipal authorities. Formulated by a local *Ordnungsamt,* such restrictions usually included a ban on uniforms or slogans that could be deemed inflammatory (such as calls for violent action against the Yugoslav state). Until 1961 there is nothing in the cursory reports of policemen and low-level *Landesamt für Verfassungsschutz* agents monitoring such demonstrations to indicate that Croatian nationalists were any different from other anti-communist émigré groups.[43]

As the experience of the Ukrainian community demonstrates, leaders of shrinking émigré communities generally relied on their allies in the Bonn political establishment rather than encouraging their grass-roots supporters to get involved in direct action. Yugoslavia's special position within the communist bloc put the Croatian community in a more complicated position. The breakdown in diplomatic relations between the Tito regime and the USSR meant that the actions of groups hostile to Yugoslavia were not going to provoke any retaliatory action from other Soviet bloc intelligence services. Even more problematic for Croatian nationalists were attempts by the United States and other Western powers to draw Yugoslavia into a tacit alliance with NATO, which enabled the Tito regime to gain leverage over West German governments. In the early 1960s, at a time when this community was expanding rapidly, anxiety among Croatian activists about a potential rapprochement between these two states became more acute. These concerns reinforced grass-roots pressure for direct and violent action against a more secure Yugoslav state.

Initially, Croatian nationalists tried to undermine the position of the Yugoslav government by reminding West Germans of the savage treatment of *Wehrmacht* soldiers and German civilians by Yugoslav partisans in 1945. Together with embittered German expellees from Yugoslav territory, Croatian émigrés provided information to the press detailing the brutal behaviour of Yugoslav communists towards ethnic Germans. Peaceful forms of direct action were also used to get this message across. In July 1963, several Croatian activists pinned large posters on a building being used for trade talks between West German and Yugoslav representatives in Munich with slogans such as:

> In the Negotiations with Yugo-Serbo Communists do not forget the many 100,000 Germans murdered in Yugoslavia!!! The Yugoslav partisans gassed German children!!![44]

This was part of a wider publicity campaign in which expellees and Croatian nationalists did their best to play down reports of *Ustascha* or *Wehrmacht* atrocities.

The growing number of Yugoslav consulates across West Germany together with the establishment of a Trade Mission in Bonn (despite the difficulties caused by the *Hallstein* doctrine) provided another target for émigrés and expellees opposed to Tito. Since most Yugoslav diplomats had been communist partisans, the likelihood remained high that an official at a consulate or Trade Mission may have been involved in the mistreatment of Germans in the latter stages of the war. With a younger generation of activists demanding concrete results, Croatian organizations were now under more pressure than ever to prove that they could damage Yugoslav interests. As a consequence, senior Croatian émigrés asked their contacts in West German ministries and the historical commissions documenting the suffering of ethnic Germans during the Second World War to release information that might tarnish the war record of Yugoslav diplomats.[45]

The greatest success the Croatian nationalist movement experienced in the course of this campaign was the so-called Grabovac affair. On 7 December 1961 Predrag Grabovac, the Yugoslav consul in Munich, fled to Austria with a police escort after several newspapers published claims that he had been involved in partisan atrocities against German soldiers, *Donauschwaben* and Croatian Catholic priests.[46] A member of the Bavarian parliament for the right-wing *Großdeutsche Partei* (GDP) called Dr Paul Wüllner had instigated this press campaign. Not only did Wüllner flaunt his strong expellee connections in the course of his speech to the *Landtag* concerning Grabovac on 29 November 1961, but he also quoted from Croatian community newsletters such as *Hrvatska Dzvora*.[47] As head of the partisan intelligence service (OZNA) in Dalmatia, Grabovac was accused of being responsible for the execution of over 500 German soldiers as well as scores of Croatian intellectuals who belonged to the *Ustascha* in 1944.[48] The Croatian nationalist newspapers cited by Wüllner also accused Grabovac of still being an active member of the UdBA (*Uprava državne Bezbednosti*) and other Yugoslav intelligence services. The fact that in 1957 Grabovac had been removed from his first diplomatic post in Buenos Aires only a few weeks after these rumours were aired in the Argentinean press even allowed Wüllner and Croatian activists to claim that he had been declared '*persona ingrata*' by the Argentine government because of his wartime past.[49]

A similar case occurred a few weeks previously when local police in Cologne arrested a Yugoslav sales representative called Ante Vracaric who was accused of war crimes by Croatian émigrés. As with the Grabovac case, the swift deportation of Vracaric to Yugoslavia before charges could be pressed quickly defused the situation.[50] Both the Grabovac and Vracaric affairs demonstrated how parties interested in harming relations between Yugoslavia and the Federal Republic used the legacy of the Second World War. Despite strenuous efforts by the Yugoslav foreign ministry to clear Grabovac's name, Bavarian newspapers picked up the story, while the Bavarian *Landeskriminalamt* began an investigation into the allegations. A desire to prevent any embarrassing revelations coming to light ultimately forced the Yugoslav foreign ministry to withdraw Grabovac.[51]

While the kind of lobbying of German contacts that most other East European émigré communities engaged in had initially brought about the Grabovac affair, the first cases of Croatian immigrant violence against Yugoslav targets a year later indicated that this community was going to travel a very different political path. The most significant of these attacks was on the Yugoslav Trade Mission in Bonn-Mehlem involving twenty-six armed Croatian nationalists on 29 November 1962. This attack was preceded over the course of 1962 by several incidents in which Croatian migrant workers insulted Yugoslav representatives in Baden Württemberg and Bavaria. The fact that migrant workers who had only recently arrived in the Federal Republic played a central role in these attacks indicated that that they were as heavily politicized as their former DPs and émigrés. Through such incidents as the tearing down of a Yugoslav flag at the Friedrichshafen trade fair in June 1962 a new generation of radical nationalist activists came to the fore.[52]

In reports on these incidents compiled by police and intelligence officials before the Mehlem attack, there is little evidence of concern that these developments might represent a significant security problem, though the Balkan desk at the *Auswärtiges Amt* wanted to prevent any worsening in the Federal Republic's delicate relations with Yugoslavia. The resulting damage limitation exercise in the summer of 1962, organized by West German diplomats, was hampered by the way in which *Borba*, the newspaper of the Yugoslav Communist League, used these incidents to attack West German 'leniency' towards Croatian nationalist groups.[53] Comments by an *Auswärtiges Amt* official in correspondence to the Interior Ministry of Baden Württemberg suggest that West German officials were worried about the possible damage the Friedrichshafen incident might do to the FRG's image in Yugoslavia rather than the implications it might have about political shifts within the Croatian community:

> Since the Yugoslav side is currently showing restraint when it comes to the German question, our side should not unnecessarily disturb this 'calm'[54]

Though in retrospect the Grabovac/Vracaric affair and the attacks on Yugoslav flags were the first indication of radicalization within the Croatian community, West German diplomats and security officials continued to describe Croatians as well meaning, if misguided, allies in the fight against communism. The increasingly conspiratorial nature of Croatian nationalist politics and the rise in the number of violent attacks on Yugoslav targets after 1962 would force West German politicians and security services to reassess this view.

On the day of the Mehlem attack itself the Trade Mission was almost empty because of a Yugoslav national holiday. The only diplomats in the building were Assistant Trade Commissioner Georgevic and his aides, who were making final preparations for negotiations with the West German government concerning financial aid for Yugoslav industry, and Albert Dovgan, a consular official who was dealing with visa matters. On the premises as well were Dovgan's eleven-year-old son Berto and the porter, Momcilo Popovic.[55] At 11.45 A.M. there was an explosion in the Trade Mission's yard as members of a Croatian nationalist group known as the *Kreuzerbruderschaft* battered the front doors down. Shouting anti-Serbian and anti-communist slogans, these Croatian activists smashed the building's furniture and equipment. While desperately trying to get his son to safety, Dovgan was overwhelmed and severely beaten by the attackers. Only the arrival of Popovic holding a gun saved Dovgan as his assailants beat a hasty retreat to the front of the building. Before Dovgan's son could drag his father to safety, one of the assailants re-entered the back hallway with a pistol.

Whether Popovic opened fire remains unclear. All that could be ascertained later is that several shots were exchanged in the hallway of the building forcing Popovic to withdraw to the back offices. Popovic then shut the door to the hallway and barricaded it with his body. The assailant carrying the pistol fired one shot as his accomplices continued to smash and burn furniture and documents; the bullet penetrated the door at waist level before hitting Popovic. Simultaneously, three of the assailants placed explosive charges in the Trade Mission's front offices. Twenty seconds after the attackers escaped through the front the explosives went off causing serious structural damage to the building.[56]

Police arriving on the scene just after the attack expected a major stand off. Yet to their surprise the assailants did not resist arrest. Even the activist who had shot Popovic, a 39-year-old trucker called Franjo Percic, surrendered meekly. The police found one participant calmly polishing off his second beer in an adjacent bar before apologizing to its flabbergasted owner for the disturbance his comrades had caused.[57] Most of the Trade Mission staff had not been physically harmed. However, Albert Dovgan had suffered serious injures that would hospitalize him for months while his son was in a state of shock. Although Popovic survived the final explosion, he was to die from his wounds twelve days later.[58]

In the aftermath of the Mehlem attack, Yugoslav newspapers such as *Borba* and *Politika* attacked the Adenauer government in articles that implied that the West German state was sliding towards fascism.[59] Popovic was posthumously awarded the title of 'Hero of the Nation' by Tito himself, who signed a condolence letter to the Popovic family. His body and family were flown back to Belgrade, where he was accorded a full state funeral attended by senior members of the regime and several thousand onlookers.[60] Under pressure from furious Yugoslav and Swedish diplomats,[61] as well as the West German press, the security services tried to make up for their failure to properly monitor the Croatian community. Yet without the quick surrender of the assailants to the local police, it is unlikely that investigators would have been able to catch those responsible for this incident so quickly. Until the Mehlem attack, West German intelligence officials knew little about growing militancy within the Croatian community or the organization involved in the attack, the *Kroatische Kreuzerbruderschaft* (in Croatian: *Hrvatski Krizari*).[62]

Founded in January 1959, the *Kroatische Kreuzerbruderschaft* had 200 members along with a wider circle of sympathizers. As an offshoot of the 'Croatian Liberation Organization' (in German the *Kroatische Befreiungsbewegung* and in Croatian the *Hrvatski Domobrani Odbor* or HDO), it had strong links to the established émigré scene.[63] In 1962 the three chairmen of the leadership committee, Franjo Percic, Father Rafael Medic-Skoko and the pharmacist Josip Alexander Jilk (who had not taken part in the attack) were aged 39, 57 and 46 respectively.[64] They had all either fought or been politically active during the Second World War and then fled to Germany in the late 1940s. Lower down the hierarchy, several members involved in the Mehlem attack, such as Ivan Starcevic, who worked as a miner, had also been old enough to fight in the war.[65]

Of the three chairmen, Father Medic-Skoko had been the most heavily involved in the *Ustascha* as Ante Pavelic's personal chaplain between 1941 and 1945. From 1945 to 1957, he had lived in exile in Madrid and Buenos Aires, two cities with heavy concentrations of Croatian nationalists and former national socialist leaders. After his return from South American exile in 1958, Medic-Skoko was personally given pastoral responsibility over all Croatians in the Ruhr region by the Bishop of Paderborn, a connection that West German investigators tried to remove from documents mentioning the Mehlem incident.[66] Medic-Skoko initially denied any involvement in the attack at the 1964 trial dealing with the Mehlem case. Despite these claims, in interrogations that took place immediately after their arrest in December 1962 several of the other key figures in the Mehlem bombing stated that Medic-Skoko had played an instrumental role in recruiting those who had been involved in the attack.[67] Though he continued to deny advance knowledge, Medic-Skoko used every opportunity he had on the witness stand to accuse the Tito regime of waging genocide against the Croatian people.[68]

By contrast, Franjo Percic had been interned in Dachau during the Second World War because of his support for Croatian language rights in parts of Croatia that had come under direct Hungarian and German control.[69] This record of resistance to the Germans did not help him much after his return to Yugoslavia, as his involvement in a nationalist student organization in Zagreb suppressed by the communists in 1946 ultimately led to his arrest. Years later he claimed that his stay in Yugoslav prisons was worse than his experiences in Dachau.[70] After his release in 1948, Percic fled to Dortmund, where he worked with Croatian nationalists like Medic-Skoko who were proud of their support for Nazi Germany. At the Mehlem trial he admitted responsibility for killing Popovic, but went on to state that he had been provoked into using his weapon by Popovic's armed response to the initial attack. Like Medic-Skoko and most of the others involved in the Mehlem bombing, both during the police interrogation and on the witness stand Percic reiterated that only a symbolic protest had been planned. Yet these claims did not square with the several kilos of explosive that the raiding party had brought with it.[71]

Others within the *Kreuzerbruderschaft*, such as Jilk and Pernar, had been involved in similar student organizations in Zagreb and became involved in émigré politics after they were granted asylum in West Germany in 1948. While Jilk was responsible for dealing with the West German authorities, effectively fronting for the *Kreuzerbruderschaft* to non-Croatians, Pernar tried to forge links with prominent Croatian nationalists such as Branko Jelic or Berislav Dezelic and Percic dealt with illicit matters such as the acquisition of guns and explosives.[72] Together with Medic-Skoko, who made much of his close relationship with Ante Pavelic, these postwar émigrés had the personal authority, contacts and organizational experience needed to set up a network capable of organized political violence.

Yet most of the *Kreuzerbruderschaft*'s 'foot soldiers' at the Mehlem attack were still in their twenties. A typical new recruit was Vladimir Murat, a 24-year-old miner who had set up the explosives during the attack. Like most of the younger members of the *Kreuzerbruderschaft* he had left Yugoslavia in the late 1950s to avoid the draft and find better paying work in West Germany.[73] Murat and other migrant workers claimed to have lost relatives to communist persecution after the war, though they openly admitted that it had resulted from their families' (low-level) affiliation with the *Ustascha* regime. Having been granted asylum, they found work in West Germany in typical 'guest worker' industries: steel, manufacturing and mining.[74] As in many other diaspora communities, young, lonely men new to German society proved susceptible to the kind of ersatz community nationalist organizations could provide.

These younger participants followed Medic-Skoko and Percic's lead in accusing Momcilo Popovic of taking part in atrocities committed against Germans in wartime Yugoslavia.[75] Such allegations, which bore great similarity to those levelled at Grabovac, helped to garner support for the *Kreuzerbruderschaft* from other Croatian nationalists as well as expellee organizations during the trial. After the attack, the *Donauschwäbischer Verband* published letters of solidarity with the arrested attackers and hired the prominent right-wing lawyer Wilhelm Schöttler to run the defence fund.[76] Confidence that 'normal' Germans supported their actions was also reflected in declarations by younger members of the *Kreuzerbruderschaft* that protests against Tito and demonstrations against the Berlin Wall in West Berlin were part of the same battle against global communism.[77] Following the example set by Percic and Medic-Skoko, Murat at one point interrupted trial proceedings with a loud monologue declaring that Tito was 'a worse war criminal than Hitler'.[78]

Such allegations were largely based on the testimony of a Croatian émigré called Ivan Boras, who alleged that he had seen Popovic organize the gassing of Croatian priests and ethnic German children in June 1945.[79] Though Boras' testimony on the witness stand at the Mehlem trial had no influence on the sentence they received, the tactic of using alleged instances of Titoist brutality in order to muddy the waters would recur in subsequent judicial cases dealing with acts of political violence committed by Croatian activists. In a manner similar to the Grabovac or Vracaric affairs, Croatian émigrés, as well as German expellee leaders, would insinuate that Yugoslav representatives attacked by Croatian nationalists had been involved in the more brutal aspects of the Tito regime's rise to power during the 1940s. When referring to alleged war crimes committed by Yugoslav partisans, émigrés and expellees used terms such as 'gassing' or 'KZ/concentration camp', in order to equate Yugoslav communist repression with atrocities committed by the SS and *Wehrmacht*.[80] This tactic helped create the impression that the assassination and bombing of Yugoslav targets was a legitimate form of self-defence by those who had suffered oppression in a communist state. While this tactic proved effective in an environment in the 1950s and early 1960s in which the West German media often made comparisons between national socialist crimes and Soviet repression, its effectiveness declined in the late 1960s once a new generation of West Germans became more open to better relations with communist regimes.[81]

The trial dealing with the attempted assassination of the Yugoslav consul Andrija Klaric on 8 June 1965 is another example of how the wartime record of the victim was used by the defence team to absolve the perpetrator of guilt. Klaric's assassin was Stanko Kardum, a migrant worker who had helped organize the desecration of the Yugoslav flag in Baden Württemberg in June 1962. Though Klaric himself had been too young to have played any major role in the partisan army during the 1940s, Kardum's defence team still focused on atrocities committed by Tito's troops in an attempt to convince the judge and public that those trying to kill Klaric were fighting for a just cause. The fact that an unregistered pistol had been discovered on Klaric after the assassination attempt was used by defence lawyers to create the impression that loyal servants of the Tito regime were capable of any crime.[82] Defence lawyers also used this strategy in another trial dealing with the fatal shooting of another Yugoslav diplomat in 1966 by a recently arrived migrant worker called Franjo Goreta. Again atrocities committed by Yugoslav partisans were mentioned throughout the trial, leading to a much lighter prison sentence than the prosecution had requested. In the subsequent decade Goreta's role in this killing increased his authority within the more violent elements of the Croatian nationalist movement.[83]

The growing influence of younger militants within the Croatian nationalist movement did not diminish its fixation on the Second World War. Migrant workers who joined the *Kreuzerbruderschaft* also emphasized their families' experiences during that conflict when it came to justifying their participation in the Mehlem attack.[84] Both in police interrogations and under cross-examination during the Mehlem trial, these participants focused on atrocities committed against Croatians and the Catholic Church by communist partisans, while rejecting any suggestion that the *Ustascha* may have perpetrated similar crimes.[85] Though migrant workers were probably vaguely hostile towards the Yugoslav state before their arrival in Germany, these attitudes were given greater cohesion once this new generation came into contact with figures of authority who promoted an extreme form of Croatian nationalism.[86]

Several migrant workers involved in the Mehlem incident and subsequent terror attacks had been in contact with other Croatian nationalist organizations before 1962. Community work by Croatian leaders who officials in the *Auswärtiges Amt* and *Bundesministerium des Innern* had considered to be moderate, such as Berislav Dezelic (who was almost killed by Yugoslav assassins in 1965), played a key role in drawing this new generation into the wider nationalist movement. Though Dezelic had fled to Germany shortly before the Second World War, his affiliation with the Peasant Party had kept him from any deeper involvement with either the *Ustascha* or the national socialists. After 1945 Dezelic established the *Kroatischer Sozialdienst* (Croatian Welfare Service), an organization that provided advice and financial aid to Croatian migrant workers and asylum seekers. It was through Dezelic's willingness to cooperate with more extreme nationalists that new arrivals came into contact with organizations such as Branimir Jelic's *Kroatische Nationalbewegung*.[87] By the early 1960s, Jelic and Dezelic's organizations lost more and more members to such splinter groups as the *Kreuzerbruderschaft* because increasingly disillusioned migrant workers and asylum seekers became frustrated with what Percic described as 'Jelic's ceaseless inaction'.[88] Jelic's reliance upon West German contacts, which pressured émigré organizations to stay peaceful in order to protect German interests, seems to have weakened his position among Croatians rather than strengthening it.

Another aspect of the Mehlem attack that was particularly shocking for West German investigators was the willingness of participants to maim or kill. Not only were several of the participants armed with guns, the four members of the raiding party who worked in mines had been able to secure the explosives used for the bombing without attracting the attention of anyone at their workplace.[89] Jilk had also managed to register the *Kreuzerbruderschaft* as a cultural club without attracting the attention of local administrators, despite the nationalist undertones of the group's name. Only after the Mehlem attack did the *Landesamt für Verfassungsschutz* decide to undertake a deeper examination of the *Kreuzerbruderschaft*'s political aims. This investigation led to the *Kreuzerbruderschaft*'s speedy dissolution by the North Rhine-Westphalian Justice Ministry, whose example was quickly followed by the other *Länder*. A more robust attitude to extreme nationalist groups was reflected in comments by the Interior Minster of North Rhine-Westphalia to *RIAS* (a West Berlin radio station):

> This [ban] is more than a warning shot for any illegal groups, which misuse the hospitality of the Federal Republic in order to carry out their political activity here in Germany.[90]

Yet even after West German security services turned against the *Kreuzerbruderschaft* they remained unable to pre-empt a growing succession of attacks upon Yugoslav targets by other Croatian nationalist groups.

Though the Mehlem trial cut short the nationalist careers of the senior leaders, the younger activists (who after the 1968 labour treaty between the FRG and Yugoslavia were classified as guest workers) went on to establish and lead nationalist organizations involved in acts of political violence long after the North Rhine-Westphalian government disbanded the *Kreuzerbruderschaft*.[91] Mile Rukavina, who was given a prison sentence for beating up Albert Dovgan, was to play a prominent enough role to merit his inclusion in a UdBA list of assassination targets discovered by the *Auswärtiges Amt* in late 1969. The list confirmed West German diplomats' worst suspicions about the activities of the Yugoslav security services, particularly since there were at least eleven attempted or successful murders of Croatian nationalists between 1965 and 1970.[92] Ten years later Rukavina was involved in a nationalist group also engaged in criminal activities under the leadership of Franjo Goreta.[93] Large community rallies commemorating the Pavelic regime or the creation of the medieval Croatian kingdom in Knin continued to provide activists with the opportunity to sustain contact as their political network spread across the Federal Republic.

The build-up to these meetings could cause massive security problems for local police forces. A typical example of these tensions was an incident involving the arrival of 500 Croatians at Munich central railway station on 12 April 1970. Consisting of activists travelling to a nationalist convention, this group assembled around a Croatian flag similar to that of the Pavelic regime (containing a chess board pattern that can be found in the flag of post-Yugoslav Croatia) that had been hoisted in the station's main concourse.[94] Yugoslav pressure had driven most *Land* governments to enforce laws concerning the licensing of political symbols, forcing Croatian activists to apply for permits not only for meetings but also for the use of flags and placards.[95] Since the spontaneous gathering and unfurling of the Croatian flag at a public place such as Munich central station took place without official permission, a handful of policemen who had been completely taken by surprise by this turn of events tried to break up the crowd. This led to a fracas that was only brought under control after riot police arrived on the scene.[96] Yet police officers had consulted émigrés organizing the convention as well as Yugoslav diplomats (who were granted heavier security during its duration) months before it actually took place. Despite all these preparations, the local police officers dealing with this unexpected gathering at the Munich train station were unable to cope with large numbers of non-German activists. This sudden switch from peaceful cooperation to violence and back again by Croatian activists, which repeatedly knocked West German police officers off balance, was described in a police report written by *Polizeiobermeister* Heinz Thurnhofer:

> I arrived at the place named above [Munich Central Railway Station] together with PM Georg Meier and PHW Teichmann (in civilian clothing), transport policeman Pregler was in uniform … In my estimation there were at least 500 people who had … assembled around the Croatian national flag … I therefore demanded that the flag bearers show me their personal identity papers including identity cards or passports. While collecting these papers, I was attacked and thrown to the ground by a man, who was later discovered to be a stateless Croatian … After searching this individual we discovered a KK revolver loaded with six bullets along with five further bullets in his clothing … While arresting and removing this man from the scene we were attacked by another Croatian, who was over 192 centimetres tall … After he was thoroughly searched a Czech pistol, caliber 7.65 and loaded with 8 bullets, was discovered.[97]

Throughout, West German police and intelligence agencies failed to anticipate and prevent acts of violence committed by Croatian activists even after they began to define the Croatian nationalist organizations as a potential security threat. Émigré leaders, conservative academics and expellees, on which security services relied for information when it came to both Yugoslavia and the Croatian community, were too closely associated with exponents of Croatian nationalism to be treated as reliable sources. Yet, a new scepticism towards old contacts did not translate into successful recruitment of reliable Croatian informers who could help prevent major acts of political violence. Investigators could only gather information about trends within the Croatian nationalist movements through the interrogation of suspects and the testimony of witnesses under cross-examination in the courtroom.[98]

Nationalists were willing to threaten anyone prepared to divulge information to outsiders with severe punishment, making it difficult for security services to keep abreast of developments within the community. As militant Croatian groups emulated other terrorist organizations emerging in the late 1960s, any successes local police did enjoy were more the result of luck than endeavour. In May 1966, only the coincidental stop and search of a car with a broken brake light, used by two Croatians to transport dynamite, warned investigators that a nationalist group was amassing a large amount of explosives.[99] Four years later a similar discovery came about through a farcical incident in Hanover. This time, the *Niedersächisches Landeskriminalamt* discovered a Croatian terrorist cell when an activist accidentally shot himself in the leg while showing off a new pistol at his daughter's christening. Investigators who subsequently searched his flat found a cache of arms as well as propaganda material from legally registered Croatian nationalist organizations.[100]

While chance events changed the course of some criminal investigations, such information could only be put into proper perspective through a comparison with material gathered from a network of reliable informers. Yet despite their best efforts, neither local police forces nor security and intelligence agencies seem to have been able to develop a reliable network of Croatian sources. Without such a regular supply of information, West German security officials were unable to exert covert influence on the internal development of the Croatian community. Each new act of political violence committed by Croatian nationalists came out of the blue for West German state officials at all levels of government, complicating their relationship with their Yugoslav counterparts, who usually had access to more comprehensive intelligence on the Croatian nationalist movement.

Yet West German diplomats and security officials were often wary of information passed on to them by Yugoslav police officers.[101] Lack of trust between West German security services and Yugoslav state representatives is reflected in a report by police officers on attempts by UdBA officials to influence investigations into the bombing of the Yugoslav consulate in Munich in 1971:

> The report of 9 June 1972 submitted to the Federal Interior Ministry from the embassy of the Socialist Federal Republic of Yugoslavia, which claimed that Stojiljko Kajevic was planning an attack on the [Yugoslav] general consulate in Munich, was not passed on directly nor did it reach the Munich police department through the local consulate. It was effectively worthless, since preventative policing measures (the only course of action that would have been in accordance with German law) would only have been possible if we had known his current location. Moreover, an unverifiable claim made by an embassy about a specific person (without the presentation of any evidence) cannot provide the basis for executive measures.[102]

Unwilling to trust the UdBA, the only intelligence agency able to infiltrate Croatian nationalist groups, West German security services were flying blind. The impression one gains is that journalists, particularly those at *Spiegel* magazine, were better informed about Croatian nationalist movements than the *Auswärtiges Amt* or the police. More often than not, information that shaped the response of the security services to Croatian nationalist activity was either incomplete or outdated.[103]

In this context, one of the more remarkable aspects of political violence committed by Croatian activists is the extent to which those involved cooperated with West German police. An extraordinary example of this willingness to trust

West German security officials was the initial Mehlem attack, where all those participating, including Franjo Percic (who had just shot Momcilo Popovic), quietly surrendered to the police. The transcripts of the ensuing interrogations are extensive since most of those involved were prepared to give detailed descriptions of their involvement in the attack. Though a few attempted to minimize their own role, the attackers' openness reflected an underlying trust in the police officers conducting the investigation. This willingness to cooperate was a product of the participants' conviction that their resistance to the Tito regime and the battle against communism in Germany were connected; an assumption that was clearly voiced by Mile Rukavina during his police interrogation:

> I plead with you to take into account that I feel that it is my duty to fight for the freedom of my homeland and against communism.[104]

It was therefore quite a shock to Rukavina and his coconspirators that prosecutors intended to jail everyone involved in the Mehlem attack. In a statement made on Rukavina's behalf, a defence lawyer indicated why members of the *Kreuzerbruderschaft* had expected to escape punishment:

> The men of 20 July [1944, i.e., the military plot to assassinate Hitler] as well as the resistance fighters of 17 June [1953, i.e., the East German workers' rebellion] and Budapest acted for the same motives as the Mehlem attackers.[105]

The fiercely anti-communist rhetoric used by West German conservatives along with anti-Yugoslav sentiment voiced by expellee organizations encouraged the belief among Croatian activists that direct action against the Tito regime would gain the support of the German public. Comparisons made by the defence team during the trial between the Mehlem attack and attempts to blow up the Berlin Wall by German right-wing radicals were designed to take advantage of such sentiment.[106] For émigrés like Branimir Jelic, West Germany should still have been a natural ally of Croatian nationalists trying to destroy a communist regime. This outlook was expressed openly in Jelic's correspondence with senior ministerial officials:

> Even in the last war we were the only nation – and we are not speaking about the [Pavelic] regime – that held out together with the Germans until the end and continued the fight against Serbian Communists after the German capitulation.[107]

The conviction that the aims of Croatian nationalists were compatible with those of the West German mainstream centre-right is the reason why participants in the first attacks on Yugoslav targets tended to surrender to the West German police.[108] Although only a small minority was directly involved in violent action, the assumption that the West German state would somehow back Croatian nationalist goals was held throughout the community; even by those who remained loyal to the Tito regime.[109]

That this proved a serious miscalculation perplexed militant Croatians. Once it became clear that Croatian nationalist support for the Federal Republic did not mean they were willing to stay within the law, West German police began to treat Croatian organizations as a major security problem. According to *Verfassungsschutz* estimates, between 1962 and 1969 there were approximately forty suspected acts of political violence committed against pro-Yugoslav individuals or Yugoslav targets by Croatian nationalists in the Federal Republic.[110] Émigrés such as Branimir Jelic believed that repressive measures taken by West German state institutions against Croatian organizations were the result of pressure from social democrats who were 'soft' on communism.[111] The increasingly draconian response of West German authorities to those involved in violence showed that in reality most centre-right politicians and officials were not prepared to back expellees and Croatian nationalists who used violence.

Some of their most loyal supporters, such as Franz-Josef Strauß, did still occasionally send expressions of support (usually couched in terms of support for the 'Croatian nation', rather then the 'Croatian state') to community gatherings. Yet this did not stop the CDU/CSU from dealing with the Tito regime in a pragmatic fashion. As with the Ukrainian community, once the aims of certain Croatian groups were seen to endanger what the centre-right considered to be the interests of the West German state, the help and solidarity they had taken for granted suddenly evaporated. At the same time that CSU members of the *Bundestag* passed on letters of support to Croatian émigrés in the early 1960s, the CSU-dominated Bavarian government was cultivating the Yugoslav regime in a bid to increase the exports of companies based in Bavaria.[112] For all their anti-communist rhetoric, neither the CDU nor CSU did anything concrete to help their Croatian allies as long as Yugoslavia seemed to have a long-term future. Where this gradual abandonment of émigré causes helped to depoliticize the miniscule and ageing Ukrainian community, it did not dampen pressure for action within expanding Croatian organizations. Even though West German police officers put their men between Croatian activists and Yugoslav diplomats on several occasions in a vain effort to maintain public order, nothing seemed to deflect nationalists who wanted to execute terrorist attacks against Yugoslav targets.

The fact that Yugoslav intelligence agencies displayed equal ruthlessness in their retaliatory measures against Croatian émigrés did not increase the sympathies of West German security services for the Croatian cause. The regular disruption caused by these bomb attacks and assassinations did, however, cause serious tension between West German police and their Yugoslav colleagues. Croatian nationalists were not the only émigrés targeted by the UdBA either. Anti-communist organizations and activists from every Yugoslav ethnic group could be found in the Federal Republic during this period.[113] While the small Slovenian and Bosnian Muslim organizations in the FRG were largely ignored by the Yugoslav government, the UdBA did all it could to interfere with political activity among Kosovo Albanian guest workers in the late 1970s. The assassination in 1981 of three Albanian activists in Heilbronn led to a quick decline in the number of Albanians involved in nationalist agitation until conditions in Kosovo deteriorated further in the late 1980s.[114]

Serb émigré groups that supported the deposed Yugoslav royal family or had connections with Četnik militias (both hostile to Croatian nationalism) that had fought both Germans and communists during the war were hit by repeated kidnappings and assassination attempts coordinated by the UdBA from the early 1950s onwards.[115] Yet while Croat nationalists could, despite tension between different leaders and organizations, at least agree on the shared goal of Croatian independence, some Serb émigrés supported a united and royalist Yugoslavia while others had a more radical nationalist agenda.[116] These deep divisions over how a post-communist Yugoslavia should be organized meant that Serb postwar émigrés opposed to the Tito regime found it very difficult to recruit newly arrived migrants and guest workers. This meant that despite the occasional strike against Serb émigrés, Yugoslav diplomats and intelligence agents in the FRG remained largely focused on destroying Croatian nationalist organizations that seemed to present the most significant threat to the interests of the Tito regime.[117]

The pressure upon police and intelligence agencies to suppress Croatian groups was made more acute by two factors. The first was the ambiguous nature of West German state sovereignty. Until 1990, the freedom of action of both the FRG and the West Berlin city government was constrained by the four occupying powers through the Yalta and Potsdam accords. Since as a member of the broader wartime alliance the Yugoslav government enjoyed certain diplomatic privileges on German territory (just as other minor powers such as Canada, Czechoslovakia or Belgium), political violence committed by Croatian groups whose predecessors had supported Nazi Germany could cause wider complications for West German foreign policy.[118] This comment made by a Bonn diplomat reporting in 1969 on the attempted assassination of the Yugoslav Military Commissioner in West Berlin by a Croatian nationalist reflects how the Auswärtiges Amt's response to such events could be affected by its endemic anxiety over sovereignty issues:

> I explained to Herr Killian [a West Berlin official], that it would be advisable if the position of the West Berlin Senate's reply would, as far as possible, match the content of the response formulated by the Allied military command.[119]

Though the special status of West Berlin accentuated the problems caused by immigrant political activity, this comment encapsulates a sense of vulnerability in West German security services that limited the extent to which police and intelligence agencies could tolerate immigrant organizations that advocated the use of violence.[120]

The second factor was growing public apprehension about immigrant crime. Though this debate was fuelled more by property or drug crime as well as popular concerns over the sexual behaviour of male immigrants (that may have reflected underlying prejudices reaching back to the national socialist era), immigrant politics also came to play a significant role. Proxy wars between immigrant communities and their homeland regimes presented a challenge to the state monopoly of violence in the Federal Republic. As a consequence, concerns that the CDU and CSU's reputation as the parties of law and order might be undermined by the unchecked growth of violent immigrant movements increased the reluctance of Christian democrat politicians to protect their émigré allies. This was compounded by the fact that SPD politicians used the contacts between Croatian nationalists and members of the centre-right for their own electoral purposes. After the Mehlem attack social democrats implied that the CDU/CSU's reluctance to distance itself from the authoritarian legacy of pre-1945 Germany meant that it was unable to maintain order within immigrant communities. Herbert Wehner, the head of the SPD parliamentary party in the *Bundestag,* insinuated as much in a debate concerning Croatian nationalists in 1963:

> Herbert Wehner (SPD): Herr Minister, is there a difference made when pursuing murderers and murder organizations because of the political beliefs of the victim and the wider political background?[121]

Wherever the SPD took power, similar accusations were made by German conservatives against prominent social democrat supporters of left-wing immigrant movements.[122] As we shall see in the fourth chapter, when it came to the Greek community, worries about being painted into such a corner often forced social democrat leaders to restrain their supporters from cooperating with friendly immigrant groups. Such worries about criminal activity had already had an impact on the attitude of West German authorities towards DPs in the 1940s and 1950s. Because cases involving immigrant criminality had great potential for public controversy neither the centre-right nor the security services were going to let violent Croatian nationalists tarnish the image of the CDU/CSU and the West German state. An official from the *Bundesministerium für Flüchtinge und Vertriebene* said as much in a discussion with a disappointed Branimir Jelic in 1969:

> The visitor (Jelic) emphasized the point that he sees his participation in the 'Friends of the CSU' group [Jelic was a member of the West Berlin CDU as well] ... as part of his role as a German citizen ... Nevertheless, Herr Dr. Wolfrum (BmfFuV) [i.e., the Ministry of Refugees and Expellees] drew his attention to the fact that there would be an inevitable and visible effect upon his Croatian posts if his work for the 'Friends' gained too much publicity.[123]

As immigrant crime became a matter of public concern, West German officials and journalists became less willing to accept political justifications of acts of violence perpetrated by Croatian activists, a trend that was compounded in the 1970s by the involvement of Croatian nationalists in a semi-criminal milieu. The kind of conspiratorial networks needed to run a terrorist organization also functioned as organized crime rackets involved in extortion and gunrunning. In 1971, journalists began to focus on this link between Croatian nationalist organizations and what came to be known as the 'Croatian Mafia'.[124] The sensationalist tones in which the actions of Croatian activists were described by the press can be seen in this *Der Spiegel* article describing a crackdown by West German police on a criminal network run by Franjo Goreta in 1981:

> In the bloody underground war between militant circles of exiled Croats in West Germany and the Yugoslav secret service, Udba, Goreta had apparently ended up on the hit list.[125]

Intriguingly, this article revealed that the Yugoslav diplomat whom Goreta had gunned down fifteen years earlier had originally recruited him as an informant.[126] By the early 1980s, CDU/CSU politicians and West German officials, whose predecessors had been sympathetic to Croatian nationalism, avoided contact with a movement that had prominent activists involved in organized crime.

Whereas militant expellees had to be taken into account by the CDU/CSU because of their electoral power, Croatian nationalists could simply be ignored or suppressed once they came to be seen as a problem. After the SPD became the dominant party of government in 1969, the position of Croatian nationalist organizations was even more precarious. With little sympathy for the unremitting anti-communism of émigré movements that were financially supported by the *Bundesministerium für Vertrieben und Flüchtlinge,* social democrat and FDP ministers cut their funding. As we have seen, negative publicity surrounding other émigré and expellee activists also hastened the end of the *Bundesminsterium für Vertiebene,* which merged with the *Bundesministerium des Innern* in 1971.[127] Not only did this have serious administrative consequences for East European émigrés and expellees, it was a symbolic act by the Brandt government designed to normalize relations with Eastern European states.

The underlying conservatism of the West German centre-right forced its representatives to avoid association with any form of violent action that embarrassed state institutions. This meant that political violence committed by Croatians helped to alienate even the most committed friends of the Croatian nationalist cause. Though such incidents encouraged many embittered Croatian asylum seekers, migrants and guest workers to join nationalist organizations, they ultimately ended whatever influence Croatian community leaders had over their German allies. Buffeted by the suspicions of the press and the hostility of the SPD, Croatian nationalists only began to be taken seriously again by the CDU/CSU in the late 1980s, at the point when the imminent collapse of the Yugoslav state became a realistic possibility rather than a nationalist dream.

****

How does the experience of the Croatian community shed light on the two questions posed at the beginning of this chapter? At what point, if at all, did Croatian organizations prepared to use violence to achieve their ideological goals break the bounds of what their German allies considered politically acceptable? Did a shift to an emphasis on collective as opposed to individual responsibility for violent acts take place when it came to the approach of the West German security services towards these communities? The key to these issues however lies in the second question posed in the introductory section of this chapter: did West German police and intelligence agencies use different forms of control for different communities based on such criteria as ideological allegiance and ethnic background? As we have seen above, security officials often used the considerable leeway at their disposal when it came to deciding how and when to clamp down upon immigrant political movements they suspected of involvement in acts of violence.

Yet the relative tolerance of the West German security services towards the actions of fellow anti-communists only provided Croatian nationalist groups with a temporary reprieve. Once West German governments began to treat the Yugoslav government as a potential strategic partner rather than a communist opponent, conservative Christian democrats distanced themselves from the Croatian nationalists' cause, which was now harming the interests of the Federal Republic. Without the protective mantle of mainstream CDU/CSU leaders even the sympathy of certain expellee organizations was not enough to keep the Croatian community from experiencing increased surveillance from local police as well as the *Verfassungsschutz*.

Of equal importance was the desire of many within the West German centre-right to avoid involvement with militant and uncontrollable elements within the anti-communist alliance that might have reminded the wider public of continuities between a national socialist past and a Christian democrat present. These pressures became more acute once the CDU began to lose control of the federal government. As the SPD gained a growing hold over West German state institutions, causes that had once been considered politically acceptable in the 1950s came to be seen as an anachronistic preserve of the extreme Right. By the late 1960s, the willingness of West German security services to cooperate with their Yugoslav counterparts, despite the assassination of several Croatian leaders by the UdBA, confirmed the extent to which the Croatian nationalist movement had lost support of the Bonn political establishment.

The fate of Croatian nationalists in Cold War Germany therefore demonstrates how even an immigrant community with the kind of anti-communist credentials that could draw support from key elements within the CDU/CSU could incur a hostile response from West German state institutions if the actions and rhetoric of its activists threatened the wider foreign policy agenda of the federal government. As we have seen in the course of this chapter, if influential figures and organizations within such a community displayed open hostility towards a major West German political party, as Croatian nationalists did towards the SPD, then the likelihood increased that violence committed by individual activists would lead to the collective punishment of the entire social infrastructure of their community.

Notes

1. H.-E. Schultz. 1990. 'Politische Justiz gegen eine "Auslandsvereinigung" und die Rolle des "Kronzeugen" als zentrales Beweismittel in schauprozeßartigen Mammutverfahren: Der PKK-Prozeß in Düsseldorf', in H. Janssen and M. Schubert (eds), *Staatssicherheit: Die Bekämpfung des politischen Feindes im Inneren*, Bielefeld: AJZ Verl., 86–88.
2. H. Aden. 1999. 'Das Bundeskriminalamt: Intelligence-Zentrale oder Schaltstelle des bundesdeutschen Polizeisystems?', *Bürgerrechte & Polizei/CILIP*, 62 (January), 8–13.
3. A. Funk. 1991. '"Innere Sicherheit": Symbolische Politik und exekutive Praxis', in B. Blanke and H. Wollman (eds), *Die alte Bundesrepublik: Kontinuität und Wandel*, Opladen: Westdeutscher Verl., 369–71.
4. K. Hartung. 1987. *Der Blinde Fleck: Die Linke, der RAF und der Staat*, Frankfurt a.M.: Neue Kritik, 17.
5. D. Schenk. 2003. *Die Braunen Wurzeln des BKA*, Frankfurt a.M.: Fischer Verl., 271–75.
6. P. Mueller and M. Müller. 2002. *Gegen Freund und Feind – Der BND: Geheime Politik und Schmutzige Geschäfte*, Hamburg: Rowohlt Verl, 65–68.
7. H. Bogs-Maciejewski. 1988. *Was Jeder vom Verfassungsschutz Wissen Sollte*, Heidelberg: Becker c.f. Müller Verl., 12–15.
8. Schenk, *Die Braunen Wurzeln des BKA*, 227, 177–80.
9. D.P. Conradt. 2001. *The German Polity*, 7th ed., New York: Longman Press, 211.
10. M. Winter. 1998. *Politikum Polizei – Macht und Funktion der Polizei in der Bundesrepublik Deutschland*, Münster: LIT (Politische Soziologie, Band 10), 21–24.
11. D. Belosevic. 1995. 'Die Minderheiten aus den ehemaligen Jugoslawien', in C. Schmalz-Jacobsen (ed.), *Ethnische Minderheiten in der Bundesrepublik Deutschland*, Munich: C.H Beck, 209.
12. J.A. Irvine. 1993. *The Croat Question: Partisan Politics in the Formation of the Yugoslav Socialist State*, San Francisco: Westview, 91–93.
13. R. Okey. 2001. *The Habsburg Monarchy 1765–1918*, London: Macmillan, 388–89.
14. J.R. Lampe. 1997. *Yugoslavia as History: Twice There Was a Country*, Cambridge: Cambridge University Press, 125–26.
15. F. Singleton. 1993. *A Short History of the Yugoslav Peoples*, Cambridge: Cambridge University Press, 162–63.
16. Irvine, *The Croat Question*, 37.
17. R. Overmans. *Deutsche Militärische Verluste im Zweiten Weltkrieg*, Munich: R.Oldenbourg Verl. (Beiträge zur Militärgeschichte Bd. 46), 284–89.
18. M. Tanner. 2001. *Croatia: a Nation Forged in War*, New Haven: Yale University Press, 130–34.
19. K.-D. Grothusen. 1977. 'Südosteuropa und Südosteuropaforschung. Zur Lage der Südosteuropaforschung in der BRD', in Nitsche, E. Oberländer and H. Lemberg (eds), *Osteuropa in Geschichte und Gegenwart*, Bohlau: Cologne, 408–26.
20. D.S., '"Aus Unsere Seele": *Spiegel*-Interview mit dem Stellvertretenden Vorsitzenden des Berliner "Freundschaftskreises der CSU" Branko Jelic', 16 February 1970, German original: 'die Tradition der deutsch-kroatischen Freundschaft'.
21. Bay. HstA. Mun., Prasidium der Bayerischen Landpolizei Nr. 111, *Brief – Bayer. Staatsministerium des Inneren to Bayer. Staatskanzlei*, Re.: 'Nationalfeiertage der Ostemigranten und der kommunistischen Ostblockstaaten', Munich, 4 February 1963.

22. For example: Pol. A.A.Ber., B 42, Nr. 569, *Prof. Dr. v. Mende – Forschungsdienst Osteuropa,* Re.: 'Darstellung der jugoslawischen Exilorganisationen in der Bundesrepublik', Düsseldorf, 10 December 1962; and Hauptstaatsarchiv Nordrhein-Westfalen (HstA. NRW), NW 308, Nr. 196, *Rundschreiben – Landesamt für Verfassungsschutz,* Re.: 'Kreuzerbruderschaft u. A.: Polizeiliche Überwachungsmaßnahmen', Cologne, 8 March 1963.

23. Pol. A.A.Ber., B12, Nr. 562, *Bericht Auswärtiges Amt an Bayerische Staatskanzlei,* Re.: 'Tatigkeit jugoslawischer Emigrantenorganisationen in der Bundesrepublik', Bonn, 25 March 1957.

24. Pol. A.A.Ber., B12, Nr. 562, *Brief Dr. Cramer – Verband der Landsmannschaften an Auswärtiges Amt,* Re.: 'Bericht zur jugoslawischen Emigration von 1914 bis zur Gegenwart', Bonn, 1 June 1956.

25. Father J. Klaric (ed.). 2003. *Hrvatska Dijaspora u Crkvi i Domovini,* Frankfurt a.M.: Spengler's Druckwerkstatt, 21.

26. B.K., B 106, Nr. 63084, *Dokumente – Bundministerium des Inneren,* Re.: 'Jugoslawien', Bonn, 1 April 1960.

27. B.K., B 106, Nr. 63088, *Berichte – Bundesnachrichtendienst,* Re.: 'Aufstellung über die in der Bundesrepublik vorhandenen Organisationen heimatloser Ausländer', Pullach, 1960.

28. Pol. A.A.Ber., B 42, Nr. 569, *Bericht Studiengruppe Südost an Auswärtiges Amt,* Re.: 'Die Kroatischen Exil-Ustaschen', Munich, 7 December 1961.

29. B.K., B 141, Nr. 30837, *Interner Bericht,* Re.: 'Kroatische Emigrantenzeitungen: Eine Analyse', Bonn, 19 June 1964.

30. Pol. A.A.Ber., B 42, Nr. 1341, *Schreiben Bundeskriminalamt an Auswärtiges Amt,* Re.: 'Zusammenstellung von Erkenntnissen über jugoslawische Emigranten und Gastarbeiter, die in sicherheitsgefährdender Weise in Erscheinung getreten sind', Bad Godesberg, 5 August 1969.

31. S.Z., 'Die Meisten distanzieren sich vom Terror', 13 December 1962.

32. Belosevic, 'Die Minderheiten aus den ehemaligen Jugoslawien', 209.

33. B. Winkler. 1994. *Was Heißt denn Hier Fremd?: Thema Ausländerfeindlichkeit und Verantwortung,* Munich: Humboldt Verl., 136.

34. B.K., B 106, Nr. 63088, *Dossier des Bundesministerium für Inneres,* Re.:'Dokumente des Verfassungsschutzes Kroatischer Organisationen in der BRD betreffend', Bonn, 24 November 1960.

35. For example: Pol. A.A.Ber., B 42, Nr. 1000A, *Polizeipräsidium Düsseldorf an Regierungspräsidium Düsseldorf,* Re.: 'Kroatische Emigrantenorganisationen – Mordversuch an 4 Exilkroaten', Düsseldorf, 18 August 1965; or B.K., B 141, Nr. 30834, *Berichte Bundesministeriums für Vertriebene,* Re.: 'Schnellbrief des Bundesministeriums für Vertriebene an Bundesministerium der Justiz', Bonn, 4 December 1962, among many examples.

36. *D.W.,* 'Zeitlose Idealisten im Außendienst für Bayerns Idol', 13 March 1970.

37. HstA. NRW, NW 308, Nr. 197, *Korrespondenzen,* Re.: 'Brief NRW Innenminister an Wilhelm Schöttler', Düsseldorf, 11 August 1965.

38. Pol. A.A.Ber., B 40, Nr. 111, *Interner Bericht Auswärtiges Amt,* Re.: 'Emigrantenzuwendungen', Bonn, 28 July 1965.

39. B.K., B 106, Nr. 63985, *Loseblattsammlung des BMI zur Ostemigration,* Re.: 'Ungarn', Bonn, 1960.

40. Pol. A.A.Ber., B 12, Nr. 562, *Bericht des Forschungsdienstes Osteuropa am Auswärtigen Amt,* Re.: 'Kroatisch-Katholischer Klerus', Bonn, 11 June 1956.

41. S.Z., 'Die Meisten distanzieren sich vom Terror', 13 December 1962.

42. Pol. A.A.Ber., B 42, Nr. 570, *Brief Geschäftsführender Präsidialmiglied vom Rat der Südostdeutschen, Dr. Josef Trischler, an das Auswärtige Amt,* Re.: 'Entschließung der Bundesdelegierten tagung der Landsmannschaft der Deutschen aus Jugoslawien e.V.'; and Pol. A.A.Ber., B 42, Nr. 570, *Bericht Forschungsdienst Osteuropa Düsseldorf,* Re.: 'Übersicht über die Organisationen der Emigranten aus Jugoslawien in der Bundesrepublik Deutschland', 31 December 1962.

43. B.K., B 106, Nr. 63084, *Sammlung des Bundesministeriums des Inneren zur Ostemigration:* 'Kroatische Nationalkomitee und andere Kroatische Organisationen', Bonn, 1961.
44. Pol. A.A.Ber., B 42, Nr. 571, *Bericht Kriminalpolizei München an Auswärtiges Amt Bonn:* 'Abschrift eines Plakats', Munich, 16 July 1963, German original: 'Bei den Verhandlungen mit den jugo-serbo Kommunisten vergesst nicht die vielen 100 000 in Jugoslawien umgebrachten Deutschen!!! Die jugoslawischen Partisanen vergasten die Deutschen Kinder!!!'
45. R.G. Moeller. 2001. 'Remembering the War in a Nation of Victims: West German Pasts in the 1950s', in H. Schissler (ed.), *The Miracle Years: a Cultural History of West Germany 1949–1968*, Princeton: Princeton University Press, 91–93.
46. S.Z., 'Grabovac verläßt München – Sicherheit des Konsuls nicht mehr garantiert, sagt das jugoslawische Generalkonsulat', 8 December 1961.
47. Bay. HstA. Mun., Stk. Nr. 13324, *Auszug:* 'Auszug aus dem Stenographischen Bericht der 104. Sitzung des Bayerischen Landtags vom 29. November 1961 über die Ausführungen des Herrn Abgeordneten Dr. Wüllner zum Haushaltsplan des Staatsministeriums der Justiz (Epl. 04)', Munich, 30 November 1961.
48. Ibid.
49. *Augsburger Allgemeine*, 'Konsul Grabovac verließ Bunderepublik – Polizeieskorte brachte jugoslawischen Diplomaten zur österreichischen Grenze', Augsburg, 9 December 1961.
50. Bay. HstA. Mun., Stk. Nr. 13324, *Auszug aus dem Stenographischen Bericht der 104. Sitzung des Bayerischen Landtags vom 29. März 1961*, Re.: 'Fall Vracaric', Munich, 30 November 1961.
51. Bay. HstA. Mun., Stk. Nr. 13324, *Auszug:* 'Auszug aus dem Stenographischen Bericht der 104. Sitzung des Bayerischen Landtags vom 29. November 1961 über die Ausführungen des Herrn Abgeordneten Dr. Wüllner zum Haushaltsplan des Staatsministeriums der Justiz (Epl. 04)', Munich, 30 November 1961.
52. Pol. A.A.Ber., B 42, Nr.568, *Emigrantenpolitik: Bericht des Innenministeriums Baden Württemberg am Auswärtigen Amt,* Re.: 'Beschädigung der jugoslawischen Flagge in Friedrichshafen', Stuttgart, 5 June 1962.
53. Pol. A.A.Ber., B 42, Nr. 568, *Fernschreiberbericht: Deutsche Botschaft Belgrad am Auswärtigen Amt Bonn,* Re.: 'Vorfälle Friedrichshafen – Grundsatzartikel Borba', Belgrade, 8 June 1962.
54. Pol. A.A.Ber., B 42, Nr. 568, *Aufzeichnung,* Re.: 'Verunglimpfung der jugoslawischen Flagge auf der internationalen Bodenseemesse in Friedrichshafen am 27.5. und 2. 6. 1962 – hier: Jugoslawischer Protest', Bonn, 22 July 1962, German original: 'Da die jugoslawische Seite zur Zeit Zurückhaltung in der deutschen Frage übt, sollte auch von unserer Seite die "Windstille" nicht unnötig gestört werden.'
55. *Bonner Rundschau (B.R.)*, 'Tür als corpus delicti', 17 April 1964.
56. HstA. NRW, NW 308, Nr. 196, *Akten des Nordrhein Westfälischen Innenministerium*, Re.: 'Verwaltungsrechtsstreit wegen Auflösung einer Vereinigung: Kroatische Kreuzerbruderschaft', 25 April 1966, 56–67.
57. *Bonner Generalanzeiger (B.G.)*, 'Bombenanschlag auf Jugoslawische Handelsmission', 30 November 1962.
58. *Frankfurter Rundschau (F.R.)*, 'Belgrad schützt Botschaftsgebäude', 14 December 1962.
59. B.K., B 141, Nr. 30834, *Zusammenfassungen Politika 2–9 Dezember 1962 and Borba 3–8 Dezember vom Forschungsdienst Osteuropa,* Re.: 'Stellungnahmen der jugoslawischen Regierung und der jugoslawischen Presse zum Godesberger Vorfall vom 29. November 1962', Düsseldorf, 11 December 1962.
60. *F.R.*, 'Im Sonnigen Belgrad Reagierte man Besonnen', 17 December 1962.
61. The Swedish embassy officially took care of Yugoslav affairs in the period between 1957 and 1967 after top-level diplomatic relations between West Germany and Yugoslavia had been suspended because of the *Hallstein* doctrine. The Yugoslav recognition of the GDR only temporarily slowed growing economic ties between both states.
62. In English: 'Brotherhood of Croatian Crusaders'.

63. HstA. NRW, NW 308, Nr. 196, *Justiz – Kroaten*, Re.: 'Verwaltungsrechtsache Kroatische Kreuzerbruderschaft Köln', 27 October 1965, 28–46.

64. HstA. NRW, NW 308, Nr. 195, *Auszüge aus Vernehmungsniederschriften*, Re.: 'Ermittlungsverfahren Percic u.a. wegen Sprengstoffverbrechens', 26 February 1963, 155–69.

65. B.K., B 141, Nr. 30834, *Antwort des Justizminister Nordrhein-Westfalens bzw. Dr. Heimeshoff (Kanzlei des Landes NRW) an Anfrage des Herrn Bundesminister der Justiz bzw. Herrn Ministerialdirigenten Dr. Dreher*, Re.: 'Ermittlungen gegen Franjo Percic in Dortmund und Andere', Düsseldorf, 5 December 1962.

66. B.K., B 141, Nr. 30844, *Untersuchungsprotokolle*, Re.: 'Informationen der Staatsanwaltschaft Bonn über Angeklagter Pastor Rafael Medic-Skoko', 4 June 1963.

67. HstA. NRW, NW 308, Nr. 196, *Staatsanwaltschaft Bonn*, Re.: 'Auszüge aus Vernehmungsniederschriften zum Ermittlungsverfahren gegen Percic und Andere wegen Sprengstoffverbrechens', 7 January 1963, 170.

68. *B.G.*, 'Ordnungsstrafe für Kroaten wegen Beleidigung Titos', 23 May 1964.

69. B.K., B 141, Nr. 30836, *Staatsanwaltschaft Bonn*, Re.: 'Strafsache gegen Franjo Percic u.A. wegen Sprengstoffverbrechens, Mordes, Geheimbündelei: Lebenslauf und persönliche Verhältnisse der Angeklagten', 25 June 1964.

70. *B.R.*, 'Attentat ohne Vorbesprechung? Haupttäter Percic: "Ich trage die Verantwortung"', 17 March 1964.

71. *B.R.*, 'Eid des Schweigens',14 April 1964.

72. HstA. NRW, NW 308, Nr. 195, *Staatsanwaltschaft – Vernehmungsprotokolle*, Re.: 'Auszüge aus Vernehmungsniederschriften zum Ermittlungsverfahre Percic u.a. wegen Sprengstoffverbrechens', 26 February 1963, 182–91.

73. HstA. NRW, NW 308, Nr. 195, *Auszüge aus Vernehmungsniederschriften*, Re.: 'Ermittlungsverfahren Percic u.a. wegen Sprengstoffverbrechens', 26 February 1963, 155–69.

74. B.K., B 141, Nr. 30836, *Staatsanwaltschaft Bonn*, Re.: 'Strafsache gegen Franjo Percic u.A.', 25 June 1964.

75. *B.R.*, 'War kein Geheimbund', 15 April 1964.

76. HstA. NRW, NW 308, Nr. 197, *Willhelm Schöttler an NRW Innenminister Minister Willi Weyer*, Re.: 'Vorschläge zur Eindämmung kommunistisch-jugoslawische Umtriebe', Recklinghausen, 11 August 1965; *Süddeutsche Zeitung*, 'Spendenlisten geben Aufschluß', 19 May 1964.

77. HstA. NRW, NW 308, Nr. 195, *Auszüge aus Vernehmungsniederschriften*, Re.: 'Ermittlungsverfahren Percic u.a. wegen Sprengstoffverbrechens', 26 February 1963, 135–204.

78. *B.G.*, 'Ordnungsstrafe für Kroaten wegen Beleidigung Titos', 23 May 1964, German original: 'ein schlimmerer Kriegsverbrecher als Hitler'.

79. Verhandlungen des Deutschen Bundestages, Drucksachen, Band 82, Bericht über 76. Sitzung des 4. Deutschen Bundestages, 15 May 1963: Boras was directly quoted by a CDU/CSU member of the *Bundestag* called Rollman who was generally complaining about the dangers of cooperating with communist states (i.e., Yugoslavia) in a question and answer session with the Minister for Refugees and Expellees (*Bundesminister für Flüchtlinge und Vertriebene*) Mischnick.

80. *B.R.*, 'Tumult der Exilkroaten', 19 June 1964; and *B.G.*, 'Ordnungsstrafe für Kroaten wegen Beleidigung Titos', 23 May 1964.

81. R.G. Moeller. 2001. *War Stories: the Search for a Usable Past in the Federal Republic of Germany*, Berkeley: University of California Press, 174–77.

82. Pol. A.A.Ber., B 42, Nr. 1000A, *Bericht Auswärtiges Amt Bonn Abteilung IIA5 and Referat V4*, Re.: 'Strafverfahren gegen Stanko Kardum wegen versuchten Totschlags/Attentat auf den jugoslawischen Konsul Klaric in Meersburg am 8. Juni 1965', Bonn, 1 December 1966.

83. Pol. A.A.Ber., B 42, Nr. 1000A, *Bericht Französische Botschaft/Schutzmachtvertretung für deutsche Interessen Belgrad*, Re.: 'Prozess gegen den Exilkroaten Franjo Goreta vor dem Stuttgarter Schwurgericht', Belgrade, 5 May 1967.

84. *B.R.*, 'Nach den Verteidiger-Plädoyers: Urteilsverkündung im Kroatenprozeß am Donnerstag', 19 June 1964.

85. While the national newspapers only covered the first and final sessions, the local Bonn newspapers *Bonner Generalanzeiger* and *Bonner Rundschau* reported daily on the progress of the Mehlem trial. Many of the more controversial allegations made by the defendants, such as the ones mentioned above, were reported verbatim in articles such as: *B.R.*, 'Attentat ohne Vorbesprechung?', 17 March 1964; *B.R.*, 'Eid des Schweigens',14 April 1964; *B.G.*, 'Ordnungsstrafe für Kroaten wegen Beleidigung Titos', 23 May 1964.

86. Pol. A.A.Ber., B 42, Nr. 569, *Bericht Studiengruppe Südost München an das Auswärtige Amt Bonn*, Re.: 'Die Kroatische Exil-Ustaschen', Munich, 1 December 1962. The first heading of this report already reflects complacency among analysts and state officials concerning Croatians in the Federal Republic: '1.) Das Mangelde Interesse der Mehrzahl der kroatischen Neuflüchtlinge für die politischen Exilgruppen.'

87. Pol. A.A.Ber., B 42, Nr. 1000A, *Polizeipräsidium Düsseldorf an Regierungspräsidium Düsseldorf – Kroatische Emigrantenorganisationen*, Re.: 'Mordversuch an 4 Exilkroaten', 18 August 1965.

88. HstA. NRW, NW 308, Nr. 195, *Vernehmungsniederschriften*, Re.: 'Auszüge aus Vernehmungsniederschriften zum Ermittlungsverfahren Percic u.A.', 135 – 204, 26 February 1963, transl.: 'dauernde Untätigkeit'.

89. *B.R.*, 'Attentat ohne Vorbesprechung?', 17 March 1964.

90. B.K., B 141, Nr. 30837, *Kommentar des Nordrhein-Westfälischen Innenministers zum Rundfunksender RIAS 'Zeitfunk'*: 'Zum Verbot der sog. Kroatischen Kreuzerbruderschaft', Düsseldorf, 12 March 1963, German original: 'Dies [the ban] soll mehr ein Warnschuss sein für irgendwelche illegalen Organe, die die Gastfreundschaft der Bundesrepublik missbrauchen um ihre politische Tätigkeit hier in Deutschland auszuüben.'

91. HstA. NRW, NW 308, Nr. 195, *Staatsanwaltschaft NRW*, Re.: 'Auflösungsverfügung gegen die "Kroatische Kreuzerbruderschaft e.v."', Düsseldorf, 8 March 1963.

92. Pol. A.A.Berl., B 42, Nr. 1324, *Bericht – Bundesinnenministerium des Innern*, Re.: 'Attentate, Brandstiftung u.A.', Bonn, 6 May 1969.

93. *D.S.*, 'Mußt du Schießen', 3 August 1981.

94. Bay. HstA. Mun., Pol. Dir. München Nr. 17234, *Bericht Heinz Thurnhofer (POM 26. Polizeirevier) an die Direktion der Schutzpolizei*, Re.: 'Ansammlung einer größeren Menschenmenge vor dem Südausgang des Hauptbahnhofes in der Bayerstraße', Munich, 12 April 1970.

95. Bay. HstA. Mun., Pol. Dir. Nr. 17234, *Bericht Direktion der Schutzpolizei an der Kriminalpolizei München*, Re.: 'Schutzvorkehrungen anläßlich des kroatischen Nationalfeiertages', Munich, 10 April 1970.

96. Bay. HstA. Mun., Pol. Dir. München Nr. 17234, *Bericht Heinz Thurnhofer (POM 26. Polizeirevier) an die Direktion der Schutzpolizei*, Re.: 'Ansammlung einer größeren Menschenmenge vor dem Südausgang des Hauptbahnhofes in der Bayerstraße', Munich, 12 April 1970.

97. Ibid., German original: 'Ich begab mich mit PM Georg Meier und PHW Teichman (in ziviler Kleidung) zu der genannten Stelle (München Hbf.), Bahnpolizeibeamter Pregler war in Uniform ... Meine Schätzung nach waren es mindestens 500 Personen, die sich ... um die kroatische Nationalfahne, versammelt hatten ... Ich forderte daher von den Fahneträgern die Personalien, bzw. die Ausweise oder Reisepässe. Während diese mir ausgehändigt wurden, wurde ich aus der Menge heraus von einem Mann, es stellte sich später heraus, daß es ein heimatloser Kroate war, zurückgerissen und zu Boden geschleudert ... Bei der Durchsuchung fanden wir bei ihm ein KK-Revolver, geladen mit 6 Schüß und weitere 5 Schuß in seiner Kleidung ... Beim Abtransport dieses Festgenommenen wurde ich von einem weiteren 192cm großen Kroaten angegriffen ... Bei seiner körperlichen Durchsuchung wurde in seiner rechten Manteltasche eine Pistole, Cal. 7.65, tschechischer Herkunft, mit 8 Schuß Munition, durchgeladen, gefunden.'

98. Bay. HstA. Mun., Staatskanzlei Nr. 13324, *Bericht Polizeipräsidium München (Kriminalabteilung III) an das Bayer. Staatsministerium des Innern*, Re.: 'Sprengstoffanschlag auf das jugoslawische Generalkonsulat', Munich, 31 July 1972.

99. HstA. NRW, NW 308, Nr. 195, *Verbotsverfügung – Bundesministerium des Innern*, Re.: 'Verbotsverfügung gegen der Kroatische Demokratische Ausschuß – Hrvatski Demokratski Odbor (HDO) – mit Sitz in Münster', Bonn, 7 September 1967.

100. NHstA. Hann., Nds. 147, Nr. 133, *Fallbericht des Niedersächsischen Landeskriminalamtes*, Re.: 'Fall Matuzic', Hanover, 19 June 1974.

101. Pol. A.A. Ber., B 42, Nr. 1000A, *Innenministerium des Landes Nordrhein Westfalen an Bundesministerium des Innern*, Re.: 'Kroatische Emigranten – Mordversuch an 4 prominenten Exilkroaten in Düsseldorf am 30.6.1965', Düsseldorf, 8 September 1965.

102. Bay. HstA. Mun., Stk. Nr. 13324, *Bericht Polizeipräsidium München (Kriminalabteilung III) an das Bayerische Staatsministerium des Innern*, Re.: 'Sprengstoffanschlag auf das Generalkonsulat in München am 15.6.1972', Munich, 31 July 1972, German original: 'Die Mitteilung der Botschaft der SFR Jugoslawien vom 9.6.1972 an das BMI, wonach Stojiljko Kajevic einen Anschlag gegen das Generalkonsulat in München plane, gelangte weder direkt noch über das hiesige Konsulat dem PP [Polizeipräsidium] München zur Kenntnis. Sie war auch insofern wertlos, als für polizeiliche Präventivmaßnahmen (und nur solche wären nach deutschem Recht zulässig gewesen) sein Aufenthalt hätte bekannt sein müssen. Darüber hinaus kann die unüberprüfbare Behauptung einer Botschaft über die Täterschaft einer bestimmten Person (ohne Vorlage irgendwelcher Beweise) nicht Grundlage von Exekutivmaßnahmen sein.'

103. *Der Spiegel* regularly reported on acts of violence committed by Croatian nationalists from 1962 onwards. The complaints of West German officials over the nature of this coverage recurs regularly in official reports such as Pol. A.A.Ber., B 42 Nr. 1000A, *Interne Anfrage des Auswärtigen Amtes an das Referat V4*, Re.: 'Strafverfahren gegen Stanko Kardum', 1 December 1966.

104. HstA. NRW, NW 308, Nr. 195, *Polizeipräsidium Bonn an Innenministerium des Landes NW*: 'Sprengstoffanschlag am 29.11.62 auf das Gebäude der Schwedischen Botschaft –Jugosl. Abt. – in Mehlem, hier: Vernehmungsprotokolle', Bonn 22 February 1963, German original: 'Ich bitte lediglich zu berücksichtigen, daß ich mich verpflichtet fühle, für die Freiheit meines Heimatlandes und gegen den Kommunismus zu kämpfen.'

105. *B.G.*, 'Exilkroaten keine kriminellen Gewaltverbrecher', 12 June 1964, German original: 'Die Männer des 20. Juli sowie die Widerstandskämpfer vom 17. Juni und Budapest haben aus den gleichen Motiven gehandelt wie die Mehlemer Attentäter.'

106. *B.R.*, 'Mildere Bestimmungen – Exil-Kroaten profitieren von Mauer-Anschlägen', 2 June 1964.

107. *B.K.*, B 106, Nr. 28217, *Brief Branimir Jelic an Bundesminister Kai Uwe von Hassel*, Re.: 'Hrvatski Narodni Odbor', Bonn, 14 June 1964, German original: 'Selbst beim letzten Krieg haben wir als einzige Nation – wir reden nicht vom Regime – bis zum Ende mit den Deutschen ausgehalten und sind nach der deutschen Kapitulation gegen serbische Kommunisten noch im Kampfe geblieben.'

108. *B.R.*, 'Kroaten an der Grenze gefaßt', 3 December 1962.

109. *B.R.*, 'Schatzmeister der Kroaten fühlt sich von Jugoslawen bedroht', 2 April 1964.

110. Pol. A.A.Ber., B 42 Nr. 1000A, *Aide Memoire Abteilung II des Auswärtigen Amtes*, Re.: 'Tätigkeit Jugoslawischer Emigranten', Bonn, 31 October 1968.

111. B.K., B 106, Nr. 28217, *Bericht Ministerialrat Dr. Wolfrum,* 'Re.: Kroatisches Nationalkomitee', Bonn, 19 March, 1970.

112. Bay. HstA. Mun., Stk. Nr. 16164, *Handelsbeziehungen*, Re.: 'Zusammenarbeit mit Slowenische und Serbische Kommissionen', 1962–1971.

113. B.K., B 106, Nr. 63084, *Loseblattsammlung des BMI zur Ostemigration*, Re.: 'Jugoslawien', Bonn, 1 April 1960.

114. *D.S.*, '"Das ganze sieht nach Hinrichtung aus" Massaker an Albanern: Wie der jugoslawische Geheimdienst Killeraufträge in der Bundesrepublik besorgt', 25 January 1982.

115. B.K., B 106, Nr. 63084, *Loseblattsammlung des BMI zur Ostemigration*, Re.: 'Jugoslawien', Bonn, 1960; and *D.S.*, '"Das Ganze sieht nach Hinrichtung aus": Massaker an Albanern – Wie der jugoslawische Geheimdienst Killeraufträge in der Bundesrepublik besorgt', 25 January 1982.

116. Bay. HstA. Mun., Präsidium der Bereitschaftspolizei Nr. 127, *Bericht Bayerisches Landesamt für Verfassungsschutz*, Re.: 'Die Politische Struktur der Ostemigration', Munich, 1 April 1960.

117. Bay. HstA. Mun., Staatskanzlei Nr. 13324, *Bericht Polizeipräsidium München (Kriminalabteilung III) an das Bayer. Staatsministerium des Innern*, Re.: 'Sprengstoffanschlag auf das jugoslawische Generalkonsulat am 15.6.1972', Munich, 31 July 1972. *Der Spiegel* regularly reported about further developments in the underground war between Serb, Albanian and Croatian nationalists and the UdBA with articles such as *D.S.*, 'Liebesgrüße aus Belgrad', 17 May 1971; *D.S.*, 'Fünfter Dan', 22 March 1981; *D.S.*, 'Hals über Kopf', 19 July 1976, among many others.

118. A. Troche. 2001. *'Berlin Wird Am Mekong Verteidigt' – Die Ostasienpolitik Der Bundesrepublik un China, Taiwam Und Süd-Vietnam 1954–1966*, Düsseldorf: Droste (Forschungen und Quellen zur Zeitgeschichte, Band 37), 8.

119. Pol. A.A.Ber., B 42, Nr. 1341, *Beratungen des Auswärtigen Amtes mit Repräsentanten des Berliner Senats*, Re.: 'Fall Kolendic', Bonn, 13 August 1969, German original: 'Ich erklärte Herrn Killian [a West Berlin official], daß es sich empfehlen würde, das Antwortschreiben des Berliner Senats in der Sache so weit wie möglich mit dem Inhalt des Antwortschreibens der Alliierten Kommandantur übereinstimmen zu lassen.'

120. The importance of occupying power pressure is particularly well described by Hans-Heinz Heldmann. 1972. 'Araber-Hatz in der BRD: Schlimme Neuigkeiten aus unserer Fremdenrechtspraxis', *Vorgänge* 10(11), 301.

121. B.K., B 141, Nr. 30834, *Auszüge aus Sitzungen des Bundestages Jugoslawien betreffend – Bundesministerium des Inneren*, Re.: 'Auszug aus der 76. Sitzung des 4. Deutschen Bundestages 15. Mai 1963', Bonn, May–July 1963, German original: 'Herbert Wehner (SPD): Herr Minister, wird bei der Verfolgung von Mördern und Mörder-Organisationen ein Unterschied im Hinblick auf die politische Haltung des Ermordeten und die politische Hintergründe gemacht?'

122. M.J. Miller. 1981. *Foreign Workers in Western Europe: an Emerging Socio-Political Force*, New York: Praeger, 63.

123. B.K., B 106, Nr. 28217, *Bericht Ministerialrat Dr. Wolfrum*, 'Re.: Kroatisches Nationalkomitee', Bonn, 19 March, 1970, German original: 'Der Besucher (Jelic) legte Wert auf die Feststellung, daß er seine Mitarbeit im "Freundeskreis der CSU" ... nur als deutscher Staatsbürger verstehe ... Gleichwohl machte ihn Herr Dr. Wolfrum (BmfFuV) auf unvermeidbare optische Nebenwirkungen auf seine kroatischen Ämter aufmerksam, wenn er seiner Tätigkeit im "Freundeskreis" zu viel Publizität gönne.'

124. *D.S.*, 'Liebesgrüße aus Belgrad', 17 May 1971.

125. *D.S.*, 'Fünfter Dan', 23 March 1981, German original: 'Im blutigen Untergrundkrieg zwischen militanten Zirkeln westdeutscher Exilkroaten und dem jugoslawischen Geheimdienst Udba war Goreta offenbar auf die Abschußliste geraten.'

126. *D.S.*, 'Terrorismus: Hals über Kopf', 19 July 1976.

127. B.K., B 106, Nr. 28217, *Brief Dr. Wolfrum (Bundesministerium des Innern) an den Bundesrechnungshof*, Re.: 'Zuwendungen an das Kroatische Nationalkomitee im Lichte der bevorstehenden Zusammenlegungen', 6 July 1970.

Chapter 3

'SUBVERSIVE' IMMIGRANTS AND SOCIAL DEMOCRATS

SHARED MEMORIES OF A 'ROMANTIC' PAST

In the immediate postwar period, a Social Democratic Party that had achieved no more than 30 per cent of the popular vote at federal elections remained unable to exert much influence over policy making in Bonn.[1] Even in those few *Länder* under social democratic control, such as Hessen or Hamburg, the police and security services were so heavily dominated by conservative holdovers from the Nazi period that they usually followed the example set for them by their federal counterparts.[2] As we have seen in the previous chapter, most members of the Left were hostile towards émigré organizations because of the authoritarian or fascist backgrounds of so many political exiles. Until the late 1950s, SPD politicians were more likely to demand a state crackdown on émigré political activity than their CDU or FDP colleagues, presenting themselves as the defenders of West Germans endangered by the actions of violent foreigners.[3]

These roles were reversed by the guest worker programme. While émigré organizations forged alliances with the CDU/CSU and the extreme right, many of the political movements that emerged from guest worker communities found allies in either the SPD or the extreme Left. For an opposition movement under pressure in a state like Spain or Iran, a rapidly expanding immigrant community in the Federal Republic was an environment in which activists could recruit and organize supporters without fear of the persecution they would encounter in their homeland. Left-wing opposition movements supported by guest workers from Southern Europe and the Third World also profited from an internationalist tradition within certain sections of the SPD after 1933. Socialists and communists who survived the Nazi purges met activists who shared their ideological world view in cities of refuge such as Prague, London, New York or Paris.[4] One of the figures involved in this international activity was Willy Brandt, who had worked for socialists in Spain during the 1930s and had helped integrate the SPD into the wider European socialist movement after 1945.[5]

This support for an internationalist approach was shared by other senior leaders such as Hans-Jürgen Wischnewski and Herbert Wehner, who used their influence to back various international causes.[6] With the SPD's rise to power on the federal level, first through the Grand Coalition with the CDU/CSU in 1966 and then as the dominant partner in a coalition with the FDP in 1969, social democratic leaders and their allies in the trade unions could exert greater pressure upon state institutions. Yet their influence was balanced by a lack of enthusiasm for international projects among more pragmatic social democrats such as Helmut Schmidt, who were more focused on domestic political and economic reform.[7] Dominated by staff that had entered the diplomatic service in the Adenauer era, the senior officials at the *Auswärtiges Amt* advising ministers on issues involving politicized immigrants were more likely to back Helmut Schmidt and other more sceptical social democrats. Such attitudes were also prevalent within the intelligence and police services, putting additional pressure on SPD politicians to maintain a tough stance when it came to immigrants involved in political violence, however sympathetic social democrats may have been to a specific cause. The fact that the *Auswärtiges Amt* and the *Bundesnachrichtendienst* (BND) were headed by free democrat coalition partners also helped to put limits on the extent to which the SPD could use the West German state to help the Left in other countries.[8]

The establishment of an organization designed to coordinate the actions of communist parties from labour-exporting countries known as the *Kampfverband zur Schutz ausländischer Arbeiter in der Bundesrepublik Deutschland,* heightened West German anxieties about potential communist infiltrators within the guest worker population.[9] When necessary, immigrant organizations close to the parliamentary Left supported condemnation of the GDR by the SPD and DGB (*Deutscher Gewerkschaftsbund*) during the Berlin Wall crisis, or joined in denunciations of the USSR when the Red Army marched into Prague.[10] Yet trade union-backed immigrant organizations were also prepared to adapt their own views concerning the GDR and the Soviet bloc after the SPD began to improve relations with Soviet bloc countries. By contrast, more conservative immigrant organizations, such as Italian workers' groups financed by the Catholic Church, were intensely hostile to anything involving communism, often organizing trips for Italian or Spanish workers to the Berlin Wall in order to illustrate the 'evils of the Communist Bloc'.[11] Yet German division was not a central issue for these organizations either, making it easier for them to work with SPD-led governments whatever their concerns about its attitude towards communist states.

Despite the doubts of the more conservative wing of the SPD, both the unions and the party bureau responsible for foreign affairs remained involved in a variety of international projects. Social democrats provided support to a wide range of groups including Spanish socialists, moderate Algerian nationalists and Greek trade union activists. However, wedded as it was to the anti-communist consensus of the West German political class, the generosity of the SPD had well-defined ideological limits. In particular, the fierce ideological battles between communists and social democrats in the interwar period and the suppression of the non-communist Left in the Soviet zone after 1946 had a major impact on SPD policy.[12] Immigrants who supported proto-communist or revolutionary movements would therefore have much greater difficulty in eliciting any sympathy from the social democratic movement.[13]

Although there were many points of disagreement between left-wing organizations from the different immigrant homelands, the sense of being part of some kind of rearguard battling the forces of oppression on behalf of socialism and liberty helped foster a sense of solidarity between the West German and immigrant Left.[14] From a post-Cold War perspective many of these anxieties may seem paranoid. But in the hothouse atmosphere of the late 1950s and 1960s, fears that democracy and greater social equality were under renewed threat from the radical Right appeared more plausible. With vivid memories of fascism on its own soil exacerbated by the survival of authoritarian regimes in several states belonging to the Western 'coalition', worries existed (even in the SPD) that the democratic basis of the FRG might be under threat.[15]

The survival of authoritarian regimes in Spain, Greece and Turkey only reinforced the impression that a state could remain a part of the Western Alliance despite the undemocratic behaviour of its ruling elite. With the Johnson and Nixon administrations (increasingly embroiled in a dirty war in Vietnam) providing crucial military aid to the Franco regime and the military junta in Greece, disdain for these governments helped strengthen negative attitudes towards their American backers. In this context, many in the mainstream West German Left, as well as more radical groups, came to treat the battles of left-wing movements in countries such as Vietnam, Iran, Greece or Spain as an extension of their own fight for power in the Federal Republic. This solidarity was often balanced by concerns among SPD and trade union functionaries that organizations they supported in Southern Europe and the Third World could potentially harbour communist sympathizers.[16]

The ambiguous relationship between the parliamentary Left and left-wing immigrant organizations had a major impact on both the Algerian and Spanish communities. Though Algerian nationalists managed to elicit considerable support from many German liberals and social democrats, they did not acquire the kind of direct institutional backing from the SPD and unions that was provided to the Spanish socialists.[17] The Algerian National Liberation Front (*Front de Liberation National* or FLN) could only rely on the support of individual SPD leaders in its guerrilla war against French colonial rule. The first part of this chapter will examine the activity of Algerian nationalists, while the second part will take a look at the relationship between Spanish opposition groups and the West German Left. In both cases, the international political context and specific nature of the immigrant communities in which these opposition movements operated imposed certain restraints on mainstream West German politicians who wished to help them.

****

In November 1954, a local uprising against French rule organized by a group of Algerian intellectuals quickly spread across North Africa. In Paris, the governing Socialist Party, as well as right-wing opposition parties, was unwilling to accommodate the demands of Algerian nationalist organizations that had crossed the threshold from peaceful activism to political violence. With a large French settler population in Algeria (the '*pieds noirs*' or '*colons*'), an anti-terrorist campaign quickly led to full-blown civil war. For the first few years of this conflict most Europeans considered it a matter of passing news interest in a world focused more on the Suez and Hungarian crises. Yet after the Battle of Algiers in 1958, in the course of which French parachute regiments tortured members of the FLN in order to restore control over that city, the Algerian nationalist cause was adopted by many left-wing Europeans. Growing criticism of human rights abuses committed by the French Army helped the FLN to establish Algerian nationalism as a 'respectable' cause.[18]

Drawing the attention of the West German public to French wars in Vietnam and Africa from the late 1940s onwards was the very large number of Germans who had joined the French Army (particularly the Foreign Legion) in the years following the Second World War. Despite serious defeats experienced by the French Army in Vietnam, Germans still made up over 40 per cent of the total in most units of the Foreign Legion in 1957.[19] The role played by German Legionnaires in French colonial wars had penetrated the popular consciousness of Adenauer Germany to the extent that a song extolling their deeds recorded by *Schlager* star Freddy Quinn rose to the top of the charts.[20] Despite the close relationship between the Federal Republic and France, both *Bund* and the *Länder* governments did everything to discourage the drift into the French Army of impressionable youths or former *Wehrmacht* soldiers unable to cope with civilian life.[21]

By the later stages of the Algerian War, West German diplomats in North Africa were dealing with a steady stream of disillusioned deserters trying to find a way home in order to avoid retribution from the FLN. While doing their best to repatriate dissatisfied ex-soldiers, West German authorities also monitored the potentially embarrassing activity of German arms traders and activists supplying the FLN with weapons, some of whom even fought side by side with the FLN in Algeria itself.[22] The considerable role played by Germans in this conflict forced the West German foreign ministry and intelligence services into a difficult balancing act. Diplomats or BND men in North Africa had to pre-empt any potential problems that German soldiers or activists might cause for a newly restored Franco-German relationship, whilst maintaining lines of communication with an increasingly successful FLN.[23] In the first years of this conflict the Algerian War was therefore largely a foreign policy issue for the Adenauer government, with little impact on the domestic scene.

The growing numbers of Algerian immigrants in the Federal Republic after 1958 quickly changed this equation. The presence of FLN functionaries and Algerian intellectuals in the Federal Republic helped to raise awareness of the Algerian conflict in the West German Left. Some senior figures within the SPD, such as Hans Jürgen Wischnewski, set up pro-Algerian solidarity associations, which portrayed the Algerian nationalists as anti-colonial freedom fighters who drew their membership from the growing West German peace movement.[24] Legal and illegal manifestations of this new Algerian nationalist presence in Germany also grabbed the attention of the press, often delivering the kind of sensationalist stories on which tabloids thrive.[25] Although there were lingering suspicions about the possible communist leanings of the FLN, the presence of active Algerian nationalists in the Federal Republic who controlled their community enabled the FLN to gain considerable left-wing support in a state that was France's closest European partner.[26]

The existence of an Algerian community in the Federal Republic was in itself the result of the French imperial project. Since Saarland was only transferred from French to West German rule in 1956 and Rheinland-Pfalz remained part of the French military zone, the borders these two *Länder* shared with France remained porous. Attracted by the good pay and conditions in factories in the Federal Republic, Algerians based in France looking for work found it relatively easy to drift over to German border towns like Saarbrücken and Kaiserslautern. The repressive measures deployed against Muslims by French security services trying to locate FLN sympathizers acted as a further incentive for Algerians to move to an environment where they were less likely to face indiscriminate arrest. The fact that Algerians were citizens of France made it easier for them to enter the Federal Republic than immigrants from other states that had not signed labour importation treaties with the Adenauer government.[27] Although they were one of the smaller guest worker groups (numbering under 10,000 in 1961), there were enough Algerians to provide a base of operations for the FLN.[28]

The ability of FLN activists to impose control over Algerians in the FRG did not mean that this was an entirely united community. Accustomed to the use of targeted attacks to 'decapitate' FLN units and organizations in North Africa, French intelligence agencies did not shrink from organizing the assassination of FLN activists on German soil.[29] Guest workers discovered to be collaborating with French security services or local German police were at risk from the kind of brutal retribution from nationalist militants that was already being meted out to informants in France or North Africa. Internal conflicts within the Algerian nationalist movement were also played out in the Federal Republic, as different factions tried to gain control over the considerable amount of cash that FLN activists were able to extort from North Africans in Germany.[30] After 1961, West German security services also had to deal with the extreme right-wing *Organisation Armeé Secrete* (OAS), which was made up of right-wing French soldiers and settlers opposed to de Gaulle's negotiations with the FLN and who were often based in West Germany. Such French and *pied noir* extremists could cause the West German authorities as many difficulties as FLN activists.[31]

Along with the diplomatic problems created by the Algerian War, the complex historical relationship between Germany and France affected the West

German state's approach towards supporters and opponents of the FLN. Both the two countries' prewar rivalry and their successful postwar rapprochement limited the room for manoeuvre for West Germans involved with North African affairs. Senior members of the SPD were careful to make sure that their support for Algerian nationalism did not imperil the new détente with France. Conversely, leaders of the CDU/CSU who were more inclined to see African and Middle Eastern liberation movements as proto-communist organizations generally accused German supporters of the FLN of undermining the Western Alliance. Yet German conservatives displayed a certain amount of *Schadenfreude* when commenting on French difficulties as well, often pointing out that the *Armée d'Afrique* was repeating the 'mistakes' made by the *Wehrmacht* in Russia.[32]

The *Auswärtiges Amt* and BND did their best to hedge the FRG's bets in case the Algerian nationalists succeeded. However much the Adenauer government needed to take action against FLN members in Germany to assuage its French allies, it did not want to go too far in order to avoid alienating members of any future Algerian elite. When confronted with criminal activity conducted by members of the FLN, *Auswärtiges Amt* officials tried to keep the punishment of activists on the ground from damaging their developing relationship with Algerian political representatives in Bonn. Yet with FLN thugs running protection rackets in Saarbrücken and Kaiserslautern that generated money for their cause, West German security officials and diplomats were regularly confronted with illegal activity organized by Algerian activists.[33] These problems were compounded by the fact that federal and local authorities did not even have the most basic information about Algerians in the Federal Republic. One of the first requests made to the *Bundesinnenministerium* by investigators from Saarland's LKA was for a survey of Algerians in the Republic:

> The Saarland government has ordered an initiative to find and register all Algerians living in the Saarland. This initiative has not been completed yet. However, it is already clear that there is a very large number of Algerians living in the Saarland on an unregistered basis. These irregularities are clearly the result of nearby cross-border traffic.[34]

This request was only sent to the BKA and the LKAs of other *Länder* after two shooting incidents in October 1958 had uncovered deep divisions within Algerian communities.[35] Subsequent acts of violence involving FLN supporters or French paramilitaries in the border regions repeatedly caught West German authorities by surprise. As a result, more thorough controls were instituted on the Franco-German border while the Federal Interior Minister instructed *Ausländerämter* to monitor the activity and movements of all Algerians. Though the BKA and *Bundesamt für Verfassungsschutz* were eventually able to compile dossiers on FLN and OAS cells in West Germany, the damage had been done.[36] Taking advantage of initial ignorance in the West German security services and the support of SPD members of the *Bundestag* hostile to 'imperialism', pro-FLN Algerians were able to take control of the embryonic North African community and use Saarland as a base of operations against the French government.

Although this was only a minor front of the Franco-Algerian War, the activity of the FLN and its supporters in the Federal Republic irritated the French government and poisoned relations between a relatively pro-Algerian SPD and a French Socialist Party whose leaders had taken a central role in the planning and execution of this conflict.[37] Luckily for both the SPD and the Adenauer government, the start of negotiations between Algerian leaders and the de Gaulle administration in 1962 led to a cessation of FLN activity in the Federal Republic. If the war had continued nothing indicates that either local or federal authorities would have been able to bring a proxy battle on German soil between the French security services and the FLN under control any more than they were able to keep Yugoslav secret services and Croatian nationalists apart. Yet, where the CDU/CSU maintained an arms' length relationship with overtly political Croatian organizations, members of the Left openly supported the Algerian cause and lobbied for greater protection of the FLN's representatives in the Federal Republic. Despite the fact that social democratic leaders such as Hans-Jürgen Wischnewski were aware of criminal rackets set up by FLN activists, they were prepared to dismiss these as the 'excesses' of a progressive revolutionary movement.[38]

Though the SPD leadership was prepared to allow individual party functionaries to lobby on behalf of Algerian nationalism, the party avoided the kind of institutional relationship with the FLN that it developed with other immigrant organizations. Worries about the FLN's ideological background and the brutality of its tactics on the battlefield meant that social democrat politicians and left-wing celebrities friendly to Algerian nationalism could only lobby the government on a personal basis rather than as representatives of the SPD or DGB. This helped to ensure that support for Algerian nationalism in the Federal Republic manifested itself in nonpartisan solidarity committees who provided humanitarian aid to the Maghreb region.[39]

Fear that anti-German resentment had not yet died down in Paris, coupled with the awareness that the Federal Republic would only be able to gain full sovereignty with French support, was a major influence of West German diplomacy. The involvement of the West German Left with Algerian nationalism in the late 1950s and early 1960s demonstrates how widespread support for a cause among prominent social democrats did not necessarily mean that the SPD or trade unions would automatically provide institutional support for it. As with the relationship between the West German centre-right and Croatian nationalism, the experience of Algerians in the Federal Republic also indicated the extent to which the historical legacy of the Second World War imposed limitations on the freedom of action of political parties and state institutions when it came to political engagement with immigrant groups.

****

Despite the continuing ascendancy of the CDU on a federal level, through the 1950s the SPD slowly strengthened its hold over a set of *Länder* and city parliaments. Over the course of the following decade this led to victories in provincial elections, which signposted the SPD's path to national power in 1969. Although the judiciary and security services were dominated by supporters of the Christian democrats until 1969, the SPD was a significant enough force to exert some influence over these institutions.[40] Thus when faced with police sanctions, immigrant groups close to the 'constitutional Left' had access to sympathetic interlocutors such as union functionaries or social democrat members of the *Bundestag*. As the small group of SPD supporters in the police and security services began to grow, immigrant leaders ideologically close to European social democracy were provided with a new set of potential partners. The campaigning experience of the SPD and unions also came in handy when it came to simple organizational tasks such as booking buildings for rallies or printing leaflets.[41]

Open support for immigrant groups that the SPD considered to be ideologically acceptable began from a very early point in the guest worker programme. A particular emphasis was put on unionizing guest workers entering new factories in order to prevent management from pitting immigrants against German employees. Students, journalists and other intellectuals from labour exporting countries found work in a variety of social democratic institutions in order to draw potential immigrant leaders away from rival political groups on both the Left and Right.[42] At times, however, this work was often undercut by the ambivalent feelings of many German union and SPD supporters towards immigrant colleagues. By the mid 1960s, several local union functionaries expressed disquiet about the possibility that German workers were losing jobs to immigrants. Petitions demanding an end to immigration (titled 'German Work for German Workers' or in the German original: '*Deutsche Arbeit für deutsche Arbeiter*') signed by the workforces of several major factories managed to hit the national headlines in 1963 and 1965. The SPD and the unions were therefore forced to balance cooperation with politicized immigrants with the need to assuage widespread fears among its working-class supporters over the effects immigration might have on their social position.[43]

While mass migration created the potential for mass protest among immigrants as well as Germans, the growing number of countries drawn into the West German labour importation programme increased the amount of possible political conflicts that the German Left had to face. While some groups such as the Algerians worked outside the trade union movement, in order to defuse some of these tensions, union functionaries tried to recruit as many immigrant workers from more cooperative communities as possible. Yet where union officials were initially faced with integrating a few hundred guest workers from one or two countries, suddenly they were dealing with tens of thousands of immigrants from two dozen states. As labour exporting states began to suffer internal political strife, social democratic and union functionaries had to make snap decisions over how to deal with the reaction of different immigrant communities to events in their homelands.

One of the first occasions in which the disenchantment of guest workers with developments in their countries of origin came to the attention of the wider German public was a set of anti-Franco protests organized by Spanish guest workers in May 1962. These were called in reaction to the suppression of an expanding network of underground union organizations, known as 'Workers' Commissions' (Comisiones Obreras), which had organized strike action. Although this movement eventually came under the control of the Spanish Communist Party, it initially covered a broad cross-section of working-class opinion, ensuring that many Spanish guest workers arriving in the Federal Republic had some personal experience of 'Worker Commission' activity.[44] As reports about police action against strikers and mass arrest of local union leaders began to filter through to West Germany, guest workers and students who sympathized with this movement decided that action was necessary in order to draw public attention to events in their homeland. Though most of those organizing the demonstrations had only arrived very recently in West Germany, on 25 May 1962 a few thousand Spanish guest workers assembled in Bonn, Frankfurt-am-Main and Hamburg in order to take part in anti-Franco rallies. Similar demonstrations took place in other European cities with major concentrations of Spanish expatriates, such as Brussels and Paris.[45]

Immigrant activists who lived in company run hostels ran a considerable risk because employers who disapproved of political activism among their workers could easily take punitive action. Such measures could involve anything from disciplinary measures within the workplace to encouraging local civil servants to take administrative action against immigrant employees. Guest workers taking part in any kind of protest against their homeland regime, particularly a state possessing good relations with the West German government, were therefore vulnerable to retaliation. The Spanish guest workers assembling at these first protests in Cologne were setting a major precedent by taking direct action despite these external pressures.[46]

Although political organizations set up by Spanish émigrés who had fled after the Civil War helped to play a role in coordinating these protests, the initiative had come from the guest workers themselves. Preoccupied with an impending conference in Munich where non-communist Spanish opposition groups hoped to build a united front against the Franco regime, it took pressure from grass-roots activists for them to take more direct involvement with the underground union movement. The new arrivals also provided more established Spanish émigrés with the lines of communication they needed to keep in touch with new opposition groups in their homeland. Thus, the events on 25 May 1962 demonstrated how the arrival of a new generation of immigrants through the guest worker programme helped to reinvigorate the Spanish opposition abroad. With more recent experience of life in Franco's Spain than opposition leaders who in many cases had not returned home for over twenty-five years, immigrants also forced organizations with an anti-Franco agenda to focus on the development of concrete policies to ameliorate poverty and mass unemployment in Spain, rather than abstract ideological conflicts.[47] At such an early point in the guest worker programme, the speedy reaction of politicized Spanish immigrants to strikes at home demonstrates how the domestic politics of labour importing and labour exporting states became increasingly interconnected.

In the initial stages, the first reaction of many civil servants was to deny the possibility that guest workers themselves could be the driving force for political action. Whereas city authorities and local security officials were well aware that pressure for action was coming from guest workers,[48] the top echelons in the *Bundesministerium des Innern* and especially the *Auswärtiges Amt* kept searching for the malevolent influence of the trade union federation (*Deutscher Gewerkschaftsbund* or DGB) or, even worse in their eyes, East German communists. Nonetheless, most reports compiled on the demonstrations of 25 May 1962 by *Verfassungsschutz* analysts and local police officers emphasized the role played by young activists in organizing these demonstrations. Typical of the tone and content of these reports is a document written by local *Verfassungsschutz* operatives in Cologne, which was passed on to junior *Auswärtiges Amt* officials two days after these demonstrations. In this document, local operatives tried to dispel worries that communists were orchestrating events:

> the Spanish [government] view, that our own extreme left-wing radicals are fostering these demonstrations, does not square with the facts to be found in the information we have collected here; however there is no doubt that the demonstrations are being aided by the DGB and the SPD.[49]

While the role of the West German parliamentary Left is acknowledged in this report, it emphasizes that the initiative was taken by guest workers.

Yet senior officials in the *Auswärtiges Amt*, who had to assuage Spanish diplomats angered by the freedoms their citizens enjoyed in Germany, remained convinced that working-class immigrants did not possess the level of political consciousness needed to organize effectively. If signs of communist involvement remained scarce, then the ample aid provided to demonstrating guest workers by prominent members of the parliamentary Left was taken as proof that these rallies had only taken place at the behest of the unions and the SPD. This tendency to underestimate the extent to which guest workers were taking the initiative themselves can be seen in the report quoted above.

In order to bring the situation under control, *Auswärtiges Amt* officials and senior officials in the *Bundesministerium für Arbeit* decided that pressure had to be put on DGB leaders to alter their anti-Franco policies:

Since the main elements involved in the politicization of Spanish workers in Federal [i.e., West German] territory are to be found in the SPD, an open discussion with appropriate figures within the SPD might be helpful.[50]

The reason for this focus on the SPD rather than the unions is made clear in a passage in an earlier part of this report:

It is clear to us in the *Bundesarbeitsministerium* that any attempt to influence the DGB in order to end political agitation among Spanish workers would be a hopeless enterprise, since the DGB would consider any efforts in this direction as meddling [by the state] in and impairment of its constitutional rights.[51]

With the individual trade unions and the DGB emphasizing their political autonomy to a CDU-led government, the scope the security services had to compel union leaders to end their support of politically active guest workers remained limited. Attempts by senior ministerial officials (who in any case tended to be supporters of the Christian democrats or the FDP) to influence the DGB's decision-making process were often counterproductive, encouraging union functionaries to use guest worker causes as a means with which to demonstrate their independence from the state. The SPD's invitation of Rodolfo Llopis, a senior socialist opposed to Franco, to hold a speech at their party conference on 27 May 1962 showed how unsuccessful state institutions were when it came to encouraging social democrats to end their support for the Spanish opposition.[52]

While supporters of the Left attracted the most attention from the start, Spanish exiles ideologically closer to the centre-right regularly visited the Federal Republic as well. From the late 1950s onwards, a number of potential contacts, such as the Christian democrat Gil Roblès, could have provided West German conservatives with the kind of confidential access to pro-opposition guest workers that the SPD already possessed.[53] It is no coincidence that one of the key meetings between the different ideological wings of the Spanish opposition in the 1960s took place in Munich only a few weeks after the demonstrations of the 25 May 1962. At the fringes of the sixth Congress of the 'European Movement' on 7 and 8 June 1962, over 118 Spanish delegates, including eighty residing in Spain itself, came together to discuss possible future political models for a putative post-Franco Spain.[54] Although this meeting did not lead to any sudden breakthrough, it did create a framework for dialogue between rival ideological movements that provided the basis for the political compromises made after the death of Franco fourteen years later. Despite this ideological diversity, the West German centre-right did not take these opportunities to develop closer relations with conservative political alternatives to the Franco regime.

It also proved the beginning of a period of unrelenting diplomatic pressure exerted on the West German government by Spanish diplomats to curb the activity of Spanish opposition movements in the Federal Republic.[55] These efforts included pressure on *Land* governments to shut down Spanish language programming aimed at guest workers on West German radio and television channels such as *Hessischer Rundfunk* or *Westdeutscher Rundfunk,* which Spanish diplomats believed was controlled by opponents of the Franco regime.[56] The attempts by West German governments to accommodate the demands of the Franco regime may have had more to do with the wider foreign policy aims of the CDU than any inherent support for the Franco regime. Yet by avoiding direct contact with immigrant leaders whose anti-Franco stance lent them great authority within this community, West German security services lost the ability to shape its internal development in their own interest.[57]

The heavy-handed intervention against Spanish language programmes on West German radio stations reflected wider concerns in the Franco regime over the risks involved in exposing Spanish workers to wealthier and more technologically advanced societies. Between the end of the Civil War in 1939 and the economic reform programme of the late 1950s, the Spanish economy went through a period of stagnation. Though this era of hardship was partly the result of the Civil War, the Falangist obsession with autarchy, combined with Allied disapproval of a government that had sympathized with the Axis powers, had exacerbated an already difficult situation.[58] With memories of this period of austerity still fresh in the minds of those who found work abroad in the 1960s, Falangist propaganda attempted to strengthen nationalist sentiment among guest workers by trying to create a sense of Spanish distinctiveness from the 'softer' societies of the north.[59]

Increasingly concerned by these challenges to its authority in countries that contained a growing number of Spanish guest workers, the Franco regime tried to set up loyal community organizations in the Federal Republic in order to maintain as much control as possible over Spaniards abroad. Spanish labour officials working from the embassy in Bonn tried to give every Spanish worker access to a cultural centre (*casas de España*) run by state-backed workers' syndicates. There were even officially sanctioned periodicals called *El Emigrante* and *7 Fechas,* written and published in West Germany by Francoist guest workers.[60] With everything from televised Real Madrid matches, Reconquista films to popular novels, this campaign covered the entire media spectrum, enveloping guest workers with information promoting the Spanish government's point of view.[61] Because remittances from Spaniards employed throughout Western Europe helped to fuel the rapid expansion of the Spanish economy in the 1960s, credit facilities were also a priority. Without this influx of hard cash, many Spanish households would have been unable to consume and invest at the furious pace that ultimately changed the face of modern Spain. One of the most important tasks of the Spanish embassy in Bonn was therefore to encourage Spanish workers to send the bulk of their earnings to their families back home.[62]

Thus, the political freedoms of Western democracies were a direct threat to the survival of the Franco regime. Having worked so hard at suppressing memories of the Civil War, the Spanish government was sending hundreds of thousands of young workers to countries where that conflict had not been forgotten by the European Left. The strenuous efforts undertaken by pro-regime diplomats to provide guest workers with a cultural programme controlled by the Spanish state was therefore an attempt to isolate them from the mainstream of the societies in which they lived and worked.[63] The Franco regime's ultimate aim was the creation of self-enclosed Spanish communities whose isolation from their host societies would prevent the more liberal political environment of Western Europe from politicizing Spanish guest workers.[64]

This policy did not fail because of any lack of demand for Spanish culture, sports or entertainment among guest workers in the Federal Republic. Spanish diplomats, who were often deceived by the number of guest workers drawn into their cultural events, believed that simple participation in regime-related activities revealed popular approval of Franco and state-sponsored labour organizations. The fact that the majority of Spaniards working in Germany came from regions such as Andalusia or Galicia, which had only recently begun to experience industrialization, increased hopes among government officials that such workers could remain 'uncontaminated' by the evils of modernity.[65] As a consequence, the Franco regime seriously underestimated the desire of Spanish guest workers to use the political freedoms available to them in the Federal Republic.

With remarkable enthusiasm, Spanish workers from the least industrialized regions of Andalusia and Galicia took the most active part in union-related activity in the Federal Republic.[66] Rather than remaining pillars of support for the state, these regions became hotbeds of socialist and communist activism. Many future socialist cabinet ministers in post-Franco governments, including Felipe Gonzalez, began their careers in Andalusia as dissident students or in the underground union movement. Arriving in the midst of an economic boom, the prosperity Spanish guest workers saw in the Federal Republic contrasted greatly with the poverty and isolation of their homeland. No amount of pro-regime literature or light entertainment in West Germany was going to be able to stem opposition towards Franco that had its origins in new developments at home.[67]

Equally significant was the role played by Spanish students studying in the Federal Republic. This student population was partly made up of academics that had left Spain in order to conduct research in a more tolerant intellectual environment as well as former workers with better than average educational backgrounds who chose to enter higher education after arriving in West Germany. Most Spanish students had close contact with their guest worker compatriots anyway, since students with middle-class backgrounds often took on part-time jobs in order to pay their way through university. They were therefore in a position to help guest workers interested in voicing their opposition to the Franco regime.[68] Some students and intellectuals who wished to leave Spain in order to seek greater political freedom even used the guest worker programme as a way out by finding jobs at West German factories before continuing their studies abroad.[69] Thus, going to film evenings organized by pro-regime activists could go hand in hand with membership of a trade union or participation in anti-Franco demonstrations in front of Spanish diplomatic buildings.

This does not necessarily mean that all Spaniards in the Federal Republic were interested in politics. Many Spanish workers decided to concentrate on their jobs or only took part in activities organized for them by the less politicized Spanish Catholic mission for the Federal Republic.[70] Others remained loyal to the regime, providing its organizations and intelligence agencies with willing recruits. Nevertheless, as with so many other immigrant or émigré communities, the number of Spanish immigrants taking part in political activity directed against their own state was enough to cause considerable problems for the Spanish and West German governments.

Yet what makes the Spanish community stand out in comparison to other immigrant groups is the support opposition movements within it received from a major West German political party. The logistical aid provided by the SPD and the DGB to Spanish socialist organizations in the Federal Republic allowed them to compete effectively with communist or pro-regime groups. The personal support for the Spanish socialists from influential figures such as Willy Brandt and Herbert Wehner guaranteed that Spaniards in the Federal Republic taking part in protests and other forms of activism could depend on a level of state solidarity that no other guest worker movement came close to attaining.[71]

The SPD continued to supply Spanish socialists with aid even after this policy began to cause serious problems between the Franco regime and the Brandt administration. The involvement of German social democrats made it considerably easier for members of the Spanish opposition to recruit supporters in the Federal Republic than under a government prepared to clamp down upon such activity.[72] Moreover, the strength of underground unions in Spain itself coupled with the involvement of members of the German union movement in the Spanish Civil War created an environment that encouraged Spanish workers to get involved in trade union activity across the Federal Republic. With this greater level of integration in the mainstream trade union movement, Spanish workers largely avoided the wildcat strikes that were organized by Greek and Turkish workers prepared to defy directives from German union functionaries.[73] With their strong relationship with the underground union movement in Spain, West German unions were therefore able to gain the trust of Spanish workers more quickly than colleagues from other immigrant communities.[74]

The unions continued to back the Spanish opposition despite the continued involvement of a considerable number of guest workers in violent anti-Franco demonstrations organized by West German students.[75] Rather than putting in place the kind of restrictive measures enacted against entire immigrant groups in similar situations, in *Länder* governed by the SPD the police only targeted specific Spanish troublemakers. A good example of this kind of leniency was a particularly turbulent demonstration in June 1973 at the Spanish consulate in SPD-governed Hanover, where the police focused more on prosecuting those participants who had thrown stones at the consulate building or tipped over a police car, rather than taking action against activists who had originally organized the demonstration.[76]

This close cooperation between the West German Left and the Spanish opposition reinforced the tendency to focus on German intermediaries instead of the guest workers among the security services and ministries monitoring immigrant activity. As their reaction to the demonstrations of 1962 indicates, this concentration on German supporters was a result of reluctance among West German state officials to acknowledge the ability of guest worker communities to organize themselves. Rather than building relationships with immigrant leaders (as they had done with East European émigré groups), state institutions consistently approached Germans close to Spanish opposition movements when confronted with evidence of the strength of anti-Franco sentiment among guest workers. As a consequence, this reliance on Germans with their own ideological agendas resulted in civil servants possessing a distorted understanding of the structure and intentions of Spanish organizations until the early 1970s.[77]

On the surface, events seemed to confirm this focus on the role of the DGB. The intervention of union officials with police directorates in Cologne and Bonn in the course of 1962 on behalf of Spanish guest workers was enough to keep local police forces from obstructing the subsequent anti-Franco campaign.[78] This convinced *Auswärtiges Amt* diplomats that their own endeavours to mollify their Spanish counterparts were unlikely to succeed:

> According to information from the Polizeipräsidium in Köln, the demonstration had been properly registered on 30 of May 1962 as a 'Silent March in Solidarity with those striking in Spain'. The registration with the authorities was dealt with by Ignacia Satelo, a Spanish student living in Köln, in conjunction with the city's Trade Union Federation (DGB) committee. The head of the Köln police stated that he had no objections to these demonstrations ... According to the opinion of the Spanish government ... the trade unions that have helped to organize these demonstrations are engaging in a systematic hate campaign directed against Spain.[79]

These demonstrations were not the only instance where the direct intervention of trade unions helped to keep local police from obstructing Spanish political events supported by the SPD. Throughout the 1960s and early 1970s, demonstrations or information evenings run by anti-Franco groups such as the *Deutsche Komittee zur Hilfe der demokratischen Flüchtlinge e.V.* (whose organizing committee was made up of both Spanish exiles and German social democrats) could count on the support of local SPD grandees if there was any trouble with the security services.[80] Many DGB functionaries were also SPD city councillors, members of provincial parliaments or the *Bundestag*. Even senior police officers would have to think twice before openly criticizing or defying union leaders who at some later point might decide the fate of their careers.[81]

Yet this focus on the direct involvement of social democrats was also a symptom of a deeper conviction among West German bureaucrats that only outside forces could be responsible for subverting apolitical guest workers.[82] Senior decision makers in federal and provincial ministries as well as the security services believed the assurances of their colleagues in labour exporting countries who often privately portrayed guest workers as uneducated peasants who were only interested in economic self-betterment. Such paternalist assumptions about the 'childlike nature' of 'southern peoples' led West German officials to assume that guest worker disaffection was caused by intervention from outside these immigrant communities rather than ideological shifts within them.[83] The comments of a head of department at the *Bundesarbeitsministerium* caught in a transcript of discussions with the *Auswärtiges Amt* encapsulate this complacency:

> According to information from the *Bundesarbeitsministerium* (particularly ORR Dahnen), Spanish workers have generally shown no interest in political questions. Their main priority has been to send the money that they have earned back to their families at home with a minimum of difficulty. However, the agitation of the DGB has now led to considerable disquiet among them. The warnings of the Spanish ambassador that his government might stop sending Spanish workers [to Germany] if the demonstrations do not come to an end, is a sign that the course of action taken by the DGB could lead to negative consequences for the labour market as well as the economy as a whole.[84]

Though this statement was correct insofar as it described the primary motivations of immigrants coming to West Germany in the early 1960s, it also indicates why the West German state was so badly prepared to deal with the political and social consequences of mass immigration.

In the ideologically charged context of the Cold War, West German security services were particularly concerned that communist infiltration of guest worker communities would strengthen the Spanish Communist Party. Not only were state officials and corporate managers well aware of the circulation of communist propaganda material among guest workers and the existence of radio programmes for immigrants broadcast from Prague and East Berlin in Spanish, Italian and Greek, newspapers such as *Bild* and *Die Welt* even claimed that pro-Soviet activists were moving to control entire immigrant communities in the Federal Republic.[85]

Though some of these articles exaggerated the extent to which communist activity was able to attract support in guest worker communities, there was enough truth in these stories to have the potential to provoke a severe response from West German authorities at the first manifestation of discontent. With almost no direct contacts in the Spanish community, *Verfassungsschutz* agents followed up any piece of evidence of pro-Soviet or PCE (the Spanish Communist

Party) activity provided to them by Spanish intelligence services. One report on conditions in Hanover in April 1962 within such a batch of surveillance documents (that in almost every case include extensive lists of supposed guest worker communists provided by Spanish diplomats) provided a particularly succinct description of these observation and control operations:

> Communist propaganda activity in the halls of residence [for workers] at Hanomag [machine tools factory] has been under observation for some time. A significant role has been played by the Peruvian Salomon Espinosa Quiroz and the Spaniard Eleuterio Ramos Elexpe. Few negative insights could be gathered about any activity directed against the Federal Republic ... when it comes to the Spaniard mentioned in the memo from the *Auswärtiges Amt*, Emeterio Calvo Martin ... The investigations concerning communist activity among Spanish guest workers in [the village of] Grevenbroich mentioned in the memo from the *Auswärtiges Amt* have not yet been completed.[86]

The possibility that immigrants might also be recruited by intelligence agencies from Warsaw Pact countries also heightened worries in West German security services about the potential political impact of the guest worker programme. Yet even here security services remained reliant on third parties or intermediaries for information until the 1970s.[87]

The fact that the moderate German Left also shared such concerns could have weakened the position of politicized guest workers even further. For the SPD and the mainstream trade unions, the communists and the New Left were the immediate rivals for the support of their own electoral and intellectual base. This anti-communist stance was strengthened by memories of the forced fusion in the GDR in 1947 of social democratic institutions with those of the Communist Party.[88] As a result of these experiences, both the leadership of the SPD as well as its rank and file still believed that communism represented an ideological threat to the social democratic movement, despite attempts by SPD-led governments to ease relations with the East German state through political dialogue.[89] Even after it became the dominant party of government in 1969, the SPD did everything to prevent the East German regime from developing further influence over the West German political process. Moreover, the fact that the SPD was dependent on its FDP coalition partner when it came to implementing domestic and foreign policy reforms ensured that pro-communists within immigrant communities still faced state hostility after 1969.[90]

These social democratic concerns about communist activity were reflected in the panicky reaction of the highest echelons of government to the planned participation of Santiago Carillo Solares and Maccaro Castillo, both senior members of the PCE, in an anti-Franco demonstration in Frankfurt on 30 April 1972. This event was the Spanish Communist Party's 'General Congress for the Spanish Emigration in Europe' ('Allgemeiner Kongress für spanische Auswanderung in Europa'), which also indicated the importance of the immigrant diaspora for Spanish opposition movements. This event was only one of several demonstrations throughout the Federal Republic organized under the motto 'Der Grosse Spanische Tag' by communists and other left-wing groups hostile to the SPD.[91] Since PCE-run events had the reputation for being disciplined and peaceful affairs, a bid by the federal Interior Ministry to have these demonstrations banned in the courts failed:

> In our general experience, such claims [about possible disturbance of public order by communists] cannot be substantiated before the planned gathering. According to the experience of the *Bundesinnenministerium*, events organized by the Communists are even characterised by good organization and disciplined behaviour.[92]

Just to be on the safe side, the event organizers had several members of the newly reconstituted German Communist Party (DKP) and New Left groups (particularly the university based '*Solidaritätskomitee für die Einheit aller antifaschistischen Kräfte*' chaired by a Prof. Heydorn of Frankfurt University) register the demonstration with the police on their behalf. The Interior Ministry directive barring Carillo and Castillo's entry into the Federal Republic also failed as both evaded border controls and made it to the Frankfurt protests on time.[93] Though with the *Bundesinnenministerium* and *Auswärtiges Amt* this unsuccessful containment strategy was coordinated by two ministries run by the free democrats, SPD leaders in the Chancellery and the party supported this course of action. Efforts to limit the influence of the PCE over the Spanish community were also accepted by social democrat members of the cabinet after they were explained by the Interior Minister, Hans Dietrich Genscher, at a cabinet meeting that took place a few days after the Frankfurt demonstrations.[94]

When it came to the PCE and other communist organizations, the SPD was as concerned as other parliamentary parties to ensure that groups potentially friendly to the GDR or other Soviet bloc states were prevented from gaining a foothold in immigrant communities. Though the Spanish Communist Party was ideologically aligned with the Italian communists and the rest of the Euro-communist movement, the SED helped its PCE counterparts with the publication of pamphlets and gave Spanish communists a weekly slot on East German radio. These links led to continuous surveillance of PCE functionaries by local police forces in SPD- as well as CDU-run *Länder*. Nothing would have seemed more likely to provoke draconian action by police and intelligence services than the thought that their East German or Soviet opponents might be using the PCE to shape the political attitudes of guest worker communities. Here, at least, there seemed to have been agreement between centre-left and centre-right about the kind of political activity among guest workers that posed a threat to the constitution.[95] Yet, by the late 1960s the security services exhibited considerable restraint when dealing with supposed communist sympathizers within the Spanish community.[96]

With their own prewar experience of revolutionary politics, SPD and DGB leaders understood that an overly repressive approach towards guest workers who supported the PCE or other more extreme left-wing groups could alienate the entire Spanish community.[97] This made it easier for the SPD and DGB to advocate a more tolerant approach towards those parts of the Spanish opposition that they considered to be ideologically problematic. The extensive nature of the SPD's commitment shows how policy could still be driven by a romantic attachment to a common revolutionary tradition, which encouraged social democrats to seek alternative means with which to combat communism in guest worker communities to the repressive measures favoured by the security services. Though initiatives designed to draw Spanish guest workers into union structures only gained momentum in the late 1960s, the SPD's aim to insulate them from communist subversion protected Spanish activists who organized anti-Franco demonstrations from any major consequences.

In this sense, the DGB backing that so frustrated labour ministry and foreign ministry officials was a reactive measure rather than some form of proactive agitation. Without the enthusiastic participation of so many guest workers and the leadership of prominent Spanish immigrants, even the greatest amount of union activity would not have been able to mobilize so much support. Instead, it was union awareness of pre-existing frustration with the legacy of the Franco regime among Spanish workers which drove senior German functionaries to take such an active role in support of guest worker organizations. The political energy existed within the Spanish community; the DGB's policy of engagement represented an attempt at channelling this energy towards the ideological traditions of German social democracy.[98]

The only other group in which a traditional Communist Party had the potential to gain mass support was the Italian community. The Italians were one of the largest guest worker communities in the Federal Republic and established themselves in large numbers relatively quickly after a labour importation treaty between Italy and the Federal Republic was signed in 1954.[99] The considerable support enjoyed by the Italian Communist Party in several Italian regions was of great concern to West German security officials, who feared that the activity of communist agitators might disrupt production at factories where there was a high concentration of Italian guest workers, such as the Volkswagen plant in Wolfsburg.[100] In order to minimize communist influence, both the Catholic Church (usually in the form of the ACLI, an Italian Catholic workers' organization) and the West German trade unions did their best to integrate Italian guest workers into their respective organizations. These efforts were largely successful, as socially conservative Italians helped reinvigorate many West German parishes, while left-wing Italians became deeply involved in the DGB.[101]

Yet the fears of West German corporate executives and security officials were also contradicted by the relatively low level of political activity in the Italian community. While the autocratic nature of the Franco regime provided a focus for resentment among Spanish guest workers, the fact that Italy was a democratic state meant that Italian guest workers were as free to express their opinions in their homeland as they were in the Federal Republic. Thus, the Italian community developed a reputation for political moderation, which was not even shaken by deteriorating industrial relations in Italy after 1969.[102] West German union functionaries trying to channel Italian guest workers away from communism were therefore confronted with far fewer complications than in their efforts to pursue the same agenda when dealing with the Spanish community.

This approach continued to be followed by social democrats and the trade unions even after many guest workers and students involved in anti-Franco activity began to work together with New Left groups. Just as the New Left drew many younger activists away from mainstream social democracy, the Spanish Left was also shaken up by the new ideological trends of the 1960s. The central place Franco and the Spanish Civil War had in the mythology of the European Left also encouraged many in the extra-parliamentary opposition to throw their support behind Spanish groups that shared their ideological stance.[103] As these New Left anti-Franco groups increasingly tried to emulate the ruthlessness of radical Basque nationalists, they began to use more violent tactics. A new emphasis on revolutionary action and a widened definition of imperialism that included NATO and other Western institutions increased the readiness of younger Spanish activists to engage in direct attacks upon Spanish diplomatic buildings and the West German police guarding them.[104]

One document put together by the *Verfassungsschutz* for the West German embassy in Madrid counted up to sixteen major demonstrations against Franco that led to violence between 26 July 1970 and 4 December 1971 and indicated that there were many other cases of more minor violent or illegal anti-Franco protest.[105] Yet once again these incidents did not lead to a general crackdown against all Spanish organizations. Following clear instructions from the Chancellery, federal and local security services focused their efforts on specific individuals suspected of pro-communist or pro-Red Army Fraction sympathies.[106] The SPD had invested too much effort in the establishment of centre-left groups in the Spanish community to risk the kind of drastic measures needed to end all political activity hostile to the Spanish government.

This reticence reflected the broader strategic goals of both the SPD and the Second Socialist International when it came to strengthening the Spanish Left. The widespread engagement of the non-communist European Left in events in Spain was also designed to weaken support for the Spanish Communist Party in order to lower its chances of ever gaining power. By bolstering the Spanish socialists, the leaders of the SPD, the French socialists and the British Labour Party did their best to foster an alternative to the communists within the Iberian Left. Of these three parties, the SPD contributed the most, covertly providing the PSOE (Socialist Party of Spain) with over twenty-two million Deutschmarks that enabled it to establish a national party infrastructure and helped fund its election campaigns after 1975.[107] With the strong financial and logistical backing of some of the most powerful political parties in Western

Europe, the PSOE was able to emerge as the dominant force in Spanish politics only six years after Franco's death. Without comparable outside support, the communists declined into a marginal force that lived off nostalgia for the 'glorious' civil war years rather than emulating the successes of their comrades in France and Italy.[108]

Beyond dealing with the problems posed by the PCE, this flexible approach was also designed to make it more difficult for organizations advocating political violence to find recruits. The Basque nationalist terrorist group ETA in particular was seen as a potential security threat by West German security organizations.[109] The major riots that took place in front of the Spanish consulate in Frankfurt after the execution in 1973 of ETA members responsible for the fatal bombing of Admiral Carrero Blanco (Franco's chosen successor) highlighted links between the extreme German Left and Basque nationalists. Those organizing this demonstration, including a young Joseph (or Joschka) Fischer, openly flaunted their contacts with ETA activists and other elements of the Spanish extreme Left. Even if ETA activity in West Germany was limited, these kinds of contacts quickly came to the attention of *Land* security services. Though there were fewer Basques in the Federal Republic than immigrants from other Spanish regions, it was hoped that bolstering Spanish socialist organizations would draw them away from ETA as well as the PCE.[110]

The importance of regional identity in Spain indicated that the SPD's approach towards the Spanish community, based as it was upon sweeping assumptions about Spanish immigrants, at times failed to take the heterogeneity of the Spanish community into account. Though opposition to the Franco regime was strong, this did not necessarily mean that the Spanish community in the Federal Republic was exclusively made up of supporters of the Left. Often groups focused on preserving regional traditions worked together with Spanish priests who still had considerable influence among devout guest workers in the FRG.[111] The Spanish Mission of the Catholic Church in Germany, which like its Croatian counterpart had its own autonomous infrastructure, still attracted large congregations in the 1980s and only saw a decline once secular attitudes began to take hold in Spain.[112] While Spanish parishes in Germany were often places in which guest workers could meet other compatriots in their town, some left-wing immigrants refused to have anything to do with the Church because of its close collaboration with the Franco regime during and after the civil war. But the critical stance taken by many 'red' priests and bishops against social injustice in Spain during the 1960s reconciled many other Spanish leftists with postwar Catholicism.[113] The Spanish Catholic Mission in the Federal Republic therefore became a more inclusive institution than the Church in Spain as many of its congregations drew immigrants from both ends of the ideological spectrum. Though it did not exert direct political influence on guest workers, the Spanish churches represented an alternative nexus of social authority to that of both the Falangists and the PSOE.[114]

Such expressions of support to either the Catholic Church or regional identities indicated that some guest workers in the Federal Republic remained close to political movements of the centre-right rather than the Left. As the decline of the Franco regime enabled the centre-right to establish its own political infrastructure, conservative and Christian democratic movements not tainted by association with the political status quo began to recruit significant numbers of guest workers. Moderate regional parties profited from the democratization process in a similar fashion. While supporters of regional autonomy or independence could only turn to politically obscure or extremist organizations before 1975, the new political order led to the foundation of a set of powerful regional movements in Catalonia, Galicia and the Basque country. Here again guest workers in the Federal Republic could openly demonstrate their support for non-socialist movements that could hardly be portrayed as a threat to the political order of the Federal Republic.[115]

Within the Spanish Left though, the aid provided to the PSOE by the SPD and others helped it to become the only movement to gain a significant following among Spanish workers in the FRG. As the above evidence indicates, members of the PSOE or affiliated organizations possessed a crucial advantage when it came to organizing and recruiting Spanish guest workers. Yet this did not secure the PSOE a monopoly of guest worker political allegiance. Because of reluctance among SPD leaders to alienate Spanish guest workers, even non-PSOE movements that belonged to the Spanish Left experienced far less intervention from the West German state authorities than comparable organizations in other guest worker communities. Despite all the attempts of PSOE officials and their SPD backers to ensure the supremacy of the social democratic Left, guest workers who had been more inclined towards the parties of the centre-right were also able to join those political movements that reflected their ideological beliefs.

Intriguingly, there is also evidence that some guest workers and students who had supported the Falangist movement before the death of Franco maintained contacts with the extreme Right throughout the Spanish democratization process. Though the regime failed to secure the loyalty of the great majority of guest workers, Falangists and diplomatic officials would never have been able to set up the regime-backed cultural and intelligence infrastructure of the 1960s and early 1970s without at least a few loyalists in the Federal Republic. Outnumbered by supporters of the Left, the Church or the centre-right opposition, the activity of these Franco loyalists was mostly ignored by the press and the government.[116] While Falangist members of the Spanish bureaucracy in Germany were gradually withdrawn, the tiny minority of Francoist guest workers maintained their loyalty to the old regime. Often this took place through the establishment of cultural clubs where old Falangists could gather and complain about the evils of 'communist' democratization or speculate about the desirability of an army coup.[117]

As long as the Falange was in power, these individuals were largely peripheral figures. The Spanish government seems to have been unwilling to use its supporters in West Germany for anything beyond surveillance of opposition supporters. The kind of internecine street warfare that took place between the different political wings of the Greek or Croatian communities rarely took place among Spaniards. With the West German radical Right too weak to provide any significant support to Francoist guest workers, they found it more difficult to gain the attention of the German public than immigrant groups with strong West German allies.[118] Spaniards opposed to the status quo therefore attracted the attention of the West German public far more effectively than those who wanted its preservation. The impact such loyalists may have had on the state's perceptions of Spanish immigrants in West Germany is more difficult to estimate. But because the great majority of state documents concerning Spanish immigrants during this period focus on the actions of the Spanish Left, one can conclude that as the bulk of Spanish guest workers came from working class or peasant communities that were either hostile or ambivalent towards the legacy of the Franco regime, there were simply not enough Franco supporters around to attract the attention of West German authorities.[119]

How then does the Spanish experience fit in the broader context of immigration to the Federal Republic? Crucially, the Spanish community was entirely the product of the guest worker programme. Though the Falangist Blue Division had contributed to the Nazi war effort until it was withdrawn from the Eastern Front in 1944, few Spaniards had directly experienced the Second World War. Those Spaniards of both the Left and Right who did find themselves caught up in the last stages of that conflict, only spent a short time in the West German DP camps before making their way to France.[120] The attitude of Spanish immigrants towards their new homeland was therefore not as strongly affected by Germany's war record as that of Ukrainian refugees or Croatian guest workers. Though in comparison to the DP communities the Spanish remained remarkably unconcerned about the legacy of the Second World War, historical memory did prove crucial in shaping the attitudes of West German political groups and parties towards this immigrant community.

With the Spanish Civil War a formative experience for so many leading figures of the West German Left, shared history between an immigrant political movement and its West German counterpart was an enormous help to the Spanish opposition in the Federal Republic. Yet even with the unreserved backing of the SPD, the Spanish socialists still remained *primus inter pares*. For the Spanish community had one characteristic in common with all other immigrant groups examined in this study, namely an extraordinary level of political and cultural heterogeneity, fully reflecting the ideological complexity of its homeland. The Falangist failure to indoctrinate guest workers was characteristic of the Franco regime's broader inability to gain any support among the Spanish working classes. The existence of different socialist, regional or Christian democrat organizations within the Spanish community simply reflected the cultural diversity that has become one of the defining characteristics of modern Spain.

The differences of opinion between the mainstream West German Left and the security services over how to deal with such a diverse and politicized community were not about the necessity of combating communism within guest worker communities, they were about the means needed to achieve this end. For SPD and trade union figures such as Hans Mathöffer or Hans Jürgen Wischnewski, the aid they provided to ideologically acceptable guest worker leaders was a better means with which to protect the Federal Republic from communist subversion than the repressive measures envisaged by the security services. Moreover, when it came to politicized guest workers the SPD and DGB were playing a much wider game than their counterparts in ministries or intelligence agencies.

While CDU policy makers and their allies in the bureaucracy were largely focused on limiting the impact of labour rotation on the political life of the Federal Republic, SPD leaders were hoping that Spanish guest workers would, after their expected return to their homelands, help the PSOE rather than the PCE to gain power after the collapse of the Franco regime. As such, the toleration of anti-Franco activity in the Spanish community was part of a wider strategy developed by the Brandt government, which also involved the rebuilding of pro-socialist union organizations through the DGB and the covert use of millions of Deutschmarks ostensibly stemming from the *Friedrich Ebert Stiftung* to help finance PSOE campaigns in Spain.[121] Even in opposition, social democrats could therefore ensure that state institutions interpreted the criteria used to determine the extent to which political activity was constitutionally acceptable with a much greater flexibility when it came to the Spanish than with any other immigrant community. At the end of the day, supporters of the Spanish Left were simply lucky that the SPD and DGB had a much clearer idea of how they could use this community for their own strategic ends than either the CDU or the security services.

****

For all the ideological differences between Spanish leftists and anti-Soviet East European émigrés, the relationships they developed with their respective West German allies bear remarkable similarities. In both cases, communities that were initially vulnerable came to enjoy the protection of West German parliamentary parties because organizations within them shared the wider ideological aims of either the CDU/CSU or SPD. The protection offered as a result of such shared political aims helped to protect both groups from the political attacks of their opponents in the Federal Republic, even when some émigrés or immigrant activists crossed the boundary from peaceful to ostensibly illegal political activity. Once political organizations within these communities were able to cement their connections with West German political parties or state institutions, their friends within the parliamentary mainstream were in a position to reinterpret the general legal framework of the Federal Republic to the benefit of their immigrant allies. As we have seen in the second chapter, these relationships put successive West German governments in a difficult foreign policy bind when homeland regimes decided to retaliate on German soil against opposition movements based in immigrant communities.

Beyond the vast differences in political outlook between Spanish socialists and émigré anti-communists, however, there was one key structural factor that was to determine the different paths these groups were to take. While the number of Ukrainians or other émigrés entering the Federal Republic quickly sank once strict border controls were established between the Allied occupation zones in 1946, the number of Spaniards settling in Germany increased from year to year after the labour importation programme was put in place in 1955. Moreover, while the Ukrainian community experienced a precipitate decline in numbers once it became clear that DPs could leave West Germany, the Spanish community continued to grow (if more slowly) despite the measures taken by West German governments to cut the numbers of guest workers in 1973 after the termination of the labour importation programme. By 1990 there were approximately 20,000 people of Ukrainian origin resident in West Germany while the number of Spanish, though down from the 250,000 of the mid-1970s, had stabilized at approximately 130,000.[122]

The opposite demographic paths of these communities had a major impact on their internal political culture. In the late 1940s, the relative youth of East European émigré communities as well as their good relations with Western intelligence services led to an upsurge of anti-Soviet activity as hopes of an overturning of the Potsdam settlement were fuelled by the conflicts of the early Cold War. Similarly, in the 1960s the large proportion of younger workers or students within the expanding Spanish community who assumed that they would return to Spain in the short- to medium-term helped to fuel a dynamic upsurge of political activity. In both cases, the assumption that a return to their home countries was imminent helped to motivate the immigrant rank and file to continue participating in homeland-oriented political activity. As the émigrés aged and decreased in number, the stability of the Cold War order led to a decline in political activity despite all the protection afforded by high-level contacts in a CDU-led government.

Thus, it was relatively easy for the Brandt government to cut East European émigré access to government resources, since it did not have to worry about facing any serious trouble from a miniscule and ageing community. By contrast, the fact that the Spanish community was expanding quickly made it easier for its social democratic allies to foster friendly political organizations within it. Social democrats could always elaborate on the risks of alienating such a large community when trying to stave off the use of repressive measures against its Spanish allies. For all the protection friendly elements in political parties and security services could provide certain immigrant or émigré organizations, such factors as demographic structure, levels of social integration or political shifts in the homeland could still push the internal development of such communities in directions that neither West German nor immigrant leaders were able to predict.

The legacy of recent history could therefore play out to the advantage of the Spanish while it at the very least did not prevent the FLN from achieving its goals in the Federal Republic. Moreover, the ideological context of the Cold War reshaped the manner in which prewar links with homeland states influenced the attitudes of both Left and Right towards immigrant movements. But while this Cold War dynamic helped to unite West German conservatives with their fellow émigré anti-communists, it complicated the SPD's relationship with left-wing immigrants as much as it increased tension between mainstream social democrats and their rivals in the extra-parliamentary New Left.

In this chapter we have seen how historical ties combined with the ideological polarization of the Federal Republic helped to create very distinct political paths for each immigrant community. The treatment of Spanish socialists and Algerian nationalists by the SPD and the West German state depended on how the historical relationships these groups had with the German Left combined with their own ideological fixations. Each movement created its own set of strategic alliances with those elements of the West German Left with whom they were (at least superficially) ideologically compatible.

While this dynamic had limited consequences for Spanish guest workers or East European émigrés because of the ideological tenets they shared with the SPD or CDU, it hindered cooperation between a whole set of other immigrant groups and the parliamentary establishment of the Federal Republic. Whereas at least some organizations within the Spanish community were portrayed as a benign force by the SPD, political organizations within most other immigrant groups found it much more difficult to dispel fears that they might present some kind of threat to the constitutional order. Unable to find unstinting support from West German parliamentary establishments, movements within the Croatian, Greek and Iranian communities were much more likely to face repressive measures from police and intelligence agencies worried about the social implications of immigrant political activity. The impact this struggle for acceptance had on immigrant organizations, and the difficulties this created for communities where such efforts failed, shall be examined in the next two chapters.

Notes

1.   P. Pulzer. 1995. *German Politics: 1945–1995*, Oxford: Oxford University Press, 50.
2.   K. Weinhauer. 1998. *Schutzpolizei in der Bundesrepublik – Zwischen Bürgerkrieg und Innerer Sicherheit: Die Turbulenten sechziger Jahre*, Paderborn: Schöningh, 4–9.

3.   See for example: *F.A.Z.*, 'München: das Dorado der Emigranten', 4 March 1963; or *Verhandlungen des Deutschen Bundestages, Anlagen zu den Stenographischen Berichten:* Bd. 82–4. Wahlperiode, 7 December 1962 to 11 January 1963.

4.   W. Brandt. 1982. *Links und Frei – Mein Weg 1930–1950*, Hamburg: Fischer Verl., 128–36.

5.   P. Merseburger. 2002. *Willy Brandt: Visionär und Realist 1912–1992*, Stuttgart: Deutsche Verlags-Anstalt, 139–43.

6.   P.O. Anaya. 2002. *European Socialists and Spain: the Transition to Democracy 1959–1977*, Basingstoke: Palgrave, 140.

7.   Best illustrated in T. Scheffler. 1995. *Die SPD und der Algerienkrieg 1954–1962*, Berlin: Verlag das Arabische Buch (Forschungsschwerpunkt Moderner Orient Nr. 7), 54–56. The readiness of leading members of the SPD to entertain governments suppressing fellow left-wing movements is also illustrated well in the admittedly extremely polemical work of G. Wallraff and A. Lengas. 1982. '"Eine Vielzahl gemeinsamer Interessen"', in G. Wallraff and E. Spoo (eds), *Unser Faschismus nebenan: Erfahrungen bei NATO-Partnern*, Hamburg: Kiepenheuer und Witsch, 116–17.

8.   Pol. A.A.Ber., B26, Nr. 452, *Aufzeichnung der politischen Abteilung des Auswärtigen Amtes* Re.: 'Vorbereitung für Besprechung der beamteten Staatssekretäre im Bundeskanzleramtes – Großveranstaltung der Kommunistischen Partei Spaniens n Frankfurt und anderen Orten des Bundesgebietes am 30. April 1972', Bonn, 7 April 1972; and Pol. A.A.Ber., B 26, Nr. 452, *Sekreteriat des Außenministers*, Re.: 'Auszug aus dem Kurzprotokoll der 109. Kabinettsitzung der Bundesregierung am 3. und 5. Mai 1972: Bundesinnenminister Genscher zum illegalen Aufenthalt des spanischen Kommunistenführers Santiago Carillo in der BRD", Bonn, 9 May 1972.

9.   *B.R.*, 'Trick mit Fremdarbeitern', 2 December 1963 (notice the use of pre-1945 term for guest workers).

10.   Bay. HstA. Mun., Pol. Dir. München Nr. 9389, *Bericht Kriminalpolizei München Bay. Landesamt für Verfassungsschutz*, Re.: 'Kongreß der Antidiktatorischen Komitees in der Bundesrepublik', Munich, 3 April 1969.

11.   *B.R.*, 'Propagandalawine erwarted die Urlauber des VW-Werks in Wolfsburg – Abstimungsergebnis der italienischen VW-Arbeiter mit Spannung erwartet', nr. 291, 16 December 1962; as well as *B.R.*, 'Gastarbeiterkinder sollen deutsche Sprache lernen – Kardinal Frings: Wohnungen für Ausländer bauen!', 2 May 1962.

12.   L. Kettenacker.1997. *Germany since 1945*, Oxford: Opus, 26.

13.   This stance encompassed movements in highly developed nations such as Britain and France as much as it did those in the Third World and the eastern bloc. See S. Milne. 2004. *The Enemy Within: the Secret War Against the Miners*, 2nd ed., London: Verso, 298–300.

14.   For a clear illustration of this outlook see or K. Hermann. 1967. *Die Revolte der Studenten*, Hamburg: Christian Wegener Verl.

15.   C. von Braunmühl. 1973. *Kalter Krieg und Friedliche Koexistenz: Die Außenpolitik der SPD in der Großen Koalition*, Frankfurt, a.M.: Suhrkamp Verl., 63–65.

16.   E. Czerwick. 1981. *Oppositionstheorien und Außenpolitik: Eine Analyse sozialdemokratischer Deutschlandpolitik 1955–1966*, Königstein: Anton Hain (Studium zum politischen System der Bundesrepublik Deutschland Nr. 27), 44–45.

17.   M.J. Miller. 1981. *Foreign Workers in Western Europe: an Emerging Socio-political Force*, New York: Praeger, 62–63.

18.   A. Horne. 2002. *A Savage War of Peace: Algeria 1954–1962*, London: Pan Books, 183–207.

19.   NHstA. Hann., Nds. 147, Nr. 794, *Berichte des Landeskriminalamtes/Werbung für Fremden Wehrdienst 1952–1961*, Re.: 'Fremdenlegion 1956–1959', Hanover 1952–1961.

20.   P. Moesser and L. Olias. 1958. *Der Legionär (Hundert Mann und ein Befehl)*, sung by Freddy Quinn, Copyright Polydor Records. Number one in the German charts for three weeks from 20 August 1958.

21.   NHstA. Hann., Nds. 147, Nr. 386, *Landeskriminalamt/Fremdenlegion*, Re.: 'Schematische Befragungen und Erlebnisberichte', Hanover, December 1957–July 1961.

22. Pol. A.A.Ber., B 25 Nr. 10, *Bericht – Bundeskriminalamt Sicherungsgruppe*, Re.: 'Erkenntnisse über eine französische Untergrundorganisation und über deren geplante Attentate gegen Waffenhändler unde andere mit den algerischen Aufständischen sympathisierenden Personen in der Bundesrepublik Deutschland', Bad Godesberg, 24 June 1959. Officials at both the BKA and the Foreign Ministry were particularly worried about the propaganda activity of a journalist from Wiesbaden called Winfrid Müller (nicknamed 'Mustapha Müller') who fought with ALN (Armée de Libération Nationale) units in Algeria and sent pro-FLN reports back to groups and publications who supported the Algerian nationalist cause in the Federal Republic.

23. Pol. A.A.Ber., B 25, Nr. 13, *Bundeskriminalamt (Bericht der Sicherungsgruppe am Auswärtigen Amt)*, Re.: 'Erkenntnisse über eine französische Untergrundorganisation (CATENA) und deren geplante Attentate gegen Waffenhändler und andere mit den algerischen Aufständischen sympathisierenden Personen in der Bundesrepublik Deutschland', Bad Godesberg, 24 June 1959.

24. Pol. A.A.Ber., B25, Nr.13, *Brief des Landesgeschäftsführers der CDU Landesverband Saar André am Legationsrat Dr. Frank (politische Abteilung des Auswärtigen Amtes)*, Re.: 'Gründung eines Hilfskomitees für algerische Flüchtlinge in Saarland', Saarbrücken, 6 February 1960.

25. A good example of such coverage is *F.R.*, 'Auch der zweite Start mißglückte – Hassan Ait Ahcene will nach Tunis zurück/Das unaufgeklärte Attentat', 8 December 1958.

26. Pol. A.A.Ber., B 25, Nr. 9, *Bericht vom Bundesministerium des Innern (Algerierfrage)*, Re.: 'Vorbeugende Maßnahmen gegen politische Attentate in der Bundesrepublik', Bonn, 16 July 1959.

27. NHstA. Hann., Nds. 100, Nr. 148, *Bericht des Landeskriminalamtes Niedersachsen*, Re.: 'Ausländerpolizeiliche Behandlung von Algerier', Hanover, 2 November 1959.

28. Pol. A.A.Ber., B 25, Nr. 10, *Aufzeichnung einer Sitzung des Bundesministeriums des Innern*, Re.: 'Algerische Umtriebe in der BRD', Bonn, 12 October 1958.

29. Pol. A.A.Ber., B 25, Nr. 13, *Abschrift eines Berichtes über Ermittlungen des Generalstaatsanwaltes bei dem Hanseatischen Oberlandsgericht an den Senat der Freien und Hansestadt Hamburg (Landesjustizverwaltung) und dem Auswärtigen Amt*, Re.: 'Ermittlungsverfahren wegen der Sprengstoffattentate auf den Waffenhändler Schlüter und auf den Dampfer "Atlas", Hamburg', 20 May 1959.

30. *F.R.*, 'Auch der zweite Start mißglückte – Hassan Ait Ahcene will nach Tunis zurück/Das unaufgeklärte Attentat', Hans Paul Lieren, 8 December 1958; and Pol. A.A.Ber., B 25, Nr. 13, *Bericht Politische Abteilung*, Re.: 'Attentat auf Ait Ahcéne', Bonn, 6 November 1958.

31. Pol. A.A.Ber., B 25, Nr. 9, *Aufzeichnung eines Gespräches mit MdB. Wischnewski (Leg. Dr. Weinhold)*, Re.: 'Algerienfrage und die BRD', Bonn, 15 May 1961.

32. Pol. A.A.Ber., B 25, Nr. 13, *Antwort an Herrn André (Landesgeschäftsführer der CDU Landesverband Saar)*, Re.: 'Gründung eines Hilfskomitees für algerische Flüchtlinge im Saarland, Bonn', 15 February 1960.

33. NHstA. Hann., Nds. 100, Nr. 148, *Vortragsvermerk für den Niedersächsischen Landesminister des Innern*, Re.: 'Ausländerpolizeiliche Behandlung der Algerier', Hanover, 2 November 1959.

34. NHstA. Hann., Nds. 100, Nr. 148, *Erfahrungsbericht des Landeskriminalamtes Saarland*, Re.: 'Die Aktivität der algerischen Aufständischen im Saarland', Saarbrücken, 19 September 1958, German original: 'Durch die Regierung des Saarlandes wurde eine Erfassungsaktion für alle im Saarland aufhaltsamen Algerier angeordnet. Die Aktion ist nicht beendet. Es ist jedoch schon jetzt zu erkennen, dass sich eine sehr grosse Anzahl Algerier im Saarland aufhält, ohne hier registriert zu sein. Dieser Mißstand ist offensichtlich eine Auswirkung des nahen Grenzverkehrs.'

35. Pol. A.A.Ber., B 25, Nr. 9, *Bericht vom Bundesministerium des Innern (Algerierfrage)*, Re.: 'Vorbeugende Maßnahme gegen politische Attentate in der Bundesrepublik', Bonn, 16 July 1959.

36. B.K., B 106, Nr. 31347, *Bundesministerium des Innern*, Re.: 'Maßnahmen gegen Französische Rechtsextremisten 1961–1967', Bonn, 1968.

37. Scheffler, *Die SPD und der Algerienkrieg*, 57.

38. Pol. A.A.Ber., B 25, Nr. 2, *Auswärtiges Amt – Aufzeichnung (gez. Leg. Janne)*, Re.: 'Unterredung mit SPD Abgeordnete Wischnewski', Bonn, 15 May 1961.

39. Pol. A.A.Ber., B 25, Nr. 13, *Schnellbrief des Bundesministeriums des Innern*, Re.: 'Gründung eines Vereines für ein freies Algerien in Saarbrücken', Bonn, 12 October 1961.

40. von Braunmühl, *Kalter Krieg und Friedliche Koexistenz*, 34–38.

41. B.K., B 141, Nr. 258524, *MdB Peter Blachstein (SPD) and Bundesminister der Justiz*, Re.: 'Anti-Franco Flugblatt', Hamburg, 26 December 1963.

42. Miller, *Foreign Workers in Western Europe*, 64, 156–59.

43. K. Schönwälder. 2001. *Einwanderung und Ethnische Pluralität: Politische Entscheidungen und öffentliche Debatten in Großbritannien und der Bundesrepublik von den 1950er bis zu den 1970er Jahren*, Essen: Klartext, 174–77.

44. Pol. A.A.Ber., B26, Nr. 206, *Diplomgerma Madrid (Drahtbericht)*: 'Bericht über Kundgebungen Spanischer Arbeiter', Bonn, 29 May 1962.

45. B.G., 'Deutsche Köche riefen "Viva España!"' – Spanische Gastarbeiter demonstrierten – Polizei: Keine Zwischenfälle', 29 May 1962.

46. Pol. A.A.Ber., B 26, Nr. 161, *Aufzeichnung Auswärtiges Amt*, Re.: 'Sympathiekundgebungen spanischer Gastarbeiter in Köln am Sonntag, den 3. Juni 1962', Bonn 1 June 1962.

47. Pol. A.A.Ber., B 26, Nr. 161, *Bericht Botschaft Madrid an Auswärtiges Amt Bonn*, Re.: 'Spanische Innenpolitik – Treffen der Opposition in München und Gegenmassnahmen des Franco-Regimes', Madrid, 16 June 1962.

48. NHstA. Hann., Nds. 100, Nr. 758, *Fernschreiberbericht Polizeidirektion Hannover an LKA Niedersachsen und LfV Niedersachsen*, Re.: 'Verfahren wegen Verdachts verräterische Beziehungen – spanischer Gastarbeiter', Hanover, 5 March 1963.

49. Pol. A.A.Ber., B 26, Nr. 206, *Diplomgerma Madrid (Drahtbericht)*: 'Sympathiekundgebungen Spanischer Arbeiter', Bonn, 29 May 1962, German original: 'Spanische Ansicht, hiesige linksradikale förderten die Demonstrationen, entspricht nach hiesigen Informationen nicht den Tatsachen, jedoch besteht kein Zweifel daran, daß die Kundgebungen seitens der Deutschen Gewerkschaften und der SPD gefördert würden.'

50. Pol. A.A.Ber., B 26, Nr. 161, *Aufzeichnung – Besprechung Auswärtiges Amt mit Bundesarbeitsministerium und Bundesministerium des Innern*, Re.: 'Demonstration spanischer Gastarbeiter im Bundesgebiet', Bonn, 7 June 1962, German original: 'Da die treibenden Kräfte bei den Aktionen zur Politisierung der spanischen Arbeiter im Bundesgebiet letzten Endes bei der SPD zu suchen sind, könnte unter Umständen ein offenes Gespräch mit einer geeigneten Persönlichkeit der SPD weiterhelfen.'

51. Ibid., German original: 'Man ist im Bundesarbeitsministerium im klaren darüber, daß jede Einwirkung auf den DGB mit dem Ziel, die Agitation unter den spanischen Arbeitern zu beenden, ein ziemlich hoffnungsloses Unterfangen wäre, da der DGB jeden Versuch in dieser Richtung als Einmischung und Versuch der Beeinträchtigung der ihm verfassungsmäßig zustehenden Rechte ansehen würde.'

52. D.W., 'Scharfe Worte gegen Franco auf dem SPD Parteitag', 27 May 1962.

53. Pol. A.A.Ber., B 26, Nr. 161, *Aufzeichnung*, Re.: 'Treffen der Opposition in München und Gegenmaßnahmen der Francoregierung', Bonn, 18 June 1962.

54. Pol. A.A.Ber., B 26, Nr. 161, *Aufzeichnung*, Re.: 'Spanische Teilnahme am IV. Kongreß der Europäischen Bewegung', Bonn, 18 June 1962.

55. Pol. A.A.Ber., B 26, Nr. 161, *Auszug*, Re.: 'Spanische Stellungnahme zum Renger-Bericht', Bonn, 13 June 1962.

56. R. Sala. 2005. '"Gastarbeitersendungen", "Gastarbeiterzeitschriften": Ein Spiegel internationaler Spannungen?', *Zeithistorische Forschungen*, 3, 373–374.

57. C.C. Seidel. 2001. *Angst vor dem 'Vierten Reich': Die Alliierten und die Ausschaltung des deutschen Einflusses in Spanien 1944–1958*, Munich: Schöningh, 78.

58. Ibid., 364–66.

59. Hauptstaatsarchiv Hessen Wiesbaden (HstA. H.W.), Abt. 503, Nr. 1192, *Abschrift des Hessischen Landeskriminalamtes*, Re.: 'Erfahrungen über das Verhalten von Ausländern in der BRD – ENO (Europäische Neuordnung)', Frankfurt, 13 April 1962.

60. NHstA. Hann., Nds. 100, Nr. 48, *Landeskriminalpolizeiamt Niedersachsachsen*, Re.: 'Ausländische Arbeitnehmer', Hanover, 8 September 1966; and Anaya, *European Socialists and Spain*, 141.

61. B. Aschmann. 1999. *'Treue Freunde...'?: Westdeutschland und Spanien 1945–1963*, Stuttgart: Franz Steiner Verlag (Historische Mitteilungen Nr. 34), 325–26.

62. Miller, *Foreign Workers in Western Europe*, 87.

63. W. Lehmann. 1988. 'Die Hypothek der Vergangenheit: Das Verhältnis der Bundesrepublik zu Spanien', *Hispanorama* 50, 78–82.

64. Pol. A.A.Ber., B 26, Nr. 181, *Aufzeichnung*, Re.: 'Betreuung Spanischer Gastarbeiter in der Bundesrepublik – Kommunistische Infiltration und Deutsche Abwehrmaßnahmen', Bonn, 11 July 1962.

65. J. Hooper. 1995. *The New Spaniards*, 2nd ed., London: Penguin, 22.

66. Pol. A.A.Ber., B 26, Nr. 161, *Bericht des Bundesamtes für Verfassungsschutz*, Re.: 'Kommunistische Infiltrationsversuche unter spanischen Arbeitern im Bundesgebiet', Köln, 16 April 1962.

67. D. Gilmour. 1985. *The Transformation of Spain: From Franco to the Constitutional Monarchy*, New York: Quartet Books, 103.

68. NHstA. Hann., Nds. 100, Nr. 148, *Bundes- und Landeskriminalämter*, Re.: 'Bericht der Unterkommission "Vorbeugende Bekämpfung terroristischer Aktionen von Ausländern"', Bad Godesberg, 7 May 1969.

69. B.K., B 136, Nr. 3799, *Bundeskanzleramt Bericht*, Re.: 'Politische Tätigkeit von Gastarbeitern', Bonn 15 October 1965.

70. G. Colosio. 1986. *Ausländische Arbeitsmigranten: Analyse und Bewertung ihrer Situation aus Theologischer und Ethnologischer Sicht*, Inauguraldissertation an der Katholisch-Theologischen Fakultät der Universität Tübingen, Tübingen, 94–95.

71. Miller, *Foreign Workers in Western Europe*, 157–58.

72. A good example is *D.W.*, 'Das rote Netz der Dolores Ibarruri – Kommunistische Agenten beeinflussen spanische Gastarbeiter', 12 July 1962. Admittedly the reporting of *Die Welt, Bild* or the *FAZ* would not be likely to approve of cooperation between the German left and Spanish immigrants, but because of their suspicion of any movement that might 'weaken' the position of the Federal Republic in the Cold War, these media groups were more likely to take notice of such activity.

73. Pol. A.A.Ber., B 26, Nr. 450, *Bericht Deutsche Botschaft and das Auswärtige Amt*, Re.: 'XI. Kongress der UGT in Toulose vom 2.–8.8.1971', Madrid, 14 September 1971.

74. Pol. A.A.Ber., B 26, Nr. 161,*Aufzeichnung Auswärtiges Amt*, Re.: 'Sympathiekundgebungen spanischer Gastarbeiter in Köln am Sonntag, den 3. Juni 1962', Bonn, 1 June 1962.

75. Pol. A.A.Ber., B 26, Nr. 450, *Bericht Auswärtiges Amt an die Deutsche Botschaft Madrid*, Re.: 'Illegale Tätigkeit spanischer Gruppen', Bonn, 6 August 1971.

76. NHstA. Hann., Nds. 721, Nr. 201, *Staatsanwaltschaft Hannover*, Re.: 'Ermittlungssache gegen Horacio Fernandez-Montez und Enrique Alonso Iglesias wegen Landfriedensbruch im spanischen Konsulat', Hanover, 16 December 1971.

77. B.K., B 136, Nr. 3799, *Bundeskanzleramt Bericht*, Re.: 'Politische Tätigkeit von Gastarbeitern', Bonn 15 October 1965.

78. Pol. A.A.Ber., B 26, Nr. 161, *Drahtbericht an der Deutschen Botschaft Madrid*, Re.: 'Sympathiekundgebungen spanischer Arbeiter', Bonn, 29 May 1962.

79. Pol. A.A.Ber., B 26, Nr. 161, *Aufzeichnung – Politische Abteilung*, Re.: 'Sympathiekundgebung spanischer Gastarbeiter in Köln am Sonntag – den 3. Juni 1962', Bonn, 1 June 1962, German original: 'Nach Auskunft des Polizeipräsidiums in Köln wurde dort die Kundgebung ordnungsgemäß am 30.5.1962 angemeldet als "Schweigemarsch zur Bekundung der

Solidarität mit den Streikenden in Spanien". Die Anmeldung wurde von dem in Köln lebenden spanischen Studenten Ignazio Satelo in Verbindung mit dem Ortsausschuß des DGB vorgenommen. Der Polizipräsident in Köln hat gegen der Kundgebung keine Bedenken geäußert ... (Nach Meinung der Spanischen Regierung) Der DGB mit dessen Hilfe diese Kundgebung durchgeführt würden, versuche damit eine systematische Hetze gegen Spanien.'

80. B.K., B 141, Nr. 258524, *Vorbereitung des Bundesministers des Innern – Fragestunde im Bundestag am 17., 18. und 19. Februar 1965*, Re.: 'Mündliche Anfrage des Abgeordneten Hans Matthöfer (SPD)', Bonn, 16 February 1965.

81. Pol. A.A.Ber., B 26, Nr. 161, *Aufzeichnung – Politische Abteilung*, Re.: 'Besprechungspunkte für das Gespräch für Herrn Erler', Bonn, 13 June 1962.

82. L.O. Michaelis. 1999. *Politische Parteien unter der Beobachtung des Verfassungsschutzes – Die Streitbare zwischen Toleranz und Abwehrbereitschaft*, Baden Baden: Nomos Verlag. (Schriften zum Parteinrecht Nr. 26), 63.

83. Examples of such value laden language can be found throughout the reports of the *Auswärtiges Amt* and other ministries. See for example: Pol. A.A.Ber., B 26, Nr. 181, *Aufzeichnung*, Re.: 'Betreuung spanischer Gastarbeiter in der Bundesrepublik – Kommunistische Infiltration und deutsche Abwehrmaßnahmen', Bonn, 11 June 1962.

84. Pol. A.A.Ber., B 26, Nr. 161, *Aufzeichnung – Besprechung Auswärtiges Amt mit Bundesarbeitsministerium und Bundesministerium des Innern*, 'Demonstrationen spanischer Gastarbeiter im Bundesgebiet', 7 June 1962, Bonn, German original: 'Nach Auskunft des Bundesarbeitsministeriuns (ORR Dahnen) haben die spanischen Arbeiter sich bisher im allgemeinen an politischen Fragen nicht interessiert gezeigt. Es wäre Ihnen in der Hauptsache darum zu tun, das hier verdiente Geld einmal ungeschoren nach Hause bringen zu können. Durch die Agitation des DGB komme nunmehr Unruhe unter sie. Der Hinweis des spanischen Botschafters, seine Regierung werde die Entsendung von spanischen Arbeitern in zukunft möglicherweise stoppen müsse, wenn die Kundgebungen nicht aufhören, sei ein Zeichen dafür, daß das Vorgehen des DGB arbeitsmarktpolitisch und volkswirtschaftlich negative Folgen haben könnte.'

85. Pol. A.A.Ber., B 26, Nr. 161, *Bericht des Bundesministerium des Innern*, Re.: 'Kommunistische Infiltrationsversuche unter spanischen Arbeitern im Bundesgebiet', Bonn, 3 July 1962; and *D.W.*, 'Pablos Freunde ließen nicht locker – Das rote Netz der Dolores Ibarruri – Kommunistische Agenten beeinflussen spanische Gastarbeiter', 8 July 1962.

86. Pol. A.A.Ber., B 26, Nr. 161, *Bericht BFV am Bundesminister des Innern:* 'Kommunistische Infiltrationsversuche unter spanischen Arbeitern', 11 April 1962, Köln, German original: 'Die kommunistische Propagandatätigkeit in der Unterkunft bei Hanomag (Maschinenbau AG) wird seit einiger Zeit beobachtet. Maßgeblich sind der Peruaner Salomon Espinosa Quiroz und der Spanier Eleuterio Ramos Elexpe. Über den im Schreiben des Auswärtigen Amtes genannten Spanier Emeterio Calvo Martin ... konnten keine nachteiligen Erkenntnisse über eine gegen die Bundesrepublik gerichtete Tätigkeit gewonnen werden .... Die Ermittlungen zu den im Schreiben des Auswärtigen Amtes geschilderten kommunistischen Umtrieben unter spanischen Gastarbeitern in Grevenbroich sind noch nicht abgeschlossen.'

87. O. Diederichs. 1993. 'Die "Arbeitsgruppe Ausländer" der Berliner Polizei – eine Sondereinheit mit Doppelfunktion', *CILIP/Bürgerrechte und Polizei*, 45.

88. Czerwick, *Oppositionstheorien und Außenpolitik*, 39.

89. Pulzer, *German Politics*, 118.

90. Pol. A.A.Ber., B 26, Nr. 452, *Aufzeichnung der politischen Abteilung des Auswärtigen Amtes*, Re.: 'Besprechung der beamteten Staatssekretäre im Bundeskanzleramt am 10. April 1972 – Großveranstaltung der Kommunistischen Partei Spaniens in Frankfurt und anderen Orten des Bundesgebietes am 30. April 1972', Bonn, 7 April 1972.

91. Pol. A.A.Ber., B 26, Nr. 450, *Besprechung der beamteten Staatssekretäre im Bundeskanzleramt am 10. April*, Re.: 'Großveranstaltung der Kommunistischen Partei Spaniens in Frankfurt und anderen Orten des Bundesgebietes', Bonn, 30 April 1972.

92. Ibid., German original: 'Erfahrungsgemäss lässt sich eine solche konkrete Feststellung vor der beabsichtigten Versammlung kaum treffen. Nach den Erfahrungen des Bundesinnenminsteriums zeichnen sich sogar von Kommunisten durchgeführte Veranstaltungen durch einen gut organisierten und disziplinierten Ablauf aus.'

93. Pol. A.A.Ber., B 26, Nr. 450, *Bericht des BfV*, Re.: 'Großveranstaltung der PCE in Frankfurt am 30. April 1972', Köln, 8 May 1972.

94. Pol. A.A.Ber., B26, Nr. 450, *Auszug aus dem Kurzprotokell der 109. Kabinettsitzung der Bundesregierung am 3 und 5. Mai 1972*, Re.: 'Illegaler Aufenthalt des spanischen Kommunistenführers Santiago Carillo in der Bundesrepublik', Bonn, 9 May 1972.

95. Pol. A.A.Ber., B 26, Nr. 452, *Sekreteriat des Außenministers*, Re.: 'Auszug aus dem Kurzprotokoll der 109. Kabinettsitzung der Bundesregierung am 3. und 5. Mai 1972', Bonn, 9 May 1972.

96. Pol. A.A.Ber., B 26, Nr. 452, *Bericht der Politische Abteilung an der Deutschen Botschaft Madrid*, Re.: 'Deutsches Komitee zur Hilfe für demokratische Flüchtlinge e.V.' and Re.: 'Illegale Tätigkeit Spanischer Gruppen', Bonn, 6 August 1971 and 6 December 1971.

97. Pol. A.A.Ber., B 26, Nr. 161, *Vermerk*, Re.: 'Einstellung der SPD zum Spanien-Problem', Bonn, 18 June 1962.

98. Pol. A.A.Ber., B 26, Nr. 161, *Aufzeichnung – Politische Abteilung*, Re.: 'Besprechungspunkte für das Gespräch für Herrn Erler', Bonn, 13 June 1962.

99. P. Panayi. 2000. *Ethnic Minorities in Nineteenth and Twentieth Century Germany: Jews, Gypsies, Poles, Turks and Others: Themes in Modern German History*, Harlow: Longman, 218.

100. NHstA. Hann., Nds. 100 Nr. 148, *Vermerk LKA*, Re.: 'Ausländer in Niedersachsen', Hanover, 23 February 1970.

101. D. Rosati. 1998. 'Von den Baracken zur Kommunalwahl: Die Arbeit des ACLI', in R. Alborino and K. Pölzl (eds), *Italiener in Deutschland – Teilhabe oder Ausgrenzung?*, Freiburg im Breisgau: Lambertus, 83–87.

102. B.K., B 136, Nr. 3799, *Bericht – Bundesamt für Verfassungsschutz*, Re.: 'Infiltration ausländischer Gastarbeiter in der Bundesrepublik Deutschland', Cologne, September 1965.

103. Gilmour, *The Transformation of Spain*, 96.

104. NHstA. Hann., Nds. 147, Nr. 1031, *Landeskriminalamt – Bericht*, Re.: 'Ausländische Organisationen – Spanier', Hanover, September 1974.

105. Pol. A.A.Ber., B 26, Nr. 450, *Bericht des BfV and Deutsche Botschaft Madrid*, Re.: 'Illegale Tätigkeit spanischer Gruppen', Bonn, 6 December 1971.

106. Pol. A.A.Ber., B 26, Nr. 450, *Bericht – Politische Abteilung*, Re.: 'Verhaftung des spanischen Staatsangehörigen Carlos Pardo in Madrid', Bonn, 28 June 1971.

107. P. Mueller and M. Müller. 2002. *Gegen Freund und Feind – Der BND: Geheime Politik und Schmutzige Geschäfte*, Hamburg: Rowohlt Verl, 472–81.

108. Anaya, *European Socialists and Spain*, 11–12.

109. NHstA. Hann., Nds. 147, Nr. 1031, *Landeskriminalamt – Bericht*, Re.: 'Ausländische Organisationen – Spanier', Hanover, September 1974.

110. HstA. H.W., Abt. 503, Nr. 3312, *Landesverfassungsschutz Hessen*, Re.: 'Verfassungsfeindliche Organisationen und Versammlungen 1950–1972', Wiesbaden , December 1973.

111. Pol. A.A.Ber., B 26, Nr. 450, *Brief des Leiters des Katholischen Büros Bonn (Prälat Wilhelm Wöste) an dem Bundesminister des Auswärtigen (Walter Scheel)*, Re.: 'Fragen der ausländischen Arbeitnehmer in der Bundesrepublik', Bonn, 18 June 1971.

112. Hooper, *The New Spaniards*, 134.

113. Gilmour, *The Transformation of Spain*, 55; and Pol.A.A. Ber., B26, Nr. 206, *Diplomgerma Madrid (Drahtbericht)*, Re.: 'Bericht über Kundgebungen Spanischer Arbeiter', Bonn, 29 May 1962.

114. Pol. A.A.Ber., B 26, Nr. 450, *Brief des Leiters des Katholischen Büros Bonn (Prälat Wilhelm Wöste) an dem Bundesminister des Auswärtigen (Walter Scheel)*, Re.: 'Fragen der ausländischen Arbeitnehmer in der Bundesrepublik', Bonn, 18 June 1971.

115. B.E. Schmitter. 1980. 'Immigrants and Associations', *International Migration Review* 14, 189.

116. HstA. H.W., Abt. 503, Nr. 1192, *Abschrift des Hessischen Landeskriminalamtes*, Re.: 'Erfahrungen über das Verhalten von Ausländern in der BRD – ENO (Europäische Neuordnung)', Wiesbaden, 13 April 1962.

117. From information provided by the Spanish embassy in Berlin, 12 June 2003. Although the cultural attaché's office had the name and address of several of these clubs on file, it was reluctant to 'officially' pass on data on 'political' clubs.

118. NHstA. Hann., Nds. 147, Nr. 1031, *Landeskriminalamt – Bericht*, Re.: 'Ausländische Organisationen – Spanier', Hanover, September 1974.

119. No mention of pro-Franco supporters can be found in key documents and reports on the activity of Spanish and other immigrant organizations such as HstA. H.W., Abt. 503, Nr. 3312, *Landesverfassungsschutz Hessen*, Re.: 'Verfassungsfeindliche Organisationen und Versammlungen 1950–1972', Wiesbaden , December 1973.

120. Gilmour, *The Transformation of Spain*, 81–82; and Hooper, *The New Spaniards*, 93.

121. Mueller and Müller, *Gegen Freund und Feind – Der BND*, 472–81. The operation to pass on millions of SPD funds secretly to the PSOE (which also involved BND operatives) was known as 'Operation Polyp'.

122. U. Schöneberg. 1992. *Gestern Gastarbeiter, Morgen Minderheit: Zur sozialen Integration von Einwanderern in einem 'unerklärten' Einwanderungsland*, Frankfurt a.M.: Peter Lang Verl. (Europäische Hochschulschriften 169).

Chapter 4

A BATTLE ON MANY FRONTS
GREEK IMMIGRANTS AND POLITICAL VIOLENCE

One of the key factors shaping West German politics between 1949 and the late 1970s was the growing power and complexity of the security services. Over this thirty-year period, police and intelligence agencies were established or expanded in reaction to a variety of perceived security threats. The three major West German intelligence services, the *Bundesnachrichtendienst*, the *Bundesamt für Verfassungsschutz* and the counter-espionage departments of the *Bundeskriminalamt* tried to maximize their influence in Bonn at each other's expense. Yet efforts to maintain a coherent security policy were often undermined by the federal structure of the West German political system. While the BND and *Auswärtiges Amt* had no provincial equivalents, the Federal Interior and Justice Ministries together with the criminal and counterintelligence services had to compete with their *Länder* equivalents for financial resources and political patronage.[1]

Similar problems were faced by local police forces. While policing was controlled by the *Länder,* the expansion of the *Bundesgrenzschutz* (BGS) in the 1970s created something akin to a national gendarmerie.[2] The amount of space immigrants and émigrés had to express their own political views depended as much on the political make up of regional and city governments or the attitude of local BGS and police commanders as it did on who determined policy at the federal level. With different party-political combinations at different levels of government, immigrant movements had to grapple with the fact that federal agencies were often at cross-purposes to provincial state institutions. A provincial government ruled by the CDU or CSU, such as Bavaria for example, could on occasion try to find ways to protect its émigré allies from the hostility of a federal government controlled by the SPD. Attempts at policy coordination involved all levels of the security hierarchy, producing ever more opportunities for information leaks and operational confusion. When one party dominated federal government and others controlled a majority of the *Länder,* these problems could also be used as a party-political weapon in the run up to federal or *Land* elections.[3]

A major criminal case would often necessitate cooperation between the BKA and a provincial counterpart in a *Landeskriminalamt,* compounding an already confused chain of command. Such potential conflict between *Land* and *Bund* agencies manifested itself even more openly between the *Bundesamt für Verfassungsschutz* and the provincial *Landesamt für Verfassungsschutz* (LfV) organizations. Incidents in which informers in immigrant or radical Right movements turned out to have worked for both the BfV and LfV, playing one organization off against the other, caused severe embarrassment for several West German governments.[4] The emergence of such 'informer duplication' in the surveillance of the extreme right-wing *Nationaldemokratische Partei Deutschlands* (NPD), along with a general lack of cooperation and trust between *Länder* and *Bund*, forced the court at the apex of the judicial hierarchy, the Federal Constitutional Court (*Bundesverfassungsgericht*), to throw out a state decree banning the NPD.[5] These institutional tensions within the West German state influenced the manner in which immigrants were administered and punished by the state.

Such judicial rulings could have a considerable impact on the life of immigrant communities. From the banning of the Communist Party in 1954 (*Kommunistische Partei Deutschlands* or KPD), to cases involving anti-terrorist legislation in the 1970s and 1980s, the *Bundesverfassungsgericht* has produced rulings that have put well-defined constitutional limits on the power of the West German state. Although police and intelligence services occasionally took measures that crossed legal boundaries, they did so with the knowledge that any judgement by the *Bundesverfassungsgericht* condemning such action could cause severe difficulty for local and federal governments. Yet since its judges were selected by a committee whose members belonged to federal and *Länder* governments, the *Bundesverfassungsgericht* often shared the general assumptions of the security services when it came to the political threat posed by organizations that did not adhere to the constitutional consensus of the Federal Republic.[6]

Though catching regular criminals was the main priority of the police and criminal intelligence agencies immediately after the Second World War, their subsequent development was shaped by an ideological environment in which the existence of the GDR challenged the political legitimacy of the Federal Republic. Intertwined with this inter-German rivalry, was the necessity to reassure West Germany's new NATO allies that the democratic experiment in the Federal Republic was strong enough to withstand those who aimed to restore the social order of pre-1945 Germany.[7] Fears that the communist bloc might attempt to subvert the political process of the Federal Republic, led the security services to monitor the activity of a wide variety of East German organizations such as its youth movement, the *Freie Deutsche Jugend* (FDJ). Any West German involved with these organizations was immediately considered a potential security threat. A look at the extensive efforts undertaken by the *Stasi* and KGB to penetrate every major element of West German society would indicate that such concerns were often well founded.[8]

Among police and intelligence officials this fear of Marxist–Leninist subversion coordinated by the GDR fostered wider paranoia over the activity of all left-wing activity in the Federal Republic. Leftist movements not under the direct control of the SPD and the unions were always at risk from further state intervention ostensibly designed to minimize 'anti-constitutional' ('*verfassungsfeindlich*') agitation, which was often a euphemism for East German involvement. Such an environment also put immense pressure on the SPD and the rest of the pro-constitutional Left to prove that it was not tainted by association with the kind of socialism propagated in the Soviet bloc.[9] In comparison, keeping the radical Right under control was less of a priority for intelligence officials. After the *Deutsche Reichspartei* was outlawed in 1953, the efforts to pursue right-wing individuals and organizations hostile to the constitution lost momentum.[10] Only after the social democrats took power on the federal level did security services begin to pay greater attention to extreme right-wing activity. The fact that senior officials within the Chancellery, federal intelligence agencies, *Länder* governments and local police forces had themselves been involved in the Nazi regime probably explains the general reluctance to tackle this problem in the 1950s.[11]

Throughout this period, the political activity of immigrants and émigrés in Germany was heavily monitored by West German security services. Police officials and governing politicians felt no qualms about using immigration law to discipline immigrants who worked with Germans hostile to the political establishment. Even peaceful activism could expose non-Germans to retributive measures at the hands of local *Ausländerämter,* which had the right to revoke residence permits. Not only were immigrant activists liable to come under surveillance from regional and national security services, they also had to deal with prying from hostile local authorities. From student activists involved in protests demanding reform of the West German university system, to senior workers fighting with their German colleagues for better pay, to shop owners protesting with the local population against re-zoning, immigrants engaged in all aspects of political life were thus far more vulnerable to state repression than their German counterparts.[12]

The fact that most immigrants could not use the ballot box to make themselves heard because of the legal hurdles that made the acquisition of citizenship so difficult meant that immigrant movements in the FRG were more dependent on local political milieus than their counterparts in other European countries.[13] The lack of an electoral outlet also encouraged the use of more radical measures, since immigrants had to go to greater lengths to gain the attention of the West German political establishment than comparable German movements. The kind of immigrant political activity that developed out of these pressures could lead to peaceful activity undertaken with the acquiescence or even support of the West German state, but in many cases it also involved the use of violent tactics by groups whose German supporters were equally opposed to the constitutional order of the FRG.

The previous chapters have demonstrated how the interaction between immigrants and state institutions did change over time, mirroring wider political shifts in West German society. Nevertheless, though the nature of political participation and the background of West German partners helped shape the approach taken by West German police and intelligence agencies towards immigrant communities, superficial similarities should not lead to generalizations about their behaviour towards politicized immigrants as a whole. As we shall see, immigrant movements who used the same techniques and had the same German contacts were often treated in very different ways.

The German Left also had difficulties dealing with the fallout from acts of political violence organized by its ostensible immigrant allies. While cooperation between German social democrats and Spanish socialists managed to keep most Spanish activists from using violent tactics, political violence remained endemic in other immigrant communities dominated by the Left. The Greek community in particular became notorious for the militant nature of its political organizations. On both the Right and Left, Greek activists were prepared to use violent means in order to achieve their political aims. The political heterogeneity of the Greek community meant that left-wing groups had to actively compete with right-wing activists for the support of the wider Greek guest worker population. By examining the political development of the Greek community, this chapter will therefore explore the tension between preserving law and order and demonstrating ideological solidarity faced by security services and German political parties confronted with internal political conflict within an immigrant community.

****

Though the first evidence of problems between left- and right-wing Greek immigrants began to emerge in the early 1960s, the number of incidents involving political violence in this community quickly increased after the Greek military coup of 1967.[14] This takeover of power by a small group of army colonels was triggered by fears on the Greek Right that an electoral victory by the left-leaning Centre Union could lead to a government coalition that would include the Greek Communist Party. In response, the parties of the Left and democratic Centre called on their supporters in the Greek diaspora to campaign for the restoration of democracy in Athens. With over 100,000 Greek guest workers in West Germany and heavy investment by West German corporations in the Greek economy, both the Greek opposition and the military junta went to considerable lengths to gain the support of Greeks living in the Federal Republic.[15] Conflict between left- and right-wing Greek immigrants continued until Greek democracy was restored in 1974. While more radical elements of the opposition set up terrorist cells, the regime organized its supporters both openly as well as covertly through the diplomatic service and the KYP, the Greek counterpart to the CIA.

Once again, a West German government found itself caught between rival political factions that both campaigned on behalf of movements in their homeland and helped their members adjust to life in the Federal Republic. Though all West German parliamentary parties claimed they wanted a restoration of democracy in Greece (that was a full member of NATO and the

Council of Europe), the underlying attitudes of most Christian democratic politicians and activists towards the military junta differed markedly from those of their counterparts in the SPD.[16] With the SPD and CDU/CSU roped together in an uneasy coalition between 1965 and 1969, the state was itself more susceptible to pressures from both sides in a conflict between Left and Right than it had been during the Adenauer era.[17]

The CDU/CSU proved particularly inclined to accept the anti-communist rhetoric of the Greek colonels. While several senior Christian democrats including Chancellor Kurt Kiesinger were genuinely shocked by events in Greece, more conservative figures such as Franz Josef Strauß actively courted the junta and lobbied for the relaxation of sanctions imposed by the European Economic Community (EEC) after the coup. Several Bavarian ministers and CSU leaders even visited Athens during this period. CDU politicians in other *Länder*, who were more doctrinally anti-communist than their counterparts on the federal level, also lobbied in support of a fellow Cold War frontline state. Moreover, the conservative wing of the CDU was prepared to accept the logic of exceptionalism deployed by the Greek junta as well as other authoritarian regimes such as Francoist Spain or various Turkish military governments. The exceptionalist argument was based on the idea that specific cultural factors in Mediterranean or the Balkan states militated against the development of 'stable' (i.e., anti-communist) democracy, necessitating authoritarian forms of government.[18]

The historical legacy of the Greek Civil War helped to cement such attitudes in CDU/CSU circles. The success of guerrilla armies in Northern Greece in 1947 that enjoyed Soviet and Yugoslav support strengthened the Truman administration's resolve to contain communist expansion through a large U.S. military presence in Western Europe. The 'Truman doctrine' ultimately ensured American support for the foundation of West Germany and the survival of West Berlin as an outpost of the Western Alliance. These direct links between the British- and U.S.-backed war against communism in Greece and the establishment of the West German state were often invoked by members of the CDU/CSU's conservative wing.[19]

Though the defeat of communist insurgents in 1949 enabled a coalition of moderate royalists and conservatives to dominate the Greek state in the 1950s, by the time thousands of Greeks began to arrive in the Federal Republic through the guest worker programme, left-wing parties such as the Centre Union or the communist KKE (*Kommunistiko Komma Elladas/Greek Communist Party*) had become a strong presence in the Greek parliament. After the coup, most European governments distanced themselves from a regime whose legitimacy they considered to be questionable. By contrast, the Nixon administration quickly restored the Pentagon's close working relationship with the Greek military after a short cooling off period.[20] While some Christian democrats expressed disgust at the junta's methods of government, conservatives defended its tactics as legitimate responses to the dangers of communist subversion. Such sentiment was best expressed by Franz Josef Strauß after one visit to Athens in the late 1960s: 'The Colonels have put an end to the chaos of the old party system and have prevented the slide into communism.'[21]

Comments on Greek affairs made by conservative German politicians such as Strauß, Barschel or Schröder, demonstrate how Colonel Papadopoulos and other members of the junta manipulated memories of the advent of the Cold War in the early 1940s and played on the centre-right's fears of the GDR and the rest of the Soviet bloc. By constantly referring back to the Greek Civil War, an otherwise unattractive military regime was able to gain support among conservative circles in Germany, enabling its representatives to get some local backing for their attempts to gain control of Greek community life in the Federal Republic. The fact that Greece remained a NATO ally and major Western states continued to conduct business with the Greek government strengthened the hand of those West Germans who wanted to support economic investment in Greece or continue military cooperation with a staunchly anti-communist regime.[22]

The free democrats and the SPD were more openly hostile towards the Greek junta. As an opposition party, the FDP was consistently critical of the Colonels, lending its direct support to opposition leaders associated with the democratic Centre such as Konstantinos Karamanlis. By contrast, the FDP avoided contact with the left-wing Centre Union and the Euro-communist KKE since most free democrats believed that these two parties bore partial responsibility for the collapse of Greek democracy. As part of the governing coalition, the SPD's room for manoeuvre was more constricted. But social democrat cabinet ministers tried to maintain distance between the West German state and what they considered to be a neo-fascist regime. However, the influence of Strauß and Barschel along with Greece's membership of the NATO alliance ensured that the Federal Republic continued to supply the Greek Army with weaponry until the collapse of the Grand Coalition.[23]

After the SPD became the dominant party of government in 1969 there were far fewer restraints upon its leadership when it came to encouraging democratic change in a variety of authoritarian states. In the Greek case this semi-official activity remained focused on improving general conditions in Greece and protecting individual dissidents. Thus, social democrat cabinet members were even prepared to use diplomats and military personnel to extract an individual dissident, Dmitri Mangakis, from Greek territory in 1971, though they tried to ensure that those involved in these kinds of schemes did not openly endorse any specific Greek movement.[24] If the KKE was beyond the pale because of its communist roots, even the radical socialist rhetoric of George and Andrew Papandreou and other Centre Union leaders was enough to make German social democrats uncertain about the ideological reliability of the Greek Left.[25] Though the SPD government's stance when it came to Greek politics led to heavy friction with the military regime, this engagement did not benefit any specific political movement.

Such political calculations were also overshadowed by the impact the Nazi occupation of Greece had on Greek society. Memories of the Second World War permeated the rhetoric of both those who supported and those who opposed the junta. As a consequence, the internal conflicts between the Greek Left and Right involved the Federal Republic in a more direct fashion than other West European states. The arrest of Max Mertens in 1957, who as a senior SS official had organized the deportation of Jews from Thessaloniki in 1943, triggered a wider debate over atrocities committed by the Germans and their Greek allies during the Second World War. The Mertens case brought these issues to the fore at a time when demands made by left-wing Greeks that the West German state should pay financial compensation to Greek victims of the German occupation were becoming increasingly strident. The emergence of Mertens's postwar contacts with right-wing circles in Greece (he had been arrested while on his regular holiday to the Greek Islands) provided further ammunition for the Centre Union and other left-wing groups in their campaign against the liberal and conservative parties that had dominated Greek politics after the Civil War.[26]

In reaction, press and politicians in the Federal Republic began to investigate how Mertens was able to continue his legal career after his release from American custody in 1946 (the Greek government had declined to ask for his extradition). Mertens had subsequently worked for the Ministry of Justice in Bonn and managed to attain some influence in centre-right politics through his association with the future *Bundespräsident*, Gustav Heinemann. The direct involvement of the *Auswärtiges Amt* in the organization of Mertens' defence attracted considerable criticism from the Greek and West German Left, along with the unwelcome attention of the East German government.[27] This trial did not have the same impact on West German public opinion that the later Eichmann and Frankfurt Auschwitz trials were to have because of the Greek government's own lack of enthusiasm for dredging up the wartime past. Mertens was quietly deported to the Federal Republic in November 1959 despite the fact that a Greek military court had sentenced him to 25 years' imprisonment in February of the same year. Alerted by the Mertens trial, left-wing groups in the Federal Republic became aware of the atrocities committed in Greece by the *Wehrmacht* and SS. Much of the propaganda material produced by the German far Left that dealt with events in Greece after 1967 emphasized continuities between the military junta and the Greek politicians and militias that had collaborated with Mertens and other *Wehrmacht* or SS officers.[28]

In this respect, the West German and European Left were simply following the lead of the Greek opposition, which portrayed the Greek junta as an ideological successor to mid-century Nazism and fascism. Commentators such as Günther Wallraff and Günther Grass called for resistance against a 'fascist' military junta whose human rights record should disqualify it from membership of NATO and other European institutions. This emphasis on 'fascist continuities' could be found throughout the West German New Left and provided opposition activists in the Greek immigrant population with a slogan that could mobilize support for their cause in the Federal Republic.[29] By claiming that cooperation between West German corporations or state institutions and the Greek government was an indicator of 'fascist tendencies' within the Federal Republic, members of the Greek opposition managed to link events in their homeland with the West German ideological battles of the late 1960s and early 1970s.[30]

Such parallels were always likely to interest members of the West German Left, because events in Greece seemed to confirm underlying fears about the future of the Federal Republic. Many young activists in New Left groups or the SPD conflated the battle against representatives of the Greek regime in Germany with their campaign against what they considered to be the 'fascist tendencies' of the political establishment. As part of this ideological conflict, more radical elements included the Springer press, major corporations, the security forces, leaders of the centre-right and even moderate social democrats such as Helmut Schmidt among their opponents. This stance fostered a tendency to emphasize connections between the German 'military-industrial' complex and the Greek junta that often led to comparisons with the structure of the Nazi regime. Some parts of the German Left went so far as to portray their involvement in the affairs of the Greek community as an extension of their own battles over the political legacy of Adenauer and the historical legacy of the Nazi era.[31]

By radicalizing many Greek immigrants, the draconian response of the Greek military government towards any form of dissent after 1967 led to a rapid rise in the number of acts of political violence directed against representatives of the Greek state in the Federal Republic. As we have seen in the case of other immigrant groups, the impact of political violence on the Greek community was dependent upon the response of the West German parliamentary Left. While the SPD leadership considered the Tito regime a necessary evil, the Greek military junta was openly criticized by senior social democrats. Despite Greece's status as a NATO ally, the Greek government therefore could not count on the backing of the West German state when it came to the military junta's efforts to take control of the Greek community.

This did not mean that SPD politicians tried to prevent West German authorities from prosecuting Greek activists involved in bombings, riots or assassination attempts. In the first years of the junta's existence, *Auswärtiges Amt* diplomats and staunchly anti-communist police and intelligence officials who wanted to maintain good relations with the Greek government tried to suppress several Greek leftist groups. Some West German diplomats even compared the activity of Greek immigrants with diplomatic difficulties caused by militant Croatian activists when it came to safeguarding West German policy interests:

> Major interests of the Federal Republic have also been damaged when it comes to its obligations set out in the NATO treaty ... The Bavarian State Ministry for the Interior would therefore like to suggest that, just as in the case of the Croatian exiles,

Greek organizations should be examined in order to determine whether their politically extreme activities are infringing association law [*Vereinsrecht*] and represent a threat to security or public order ... These consultations should also include the use of relevant mechanisms provided by immigration law (for example a ban on the entry [into West Germany] of certain foreign agitators).[32]

Yet while regional and federal intelligence agencies identified the Greek Left as a potential security threat, senior officials in these agencies believed that local police services were more susceptible to pressure from social democratic politicians who opposed the Greek junta.[33]

Where did this leave the Greek immigrants themselves? In the months after the guest worker programme began to attract labour from Greece, in the first months of 1962 workers from all Greek regions began to arrive in West Germany, making this community one of the most visible of guest worker groups.[34] Accompanying the speedy growth in the number of Greek workers, many students from universities in Athens and Thessaloniki decided to do graduate work in West German universities. As in the case of the Spanish community, the Greek student body was augmented by better educated guest workers who chose to begin or continue their university careers in Germany after having earned some extra money on the factory floor.[35]

With their more comprehensive understanding of the workings of West German society, these students often acted as mediators between less educated guest workers and the state. They were also instrumental in helping to set up the kind of cultural clubs that provided the Greeks with a local community infrastructure.[36] Better educated guest workers and students on both sides of the Greek political divide also worked as translators for German civic or police authorities. Despite the fact that Greek consulates tried to ensure that such translators would not make any trouble for their own diplomatic staff by recommending individuals with known right-wing credentials, opposition groups and West German trade unions were always able to find left-wing Greek students prepared to volunteer for translation work as well. Greeks dealing with local or federal bureaucrats would often request that officially sanctioned translators be replaced by more 'neutral' individuals associated with the local DGB office.[37] This kind of close contact between Greeks of very different educational backgrounds meant that Greek political organizations in West Germany possessed a high level of social diversity. While Greek students brought working-class guest workers into contact with West German student politics, politically aware *Gastarbeiter* who originated from the slums of Athens and rural Greece put students in touch with West German trade unions and the Greek workers' movement.

The prominent role played by Greek diplomats in the efforts of West German managers to prevent the unionization of their guest worker employees meant that cultural clubs and other community institutions became heavily involved in organizing strikes and walkouts.[38] Acting as translators or organizers, Greek students and academics emphasized the brutal working conditions endured by their guest worker compatriots in order to gain the support of West German union officials and students. In doing so they used the charged language of 1960s student politics, with its focus on perceived remnants of the Nazi past and a revisionist approach towards the origins of the Cold War. As most members of the Greek opposition shared such assumptions, this recourse to common rhetorical devices helped to shore up the firm support of the West German extraparliamentary opposition.[39]

Along with this mobilization of support against the junta, many left-wing Greek students were heavily involved in direct action protests organized by their German counterparts in the SDS (Socialist German Student Union) and other student groups. When Greek undergraduates became involved in Hanover's 'Roter Punkt' protests against hikes in ticket prices for local transport in 1969, many of their guest worker acquaintances took part as well. This proved a major contribution to one of the few successes enjoyed by the New Left in the 1960s.[40] On the other side of the political divide, the Greek diplomatic corps' partially successful attempt to recruit guest workers into pro-junta groups meant that these right-wing organizations, which also contained several Greek businessmen and intellectuals who worked in Germany, also possessed a strong social mix.[41] The important role played by Greek academics and students in the construction of the social and political infrastructure of their community meant that ideological concerns not usually associated with the guest worker milieu were adopted by many Greek workers' organizations. Greek immigrants therefore had started to establish their own culture clubs and political discussion groups before the SPD and the trade unions became involved in the life of this community.

This reflected the high level of political mobilization in Greece in the run up to the 1967 military takeover, which meant that any major political shifts in their homeland were going to have serious consequences for the Greek diaspora.[42] Though rumours of a coup had been circulating since the early 1960s, the speed with which the military junta managed to take control of the state surprised many Greeks.[43] Once it became clear that the regime had cemented its grip on power, those opposed to it did their utmost to draw international attention to their cause. While centre-right politicians who fled Greece, such as Konstantinos Karamanlis, condemned the use of violence, exiled leaders of the Greek Left, including George Papandreou and his son Andreas, made ambiguous statements about the necessity for 'active' resistance. Following this lead, many opposition activists began to ask whether violent methods were needed to bring about the downfall of the military junta.[44]

Right-wing Greek immigrants who supported the regime were also prepared to use violent tactics. Pro-junta culture clubs and workers' associations had considerable resources at hand because of the financial backing they enjoyed from the Greek government.[45] Each Greek consulate had a labour attaché responsible for Greeks recruited by the labour importation programme who did his best to ensure that Greek immigrants joined workers' associations loyal to the regime. Senior figures in extreme right-wing immigrant organizations were even given financial aid by the Greek embassy and pensions from the labour ministry in Athens. After 1969, annual conventions took place in Greece where hundreds of pro-regime guest workers came together at the junta's expense in order to meet leading government figures and coordinate further action in the Federal Republic.[46] With this kind of support, right-wing Greek guest workers and students were able to mount an open challenge to their left-wing opponents.[47] Conversely, Greek workers who chose to join left-wing organizations or trade unions were faced with threats of retaliation from Greek consular staff such as the withdrawal of identity documents or the arrest of relatives still living in Greece.[48]

However, it was the open conflict between Greek and Turkish immigrants (of the Left and Right in both ethnic groups) in 1964, rather than subsequent political conflict within the Greek community, that provided the first indications of the growing militancy of Greek guest workers.[49] When ethnic tension between Greeks and Turks in Cyprus led to civil war in the mid-1960s, several factories in Germany witnessed heated disputes between Greek and Turkish guest workers. At one factory in Baden-Württemberg a mass brawl between Greeks and Turks erupted after one guest worker put up a pro-Greek Cypriot banner in the canteen.[50] The fact that the Turkish community became the largest of all the guest worker groups in the late 1960s, numbering over a million after 1972, meant that Greeks were likely to encounter and often come into conflict with Turkish counterparts wherever they lived and worked in the Federal Republic.[51]

Paradoxically, though relations between these two communities were often fraught, the manner in which the 1967 military takeover in Athens triggered an upsurge of political violence involving Greek immigrants presaged developments in the burgeoning Turkish community after the Turkish Army took power in a bloodless coup d'état on 12 March 1971. Though army leaders restored civilian rule after a few months, they systematically rewrote the Turkish constitution in order to strengthen their own position. Rather than damping down extremist political activity, this intervention destabilized Turkish society. During this brief period of military rule extreme left-wing organizations grew in strength, while police collusion with right-wing terrorist groups affiliated to the neo-fascist Nationalist Movement Party (*Milliyetçi Hareket Partisi* or MHP) and the ultra-nationalist Grey Wolves organization led to violent attacks upon targets affiliated with trade unions and the moderate Left.[52]

Immediately after the Turkish military coup, left-wing union activists and intellectuals fled to Germany, where they found refuge among sympathetic guest workers who helped build an extensive political infrastructure throughout the Turkish diaspora. The Grey Wolves were quick to react, and by 1975 had established their own network of guest worker organizations. This led to the final breakdown of the dormitory system as different Turkish political groups tried to take control of buildings in which companies housed guest workers.[53]

At the same time, Kurdish nationalist movements banned in Turkey established their own organizations in the Federal Republic, which would later be absorbed by the extreme nationalist PKK. The turf battles that accompanied the growth of a variety of such political organizations led to considerable street violence in cities with large Turkish populations, which occasionally involved gun battles and bombings between rival groups. As in the case of the underground war between supporters of the junta and opposition activists in the Greek community, a sudden shift in the political conditions of a labour exporting state meant that German law enforcement agencies suddenly found themselves in the middle of a conflict that they had not anticipated.[54]

The battles between the Left and Right in the Turkish community and between Turks and Kurds, examined in the work of Eva Østergaard-Nielsen[55] and Ertekin Özcan,[56] only reached their height around the time of the third postwar Turkish military coup of 1980.[57] The development of the Turkish and Kurdish communities demonstrates how the experience of Greek immigrants a decade earlier foreshadowed the kind of tensions that enveloped other politically diverse immigrant groups. While the undercurrent of tension between Turks and Greeks in the Federal Republic showed how the ethnic diversity of the immigrant population as a whole could lead to inter-communal political violence, the similarities in the manner in which political conflict manifested itself in these two communities is evidence of how much they had in common.

The period between 1964 and 1967 saw an increase in the number of Greek immigrant organizations in Germany.[58] This was partly the result of a desire among many Greek workers and students to seek out the company of their fellow nationals in what was often a hostile environment. Nevertheless, the fact that these organizations were founded along ideological lines sowed the seeds for continuing political conflict within the Greek community.[59] Battles between members of different workers' associations or culture clubs for control of places and events attended by the wider community were not just the manifestation of vague gang rivalries. Throughout the Greek community such intra-communal violence was seen as part of a wider battle for political dominance of the Greek diaspora. Thus a cinema playing Greek films or a site for a community event on an Orthodox saint's day would be treated by immigrant activists as bastions, which had to be conquered and protected from political opponents in order to attract the support of undecided or apolitical Greek immigrants.

Such political rivalries often became intertwined with personal disputes between individual Greeks. Thus many public disturbances involving Greeks could be portrayed both as acts of political violence or as the settling of personal vendettas between rival gangs.[60] Supporters of the Greek opposition as well as pro-junta activists usually emphasized the former when describing acts of violence in the Greek community. By contrast, police officials and the *Auswärtiges Amt* tried to play down the political nature of such incidents in order to avoid trouble with the Greek government. There was also a strong tendency on the part of the SPD as well as the New Left to portray anti-junta activists as the aggrieved victims of a proto-fascist regime. Conversely, West German officials and politicians close to the military regime in Athens often claimed that the Greek opposition had been subverted by the Communist Party and presented a threat to the Western Alliance.[61] These differences within the West German political establishment when it came to dealing with politicized Greek immigrants became particularly visible in a succession of violent incidents involving Greeks in Hanover and Munich between 1967 and 1973.

The heavy concentration of Greek immigrants and students in Hanover and other Lower Saxon cities was the result of the labour recruitment practices of major corporations based in Northern Germany. While Volkswagen (VW) had initially focused on the recruitment of Italian and Spanish workers, it also hired a large number of Greek immigrants for its factories in Hanover.[62] The Preussag steel plants in Salzgitter and Braunschweig, the Continental tire plant and the machine tool company Hanomag in Hanover hired workers from the same three ethnic groups. Following this example, several smaller companies supplying parts and equipment to these major corporations also started to hire workers from Greece.[63] In parallel, a growing number of Greek students were matriculated at local universities and polytechnics. Across West Germany, such regional concentrations became entrenched as subsequent waves of guest workers tried to settle in places where they could find relatives and friends.

The tensions that emerged in Hanover's Greek community after the military coup quickly came to the attention of police officers and local trade union officials in Lower Saxony. The first major brawls between left-wing and right-wing groups for control of a Greek cinema in Hanover were already reported in 1965, two years before the military takeover in Athens.[64] Militant Greek student groups in Hanover began to work with underground organizations formed in Greece in the immediate aftermath of the coup.[65] These included anarchist and communist groups such as PAM (Patriotic Antidictatorial Front) or PAK (Panhellenic Liberation Movement) that advocated the bombing of Greek diplomatic buildings and other state targets. By late 1967, the Hanoverian police force had already discovered a bomb buried in the garden of the Greek consulate, the first of a succession of bomb attacks on Greek diplomatic property and staff.[66] At the same time police investigators in Munich found a small brochure in a guest worker flat containing detailed bomb-making instructions for anti-junta groups. The preamble of this document clearly described the ultimate aims of opposition activists who organized these attacks on Greek government targets. Its terminology, with its emphasis on fascism and 'Praxis' was remarkably similar to the literature produced by the German *Rote Armee Fraktion* (RAF):

> Greek, oh You who are being oppressed by the fascist dictatorship and who has no other means at hand against the brutal violence, we deliver to You this small brochure, which represents a successful weapon against the dictatorship because it

is based on *Praxis* and nothing but *Praxis*. With this weapon – the recipe for catastrophes – You can take action that dictators and oppressed people will feel equally.[67]

Lower Saxon LKA investigators together with their colleagues on a federal level were quick to link the Greek activists who had written this brochure with attempted bombings in Hanover as well as other terrorist incidents across Western Europe perpetrated by supporters of the Greek opposition.[68]

As with the Croatian community, the inability of West German security services to recruit reliable informants in the Greek community made them heavily dependent on information supplied by Greek intelligence agencies. Although the BfV and BKA were able to acquire information about the structure and aims of more extreme groups through raids on flats and offices used by Greek activists, these searches were usually the product of tips passed on by Greek diplomats or German managers who wanted to prevent the spread of communism among their guest workers. Such cooperation between foreign diplomats and business circles enjoyed the tacit backing of conservative CDU/CSU politicians.[69] With the help of Greek officials, the BfV discovered links between the PAM and the more widespread *Lambrakis* youth organization run by the Greek Communist Party, which had offices in East Berlin. For senior members of the West German security services, such a discovery indicated that there were connections between the wider Greek opposition, anti-junta terrorist groups and the Soviet bloc.[70] In 1971, the arrest of two West German students at the Greek border by Yugoslav border guards after bomb-making equipment was found in their car also seemed to confirm that Greek opposition activists were cooperating with West German terrorist groups.[71]

The *Verfassungsschutz* and the *Kriminalämter* therefore tended to assume that left-wing Greeks should automatically be counted as potential pro-communist security risks. This stance was reflected in a number of reports produced by LKAs and LfVs exploring potential links between Greek anti-junta groups and the East German government in 1968 and 1969.[72] The fact that circumstantial evidence was often taken as proof of communist or East German intervention can be seen in this description of the nature of anti-junta activity in one memorandum circulated by the *Bundeskriminalamt*:

KOUNALAKIS [a functionary for the proto-communist EDA in West Germany], possesses, at the behest of and in cooperation with communist functionaries in Greece, covert contacts with a wide variety of collaborators in a wide variety of German cities. While the goals of their activity are not specifically directed against the political order of the Federal Republic of Germany, the nature, extent and effectiveness of the organization under their control in general, and the conspiratorial working methods used by KOUNALAKIS and his ideological allies in particular, represent a threat to the security of the state. It would be unrealistic to assume that a coming together of [Greek] émigrés and *Gastarbeiter* brought about by the communists would not, in the longer term, have a lasting impact on the existing democratic order of the FRG.[73]

This report went on to claim that other guest worker groups within the Turkish or Spanish communities were similarly vulnerable to communist infiltration and described the potential threat immigrants presented to West German democracy in the darkest terms:

> There are also indications [in the case of Turks and Spaniards], that the illegal KPD [the West German communists] and the SED [the East German Communist Party] have provided support to this infiltration of *Gastarbeiter* in the FRG in cooperation with respective central leaderships that are located abroad. This work [by the KPD and SED] is designed to have an impact on businesses as well as the wider economy.[74]

While security officials remained focused on the conflict between pro-junta groups and left-wing organizations, they largely ignored tensions within the anti-junta coalition. A heterogeneous assortment of political movements, including the orthodox Marxist EDA (United Democratic Left), the ideologically eclectic Centre Union or anarchist terror groups such as the PAM, competed for ascendancy within the Left.[75] In comparison, social democratic members of regional and federal parliaments were much better informed about developments within the Greek community than the professionals in the West German security services. Sharing anti-junta activists' disdain for the military regime in Athens, SPD and trade union functionaries intervened in the internal politics of the Greek community. In the process, tension between security officials and SPD leaders arising from such differing attitudes towards Greek immigrants came to the fore as a result of some of the less spectacular day-to-day violence dividing the Greek community in cities like Hanover.

Though bomb attacks on Greek consulates bearing all the hallmarks of urban terrorism drew the most attention from police and press in Lower Saxony, street fighting and violent protests made up the bulk of political violence involving the Greek community. One case that drew the attention of the West German press was two connected street brawls between rival groups of Greeks in Neustadt (a suburb of Hanover) on 11 and 12 April 1970. The first of these took place on the evening of 11 April as fifteen Greeks opposed to the junta confronted and then attacked another group of about twenty pro-regime guest workers sitting at a restaurant in Neustadt. This kicked off a set of fistfights outside the restaurant in which two participants were so heavily injured that they had to be taken to hospital.[76] On the following evening several pro-junta Greeks retaliated, dragging three known supporters of the Greek opposition out of a bar in another part of Hanover and beating them so severely that they had to be hospitalized as well.[77]

In the police inquiry that followed, German bystanders were unable to give any evidence about what the participants actually said since they had not spoken any German. Compounding these problems, investigators were almost unable to find a translator who was considered acceptable by both sides. The young student who finally did this work was herself worried about the impact her cooperation with German police might have on her family in Greece.[78]

When it came to the participants, the only point of agreement was that a discussion at the restaurant in Neustadt over a proposal to found a Greek cultural centre in Hanover backed by the Greek consulate had triggered this bout of fighting. Moreover, while pro-regime Greeks stated that the meeting in Neustadt had been stormed by supporters of the opposition, anti-junta activists (almost all of them members of the West German *IG Metall* union) as well as German trade union functionaries claimed that opposition activists who had attended this meeting had only become drawn into a brawl after provocation by junta supporters.[79]

Such contradictory testimony is not unusual when it comes to street brawls, be they politically driven or not. The fighting on 11 and 12 of April 1970 also had some precedent in Hanover. Two years before, fighting between pro and anti-junta Greeks at a cinema showing Greek-language films led to many arrests. Triggered by a shouting match between individual Greek workers, this brawl drew several dozen guest workers from both sides of the political divide who were drinking in nearby bars into a rolling street battle that had to be broken up by the riot police.[80] Yet the incidents on 11 and 12 of April 1970 did differ from previous confrontations when it came to the subsequent involvement of third parties. With a project supported by the consulate being the initial point of contention, it was not surprising that the Greek consul decided to intervene. A week after this incident he wrote several letters to the local press, which claimed that the Greek opposition was using organized street gangs akin to the SA and communist action groups of the 1930s:

> We Greeks who come from the cradle of democracy can recognise the true face of these groups of thugs, a mug which our German friends ought to know from the past.[81]

The consul's attempt to use recent German history to condemn his political opponents was not crowned with any great success outside the small circle that already supported the junta. However much press commentators expressed disapproval of the behaviour of both sides involved in these brawls, these aggressively partisan comments did not improve the image of the Greek government in Hanover. Rather, the overwrought rhetoric used by Greek diplomats even provoked centre-right commentators, irritated by such historical analogies, into highlighting the junta's poor human rights record.[82] Aware of the close links between consular officials and the pro-junta activists embroiled in this affair, the state prosecutor delayed the interrogation of local Greek diplomats as long as possible. The Greek ambassador did not necessarily help junta supporters by declaring that in comparison to Athens the city of Hanover was an insignificant and barbarous place.[83]

The Greek foreign ministry was forced to pay attention to this street brawl because of the support given by Lower Saxon trade union functionaries to the victims of the assault on 12 April. On 13 April, a representative of the *IG Metall* manufacturing union accompanied one of the victims of the attack at the

Ratskeller bar to the local police station. Together with three other Greek union members, this *IG Metall* official helped this severely injured anti-junta activist with the paperwork needed to press charges against his attackers. This was quickly followed by an official complaint made by the Lower Saxon *IG Metall* to the Hanoverian police department about the lack of police protection for vulnerable anti-junta activists.[84] Union officials also produced a Greek consular employee who claimed that the consul himself had helped organize gangs of pro-junta thugs whose job it was to intimidate supporters of the opposition, an intervention that dismayed police officers investigating the case.[85]

Reaffirming the commitment of West German trade unions to the Greek opposition (despite its ambivalent attitude towards the use of violence), a lengthy report about developments in the Greek community in Hanover after 11 April 1970 was compiled by *IG Metall* called '*Gefahr für griechische Demokraten in der Bundesrepublik Deutschland*' or, in English, 'Danger for Greek Democrats in the Federal Republic of Germany'. This document was sent to trade union centres and major newspapers across West Germany and contained interviews with anti-junta Greeks who were either involved in the fighting over the proposed community centre or were caught up in similar incidents in 1970.[86] Whereas police reports tended to interpret such cases as manifestations of personal rivalries within the Greek community, the *IG Metall* report focused on the union background of the anti-junta participants. It also went on to condemn the Greek military government and implicitly criticized the West German police for not doing enough to defend the rights of Greek workers. The vehement tone of this document is set out in the introductory note written by Heinrich Menius, the most senior *IG Metall* functionary in Lower Saxony at that time:

> The Circumstances of Greek Union Members in their Guest Country the Federal Republic of Germany.

There are well founded suspicions that the acts of terror directed against Greek citizens and employees described in this document were centrally coordinated by officials at the [Greek] consulate. We demand that the General Consul in Hanover and his helpers be expelled from the Federal Republic of Germany ... We demand the punishment of the perpetrators named here and that they be expelled from the Federal Republic of Germany! Foreign employees working in our country must receive guarantees that they will enjoy the same constitutional rights possessed by every German citizen. All of those residing in our country should be equal before the law and protected from acts of terror and revenge. We demand from the responsible institutions, that action should be taken as quickly as possible to ensure the security of our guests ['Gäste'] and citizens.[87]

This introduction in itself provides quite a revealing insight into the relationship between trade union leaders and politicized guest workers. On the one hand, it stakes out the claim of *IG Metall* as the defender of the rights of Greek democrats in the Federal Republic. Yet by using the terms '*Gastland*' for the Federal Republic and '*Gäste*' for Greek workers, German union functionaries signalled that they shared the general consensus within the West German political establishment that migrant workers should only stay in the Federal Republic for a limited period of time. For trade union leaders as well as rank and file German workers, there was no contradiction between backing immigrant political causes such as opposition to the Greek junta and pressuring the government to foster the eventual return of economic migrants to their homelands. According to trade union logic, helping to bring about political change in Greece and other authoritarian regimes in Southern Europe would hasten the voluntary repatriation of guest workers who might otherwise have preferred to remain in a democratic Federal Republic.[88]

This document blamed the escalation of political conflict within the Greek community upon the arrival in Hanover of a new general consul called Athanosios Exintaris at the beginning of 1970. The testimony of several former employees at the consulate (that was repeated in much of the press reporting on the events of 11 and 12 April 1970) is used in this *IG Metall* document to emphasize Exintaris' desire to destroy Greek opposition groups in Lower Saxony. In contrast to the portrayal of the incident on 11 April by pro-junta groups, the trade union brochure repeated claims made by opposition supporters that they had been attacked by government supporters at the meeting in Neustadt.[89] In the brochure as well as subsequent interviews with the press, *IG Metall* functionaries portrayed incidents like the fighting on 11 and 12 April 1970 as evidence of a campaign of intimidation by the Greek government and its German allies designed to stop the successful unionization of Greek immigrant labourers. Trade union leaders believed that this campaign could cause a split between unionized German workers and non-union immigrants, which would enable corporations and businessmen to erode workers' rights. Thus, a link was created between German business circles hostile to West German unions and a Greek authoritarian regime that had destroyed the Greek union movement.[90]

Attempts by Greek labour attachés to punish Greek guest workers who decided to join West German trade unions confirmed these fears. This issue came to a head in Lower Saxony, where managers at several manufacturers in Hanover openly expressed support for the Greek consulate. At these factories, Greek employees known to be supporters of the regime were given considerable opportunity by management to intimidate guest workers close to the trade unions. Supporters of the opposition regularly experienced shop-floor bullying while the process to elect the guest workers' representative committee was rigged in favour of right-wing Greeks.[91] Such cases of collusion between German managers, Greek diplomats and pro-junta guest workers were already causing considerable disquiet among trade unionists before April 1970. At VW, managers even fired pro-regime Greeks involved in acts of political violence who worked at VW factories in order to avoid any problems with *IG Metall*.[92] Nevertheless, the arrest by Hanoverian police of a Greek diplomat for blackmailing Greek union members in August 1970 showed that such intimidation was still taking place at other companies. In collusion with the German owner of an auto parts factory, this diplomat had tried to force Greeks to leave *IG Metall* by cutting their bonus pay, having them beaten up by regime loyalists in the dormitory and threatening state retribution against their relatives in Greece.[93]

The fact that the Lower Saxon employers' federation condemned the German managers entangled in this affair indicated that such anti-union measures did not necessarily meet the approval of other businessmen in the region. When asked by the press about the blackmail case in August 1970, a VW director pointed out that some senior executives valued the ability of union functionaries to maintain discipline among their guest worker employees and reduce tension between German and non-German colleagues:

> We highly value the work of the unions when it comes to integrating Greek *Gastarbeiter* in their workplace.[94]

The partnership between Greek regime loyalists and conservative German businessmen backfired badly for the junta. The moderate stance taken by West German corporations such as VW meant that junta supporters had to focus their efforts on smaller companies.[95] By encouraging West German trade unions to view conflicts within the Greek community as an issue involving key interests of their own German clientele, the concerted attack coordinated by Greek diplomats upon immigrant union members increased the support of the SPD, DGB and *IG Metall* for the Greek opposition. Even acts of violence committed by anti-junta activists in the Federal Republic did not deter trade union functionaries and social democratic politicians from providing law-abiding Greek groups with financial and logistical support.[96]

Indirect links between SPD and union functionaries and the more violent elements of the Left in the Greek community were particularly evident in late 1960s Munich. Senior members of the Greek opposition in Bavaria who supported the Centre Union or Christian democratic organizations were either unable or unwilling to exclude groups close to the New Left or the communist KKE. More radical left-wing groups in turn worked together with their counterparts in the West German New Left as well as organizations that were covertly backed by the East German government such as the *Vereinigung der Verfolgten des Naziregimes* (VVN) or the *Deutsche Kommunistische Partei* (DKP). As long as the junta condemned all opposition activity as potentially communist, opposition organizations in Greece and throughout the Greek diaspora were prepared to cooperate against it despite deep underlying ideological differences.[97] The campaign against the military regime in Greece therefore became one of the few political issues after 1969 in which senior union and SPD officials found themselves working cheek by jowl with the kind of socialist, communist and anarchist militants whom they otherwise considered to be dangerous rivals for control of the Left.

Meetings with unions and social democrat participation repeatedly witnessed calls for armed resistance against the junta by a variety of Greek and German speakers.[98] Following such political rallies, militant guest workers and students would often move on to vandalize Greek diplomatic property or surround bars and restaurants frequented by supporters of the military regime. The resulting potential for serious mayhem led police in Munich to impose major security restrictions on meetings and demonstrations organized by Greek opposition groups and their German allies.[99] Such rallies could have anything from 300 to 1000 participants, with a fifth of these demonstrators usually German supporters and the rest Greek guest workers and students. One or two plainclothes policemen would also be in attendance in order to ensure that nothing took place that could be construed as a call for violent action.

A rally at the *Franziskanerkeller* on 20 April 1968 that was followed by a march to the Munich memorial commemorating the victims of fascism was typical of these kinds of meetings organized by the Pan-Hellenic Antidictarorial Movement (*Gesamtgriechische antidiktatorische Union* or PAE in Greek). The PAE was mostly made up of students close to the *Sozialistischer Deutscher Studentenbund* (SDS) and other bastions of the West German New Left. With (according to police figures) 500 participants, including fifty Germans, this was one of several rallies in that month to mobilize Greeks opposed to the junta.[100] After a few words of greeting by the local head of the PAE, a mid level functionary from the printing unions (*Gewerkschaft Druck und Papier*) declared that he and his organization supported the Greek opposition. He was followed by a much younger student representative of the SDS, who also pledged solidarity with Greek anti-fascists and (according to the police report) ended his speech with this slogan:

> 'Oppressed of all nations unite!' ... and received a noisy ovation. Cries of 'Ho-Ho-Ho Chi Minh' were also heard.[101]

Even more incongruous than a union functionary attending a meeting at which much of the crowd punctuated speeches with shouts of 'Ho-Ho-Ho Chi Minh', a member of a Turkish student organization also declared his support for the anti-junta cause. An attack on a Greek academic who was subsequently spirited away by the police by several participants who believed that he was an informer working for the Greek consulate was the only violent incident at this event.[102]

Another anti-junta rally at the *Franziskanerkeller* on the following day showed how social democrats and radical members of the New Left could end up sitting next to each other because of their support of the Greek opposition. This meeting was put together by the Munich district organization of the SPD together with guest workers who belonged to the local Centre Union organization. There were, however, a number of Greek and German students among the 350 participants that police observers suspected to be SDS members. The two main speakers at this meeting were Wilhelm Hoegner, a former *Ministerpräsident* of Bavaria in the early 1950s, and Hans Kolo, who was head of the social democratic youth organization in Munich. Both spoke at length about the need to integrate Greece further into Western European political institutions such as the EEC once the junta was removed from office. In the middle of the former *Ministerpräsident*'s speech, the same Greek academic who had been identified as an informer for the consulate at the PAE protest march had to be escorted out of the *Franziskanerkeller* after several participants tried to beat him up again.[103]

While this tussle demonstrated the latent potential for violence among politically moderate supporters of the Greek opposition, the heckling that accompanied Kolo's speech uncovered ideological strains within the anti-junta coalition. These interruptions, which mostly consisted of shouts of 'Ho-Ho-Ho-Chi Minh', came from SDS members in the audience. In order to distance himself from these hecklers and shift the focus of the meeting away from conflicts within the Left over the role of the United States, Kolo finally faced down one SDS activist:

> The German participants ought to solve their own problems and leave the Greeks in peace.[104]

As long as Germans allied to the Greek opposition believed that the Greek military regime marked the beginning of a resurgence of fascism across Europe, such efforts to separate the campaign against the junta from ideological conflict within the West German Left were unlikely to succeed.

The spectre of violent political action at the *Franziskanerkeller* emerged in an even more open fashion at an anti-junta rally on 14 September 1968. Organized by Greek émigrés close to the SPD, according to police reports there were 400 participants, of which fifty were Germans associated with the radical Left. While the main Greek speaker was Dr Carlos Papoulias, a well-known left-wing academic, the only German to hold a speech was Herbert Klinger, who in his role as head of the *Karl-Marx-Gesellschaft* and the VVN was a prominent member of the old Stalinist Left. While the speeches were relatively uncontroversial declarations of solidarity, the slogans chanted by the crowd in the course of the rally were open calls for armed resistance to the Greek military regime at home and abroad. A recording made by the police contains chants in Greek such as:

> 'We want weapons!!' … 'Give us weapons!!' … 'Resistance!!'[105]

Intriguingly, the Greek student acting as a translator for the police at this rally did not translate these slogans even after being asked about them several times by the senior police officer at the scene.[106] Nonetheless, this incident indicates the extent to which the police response to such events could be dependent upon immigrant intermediaries. A recalcitrant translator or interlocutor could mislead German policemen or intelligence agents who did not speak any of the major guest worker or émigré languages.

The point at which violent rhetoric was most likely to lead to violent action was when both sides of the Greek political divide faced off against one another. A meeting that resulted in the kind of street fighting that most worried West German police took place on 3 November 1968, at a rally organized by the Greek labour attaché in remembrance of the Italian declaration of war upon Greece in 1940. The Greek general consul held a speech that (as related in a police report) illustrated the world view of many Greek guest workers who remained loyal to the junta:

> In his speech, the Greek General Consul emphasized the historical significance of this day [the Italian invasion in 1940] and expressed the opinion that Greece has been, at that time, preserved from fascism and, by the current government, from communism.[107]

After an hour of relative peace, the 650 guest workers attending this event were suddenly confronted by 200 counter-demonstrators (eighty of them were German students) who stormed the *Hackerkeller's* beer garden. Despite the best efforts by the organizer to turn up the volume of the sound system inside, anti-junta slogans such as 'Nieder mit dem Faschismus' (down with fascism), 'Pathakos Mörder' (Pathakos murderer) or 'Freiheit für Griechenland' (freedom for Greece) were heard inside the *Hackerkeller* hall. Pro-junta guest workers sitting in the beer garden got into fistfights with opposition activists before the police were able to divide the two groups. To confuse matters further a group of so-called 'Rockers', working-class youths interested in motorcycles, hard rock and hostile towards 'long-haired' middle-class students, arrived on the scene and promptly attacked several left-wing Germans demonstrating with the anti-junta Greeks. Some of these 'Rockers' tried to forcibly cut off the hair of one young anti-junta German before he managed to escape under police protection.[108]

Such confrontations between pro- and anti-junta activists made up the bulk of violent incidents involving the Greek community. The actions of small terror groups such as the PAK could lead to a drastic reaction from West German security services against the most militant elements of the Greek opposition in the Federal Republic. However, political rallies such as those in Hanover and Munich show how in the Greek community political violence was not just perpetrated by small conspiratorial groupings. Rather, it was a widespread response to the threat posed by an authoritarian government and its representatives in the Federal Republic towards those who did not support the junta. Only in this context can the continuing support of large elements of the West German parliamentary Left for the Greek opposition be understood.

The DGB, which considered the close relationship between Greek diplomats and conservative German businessmen to be a threat to its own position, ignored the ambivalent stance of its Greek allies when it came to acts of violence directed against the Greek state. Bombings or shootings may have attracted the attention of the wider West German public, but these remained isolated incidents whose effects on most Greeks in the Federal Republic were limited. Forcing local police services as well as LKAs and LfVs to deal with the divisions within the Greek diaspora, recurring brawls, street battles and minor scuffles were what ultimately led West German security officials to treat the Greek community as a major security risk despite SPD support for the anti-junta cause. The kind of low-level street violence examined here and its intermingling of ideological commitment with personal vendettas had a far greater impact on the lives of Greek students and guest workers.

****

What made the Greek case different from other immigrant communities was the fundamental political changes that took place in Greece after Greek guest workers had become a considerable presence in West Germany. Though Algeria had also gone through a period of upheaval after 1945, this process had largely worked itself out before the guest worker process had really gained momentum. Ironically, perhaps the only other state that experienced a similarly sudden set of political shifts between 1945 and 1973 was Turkey, where the military took power in 1961, 1970 and 1982.[109] Yet, while the turmoil in Turkey did not lead to any close cooperation between Turkish activists and West German political groups, the impact of the military coup of 1967 in Greece had a direct impact on both the West German political establishment and the German New Left because of the ambiguous historical legacy of the 1940s. As a result, the large and socially diverse Greek community was quickly drawn into the domestic political conflicts of the FRG.[110]

The reticence displayed by West German security services towards the Greek community confirms the importance of broader political factors, rather than any specific concerns about 'Innere Sicherheit', or 'homeland security', when it came to state responses to immigrant political violence. Until the late 1960s, a West German state dominated by the vehemently anti-communist CDU/CSU was faced with a Greek guest worker community whose homeland political system was a constitutional monarchy. In that context, the influence of the Greek Communist Party over Greek guest workers and students triggered anxieties among centre-right politicians and security officials that the importation of labour could lead to the rise of a pro-Soviet fifth column in the Federal Republic. As a result, the activity of legally registered Greek leftist organizations and covert communist networks (described in the 1965 report on the EDA) came under heavy surveillance from West German intelligence agencies.[111] The fact that several of these networks had contact with the office of the EDA in East Berlin only helped to heighten the concerns of the BKA and

BfV over the ideological reliability of Greek guest workers. This tendency in the security services of equating all left-wing activity among guest workers and émigrés with support for communism, rather than differentiating between the EDA and the more socially democratic oriented Centre Union, was extraordinarily clumsy. It also had the potential to alienate the wider Greek community.

Both the coalition between the CDU/CSU and SPD and the Athens military coup of 1967 changed this state of affairs. The presence of social democrats in key ministries and the SPD's subsequent role as the dominant party of government after 1969 meant that a more subtle approach towards the communist bloc and communist parties began to take root. Though social democrats were keen to thwart the recruitment of Greek guest workers by communist organizations, they were better prepared to take a more measured and balanced approach towards the activity of other leftist organizations than the security services. Of equal significance were the ideological implications of the military coup in Athens. Whereas in the early 1960s West German security services and the *Auswärtiges Amt* believed that Greek democracy seemed to be under threat from a communist uprising, in reality the democratic framework of the Greek monarchy was shattered by anti-communist army officers. Such a seminal event was bound to change attitudes across the West German political spectrum towards Greek politics and the political life of the Greek diaspora.[112]

The strength of the German Left's dislike for the junta can be seen in the strong support given by union functionaries to Greek guest workers facing intimidation from Greek diplomats and regime loyalists in Hanover and Munich. The active support of Greek diplomats and intelligence agents (occasionally in cooperation with conservative German business managers) for right-wing Greek guest workers only provoked the more moderate elements of the West German Left, which believed that such intervention was a potential threat to the democratic order of the Federal Republic, rather than just an internal Greek issue. However much anti-junta activists involved in political violence were pursued by the Munich police or the Lower Saxon *Landeskriminalamt,* West German security services became more careful in their dealings with the political organizations to which these activists belonged. The suppression of Greek left-wing organizations would therefore remain unlikely as long as they and their leading members remained close to the SPD and the trade unions.

Ultimately, the approach taken by West German state institutions and political organizations towards violent immigrant activists was not that different to their approach towards their peaceful counterparts in other immigrant communities. West German state policy concerning immigrant political violence was not determined by any deep abhorrence of violent action and the threat it represented to the stability of the Federal Republic. Rather, the response of the West German state was shaped by a combination of strategic ideological concerns and pragmatic tactical considerations. For all the ritualized uniformity of the shock and horror expressed by West German politicians and journalists in reaction to political violence committed by worker or émigré 'guests', German state institutions and political organizations were not neutral arbitrators of conflict within these new immigrant societies. In reality, by either backing one group over another or cooperating with homeland regimes, West German political parties, unions, employers' federations, security services and nongovernmental organizations were as much participants in the battles going on within immigrant communities as immigrants themselves.

Notes

1.   H. Prantl. 2002. *Verdächtig: Der starke Staat und die Politik der inneren Unsicherheit*, Hamburg: Europa Verl., 53–54.
2.   P. Pau and K. Schubert. 1999. 'Bundesgrenzschutz: Eine omnipräsente und omnipotente Bundespolizei?', *Bürgerrechte & Polizei/CILIP* 62, 19–25.
3.   P.J. Katzenstein. 1990. *West Germany's Internal Security Policy: State and Violence in the 1970s and 1980s*, Cornell: Western Societies Program (Cornell Centre for International Studies nr. 28), 27–29.
4.   C. Gröpl. 1993. *Die Nachrichtendienste im Regelwerk der deutschen Sicherheitsverwaltung – Legitimation, Organisation und Abgrenzungsfragen*, Berlin: Duncker und Humblot (Schriften zum Öffentlichen Recht, Band 646), 214.
5.   W.-D. Narr. 2001. 'Die arme Verfassung: Verfassungsschutz, V-Leute und NPD-Verbot', *Bürgerrechte und Polizei/CILIP*, 71, 78.
6.   A. Funk. 1991. '"Innere Sicherheit": Symbolische Politik und exekutive Praxis', in B. Blanke and H. Wollman (eds), *Die alte Bundesrepublik: Kontinuität und Wandel*, Opladen: Westdeutscher Verl, 371.
7.   T. Naftali. 2004. 'Berlin to Baghdad: the Perils of Hiring Enemy Intelligence', *Foreign Affairs* 83(4), 127.
8.   P. Mueller and M. Müller. 2002. *Gegen Freund und Feind – Der BND: Geheime Politik und Schmutzige Geschäfte*, Hamburg: Rowohlt Verl, 254–60.
9.   C. von Braunmühl. 1973. *Kalter Krieg und Friedliche Koexistenz: Die Außenpolitik der SPD in der Großen Koalition*, Frankfurt, a.M.: Suhrkamp Verl, 38–42.
10. D. Schenk. 2003. *Die Braunen Wurzeln des BKA*, Frankfurt a.M.: Fischer Verl, 304.
11. Ibid., 271.
12. H.-H. Heldmann. 1989. *Verwaltung Versus Verfassung: Ausländerrecht 1965–1988*, *Europäische Hochschulschriften* Vol. 882, Frankfurt a.M.: Peter Lang Verl, 92–95. Heldmann was also part of the defence team at the RAF trials at Stammheim in the mid-1970s.
13. B.E. Schmitter. 1980. 'Immigrants and Associations', *International Migration Review*, 14, 185–86.
14. Pol. A.A.Ber., B 26, Nr. 256, *Brief des Bayerischen Staatsministeriums des Innern an Herrn Andreas Borakos*, Re.: 'Tätigkeit des "Koordinationskomitee für Cypernfragen" (SEKA) in München', München, 19 October 1964.
15. *D.S.*, 'Gastarbeiter: Lieber Piano', 10 April 1967.
16. B. Spengler. 1995. *Systemwandel in Griechenland und Spanien: Ein Vergleich*, Saarbrücken: Peter Lang Verl. (Saarbrücker Politikwissenschaft Nr. 20), 108–110.
17. M. Balfour. 1982. *West Germany: a Contemporary History*, London: Croom Helm, 224–29.
18. Bay HstA Mun., Stk. Nr. 13173, *Brief Erwin Lauerbach (Staatssekretär im Bayer. Staarsministerium f. Unterricht u. Kultus) an Dr. hc. F.-J. Strauß a.D. MdB.*, Re.: 'Unterredung mit Griech. Ministerpräsident', Munich, 23 April 1972.

19. Bay. HstA. Mun., Stk. Nr. 13173, *Bayerischer Landtag, 7. Wahlperiode, Stenographischer Bericht*, 20. Sitzung: Fragestunde, Munich, 24 November 1971.

20. K. Featherstone and D. Katsoudas. 1987. *Political Change in Greece: Before and After the Colonels*, New York: St. Martin's Press, 221, 233.

21. G. Wallraff and E. Spoo (eds). 1982. *Unser Faschismus nebenan: Erfahrungen bei NATO-Partnern*, Hamburg: Kiepenheuer und Witsch, 96, German original: 'Die Obristen haben das Chaos des alten Parteiensystems eingedämmt und das Abgleiten in den Kommunismus verhindert.'

22. Pol. A.A.Ber., B 26, Nr. 437, *Bericht (der Botschaft Athen)*, Re.: 'Kongress der Vereinigung der Griechen in Westdeutschland (in Saloniki)', Athens, 17 December 1971.

23. Spengler, *Systemwandel in Griechenland und Spanien*, 83.

24. Pol. A.A.Ber., B 26, Nr. 432, *Bericht der Botschaft Athen*, Re.: 'Freilassung von Mangakis', Athens, 18 March 1972.

25. Featherstone and Katsoudas, *Political Change in Greece*, 118–19.

26. S.-S. Spiliotis. 1997. '"An Affair of Politics, Not Justice": The Mertens Trial (1957–1959) and Greek-German Relations', in M. Mazower (ed.), *After the War Was Over: Reconstructing the Family Nation and State in Greece 1943–1960*, Princeton: Princeton University Press, 298–300.

27. Pol A.A.Ber., B 26, Nr. 134, *Bericht Legationsrat Walters an der Zentrale Rechtsschutzstelle*, Re.: 'Mertens', Bonn, 23 April 1959.

28. Bay. HstA. Mun., Stk. Nr. 16656, *Berichte über Innere Angelegenheiten*, Re.: 'Fall Mertens', Munich, April 1961.

29. Wallraff and Spoo, *Unser Faschismus Nebenan*, 28–31; or Pol A.A.Ber., B 26, Nr. 437, *Bericht Botschaft Athen*, Re.: 'Günther Grass – Besuch und Vortrag', Athens, 18 June 1971.

30. Pol. A.A.Ber., B 42, Nr. 435, *Griechenland – Innere Angelegenheiten*, Re.: 'Teilnahme von Theodorakis an einer Veranstaltung in Bonn', Bonn, 1 June 1972.

31. For a good example of the manner in which this rhetoric was deployed see *D.S.*, 'Griechen: Schwarze Krallen', 14 April 1969; and *D.S.*, 'Griechische Gastarbeiter: Lieber Piano', 28 April 1967.

32. Pol. A.A.Ber., B 26, Nr. 420, *Bericht Bayer. Staatsministerium des Innern am Auswärtigen Amt*, 'Re.: Politische Betätigung von Exilgriechen in der Bundesrepublik Deutschland', Munich, 22 November 1968, German original: 'Auch werden im Hinblick auf die Bündnisverpflichtungen aus dem NATO-Vertrag erheblich Belange der Bundesrepublik verletzt ... Das Bayer. Staatsministerium des Innern möchte daher anregen, ebenso wie das für Exilkroaten geschehen ist, die Tätigkeit derjenigen griechischen Organisationen vereinsrechtlich zu prüfen, von deren extrem-politischen Umtrieben eine Gefährdung der Sicherheit oder der öffentlichen Ordnung ausgeht ... In die Überlegen sollten zweckmäßigerweise auch ausländerrechtliche Maßnahmen (z.B. Einreisesperre für Agitatoren aus dem Ausland) einbezogen werden.'

33. Pol. A.A.Ber., B 26, Nr. 420, *Brief Bayer. Staatsministerium des Innern an den Bundesminister Herrn Dr. Ernst Benda*, Re.: 'Politische Betätigung von Exilgriechen in der Bundesrepublik Deutschland', Munich, 5 October 1968.

34. U. Herbert and K. Hunn. 2001. 'Guest Workers and Policy on Guest Workers in the Federal Republic', in H. Schissler (ed.), *The Miracle Years: a Cultural History of West Germany 1949–1968*, Princeton: Princeton University Press, 193.

35. NHstA. Hann., Nds. 100, Nr. 9, *Berichte über Studentendemonstrationen*, Re.: 'Griechen', Hanover, November 1969.

36. Bay HstA. Mun., Stk. Nr. 13173, *Deutsch-Griechische Beziehungen*, Re.: 'Griechische Vereine und Arbeiterkommissionen', April 1972.

37. NHstA. Hann., Nds. 147, Nr. 225, *Ermittlungsakte zu Sprengstoffanschlag am Griechischen Konsulat*, Re.: 'Beschwerden wegen Übersetzungspersonal', 7 September 1970.

38. NHstA. Hann., Nds. 147, Nr. 386, *Berichte zu Gewerkschaftsangelegenheiten*, Re.: 'Ermittlungsverfahren gegen griechischen Beamten wegen Erpressung griechischer Gastarbeiter um Austritt aus der Gewerkschaft zu erzwingen', Hanover, 24 August, 1970.

39. Pol. A.A.Ber., B 26, Nr. 438, *Berichte des BKA zur illegalen Tätigkeit griechischer Gruppen*, Re.: 'Zusammenarbeit mit SDS u.a.', Bonn, 31 January 1970 to 20 February 1971.

40. NHstA. Hann., Nds. 100, Nr. 6, *Berichte zu Studentenunruhen*, Re.: 'Aktion Roter Punkt', May 1969–October 1969.

41. The development of state-backed *Gastarbeiter* organizations was tracked by the *Auswärtiges Amt* with a surprising amount of concern. This reflected suspicions even among more conservative diplomats that the military regime was not a reliable partner. See Pol. A.A.Ber., B 26, Nr. 437, *Berichte: Deutsches Generalkonsulat Thessaloniki*, Re.: 'Kongress der "Vereinigung der Griechen in Westdeutschland" in Saloniki', Thessaloniki, 30 August 1971 and 17 December 1971.

42. C.M. Woodhouse. 1985. *The Rise and Fall of the Greek Colonels*, London: Granada, 36–38.

43. D.H. Close. 2000. *Greece since 1945: Politics, Economy and Society*, London: Pearson Education, 240–51.

44. Woodhouse, *The Rise and Fall of the Greek Colonels*, 16–19.

45. *D.S.*, 'Griechen – Schwarze Krallen', 14 April 1969.

46. Pol. A.A.Ber., B 26, Nr 437, *Berichte: deutsches Generalkonsulat Thessaloniki*, Re.: 'Kongress der Vereinigung der Griechen in Westdeutschland', Thessaloniki, 30 August 1971 and 17 December 1971.

47. *D.S.*, 'Verbrechen: Griechen-Terror – Arm der Obristen', 27 April 1970.

48. Bay. HstA. Mun., Polizeidirektion München Nr. 9374, 'Dokumentation – Gefahr für griechische Demokraten in der Bundesrepublik Deutschland – Herausgeber IG Metall, Ortsverwaltung Hannover, H. Menius', Hannover, 7 June, 1970.

49. Pol A.A.Ber., B 26, Nr. 256, *Bericht des Bayerischen Staatsministeriums für Bundesangelegenheiten*, Re.: 'Politische Betätigung griechischer Arbeiter und Studenten in München', Munich, 2 November 1964.

50. Pol. A.A.Ber., B 26, Nr. 256, *Brief des Bayerischen Staatsministeriums des Innern an Herrn Andreas Borakos*, Re.: 'Tätigkeit des "Koordinationskomitee für Cypernfragen" (SEKA) in München', München, 19 October 1964.

51. F. Sen. 1994. *Ausländer in der BRD: Ein Handbuch*, Opladen: Lesle und Budrich, 15–16.

52. H. Pope and N. Pope. 1997. *Turkey Unveiled: Atatürk and After*, London: John Murray Ltd., 133–37.

53. *D.S.*, 'Ausländer: Graue Wölfe', 23 August 1976.

54. E. Özcan. 1989. *Türkische Immigrantenorganisationen in der Bundesrepublik Deutschland*, Berlin: Hitit Verl, 171–74.

55. E.K. Østergaard-Nielsen. 1998. *Diaspora Politics: the Case of Immigrants and Refugees from Turkey Residing in Germany since 1980*, Thesis (D.Phil.), Oxford: University of Oxford.

56. Özcan, *Türkische Immigrantenorganisationen in der Bundesrepublik Deutschland*.

57. Ibid., 288–92.

58. NHstA. Hann., Nds. 147, Nr. 225, *Akten des Landeskriminalamtes zu Politische Bedrohungen/ Anschläge 1960-1975*, Re.: 'Gewaltfälle – Griechen I 1965–1967', Hanover, June 1976.

59. *D.S.*, 'Gastarbeiter: Lieber Piano', 10 April 1967.

60. Bay. HstA. Mun., Pol. Dir. Nr. 9374, *Bericht – Polizeipräsidium Hannover an Regierungspräsident München*, Re.: 'Gewalttätige Ausseinandersetzungen zwischen Griechen am 11. und 12.4.1970 in Neustadt/Rbge.', Hanover, 26 June 1970.

61. Pol. A.A.Ber., B 26, Nr. 420, *Bericht Auswärtiges Amt Referat V3*, Re.: 'Politische und terroristische Betätigung von Ausländern und Emigrantenorganisationen in der Bundesrepublik Deutschland', Bonn, 10 September 1969.

62. NHstA. Hann., Nds. 100, Nr. 148, *Vermerk LKA*, Re.: 'Ausländer in Niedersachsen', Hanover, 23 February 1970.

63. NHstA. Hann., Nds. 100, Nr. 148, *Innenministerium – Ausländerangelegenheiten 1969–1979*, 'Re.: Vorbeugende Bekämpfung terroristischer Aktionen von Ausländern: Hintergründe', Hanover, 6 May 1967.

64. NHstA. Hann., Nds. 147, Nr. 225, *Akten des Landeskriminalamtes zu Politische Bedrohungen/ Anschläge 1960–1975*, Re.: 'Gewaltfälle –Griechen I 1965–1967', Hanover, June 1976.

65. NHstA. Hann., Nds. 100, Nr. 148, *Innenministerium – Ausländerangelegenheiten 1969–1979*, 'Re.: Vorbeugende Bekämpfung terroristischer Aktionen von Ausländern: Hintergründe', Hanover, 6 May 1967.

66. NHstA. Hann., Nds. 100, Nr. 148,*Bundes- und Landeskriminalämter*, Re.: 'Bericht der Unterkommision "Vorbeugende Bekämpfung terroristischer Aktionen von Ausländern"', Bad Godesberg, 7 May 1969.

67. Bay. HstA. Mun., Pol. Dir. Nr. 9374, *Bericht KK III vom 13.4. 1970*: 'Übersetzung', Munich, 13 April 1970, German original: 'Grieche, der Du von der faschistischen Diktatur unterdrückt wirst und keine anderen Mittel gegen die brutale Gewalt in die Hand hast, wir liefern Dir diese kleine Broschüre, die eine erfolgreiche Waffe gegen die Diktatur darstellt, weil sie auf Praxis und nichts anderem als Praxis beruht. Mit dieser Waffe – dem Rezept bei Katastrophen – kannst Du Aktionen unternehmen, die Diktatoren und unterdrückte Menschen genauso spüren.'

68. NHstA. Hann., Nds. 100, Nr. 148, *Bericht einer Tagung des BKAs und der LKAs*, Re.: 'Der Unterkommission "Vorbeugende Bekämpfung terroristischer Aktionen von Ausländern"', Bad Godesberg, 7 May 1969.

69. *D.S.*, 'Griechenland Regime-Werbung: Reise Gratis', 8 June 1970. The bulk of this article however describes how the Greek military regime successfully bought the loyalty of several CSU members of the *Bundestag* by offering them free vacations on the Aegean Islands.

70. Pol. A.A.Ber., B 26, Nr. 420, *Bericht des Bayer. Staatsministerium des Innern*, Re.: 'Politische Betätigung von Exilgriechen in der Bundesrepublik Deutschland', Munich, 5 November 1968.

71. Pol. A.A.Ber., B 26, Nr. 438, *Bericht Deutsche Botschaft Athen an Auswärtiges Amt Bonn*, Re.: 'Festnahme eines dt. Ehepaares, das 15 Plastikbomben nach Griechenland einführen wollte', Athens, 18 December 1971.

72. One of a succession of reports, for example, is this eighteenth report by a commission examining the terrorist threat posed by immigrant communities, NHstA. Hann., Nds. 100, Nr. 148, *Bundes- und Landeskriminalämter*, 'Bericht der Unterkommission "Vorbeugende Bekämpfung terroristischer Aktionen von Ausländern"', Re.: 'Verbesserung der Bekämpfung terroristischer Aktionen von Ausländern in der Bundesrepublik Deutschland', Bad Godesberg, 7 May 1969.

73. Bay. HstA. Mun., Polizeidirektion München Nr. 9381, *Bericht vom Bundeskriminalamt – Sicherungsgruppe 1Bad Godesberg*, Re.: 'Auswertungsbericht zu dem im Ermittlungsverfahren 2 BJ.s 22/65 des Herrn Generalbundesanwalts sichergestellten Beweismaterial – Tätigkeit des KOUNALAKIS für die "ENIAA DIMOKRATIKI ARISTERA (EDA)"', Bad Godesberg, 31 October 1965, German original: 'KOUNALAKIS [a functionary for the proto-Communist EDA in West Germany] unterhält im Auftrage und im Zusammenwirken mit kommunistischen Funktionären in Griechenland Geheimverbindungen zu zahlreichen Mitarbeitern in den verschiedensten Städten Deutschlands. Wenn sich auch die Zielsetzung ihrer Tätigkeit nicht unmittelbar gegen die politische Grundordnung der Bundesrepublik Deutschland richtet, so bedrohen Art, Umfang und Wirksamkeit der von ihnen gesteuerten Organisationen, insbesondere aber die konspirative Arbeitsweise des KOUNALAKIS und seiner kommunistischen Gesinnungsfreude, die Sicherheit des Staates. Es wäre unrealistische anzunehmen, daß ein kommunistische gesteuerter Zusammenschluß von Emigranten und Gastarbeiter auf die Dauer ohne Einfluß auf die bestehenden demokratischen Verhältnisse der BRD bleiben wird.'

74. Ibid., German original: 'Es liegen auch dort [Turks and Spanish] Hinweise vor, daß die illegale KPD und die SED diese Infiltrationstätigkeit der Gastarbeiter in der BRD in

Zusammenarbeit mit den zentralen Führungsstellen im Ausland unterstützen. Auswirkungen auf die betrieblichen und wirtschaftlichen Verhältnisse werden [by the KPD and SED] angestrebt.'

75. Spengler, *Systemwandel in Griechenland und Spanien*, 87–93.

76. Bay. HstA. Mun., Pol. Dir. München Nr. 9374, *Bericht – Polizeipräsidium Hannover an Regierungspräsident München*, Re.: 'Gewalttätige Ausseinandersetzungen zwischen Griechen am 11. und 12.4.1970 in Neustadt/Rbge.', Hanover, 26 June 1970.

77. Ibid.

78. Bay. HstA. Mun., Pol. Dir. München Nr. 9374, Re.: 'Dokumentation – Gefahr für griechische Demokraten in der Bundesrepublik Deutschland – Herausgeber IG Metall, Ortsverwaltung Hannover, H. Menius', Hannover, 7 June, 1970.

79. Ibid.

80. NHstA. Hann., Nds. 721, Hann. Nr. 86, *Staatsanwaltschaft Hannover*, Re.: 'Strafsache wegen Körperverletzung 24. November 1968', Hanover, 12 August 1969.

81. *Hannoversche Neue Presse (H.P.)*, 'Griechische Botschaft: Wir Brauchen Keine Schläger', 21 April 1970, German original: 'Wir Griechen aus der Wiege der Demokratie können das wahre Gesicht dieser Schlägertrupps erkennen, eine Fratze die unsere deutschen Freunden schon aus der Vergangenheit bekannt sein müßte.'

82. *Hannoversche Allgemeine Zeitung (H.A.Z.)*, 'Hannover ist nicht Athen', 16 April 1970; *Der Spiegel*, 'Verbrechen: Griechen-Terror – Arm der Obristen', 27 April 1970; *S.Z.*, 'Griechische Botschaft in Bonn attackiert Greulich', 23 April 1970; *Konkret*, 'Messer, Knüppel, Eisenstange', Nr. 11, 21 May 1970, among others.

83. *H.P.*, 'Griechische Botschaft: Wir Brauchen Keine Schläger', 21 April 1970.

84. Bay. HstA. Mun., Pol. Dir. München Nr. 9374, *Bericht des Regierungspräsidiums Hannover*, Re.: 'Gewalttätige Auseinandersetzungen zwischen Griechen am 11. Und 12. 4. 1970 in Neustadt/Rbge.', Hanover, 26 June 1970.

85. Ibid.

86. Bay. HstA. Mun., Pol. Dir. München Nr. 9374, Re.: 'Dokumentation – Gefahr für griechische Demokraten in der Bundesrepublik Deutschland – Herausgeber IG Metall, Ortsverwaltung Hannover, H. Menius', Hannover, 7 June 1970.

87. Ibid., German original: 'Die Lage griechischer Gewerkschafter in ihrem Gastland Bundesrepublik Deutschland ... Es besteht der begründete Verdacht, daß die in der Dokumentation dargelegten Terrorakte gegen griechische Staatsbürger und Arbeitnehmer von zentraler Stelle gelenkt und von konsularischen Stellen unterstützt werden. Wir fordern Ausweisung des hannoverschen Generalkonsuls und seiner Helfer aus der Bundesrepublik Deutschland ... Wir verlangen Bestrafung der von uns benannten Täter und anschließend die Ausweisung aus der Bundesrepublik Deutschland! Die in unserem Land tätigen ausländischen Arbeitnehmer müssen die gleichen verfassungsmäßigen Rechte garantiert bekommen wie jeder deutsche Staatsbürger. Alle in unserem Lande Lebenden sind vor dem Gesetz gleich und vor Rache- und Terrorakten zu schützen. Wir fordern von den verantwortlichen Instanzen, daß schnellstens gehandelt wird um die Sicherheit unserer Gäste und Bürger zu gewährleisten.'

88. Ibid.; as well as Pol. A.A.Ber., B 26, Nr. 161, *Aufzeichnung Auswärtiges Amt Bonn*, Re.: 'Sympathiekundgebung spanischer Gastarbeiter in Köln am Sonntag, den 3. Juni 1962', Bonn, 2 June 1962.

89. Pol. A.A.Ber., B 26, Nr. 437, *Berichte: Deutsches Generalkonsulat Thessaloniki*, Re.: 'Kongress der "Vereinigung der Griechen in Westdeutschland" in Saloniki', Thessaloniki, 30 August 1971 and 17 December 1971.

90. Bay. HstA. Mun., Pol. Dir. München Nr. 9374, Re.: 'Dokumentation – Gefahr für griechische Demokraten in der Bundesrepublik Deutschland – Herausgeber IG Metall, Ortsverwaltung Hannover, H. Menius', Hannover, 7 June, 1970; or NHstA. Hann., Nds. 721 Hann. Nr. 86, *Staatsanwaltschaft Hannover*, Re.: 'Strafsache wegen Körperverletzung 24. November 1968', Hanover, 12 August 1969; or *H.P.*, 'Griechen-Spitzel im Arbeitsamt?', Hanover, 4 March 1969.

91. Ibid.
92. Bay. HstA. Mun., Pol. Dir. München Nr. 9374, 'Dokumentation – Gefahr für griechische Demokraten in der Bundesrepublik Deutschland – Herausgeber IG Metall, Ortsverwaltung Hannover', Hanover, 7 June 1970.
93. NHstA. Hann., Nds. 147 Hann. Nr. 386, *Untersuchung*, Re.: 'Staatsanwaltschaft Hannover – Ermittlungsverfahren gegen griechischen Beamten, u.a. wegen Erpressung griechischer Gastarbeiter (um Austritt aus der Gewerkschaft zu erzwingen) August 1970 – Juli 1971', Hanover, 24 August 1970 and 18 July 1971.
94. *Göttinger Tageblatt,* 'Griechische Arbeiter Erpresst?', 25 February 1968, German original: 'Wir schätzen die Mitarbeit der Gewerkschaften sehr wenn es darum geht griechische Gastarbeiter in ihrem Arbeitsplatz zu integrieren.'
95. NHstA. Hann., Nds. 147 Hann. Nr. 386, *Untersuchung*, Re.: 'Staatsanwaltschaft Hannover – Ermittlungsverfahren gegen griechischen Beamten, u.a. wegen Erpressung griechischer Gastarbeiter (um Austritt aus der Gewerkschaft zu erzwingen) August 1970 – Juli 1971', Hanover, 24 August 1970–18 July 1971.
96. Bay. HstA. Mun., Pol. Dir. München Nr. 9394, *Rundschreiben des BKA an das Bay. Landeskriminalamt usw.,* Re.: 'Griechische Zentrumsunion, Parteiorganisation in der Bundesrepublik Deutschland', Munich, 5 February 1968.
97. Bay. HstA. Mun., Pol. Dir. München Nr. 9394, *Rundschreiben des Polizeipräsidiums am BKA und sämtliche Landeskriminalämter,* Re.: 'Griechische Zentrumsunion, Parteiorganisation in der Bundesrepublik Deutschland', Bonn, 29 January 1968.
98. Bay. HstA. Mun., Pol. Dir. München Nr. 9377, *Bericht KK III,* Re.: 'Veranstaltungsbericht – Protest gegen die Militärjunta in Griechland und die Wahlen am 29.9.1968', Munich, 26 September 1968.
99. Bay. HstA. Mun., Pol. Dir. München Nr. 9374, *Bericht Kriminalabteilung III,* Re.: 'Veranstaltungen griechischer Vereinigungen', Munich, 11 August 1968.
100. Bay. HstA. Mun., Pol. Dir. München Nr. 9394, *Bericht Abteilung KK III,* Re.: 'Veranstaltungsbericht – Protestversammlung aus Anlaß des Jahrestages der Machtübernahme in Griechenland – 21. April 1968', Munich, 25 April 1968.
101. Bay. HstA. Mun., Pol. Dir. München Nr. 9389, *Bericht Abteilung KK III,* Re.: 'Veranstaltungsbericht – Kundgebung gegen den Faschismus des PAE (Gesamtgriechische antidiktatorische Union=GAU)', Munich, 21 April 1968, German original: '"Unterdrückte aller Länder vereinigt Euch!" ... und erntete lautstarken Beifall. Auch wurden "Ho-Ho-Ho Tschi" Minh-Rufe laut.'
102. Bay. HstA. Mun., Pol. Dir. München Nr. 9389, *Bericht Abteilung KK III,* Re.: 'Veranstaltungsbericht – Kundgebung gegen den Faschismus des PAE (Gesamtgriechische antidiktatorische Union=GAU)', Munich, 21 April 1968.
103. Bay. HstA. Mun., Pol. Dir. München Nr. 9394, *Bericht Abteilung KK III,* Re.: 'Veranstaltungsbericht – Protestversammlung aus Anlaß des Jahrestages der Machtübernahme in Griechenland – 21. April 1968', Munich, 25 April 1968.
104. Ibid., German original: 'Die deutschen Teilnehmer möchten ihre Probleme selbst lösen und die Griechen in Ruhe lassen.'
105. Bay. HstA. Mun., Pol. Dir. München Nr. 9377, *Bericht KK III,* Re.: 'Veranstaltungsbericht – Protest gegen die Militärjunta in Griechland und die Wahlen am 29.9.1968', Munich, 26 September 1968, German original: '"Waffen wollen wir!!"... 'Gebt uns Waffen!!'... 'Widerstand!!"'
106. Bay. HstA. Mun., Pol. Dir. München Nr. 9377, *Bericht KK III,* Re.: 'Veranstaltungsbericht – Protest gegen die Militärjunta in Griechland und die Wahlen am 29.9.1968', Munich, 26 September 1968.
107. Bay. HstA. Mun., Pol. Dir. Nr. 9374, *Bericht Abteilung KK III,* Re.: 'Veranstaltungsbericht – Nationalfeier 28.10.1940 am 3.11.1968 im Hackerkeller', Munich, 13 January 1969, German original: 'Der griech. Generalkonsul wies in seiner Ansprache auf die historische Bedeutung

dieses Tages hin und meinte, damals sei Griechenland vor dem Faschismus und durch die jetzige Regierung vor dem Kommunismus bewahrt worden.'

108. Bay. HstA. Mun., Pol. Dir. Nr. 9374, *Bericht Abteilung KK III*, Re.: 'Veranstaltungsbericht – Nationalfeier 28.10.1940 am 3.11.1968 in Hackerkeller', Munich, 13 January 1969.

109. W. Hale. 1990. 'The Turkish Army in Politics 1960–1973', in A. Finkel and N. Sirman (eds), *Turkish State, Turkish Society*, Routledge: London, 70–78.

110. Özcan, *Türkische Immigrantenorganisationen in der BRD*, 171–74.

111. Bay. HstA. Mun., Pol. Dir. München Nr. 9381, *Bericht vom Bundeskriminalamt – Sicherungsgruppe 1Bad Godesberg*, Re: 'Auswertungsbericht zu dem im Ermittlungsverfahren 2 BJ.s 22/65 des Herrn Generalbundesanwalts sichergestellten Beweismaterial – Tätigkeit des KOUNALAKIS für die ENIAA DIMOKRATIKI ARISTERA (EDA)', Bad Godesberg, 31 October 1965.

112. von Braunmühl, *Kalter Krieg und Friedliche Koexistenz*, 41.

Chapter 5

BOTH LOSERS AND WINNERS?
THE IRANIAN COMMUNITY AND THE STUDENT MOVEMENT

The existence of a communist East German state overshadowed West German public debate as each political party or organization in the Federal Republic tried to respond to the ideological challenge it posed.[1] As we have seen in the case of Spanish and Greek guest workers, the anti-communist stance that prevailed in all three West German parliamentary parties could affect the fate of many immigrant political movements. Fears that immigrant communities might be vulnerable to communist infiltration were fed by wider anxieties about the extent of covert East German influence over the West German political process. The political division of Germany was therefore in itself a key factor shaping state and party responses to immigrant groups.[2]

In this context, political turmoil in immigrant communities and their homeland states would always be scrutinized by the security services for its potential impact on the delicate power balance between the GDR and the FRG. When it came to individual immigrant leaders or political organizations, their stance towards the East German regime could often determine whether agencies such as the BKA or BfV were prepared to tolerate their presence or even provide them with support. As the experience of the Spanish community has shown, if the security services suspected that an émigré leader or immigrant organization might either be too friendly with the East German regime or a threat to West German foreign policy goals such an individual or group quickly faced great difficulties from police and intelligence agencies.

The *Auswärtiges Amt* played a crucial role in helping other state institutions determine whether the actions of immigrant activists and organizations were detrimental to West German foreign policy.[3] From the policing of immigrants to negotiations with labour-exporting states, *Auswärtiges Amt* officials came into contact with all aspects of the immigration process. Diplomats and security officials from labour-exporting states were quite aware of how the division of Germany dominated policy making in the *Auswärtiges Amt*. They often did their best to use this to their own advantage by trying to prove that immigrant movements to which they were hostile enjoyed the covert backing of the

East German state. Of crucial importance was the shift from the 'Hallstein doctrine', a policy under the Adenauer government based on the nonrecognition of the existence of the GDR, to the more flexible approach towards the Soviet bloc championed by Willy Brandt and the SPD, which came to be known as *Ostpolitik*. The *Hallstein* doctrine limited the number of policy options open to the *Auswärtiges Amt* since one of its main tenets stipulated that the Bonn government must cease diplomatic relations with any country that recognized the existence of East Germany as a separate state. By contrast, *Ostpolitik* did not just transform relations with the Soviet bloc, it enabled the West German government to develop stable relations with Third World states who did not want to have to choose between East and West.[4]

While most immigrant movements associated with guest worker communities were not particularly interested in German unity, almost every labour exporting government had become accustomed to dealing with or even manipulating the concerns of the West German state when it came to their relations with the GDR. As long as the *Hallstein* doctrine maintained its hold over West German foreign policy, even governments belonging to the Western alliance could put their West German counterparts under pressure. Although most realized that diplomatic recognition would represent a step too far for the West Germans and their American backers, there was a variety of less drastic options available when it came to dealing with the East Germans. Exploring potential trade links, cultural exchanges or the toleration of the presence of East German officials on their soil could do much to worry West German diplomats about their own position in a labour exporting state. Third World states not allied with NATO or the United States on occasion even threatened to purchase arms from East German suppliers.[5] Despite its dependence on Western support, one state that was particularly adept at manipulating West German concerns when it came to the GDR was the autocratic regime under Shah Mohhamad Reza Pahlevi that governed Iran until 1979. Yet this complex relationship between the Federal Republic and an autocratic oil monarchy was ultimately defined and then undermined by the emergence of an Iranian community in Germany.

****

The activity of Iranian students who opposed the Iranian government quickly gained the attention of the German public in the course of the 1960s. From 1958, Iranians quickly became the largest non-European group in West German higher education, and by the mid 1960s most of the 20,000 Iranians in West Germany were either students or had decided to settle in the Federal Republic after completing their studies.[6] Apart from this student community there were also a small number of expatriates concentrated in larger urban centres such as Hamburg, Munich or Cologne. Some of them were exiled dissidents who ended up in West Germany after being forced to find employment in Europe while others were businessmen who were usually active in the import/export or textiles trades.[7] Throughout this period Iranian activists also profited from the backing of well connected German leaders of the 'New Left', such as Hans Magnus Enzensberger. With this kind of support, the anti-Shah cause was, like Vietnam, quickly adopted by the student movement, which saw the American-backed Pahlevi regime as an example of the kind of 'imperialism' and 'capitalist exploitation' they were trying to fight in the Federal Republic.[8]

In terms of social structure, Iranians probably diverged most from the image of the working-class economic migrant since only a small number of Iranians in the Federal Republic conformed to the classic guest worker stereotype. Of approximately 20,000 Iranians in West Germany in 1967, 5,027 were in the country on student visas while many others were pursuing some form of academic study.[9] While most other immigrant groups contained students as well, the fact that the great majority of Iranians had come to Germany to go to university meant that this was a community with a predominantly middle-class background.[10] This sudden upsurge in Iranian student numbers in West Germany and Europe after 1959 was the result of the emphasis placed upon education by the embryonic Iranian middle and upper classes, which led to a growing number of students who could not be absorbed by a relatively small Iranian higher education system.[11] While for the religiously minded the only options were the seminaries of Mashad and Qom, secular Iranians without access to aristocratic patronage had to go abroad in order to pursue a university degree. Another factor that compounded these pressures was that the middle-class background of most students meant that few could attain access to the upper echelons of the bureaucracy in a political system so heavily dominated by a small clique loyal to the Shah.[12]

Within this community most politically active Iranian students were members of left-wing organizations close to the German student movement. However, the political aims of many of those opposed to the Shah were not necessarily identical with those of the radical Left. Iranians close to the nationalist tradition of Mossadeq shared his suspicion of the communists, while some conservatives who lost out in the internal power squabbles that dogged the Shah regime also found their way to the Federal Republic. A minority of expatriate students were even members of a pro-Shah group sponsored by the Iranian embassy.[13] There is also evidence of support for the kind of Shi'a fundamentalist movements that were later to propel Ayatollah Khomeini to power. In 1979, West Germans whose attitudes towards the Middle East were shaped by their contact with the Iranian student movement in Europe were caught by surprise when the Pahlevi regime was toppled by religious revolution rather than class war.[14]

Iranians involved in anti-regime activity were faced with an autocratic government that enjoyed the support of the United States and most of the Western Alliance. From his accession to the throne in 1942 until the collapse of his regime in 1978, the Shah would remain politically dependent upon American support.[15] After surviving a challenge for dominance from a republican nationalist movement, the proto-communist Tudeh Party (that had been directly backed by the Soviets in 1945) and the Shi'ite religious establishment, the survival of the Shah regime seemed to be assured. With some of the largest oil reserves in the world and the fastest population growth in the Middle East, the continuing existence in Iran of a regime friendly to the West was considered to be of vital strategic importance to the Western Alliance. Equally significant was the long land border Iran shared with the USSR, giving it a crucial role in the wider effort by the United States to 'contain' Soviet expansionism. As a consequence, the Americans actively supported an extensive Iranian programme of weapons procurement through which the Shah hoped to extend his power throughout the Middle East by the early 1970s.

With competition for contracts growing more intense, Western governments directly lobbied the Shah on behalf of West German businesses that hoped to profit from the surge in Iranian government and private spending.[16] For its part, the West German government bankrolled joint educational and scientific programmes in order to raise the profile of the Federal Republic and strengthen what they considered to be a tradition of friendship between Germany and Iran. These efforts paid off for several West German companies, such as Siemens or Bosch, as a number of multi-million dollar joint ventures designed to speed Iranian industrialization and military modernization got off the ground.[17] Major West German banks also provided financial services for an Iranian government whose spending seemed to have no limits, though only a small part of this expenditure seems to have been used to improve economic conditions for the majority of the Iranian population. As a customer, the Iranian government was the big spender any corporation dreamed of, purchasing industrial equipment worth over 500 million Deutschmarks in 1960 alone.[18] The growing number of contracts flowing out of Teheran was more than enough to provide the Iranian government with a strong lobby in Bonn and Frankfurt.

On the surface, the Iranian-German relationship seemed to be entirely based on commerce, making the historical legacy of the Second World War far less significant for the Iranian community than most other immigrant groups. For many Iranians, that conflict was simply one of a succession of direct Western interventions in the political development of their nation. The first, Pahlevi Shah's support for the Axis, led to the occupation of Iran by the Allies and his replacement by his son, Mohhamad Reza, bringing Iranian oil supplies under Anglo-Soviet control. After the withdrawal of Soviet troops in 1945, the British and Americans tried to ensure that Iran remained a part of the Western Alliance by supporting the young Shah's government through the sale of arms to the Iranian military and covert aid to the Iranian security services.[19] In 1953, the CIA and MI6 went so far as to finance the toppling of Mossadeq, Mohhamad Reza's Prime Minister and political rival, who had offended Western corporations and governments by nationalizing the oil industry. Anxious to be of service to the two states in the Western Alliance that guaranteed its security, the West German state enthusiastically supported the actions of the British and Americans in Iran.[20]

Yet it combined its own Cold War aid to the Shah with efforts to encourage his government to provide West German corporations with civilian and military contracts, often using rhetoric such as that of *Bundespräsident* Lübke, who referred back to the 'long friendship between the Iranian and German peoples'.[21] While backing the postwar involvement of the U.S. and U.K. in Iran, the Adenauer and Kiesinger governments tried to use the history of cooperation between prewar Germany and Reza Pahlevi to their own economic advantage. Though these historical ties may not have directly affected the development of the Iranian community in the Federal Republic, they did influence the kind of political alliances anti-Shah groups struck with West German counterparts.

After the occupation of the Iranian consulate in Munich by Iranian students in 1961, West German security services had to deal with regular protests against the Shah regime. The frequency and violence of these demonstrations rose after 1965, possibly reflecting radicalization caused by the mass arrest of students in Teheran who had returned from Europe.[22] In the aftermath of these arrests, the great majority of those studying abroad had to face the fact that if they wanted to begin a career in the profession of their choice they would probably have to remain in Europe or America for an indefinite period.[23] Though they found themselves in a relatively disadvantageous position, their educational experience and middle-class background meant that they had very little in common with the Iranian peasantry and working class they so fervently championed. Quite a few of these Iranian exiles in fact seem to have envisioned themselves as part of the ruling elite of the future. For many, achieving regime change in Iran was considered to be the only possible way to return home and find a social role worthy of their educational training.[24]

The bulk of anti-Shah activism took place on university campuses under the leadership of better established students, some of whom had effectively abandoned their studies for a political career. The 1961 sit-ins staged in the Munich consulate marked the beginning of the regular use of direct action tactics, demonstrating how close this community's student leadership was to its German counterparts.[25] The attention paid by the German media to the anti-Shah cause enabled dissident students from a smaller immigrant community to reach a broader, if still left-wing, audience. With these kinds of supporters, the anti-Shah cause was (like Vietnam and Greece) quickly adopted by the student exponents of the New Left, who saw the American-backed Pahlevi regime as an example of the kind of 'imperialism' and 'capitalist exploitation' they were trying to fight in the Federal Republic.[26] It also helped Iranian students to gain a role within the general student Left that was disproportionate to the size of their community. Many German students adopted the anti-Shah cause believing that these dissidents were victims of an authoritarian regime backed by 'global imperialism'.[27]

There was a strong historical subtext both to the activity of Iranian opposition groups and the enthusiastic adoption of their cause by the West German New Left. In addressing their German counterparts, Iranian members of the Tudeh Party and Mossadeq's Second National Front drew on historical imagery from 1930s Europe by claiming that the Shah governed a fascist regime and comparing human rights abuses committed by SAVAK (Organization for Intelligence and National Security) and other Iranian security services with Nazi atrocities.[28] In language similar to that of Greek opposition activists, investment by West German corporations in the Iranian economy was taken as proof that the German business elite of the 1960s was prepared to cooperate with authoritarian regimes in much the same way as its predecessors had collaborated with the Nazis between 1933 and 1945. Such rhetoric and symbolism could be found in anti-Shah pamphlets, posters and other written material as well as the many speeches made by Iranian activists at protests organized by the New Left during this period.[29]

It is difficult to ascertain the extent to which this represented a deliberate strategy on the part of politicized Iranians. When it came to the work of the moderate academic Bahman Nirumand and the circle of students who joined German New Left groups, the use of such rhetorical devices was partly the result of their immersion in a general environment where such language was commonplace. The political language used by Nirumand at teach-ins in 1960s West Berlin involving both Germans and Iranians shows how the attitudes of the German New Left were adopted by Iranian students. At several of these events, Nirumand emulated German activists by using examples from the Nazi era in order to underline a description of conditions in his homeland.[30] By contrast, the actions of leading activists more closely associated with the National Front and the proto-communist Tudeh Party harnessed ideological conflicts over history in a more premeditated fashion. Position papers sent out in 1967 by CISNU leaders (the student representatives of the National Front), openly recommended the use of examples from the Nazi past to members trying to explain the structure of the Shah regime to Germans.[31]

Yet the very success such rhetoric had in attracting the German Left to the anti-Shah cause points to a wider phenomenon shaping the attitudes of its younger members towards left-wing immigrant movements. Many Germans who had been born either during or after the Nazi era felt a deep obligation to prevent right-wing totalitarianism from enjoying any further successes in Europe. Feeding into such sentiment were fears that bureaucrats and politicians who had served the Nazis in the 1930s were now using their position to roll back democratic freedoms in the Federal Republic. In this context, any cooperation with authoritarian regimes, such as the Iranian monarchy, could be taken as evidence of the 'fascist tendencies' (to quote Rudi Dutschke) that were supposed to be inherent within the 'restored' Germany of Adenauer.[32] For some who had been too young to resist the Nazis, the campaign against the Shah's visit in 1967 was perhaps an opportunity to prove that they would have been capable of meeting challenges from the Right that the previous generation had been unable to cope with. Aiding the Iranian opposition was therefore seen by many in the New Left as an intrinsic part of the wider battle for the political soul of West Germany itself.[33]

The New Left was not the only movement that believed that it had learned the 'lessons of history'. Leading CDU/CSU politicians and conservative bureaucrats tried to legitimize their relationship with the Iranian government through their own selective interpretation of the recent past. Many Middle East specialists in the prewar *Auswärtiges Amt* and intelligence services who had been able to continue their careers after 1945 remained wedded to the idea that a 'special relationship' between Germans and Iranians had been established by the first Pahlevi Shah.[34] Although attempts by the Hitler regime to exert influence over Iran had ended in failure, the influence of those associated with this wartime initiative provided the Pahlevi regime with a natural support base within the West German state. Such continuities, bolstered by the prevailing academic (particularly among Middle East specialists) consensus of the Adenauer era, underpinned the belief among conservative bureaucrats and politicians that monarchy was the 'natural' political system for Iran. These attitudes led West German diplomats and intelligence officers in Teheran to underestimate rival sources of power to the Shah regime such as the religious establishment.[35]

Believing in both the existence of a tradition of German-Iranian friendship and the regime's claims of reform, even governments dominated by the social democrats turned a blind eye to human rights violations in Iran. Characteristic for the regime was the response to mass demonstrations in the university town of Qom in 1961, where the army killed hundreds of demonstrators after firing into crowds with live ammunition. Dissidents who refused to be coopted by the Iranian state had to choose between exile, as in the case of Ruhollah Khomeini, or imprisonment.[36] Rather than obtaining independent intelligence on a state that was becoming economically important for the Federal Republic, the BND relied on the information it received from the Iranian government and SAVAK or reports that the Americans and British (very much the senior partners in Teheran) deigned to pass on.[37] Not surprisingly, much of this information was unlikely to put the Pahlevi regime in an unfavourable light. Even when members of the small German community in Iran passed on information that contradicted the Pahlevi line, it was often ignored by the *Auswärtiges Amt* since most diplomats in Teheran believed that mere 'civilians' were ignorant of the bigger picture.[38] There were also some within the *Bundestag* and the left-liberal press critical of the close relationship between West German governments and the Shah regime. As long as these doubts remained confined to the small number of German political activists and academics with an interest in Middle Eastern affairs, expressions of disapproval of the Shah regime in the broadsheet press or academic journals did not worry diplomats stewarding West German-Iranian relations.

By the early 1960s, however, anti-Shah demonstrations began to involve a growing number of left-wing Germans and Iranians from outside the small circle of academics working on Middle Eastern affairs. These demonstrations included sit-ins at Iranian consular buildings and protests on university campuses that managed to gain considerable coverage from the German news media. Even minor incidents of this nature were followed by demands from Iranian diplomats that their West German colleagues crack down on Iranian dissidents.[39] The rapid growth of trade links with Iran in the course of the 1960s only heightened sensitivity among West German diplomats and politicians over the concerns of the Pahlevi regime. With each critical newspaper article or demonstration, the small group of diplomats in the *Auswärtiges Amt* and the West German embassy in Teheran responsible for administering day-to-day relations with the Iranian government became increasingly anxious about the possible damage Iranian students in the FRG might be doing to the position of West German corporations in Iran.[40]

Typical of the extent to which Bonn ministries tried to avoid any potential problems with the Shah regime was the reaction of the *Auswärtiges Amt* when it was informed by the German Student Confederation (*Verband Deutscher Studentenschaften* or VDS) that one of its representatives was about to go to Iran on a fact finding mission. The VDS was an organization that (much like the British National Union of Students) officially represented the interests of all students in the Federal Republic. Disturbed by the information it was receiving from Iranian students in Germany about human rights abuses on Iranian campuses, it decided to send a doctoral student in oriental studies called Christof Jaeger to Teheran. In order to ensure that he saw things from their point of view, *Auswärtiges Amt* officials met with Jaeger several times and put him in touch with various Iranian education officials. They also informed SAVAK about his presence in order to steer him away from what they euphemistically called 'unhelpful elements'.[41] Grateful to the West German embassy officials who had been so obliging, Jaeger sent an extensive report on his trip to the *Auswärtiges Amt,* which even included the names of dissidents he had met. In subsequent reports to their superiors, the Iran experts in the *Auswärtiges Amt* in Bonn expressed great relief at having successfully denied the Iranian opposition a propaganda victory. Throughout this storm in a teacup it becomes clear that these West German diplomats largely agreed with the Pahlevi regime's assertion that Iran was not ready for democracy.[42]

The ability of Iranian activists to put their case across despite this hostility from West German state officials was enhanced by their high level of organization. For a time, the Iranian Left in Germany was dominated by the Confederation of Iranian Students/National Union, or CISNU. Founded in 1963, CISNU was effectively a broad federation of ideological, political and religious student organizations that were only held together by their dislike of the Pahlevi regime. Though tensions between this movement's more religious elements and its Marxist–Leninist wing led to its collapse in the early 1970s, for a while it provided Iranian dissidents with a platform to organize anti-Shah activity.[43] Yet despite the more moderate views of many of CISNU's supporters, its leadership was largely dominated by members of the proto-communist Tudeh Party, whose European headquarters were in East Germany.[44] As a result, it did not need much to convince West German security that Iranian dissidents represented a potential danger to the Federal Republic. Iranian diplomats were quick off the mark, handing information to the German Foreign Ministry that tried to connect CISNU activists with either the extreme New Left or the *Stasi*.[45]

A good example of the kind of Iranian activists that particularly interested Iranian diplomats and West German officials was a student called Hassan Massali. After initially coming to the Federal Republic in 1958 in order to study medicine at Kiel University, Massali came to the fore of the Iranian community after being elected to the chairmanship of CISNU and joining several Tudeh front organizations in 1964.[46] Nonetheless, figures such as Massali had to work with a wide variety of different groups, some of which disapproved as much of the Tudeh tradition as they did of the Pahlevi regime. Despite an explicit Iranian request and the *Auswärtiges Amt*'s best efforts, his residence permit was restored after 1967 on the strict condition that he must stop taking part in political activity, a restriction that he ignored.[47] Moving around Germany in order to avoid arrest, Massali became a leading member of Communist Unity, a group that supported and financed Iranian guerrilla organizations in the years leading up to the Islamic Revolution.[48] Under regular surveillance by SAVAK and European security services because of his involvement in arms smuggling, Massali became part of a terrorist demi-monde, a world in which left-wing extremists from the Red Army Fraction to George Habash's Popular Front for the Liberation of Palestine cooperated in what they believed was a common war against 'Western imperialism'.[49]

With both dominant political groupings in the Federal Republic inclined to give the Shah regime the benefit of the doubt, those elements of the security and foreign policy establishment most directly involved in shaping relations with Iran could easily pursue their pro-Shah agenda. Starting with the first anti-Shah demonstrations in 1961, *Auswärtiges Amt* officials acceded to the demands of Iranian diplomats for the suppression of opposition activists in the Iranian community. In the years that followed, every major protest by anti-Shah activists led to further pressure on provincial ministries and local police forces to get Iranian dissidents under control. With the help of the *Auswärtiges Amt,* the Iranian embassy seems to have been able to consistently prod local officials into action when it could point to cooperation between German leftists, East German institutions and Iranian exiles.[50] In Iran, West German embassy officials were occasionally invited to the Iranian Interior Ministry, where SAVAK officers handed them lists of those Iranian dissidents in West Germany whom they wished to have deported, which were usually accompanied by snippets of information designed to show how these individuals could be of danger to the Federal Republic.[51]

The counter-productive nature of these kinds of measures can be seen in the trial of three Iranian medical students in September 1963. Put under pressure by the West German Foreign Ministry, the Cologne prosecutor's office arrested Iradj Nazemi, Houchang Hamzawi-Abedi and Manoutcher Bouzari, who were medical students at Cologne University and belonged to the Tudeh Party, for being members of an 'anti-constitutional' political organization. One of the main pieces of evidence buttressing the prosecution's case against these two students was a set of visits they had made to East Berlin in 1960.[52] The North Rhine-Westphalian courts rejected the prosecution's case, pointing out that anti-extremism laws dealt with direct threats to the West German constitutional order, not indirect threats to a government's foreign policy. Not only did the trial end in failure, it attracted the attention of many West German left-wing figures and helped Iranian dissidents to develop links with the New Left.[53]

An alternative path was taken by Bahman Nirumand, a young writer and academic who in many ways typified the Iranian dissidents who were drawn into the New Left through their close relationships with West German intellectuals.[54] Initially a junior lecturer at Teheran University, Nirumand fled Iran in 1962 after being interrogated by SAVAK and settling in West Berlin, where he continued his research and published a book highly critical of the Pahlevi regime and its American supporters in March 1967.[55] Through this work as an academic and journalist, Nirumand developed close relationships with leading German intellectuals such as Hans Magnus Enzensberger or Ulrike Meinhof. His status as one of the New Left's most prominent academics was confirmed when he was invited to speak at the 'International Vietnam Conference' in February 1968, which almost led to his deportation from the Federal Republic. This was a meeting that has attained legendary status in German left-wing circles because it brought the different strands of the extra-parliamentary opposition together at the beginning of a tumultuous year.[56] Nirumand's ability to develop contacts with leading German intellectuals demonstrates how immigrants could rise to prominence through activism focused on their country of origin. That such Iranian students were not necessarily representative of an oppressed peasantry or working class did not matter. The claim made by their leaders that the entire Iranian people had been victimized by Western imperialism and the very real oppression they faced if they returned home was enough to integrate them into a radical milieu through the help of student leaders such as Joschka Fischer and Daniel Cohn-Bendit.

As a consequence of this growing cooperation between German and Iranian student militants, the event involving the Iranian community that finally grabbed the attention of the wider public also proved to be one of the crucial moments in the development of the New Left. This was the tour of West Germany by the Shah in 1967, which triggered the first of a succession of student-led demonstrations and riots across the Federal Republic. The Kiesinger/Brandt government had initially hoped that this tour would enhance economic links and boost West German political influence over the Pahlevi regime. Scared that the Shah might react extremely badly to any contact with Iranian or German demonstrators, Iranian diplomats in Bonn and Teheran as well as *Auswärtiges Amt* officials put heavy pressure on the security services to suppress anti-Shah organizations before the visit.[57] This resulted in a set of exclusion orders against known dissidents, wide powers of arrest for police and a heavy and well advertised security presence along the Shah's route in order to deter demonstrators.

In Munich scores of Iranians were ordered to register with the police and temporarily leave their districts.[58] Regensburg city council instructed local Iranians to stay in the city and report twice a day to the *Ausländerbehörde*. Erlangen and Düsseldorf put out similar curfews while in Frankfurt, Wiesbaden, Bonn and Cologne potential non-German troublemakers were ordered to visit their local police station once a day throughout the visit and other non-Germans were threatened with deportation if they were caught taking part in demonstrations.[59] West German police forces had some reason to worry despite these measures. New Left activists had proven themselves adept at using extremely confrontational tactics in their run-ins with the police. Though most student activists believed that Soviet communism was an authoritarian dead end, there was enough evidence of SED or *Stasi* meddling in the New Left (such as funding the satirical magazine *Konkret*) to confirm the suspicions of the *Auswärtiges Amt* when it came to the influence of the GDR over the extraparliamentary opposition. By instructing local police to be prepared to defend the royal entourage from attacks by ultra-violent Iranian communists, Foreign Ministry officials only helped to heighten the tension. Tabloid journalists (particularly from the *Bild* newspaper) were also briefed in similar terms by the *Auswärtiges Amt*. By the time the Shah arrived in Bonn on 25 May 1967, in the eyes of regular policemen or average tabloid readers the Iranian opposition represented a menace to society, no better in fact than German student radicals.[60] Rather than preventing trouble, such pre-publicity rallied the support of a wider spectrum of people than the socialist students' organization SDS (*Sozialistischer Deutscher Studentenbund*) could have done on its own.[61]

The *Auswärtiges Amt* had already encouraged newspapers and magazines such as *Bild, Bunte* or *Neue Revue* to give the Shah's visit positive coverage long before the anti-Pahlevi protests. Throughout the 1950s and 1960s the Shah's court had been regular fodder for the German tabloid press, which made copy out of his marriages, first to half-German, half-Iranian Soraya and then to Farah, the consort who accompanied him on the 1967 trip. When Iranian politics were touched upon, these papers usually mentioned the so-called 'White Revolution', a half-hearted attempt at land reform.[62] While the dark side of the Pahlevi regime got some mention in left-liberal papers such as the *Süddeutsche Zeitung* and the *Frankfurter Rundschau, Bild* readers were more likely to find out about Shahbanu Farah's wardrobe and the Shah's steadfast anti-communism. In an attempt to generate popular excitement about the Shah's visit, the government even persuaded *Bild* to publish the itinerary of the tour with an article encouraging *Bild* readers to come out and welcome this glamorous ally.[63] The tabloids and centre-right broadsheets such as the *Frankfurter Allgemeine Zeitung* were heavily influenced by conservative orientalists in West German academia, who set much store in the 'traditional' friendship between Germany and Iran.[64] Anti-Shah protests were mentioned too, but like other cases where left-wing students were involved, the tabloid readership was left with the impression that anti-Shah activists were all dangerous hooligans out to get at the police and ruin West Germany's reputation.[65]

From the outset it was clear that this state visit was not going to be the success diplomats and politicians had hoped for. In North Rhine-Westphalia the Shah's motorcade elicited complaints from delayed motorists rather than popular enthusiasm, while in Munich the crowds flocking to the city centre were there to greet a cup-winning FC Bayern side rather than the Shah.[66] With such thin crowds, the noisy contingent of demonstrators shadowing the Shah's entourage was able to make itself seen and heard. Constant checks by rifle-toting policemen only served to further dampen the enthusiasm of onlookers and ratchet up tension with the protesters.[67] Each of these failures was commented upon acidly by East German newspapers, which did their best to equate the social order of the Federal Republic with that of Iran.[68]

On the evening of 1 June 1967 (the fourth day of the tour) a 'teach-in' at the Free University of Berlin took place that gave an indication that the protests in West Berlin were going to top the preceding ones in West Germany proper. In a packed lecture theatre, prominent West Berlin radicals such as Horst Mahler, Rudi Dutschke and Bahman Nirumand described the human rights situation in Iran and decried the extensive contacts between West German corporations and the Iranian state. At the end of this teach-in, copies of the Shah visit's official schedule published in the *Bild Zeitung* were handed out to hundreds of participants. The students also received a pamphlet in which one New Left activist called on protestors to do their utmost to be heard:

> The friendly welcome the Shah received from our politicians … is a blow to democracy and justice. Demonstrate against this! Explain your position to the members of parliament from the different parties! Demonstrate against the fact that the [West] German authorities have allowed and at times even actively helped the Persian Gestapo (SAVAK) to monitor and suppress Iranian students![69]

During the Shah's tour of the office of the Mayor of West Berlin, Heinrich Albertz (a social democrat), in Schöneberg at noon the next day, both witnessed how successful this 'teach-in' had been in mobilizing the West Berlin Left. Several hundred protestors picketed Schöneberg city hall, including many older Berliners from the social democrat pensioners association. Also present were supporters of the Shah who had been specially bussed in for the occasion by the Iranian government, who drew batons and attacked the anti-Shah protesters in full sight of the assembled press corps after the Shah entered the building.

Rather than arresting the pro-Shah assailants, almost instantly dubbed 'Hurrah-Persians' by the left-liberal press, the police focused their attention on several anti-Shah protesters who were arrested for 'insulting a foreign head of state'.[70] After the Schöneberg scuffles, the Chief of Police, Erich Duensing, assured the *Auswärtiges Amt's* Head of Protocol that the situation would not escalate.[71] At seven in the evening the first guests began to arrive at the *Deutsche Oper,* where the Shah and the *Bundespräsident* were supposed to watch a premiere of *The Magic Flute.* Behind the crowd barriers the first melées broke out between the 'Hurrah-Persians' and anti-Shah demonstrators. The participation of prominent representatives of the New Left such as Fritz Teufel and members of *Kommune 1* helped to increase the tension. As political leaders entered the opera, protesters threw eggs, tomatoes and flour bombs.[72]

Once the opera doors had closed, riot police under Duensing's command attacked the protesters without warning. While anti-Shah Iranians and Germans were speedily arrested, pro-Shah Iranians were able to get away with attacks upon demonstrators right in front of watching policemen.[73] Many Germans and Iranians were beaten senseless, often as they lay helpless on the ground. The fact that the national and international press was there to record everything did not seem to bother the police in the slightest. In the midst of this chaos a plainclothes policeman, Karl-Heinz Kurras, pulled his pistol and fired several shots at a group of students for reasons that have never been adequately explained. One of the bullets mortally wounded Benno Ohnesorg, an apolitical theology student. News of these street battles and the death of Ohnesorg on 2 June 1967 sparked riots at campuses across West Germany, radicalizing many previously moderate students.

These riots did far more than damage German-Iranian relations. In his desire to restore order, Erich Duensing instigated one of the most famous of the many street battles that shook West German society in the late 1960s and early 1970s. The judicial exoneration of Kurras in November 1967 only made things worse, though *Bild* and other tabloids owned by Axel Springer continued to blame the student anti-Shah activists for the riots and the death of Ohnesorg.[74] For students and much of the Left it looked as if the West Berlin government was trying to cover something up. Though there had already been considerable political activity in the universities before 2 June 1967, the brutality of the West Berlin police and the death of Benno Ohnesorg became a key moment in the radicalization of the extra-parliamentary Left. Through it, senior New Left activists such as Rudi Dutschke and Horst Mahler gained national prominence and it was no coincidence that one of the first extreme Left terrorist cells later drawn into the Red Army Fraction initially called itself the 'Movement 2nd June'.[75] Yet, while members of the Iranian opposition in Germany remained focused on their campaign against the Shah, the rest of the New Left shifted its attention to the Vietnam War and internal battles over the political direction of the Federal Republic.

The demonstrations also left a profound impression upon the Shah and his entourage. With West Berlin still smouldering, the last two days of the tour in Hamburg continued to be marred by street violence.[76] Angry and humiliated, after returning to Teheran the Shah publicly demanded an apology from the Kiesinger/Brandt administration as well as the arrest of all those demonstrators who had insulted him and the Iranian state. Under strict instructions not to let the matter drop, the Iranian Foreign Ministry put pressure on the West German government to take action that could compensate for so serious a blow to the Shah regime's prestige. The Shah publicly criticized the West German government in interviews with German journalists for its (in his opinion) inability to maintain proper security.[77] More worryingly for West German ministers who had hoped that the Shah's visit would strengthen the FRG's position in the Middle East, he privately threatened the West German ambassador with retaliatory steps that would have led to a serious deterioration in relations between the two states. In the presence of German diplomats, the Shah and senior Iranian officials mooted measures such as the cancellation of state contracts with West German corporations or the rejection of West German military aid.[78] Yet the threat that most excited West German diplomats in Teheran and Bonn was the Shah's suggestion that he might 'review' Iranian policy towards the GDR.

Beyond any difficulties for West German businesses, it was the possibility that there might be gains for East German diplomacy that bewildered West German officials. In the weeks after the Shah's return, several Iranian diplomats hinted to *Auswärtiges Amt* colleagues that the East Germans might be permitted to open a trade office in Teheran; there was even a suggestion that the Iranian state-owned businesses might set up joint ventures with East German companies. This caused serious concern among many West German diplomats:

> There is no doubt in the fact that several months ago, two gentlemen from the Eastern Zone [i.e., the GDR] were in Teheran in order to conduct the kind of discussions described in these newspaper reports ... When it comes to the question about the willingness of the Iranian government to give the SBZ ['Sowjetisch besetzte Zone', a euphemism for the GDR] a limited amount of access to Iran, then its actions will largely be dependent upon any political concessions or economic offers made by the SBZ ... When it comes to such a decision, the Iranian government will be less inclined to take our expressed interests into account as was once the case ... At the time of the visit of *Bundesinnenminister* Lücke [13 September 1967] it was made clear to us that along with the normalization of German press reporting on Iran, in Iranian eyes it is essential that we actively support it in the fight against the forces of the Iranian opposition in the Federal Republic of Germany if there is to be any chance of restoring our traditionally good relationship.[79]

Any further moves to court the GDR, such as the establishment of full diplomatic relations, were less likely. Permitting the opening of an East German embassy before the West Germans themselves had taken that step would have been too blatant a contradiction of the Shah's image as a stalwart friend of the

Western Alliance. It would also have put major arms procurement contracts with West German and American companies at risk, since the American Department of Defence wanted to have confidence in the reliability of a state to which U.S. defence contractors were selling their newest military equipment.[80]

Even the merest suggestion of an Iranian initiative to develop contacts with East Germany was seen by diplomats and politicians in Bonn as a potential setback for West German foreign policy. Despite moves by the SPD towards a more flexible approach, the effort to systematically isolate the GDR, which was the cornerstone of the *Hallstein* doctrine, still dominated West German foreign policy thinking. Any accommodation with East Germany by a state as influential in the Middle East as Iran would have been perceived by Bonn as a major blow to the Federal Republic's claim to be the sole representative of the German nation. Worried that the actions of the Shah might be emulated by other Middle Eastern states, officials in the *Auswärtiges Amt* did their best to assuage the Shah. There was more than a hint of irony in an authoritarian monarchy pressuring the West Germans into prosecuting extreme left-wing activists by flirting with a communist East German regime.[81]

Even before the Shah made his displeasure clear, the *Auswärtiges Amt* and BND officials were already pushing municipal prosecutors' offices to do something, anything, about Iranian and German anti-Shah activists. As the Iranian government began to make noises about initiating dialogue with the GDR, the requests from Bonn to local judicial and law enforcement agencies for stricter punishment of demonstrators became more urgent.[82] Though many demonstrators had already been charged for various offences related to the street violence surrounding the tour, several federal ministries requested a more symbolic punishment of demonstrators that could directly appease the Shah. With few tools in their judicial armoury, local prosecutors in Munich and West Berlin revived an obscure law in August 1967 banning the insulting of a foreign head of state and initiated what were effectively libel cases against many of those who had participated in the demonstrations. Jail loomed for those defendants unable to pay the exorbitant fines for infractions against this law.[83]

This attempt to punish Iranian and West German demonstrators backfired badly. A fiery article by Bernhard Schütze, a columnist at the *Frankfurter Rundschau*, started a campaign in the course of which thousands of individuals across the country admitted to their local police authority that they had at some time insulted the Shah in order to clog up the courts.[84] By this point even the influential and conservative *Frankfurter Allgemeine* was condemning the Kiesinger/Brandt coalition for buckling under pressure from a foreign government, as the Shah's demand that the West German government muzzle his critics managed to antagonize many in conservative circles who had previously been his natural supporters.[85] However much conservative commentators and members of the *Bundestag* may have wanted to increase West German influence in Teheran, many of them found the spectacle of their government giving in to a Third World regime rather embarrassing. After a few weeks of sustained Iranian pressure, most *Bundestag* deputies and newspaper columnists believed that the Kiesinger government had done enough to assuage the Shah's concerns.[86] In a final damage limitation exercise, the CDU Federal Interior Minister, Paul Lücke, flew to Teheran on 12 September 1967 and personally handed over an official apology for the protests in an effort to get the Shah to withdraw his demands. An exchange at one meeting with the Shah was recorded by the West German ambassador in Teheran:

> *Bundesinnenminister* Lücke implored the Shah to show understanding for the situation in the Federal Republic … He [Lücke] himself believed that the Shah's complaints about the Federal Republic did have some justice to them. He could only guarantee that the federal government would make the strongest efforts to repair the damage to relations. He called upon the Shah to follow his heart and help restore the old trusted friendship [between both nations].[87]

Informed that libel trials would give his opponents another platform from which to vent their criticisms and mollified by the grovelling of a German cabinet minister, the Shah assented to Lücke's request and the libel investigations died a quiet and unmourned death.[88]

Even though the Shah's tour had proven such a disaster, the Cold War logic that had fostered Anglo-American support for the Iranian monarchy still shaped West German foreign policy. Continuing support for the Shah was not only based upon a desire to be seen as part of the Western 'club', but also upon the experience of the early Cold War. Consequently, many within the West German political establishment believed that Iran, like the Federal Republic, was part of the anti-communist 'frontline'. Even though many of its members were traditionally suspicious of authoritarian regimes, some senior SPD leaders accepted such analogies, seeing Iran as a 'force for modernity' in an otherwise 'primitive' Middle East.[89] Despite their own doubts over the Shah's disastrous human rights record, the belief that his regime contained 'progressive' elements led social democratic politicians to take an active role in providing the Iranian government with financial aid for projects that they considered to be essential to the modernization of Iranian society.[90]

By pointing to possible links between Iranian opposition movements and various communist states, SPD leaders were able to play on the deep-seated anti-communism of many social democrats who detested the way many of their fellow party comrades had experienced repression in the GDR.[91] Such comparisons with events in late 1940s Germany helped to discourage expressions of support for anti-Shah activists from members of the parliamentary Left until the late 1960s. The tendency of West German state institutions to equate the behaviour of the German and immigrant New Left with the actions of German communists after 1945 explains the vehement denunciation of anti-Shah organizations by mainstream politicians and media commentators. In a political environment where references to national socialism and communism were regularly used in political debate, it is not surprising that analogies with both totalitarian ideologies were invoked so often when politicians or the German media discussed left-wing Iranians.

In the aftermath of major incidents involving Iranians and the West German New Left such as the Shah's visit, the reaction of members of West German state institutions or mainstream political parties was vitriolic. Conservative journalists, diplomats and politicians often compared the tactics used by the (mostly peaceful) anti-Shah activists to the methods of Nazi and communist storm troopers during the Weimar era in order to discredit them in the eyes of the wider German public.[92] Using remarkably similar language to their ideological opponents, New Left activists accused the Kiesinger/Brandt government of appeasement in the aftermath of the Shah's visit. For many German and Iranian members of the New Left the brutal response of the West Berlin police towards anti-Shah demonstrators in June 1967 was final proof that the Federal Republic possessed the same 'fascist tendencies and continuities' that they believed existed in Iran.[93] Though not as vehement as the radical Left, critical columnists and commentators in the left-liberal press also used language and imagery that referred back to the national socialist legacy.[94] Such allusions to recent history are encapsulated in Peter Wapnewski's description of police brutality during the protests against the Shah in 1967:

> During these events they [the students] have begun to understand the nature of uncontrolled violence, which seeks to destroy human dignity and freedom out of a lust for brutality and a delight in destruction. They consider this to be 'fascist' and are scared: of the batons – and of the future.[95]

In a political culture so suffused with coded (and not so coded) references to recent history, the ability of new immigrant political movements to understand and manipulate the legacy of the Nazi era and its immediate aftermath could enhance their ability to attract attention to their own agenda. Although the Second World War only had an indirect impact on Iran, the astute manner in which many anti-Shah activists managed to draw parallels between events in their homeland and the Nazi regime proved instrumental to their ability to attract wide support in the West German Left for their campaigns against the Shah regime.

The Shah riots were a mixed blessing for Iranian dissidents in the Federal Republic. The demonstrations surrounding the Shah's visit had provided Iranian dissidents with a priceless opportunity to make themselves heard. But the conflict between the more radical elements of the student movement and the West German state in the aftermath of Benno Ohnesorg's murder pushed the Shah and his opponents out of the headlines. Though individual Iranians still had positions of influence in the New Left after 1967, Vietnam quickly superseded Iran as the student movement's cause célèbre. When reading many of the statements made by German members of the New Left, one gains the impression that they were more interested in using the Shah regime as a stick with which to beat the West German political establishment rather than really engaging with the ins and outs of Iranian politics. Though public attention quickly drifted away from Iran, militant Iranian students and academics continued to demonstrate and engage in direct (if nonviolent) action against Iranian diplomatic property.

Nine years after the first occupation of the Iranian consulate in 1961, a second occupation took place in August 1970. Dozens of hooded Iranian Maoists stormed the consulate, only to be violently removed by Munich police who threatened many of the participants with deportation.[96] In the 1970s such incidents still tended to cluster around major events in Iran, like the vast celebrations to celebrate the 2500th anniversary of the Persian monarchy organized by the Shah regime in 1973. In both 1970 and 1973, BND officers passed on lists to their colleagues in SAVAK with the names of the Iranians who participated in these protests, thereby endangering their lives and their families and breaking several federal laws concerning the use of police information by the security services.[97]

Paradoxically, given their focus on toppling the Shah regime, despite such confrontations the participation of many young Iranian newcomers in the German student movement in the years after 1967 helped to speed their integration into West German society. Though the New Left remained outside of the social mainstream of the Federal Republic, it acted as a stepping stone for many in the Iranian community towards greater involvement in both German political life as well as wider social integration. The speedy expansion of the Iranian community after the late 1970s (by 1989 it would number over 130,000) did not alter this dynamic. On the contrary, the strong interaction between many Iranian activists and German left-wing groups helped the thousands of Iranian refugees who fled to the Federal Republic after 1979 because of the Islamic Revolution to integrate into German society. This process was accompanied by continuing harassment from security services that used every means they could find within the framework of West German immigration law to suppress Iranian organizations that they considered to be politically or religiously extreme.[98]

In the tense atmosphere after the first Red Army Faction offensives and the killing of Israeli athletes at the Munich Olympics by Palestinian militants on 4 September 1972, West German security services were able to use immigration law in order to take drastic action against other immigrant political movements. Suddenly, measures with which Iranian activists had become familiar were applied against Palestinian as well as other Arab activists opposed to Israeli policies. Though Palestinian, Jordanian and Lebanese students had been protesting peacefully against Israeli and American 'imperialism' since the Lebanese crisis of 1958, few Arabs in West Germany were directly involved with Palestinian terror networks.[99] Faced with their own massive public failures, West German security services responded to the crisis at the Munich Olympics with what amounted to collective punishment, expelling a large number of Arab activists (from many different political backgrounds) from Bavaria in late

September 1972.[100] On the Iranian side, once the Mojahedin movement in Iran began a guerrilla offensive directed against the Shah's security services, anti-Shah activists in Germany who wanted to emulate the urban guerrilla tactics used by the RAF and the Red Brigades returned to their homeland instead of attacking Iranian targets in the Federal Republic. The relative moderation of anti-Shah activists who remained in Germany did not, however, mollify the West German police and intelligence agencies, which continued to monitor former Iranian activists until the mid 1980s.[101]

Legal commentators such as Hans Heinz Heldmann believed that the relentless pressure exerted upon Iranian and Arab activists by the West German executive and judiciary betrayed an inherent xenophobic bias against immigrants.[102] Though contempt for Muslims certainly existed among German policemen and bureaucrats, the evidence examined in this chapter indicates that Iranian activists were policed so heavily because of who their West German allies were. With worries running high in the Kiesinger/Brandt government that German student radicals might represent some kind of GDR backed fifth column, any immigrant grouping working closely with the extra-parliamentary opposition was liable to be identified as another potential threat to the constitutional order. Though the major shift in policy towards East Germany that was initiated by Willy Brandt's *Ostpolitik* may have led to a diplomatic thaw, security services, state institutions and the parliamentary parties still did their utmost to limit the influence of the East German state over the West German political process.

In a political environment in which even the slightest contact with the East German state could lead to serious legal consequences for West German citizens, even the most peaceful forms of protest by Iranian activists indirectly associated with the GDR led to mass arrests and threats of deportation. Exposing them further, Iranians did not have the kind of parliamentary allies prepared to lobby on their behalf that had managed to protect Spanish organizations from the suspicion of the security services. With the Iranian embassy passing on information to support these suspicions, it is therefore not surprising that Iranian political movements far less violent than their Greek or Croatian counterparts were treated far more harshly.

****

As the experiences of émigré groups and the Iranian community illustrate, the division of Germany affected the internal development of every immigrant community in West Germany. Whatever other national agendas an immigrant movement may have had, the key factor deciding the kind of partners it would find in Germany was its attitude towards the 'German Question' and Soviet communism in general, and, with the notable exception of the Poles, East Germany in particular. Moreover, ideological polarization fuelled by the Cold

War affected every immigrant community in West Germany. Cutting across differences in national culture and religious tradition, the common language of Cold War conflict provided a basis with which immigrant movements could position themselves in the political framework of the Federal Republic. The debate surrounding the division of Germany had a particularly strong impact on the position of immigrant activists and organizations during the late 1960s and early 1970s, the years marking a shift in West German foreign policy from the CDU/CSU's focus on the *Hallstein* doctrine to the SPD's increasingly open espousal of détente enshrined in Willy Brandt's *Ostpolitik*. While the SPD's growing participation in government diminished the influence of East European émigrés unwilling to compromise with the communist bloc, left-wing Iranian students, whose putative contacts with East Berlin had caused them such difficulties with the security services, did not benefit from *Ostpolitik*. The gradual rejection of the émigré and expellee agenda by the state did not ultimately improve the position of immigrant groups believed to be open to East German influence.

Faced with the hostility of the West German political establishment because of the influence of communist ideology upon their homeland organizations and the interest their young activists displayed in fashionable forms of neo-Marxism, Iranian groups opposed to the Shah regime had no alternative to cooperation with the New Left. Allusions to the Nazi regime were used by supporters of the Iranian opposition as a means to attack the West German establishment as much as to criticize the Shah regime. In response, those who advocated the suppression of such 'ideologically unreliable' elements used Nazi analogies to compare the actions of anti-Shah activists with those of the Nazi and communist street gangs of the Weimar era. Justifiable West German concerns about the actions of the East German state could, as in the case of Iran, still be manipulated by homeland regimes after the SPD became the dominant party in 1969. To paraphrase an expression much used by historians, when it came to the West German state's fear of the GDR, *continuity* alienated immigrants close to the New Left, while *change* in its wider foreign policy approach marginalized right-wing immigrant and émigré organizations.

Notes

1.   W.E. Paterson and D. Southern. 1992. *Governing Germany*, Oxford: Blackwell, 282–83.
2.   C. Gröpl. 1993. *Die Nachrichtendienste im Regelwerk der deutschen Sicherheitsverwaltung – Legitimation, Organisation und Abgrenzungsfragen*, Berlin: Duncker und Humblot (Schriften zum Öffentlichen Recht, Band 646), 84.
3.   Eric D. Weitz, 'The Ever-Present Other: Communism in the Making of West Germany', in H. Schissler (ed.), *The Miracle Years: a Cultural History of West Germany 1949–1968*, Princeton: Princeton University Press, 228–29.
4.   C. von Braunmühl. 1973. *Kalter Krieg und Friedliche Koexistenz: Die Außenpolitik der SPD in der Großen Koalition*, Frankfurt, a.M.: Suhrkamp Verl., 34–6.

5. P. Mueller and M. Müller. 2002. *Gegen Freund und Feind – Der BND: Geheime Politik und Schmutzige Geschäfte*, Hamburg: Rowohlt Verl., 522–34.

6. K. Amiri. 1995. 'Die Iranische Minderheit', in C. Schmalz-Jacobsen (ed.), *Ethnische Minderheiten in der Bundesrepublik Deutschland*, Munich: C.H. Beck, 203–6.

7. M. Ghaseminia. 1996. *Zur Lebensituation und Integration Iranischer Staatsangehöriger in Niedersachsen*, Hanover: Universität Hannover, 33–34.

8. K. Hermann. 1967. *Die Revolte der Studenten*, Hamburg: Christian Wegener Verl., 11–19.

9. Amiri, 'Die Iranische Minderheit', 203–6.

10. Ghaseminia, *Zur Lebensituation und Integration Iranischer Staatsangehöriger in Niedersachsen*, 33–34.

11. Amiri, 'Die Iranische Minderheit', 200.

12. N. Keddie. 1981. *Roots of Revolution: an Interpretative History of Modern Iran*, New Haven: Yale University Press, 67–71.

13. Bay HstA. Mun., Staatskanzlei Nr. 16187, *Beziehungen zu Iran*, Re.: 'Feier des 2500 jährigen Bestehens der Persischen Monarchie in München', Munich, October 1973; and *D.S.*, 'SAVAK: Spur in den 4. Stock', 12 October 1967. Among those disillusioned members of the regime who fled to Germany, Switzerland and Austria were the Shah's former consort, Soraya, and a former head of SAVAK itself, General Amir Teymour Bakhtiar.

14. Dieter Wild, 'Chomeini soll Leben', *D.S.*, 23 November 1979.

15. M.J. Gasiorowski. 1990. 'Security Relations between the United States and Iran, 1953–1978', in N.R. Keddie and M.J. Gasiorowski (eds), *Neither East Nor West: Iran, The Soviet Union, And The United States*, New Haven: Yale University Press, 148–53.

16. M.H. Pesaran. 1985. 'Economic Development and Revolutionary Upheavals in Iran', in H. Afshar (ed.), *Iran: a Revolution in Turmoil*, London: Macmillan, 19–20.

17. Pol. A.A.Ber., B 36, Nr. 40, *Aufzeichnung des Bundespräsidialamtes*, Re.: 'Informationsaufzeichnung für den Staatsbesuch des Herrn Bundespräsidenten in Iran', Teheran, 3 September 1963.

18. Ibid.

19. G.R. Fazel. 1985. 'Tribes and State in Iran: From Pahlavi to Islamic Republic', in H. Afshar (ed.), *Iran: a Revolution in Turmoil*, London: Macmillan, 82–85.

20. A. Mahrad. 1985. *Die Außenpolitik Irans von 1950 bis 1954 und die Aufnahme der Beziehungen zwischen Iran und der Bundesrepublik Deutschland (Sozialwissenschaftliche Studien zu internationalen Problemen Nr. 103)*, Saarbrücken: Breitenbach Verl., 62–73.

21. Pol. A.A.Ber., B 36, Nr. 40, *Botschaft Teheran/Bundespräsident Lübke*, Re.: 'Aufenthalt in Teheran', Teheran, 13 September 1963, German original: 'lange Freundschaft zwischen den Iranischen und Deutschen Völkern'; and *F.A.Z.*, 'Bei den Kaiserlichen Majestäten aus Persien – Über den Gala-Empfang im Brühler Schloß Augustusburg', Nr. 121, 29 May 1967. What is so surprising in much of the coverage of the 1967 visits and similar events involving Iran, is the openness with which West German politicians and businessman referred back to prewar contacts in order to cement the notion of some kind of traditional Iranian-German friendship.

22. Bay HstA. Mun., Staatskanzlei Nr. 13316, *Iranisches Generalkonsulat 1953–1964, Berichte über Studentenunruhen*, Re.: 'Iranischen Studenten im Sitzstreik – vom Überfallkommando (der Polizei) aus dem Konsulat gewiesen', Munich, 11 July 1961.

23. B.K., B 141, Nr. 26028, *Bundesministerium der Justiz – Hintergrundberichte über Iranische Studenten*, Re.: 'Teilnehmer an Demonstrationen beim Schahbesuch', Bonn, 19 October 1967.

24. M. Behrooz. 2000. *Rebels with a Cause: the Failure of the Left in Iran*, New York: I.B. Tauris, 34–37.

25. Bay. HstA. Mun., Staatskanzlei Nr. 13316, *Iranisches Generalkonsulat 1953–1964, Berichte über Studentenunruhen*, Re.: 'Iranischen Studenten im Sitzstreik – vom Überfallkommando (der Polizei) aus dem Konsulat gewiesen', Munich, 11 July 1961.

26. Hermann, *Die Revolte der Studenten*, 11–19.

27. I. Gilcher-Holtey. 2001. *Die 68er Bewegung*, Munich: C.H. Beck, 65–68.

28. B.K., B 106, Nr. 26030, *Bericht Bundesministerium der Justiz (Referent MR Götz) weitergereicht am Auswärtigen Amt*, Re.: 'Beleidigung des Schah', Bonn, 29 September 1971.

29. B.K., B 141, Nr. 26028, *Generalstaatsanwalt Berlin an Bundesminister der Justiz*, Re.: 'Ermittlungsverfahren wegen Beleidigung des Schahs', Berlin (West), 19 June 1967. Pamphlets by CISNU and other Iranian opposition groups can still be found in most German state libraries. One of the best examples of how such documents tried to show a connection between events in the BRD and Iran is: Conföderation Iranischer Studenten/National Union (hrsg.). 1976. *Iran Report Extra: Ausverkauf eines unterentwickelt gehaltenen Landes – am Beispiel der wirtschaftlich-politischen Beziehung der BRD zum Iran*, Franfurt am Main: CISNU.

30. L.B., B Rep. 015, Nr. 317, *Berichte über Verfassungsfeindliche Veranstaltungen*, Re.: 'Bericht über die auf der "Internationalen Vietnam-Konferenz" gehaltenen Reden, Berlin (West)', 17 February 1968.

31. B.K., B 166, Nr. 1173, *Brief der Föderation der Iranischen Studenten an Verband Deutscher Studentenschaften*, Re.: 'Schikanen gegen Iranischen Studenten', Bonn, 4 June 1964.

32. L.B., B Rep. 015, Nr. 317, *Berichte über Verfassungsfeindliche Veranstaltungen*, Re.: 'Bericht über die auf der "Internationalen Vietnam-Konferenz" gehaltenen Reden, Berlin (West)', 17 February 1968, German original: 'faschistische Tendenzen' and 'Restauration'.

33. An excellent example of how these attitudes were reflected in the coverage by the Left-Liberal press of the Shah visit is an article by Bernhard Schützein *F.R.*, 'Ich nenne den Schah einen Mörder und bitte um Strafe', 2 August 1967; and in Hermann, *Die Revolte der Studenten*, 16–18.

34. B. Nirumand. 1967. *Persien: Modell eines Entwicklungslandes – Oder: Die Diktatur der Freien Welt*, Frankfurt a. M.: RoRoRo aktuell, 87.

35. Pol. A.A.Ber., B 42, Nr. 294, *Berichte über Iranische Angelegenheiten*, Re.: 'Majlis/Wahlen', Teheran, 25 October 1967.

36. M. Zonis. 1991. *Majestic Failure: the Fall of the Shah*, Chicago: University of Chicago Press, 134–37.

37. Pol. A.A.Ber., B 36, Nr. 108, *Berichte zu Beziehungen mit dem Iran*, Re.: 'Ermittlungsverfahren gegen persische Studenten: Berichte des Bundesamt für Verfassungsschutzes', Bonn, 1963–67.

38. B.K., B 141, Nr. 26028, *Legationsrat Bach an das Auswärtige Amt Bonn*, Re.: 'Bericht über Deutsch – Iranische Beziehungen nach dem Schahbesuch', Teheran, 10 August 1967.

39. Pol. A.A.Ber., B 36, Nr. 40, *Botschaftsangelegenheiten*, Re.: 'Verbalnoten der Iranischen Botschaft', March 1962–September 1967.

40. Pol. A.A.Ber., B 36, Nr. 40, *VLR Dr. Meyer Lindenberg an den Stellvertetenden Chef des Protokolls von Borries*, Re.: 'Bericht über Demonstrationen von ausländischen Studenten im Raum Bonn', Bonn, 30 October 1963.

41. B.K., B 166, Nr. 1173, *Briefe des Auswärtigen Amtes am Verband Deutscher Studentenschaften und Bericht eines VDS Vertreters über Lage Im Iran*, Re.: 'Mitteilung Ungern-Stermberg an Dr. Gehlhoff, Bonn, 18 January 1964, German original: 'Wir sollten den Herren Jaeger von störrerischen Elementen fern halten.'

42. B.K., B 166, Nr. 1173, *Verband Deutscher Studententschaften*, Re.: 'Briefe des Auswärtigen Amtes am Verband Deutscher Studentenschaften und Bericht eines VDS Vertreters über Lage im Iran', Bonn, 18 January 1964.

43. Ghaseminia, *Zur Lebensituation und Integration Iranischer Staatsangehöriger*, 128–32.

44. Ibid., 139–41.

45. B.K., B 141, Nr. 26030, *Bayerische Staatsministerium des Inneren am Bundesministerium des Inneren*, Re.: 'Bericht über Aktionen und Demonstrationen Iranischer Studenten', Bonn, 2 November 1971.

46. Pol. A.A.Ber, B 36, Nr. 108, *Bundesamt für Verfassungsschutz – Abteilung Schleswig-Holstein*, Re.: 'Vermerk über Tätigkeit des Iranischen Staatsangehörigen Massali', Kiel, 1 April 1964.

47. B.K., B 141, Nr. 26028, *Interne Mitteilungen Bundesministerium Justiz*, Re.: 'VDS und Massali', Bonn, October 1967.

48. Behrooz, *Rebels with a Cause*, 91.

49. Ibid., 90–94.

50. Pol. A.A.Ber., B 36, Nr. 108, *Berichte des Bundesamt für Verfassungsschutzes*, Re.: 'Ermittlungsverfahren gegen persische Studenten', Bonn, 1963–1967.

51. One example of which is: Pol. A.A.Ber., B 36, Nr. 107, *Dr. Ungern-Stermberg (Botschaft der BRD Teheran) an das Auswärtige Amt Bonn*, Re.: 'Politische Betätigung iranischer Studenten in der Bundesrepublik Deutschland', Teheran, 30 April 1964.

52. B.R., 'Persische Ärzte sollen KPD unterstützt haben: Gefängnis gefordert – Verteidiger: Die Angeklagten verdienen Respekt', 28 May 1964.

53. Pol. A.A.Ber., B 36, Nr. 41, *Interner Bericht des Auswärtigen Amtes*, Re.: 'Kommunistische Elemente unter iranischen Studenten', Bonn, 7 October 1963.

54. Pol. A.A.Ber., B 36, Nr. 294, *Bericht Abteilung I des Auswärtigen Amtes (VLR I Dr. Gehlhoff) an den Herrn Staatssekretär (i.V. Caspari)*, Re.: 'Hintergrund der Opposition iranischer Studenten gegen den Schah', Bonn, 3 September 1968. This report goes on to express the opinion of Middle East experts in the Foreign Ministry such as Gehlhoff that Nirumand as well as other Iranian dissidents had only claimed asylum in order to get access to better academic jobs in Europe and that the students would come to support the Shah regime after they had found jobs in Iran.

55. Nirumand, *Persien: Modell eines Entwicklungslandes – Oder: Die Diktatur der Freien Welt*.

56. L.B., B Rep. 015, Nr. 317, *Bericht über die Internationale Vietnam-Konferenz am 17. Februar 1968 in West Berlin*, Re.: 'Gehaltenen Reden', West Berlin, 21 February 1968.

57. Pol. A.A.Ber., B 36, Nr. 294, *Botschaftsangelegenheiten*, Re.: 'Besuche des iranischen Botschafters', March–May 1967.

58. The extensive nature of these preparations can be seen in memos by the Bavarian *Landpolizei*, timing the visit in twenty minute slots and giving a special code word for the possibility of assassination in Bay. HstA. Mun., Präsidium der Bayerischen Landpolizei: Nr. 9/1, *Staatsbesuche*, Re.: 'Staatsbesuch des Persischen Kaiserpaares', Ansbach, 26 May 1967.

59. S.Z., 'Peseraustausch Zum Schahbesuch – 107 müssen die Stadt verlassen/Kaisertreue Ersatzgruppe', 30 May 1967.

60. Bay. HstA. Mun., Präsidium d. Bayer. Landpolizei: Nr. 9/1, *Staatsbesuche*, Re.:'Staatsbesuch des persischen Kaiserpaares: vorbeugende Maßnahmen', Munich, 23 May 1967.

61. Bay. HstA. Mun., Präsidium der Bayerischen Landpolizei: Nr. 9/1, *Staatsbesuche*, Re.: 'Staatsbesuch des Persischen Kaiserpaares: vorbeugende Maßnahmen', Ansbach, 26 May 1967.

62. For Example: *Neue Revue*, 'Ein Tag im Leben der Shahbanu Farah', 28 May 1967.

63. *Bild*, 'Farah wird zweimal verzaubert', 27 May 1967.

64. *Bild*, 'Buh-Rufe: Maskierte Männer an der Straße', 29 May 1967.

65. Ibid.

66. S.Z., '"Die hat ja gar keine Krone auf": Schah Reza und Farah wurden von Prominenten begrüßt, von Polizisten abgeschirmt und vom FC Bayern besiegt', 2 June 1967.

67. S.Z., 'Ein Strauß vom persische Paradestudenten: umfangreiche Sicherheitsvorkehrungen beim Schah-Besuch behindern einen herzlichen Empfang des Kaiserpaars durch die Bevölkerung', 29 May 1967.

68. *Neues Deutschland*, 'Empörung und Erbitterung in der Studentenschaft', 4 June 1967.

69. Bundesbeauftragte für Staatssicherheitsunterlagen (BStU) Berlin, Aktenreihe 000053/ Ohnesorg, Re.: 'Schriftmaterial: "Folter und Terror", A. Hamann', Berlin, 1 June 1967, German original: 'Die freundliche Begrüßung des Schahs durch unsere Politiker ... ist ein Tritt für Demokratie und Gerechtigkeit. Protestieren sie dagegen! Tragen Sie die Abgeordneten der Parteien, wie sie dazu stehen! Protestieren Sie dagegen, daß deutsche Behörden der persischen Gestapo (SAVAK) die Überwachung und Verfolgung iranischer Studenten erlaubt und ihr sogar Amtshilfe leistet!'

70. *S.Z.*, 'Offene Fragen im Fall Ohnesorg', 7 June 1967, German original: 'Jubelperser' and 'Beleidung eines Staatsoberhauptes'.

71. *D.S.*, 'Knüppel Frei', 9 June 1967, German original: 'Wir werden schon mit diese Persische Sache fertig werden.'

72. *D.S.*, 'SAVAK: Spur in den 4. Stock', 12 October 1967.

73. *S.Z.*, 'Der Todessschuß fiel während der Zauberflöte', 5 June 1967.

74. Hermann, *Die Revolte der Studenten*, 16–17.

75. Gilcher-Holtey, *Die 68er Bewegung*, 69–70, German original: 'Bewegung 2. Juni'.

76. *D.W.*, 'Weichmann zog Bilanz des Schah-Besuchs – Dank an Hamburger – Trotzdem: "Schwarzer Tag für das Tor zur Welt"', 5 June 1967.

77. *F.A.Z.*, 'Kritik an der persischen Note', 28 July 1967.

78. Pol. A.A.Ber., B 36, Nr. 294, *Vermerk, Botschaftsangelegenheiten*, Re.: 'Vorsprache des iranischen Botschafters', Bonn, 14 July 1967.

79. Pol. A.A.Ber., B 36, Nr. 294, *Mitteilung – Botschaft der Bundesrepublik Deutschland in Teheran an Auswärtiges Amt Bonn*, Re.: 'Beziehungen des Irans zur sowjetischen Besatzungszone', Teheran, 28 November 1967, German original: 'An der Tatsache, daß vor einigen Monaten zwei Herren der Ostzone in Teheran gewesen sind und offensichtlich Gespräche im Sinne der Eingangs erwähnten Zeitungsmeldung führen wollten, wird nicht zu bezweifeln sein ... Bei der Frage, ob die iranische Regierung es zulassen wird, der SBZ die Tür zum Iran einen Spalt zu öffnen, wird sie sich weitgehend von den politischen Konzessionen und evtl. wirtschaftlichen Angeboten der SBZ leiten lassen ... Bei einer solchen Entscheidung wird sich die iranische Regierung jedenfalls nicht mehr im gleichen Maße wie bisher von der Rücksichtnahme auf unsere Wünsche beeinflussen lassen ... Zur Zeit des Besuchs von Herren Bundesinnenminister Lücke (13 September 1967) war zu verstehen gegeben worden, daß neben der Normalisierung der deutschen Presseberichterstattung über Iran eine Unterstützung der Bemühungen bei der Bekämpfung oppositioneller iranischer Kräfte in der Bundesrepublik Deutschland in iranischen Augen zur Wiederherstellung des alten guten Verhältnisses erforderlich erachtet würden.'

80. A. Sampson. 1988. *The Arms Bazaar*, London: Cornet (Hodder and Stoughton), 244–45.

81. Pol. A.A.Ber., B 36, Nr. 294, *Bericht – Botschaft der Bundesrepublik in Teheran and Auswärtiges Amt Bonn*, Re.: 'Deutsch-iranische Beziehungen', Teheran, 30 September 1967.

82. Pol. A.A.Ber., B 36, Nr. 323, *Bericht Auswärtiges Amt Bonn an die Deutsche Botschaft Teheran*, Re.: 'Ausländerrechtliche Maßnahmen (Ausweisung) gegen iranische Staatsangehörige in Berlin', Bonn, 10 January 1967.

83. B.K., B 141, Nr. 26028, *Iran/Schahbesuch*, Re.: 'Ermittlungsverfahren wegen Beleidigung des Schahs', Generalstaatsanwalt Berlin, 19 June 1967.

84. Bernhard Schütze, 'Ich nenne den Schah einen Mörder und bitte um Strafe', *F.R.*, 2 August 1967; *F.R.*, '2000 erstatteten Selbastanzeige: Lauterkeitskampagne der "Schah-Beleidiger"', 10 August 1967; *F.R.*, 'Persische Pervesion', 28 July 1967; H.-H. Heldmann. 1989. *Verwaltung Versus Verfassung: Ausländerrecht 1965–1988, Europäische Hochschulschriften* Vol. 882, Frankfurt a.M.: Peter Lang Verl., 93–95; and N. Thomas. 2003. *Protest Movements in 1960s West Germany*, Oxford: Berg, 115–17.

85. *F.A.Z.*, 'Für Persien Tragbar', 17 August 1967.

86. B.K., B 141, Nr. 26028, *Iran/Schahbesuch*, Re.: 'Bericht über mündliche Anfrage des Abgeordneten Borm über Demonstrationen beim Schahbesuch', 8 November 1967.

87. B.K., B 141, Nr. 26028, *Brief des Deutschen Botschafters an das Auswärtige Amt*, Re.: 'Besuch des Bundesinnenministers in Iran vom 9.–14. September 1967', Teheran, 13 September 1967, German original: 'Bundesinnenminister Lücke appellierte an den Schah, Verständnis für die Lage in der Bundesrepublik zu haben ... Er (Lücke) selbst glaube an die Berechtigung der Vorwürfe, die der Schah gegenüber der Bundesrepublik erhöbe. Er könne nur versichern, daß die Bundesregierung mit allen Kräften bemüht sei, die gestörten Beziehungen wieder in

Ordnung zu bringen. Er appelliere an das Herz des Schahs mitzuhelfen, daß das alte vertrauensvolle Freundschaftsverhältnis wieder hergestellt werde.'

88. B.K., B 141 Nr. 26028, *Iran/Schahbesuch, Deutsche Botschaft Teheran (Botschaftsrat Bach) an Bundesinnenministerium (Abteilungsleiter Winnefeld)*, Re.: 'Bericht der Deutschen Botschaft in Teheran über Besuch des Deutschen Innenministers den Schahdemonstrationen betreffend', 13 September 1967, 115–24.

89. B.K., B 141, Nr. 26028, *Schahdemonstrationen*, Re.: 'Bericht der Deutschen Botschaft Teheran über Besuch des Innenministers Lücke', Teheran, 13 September 1967.

90. *F.A.Z.*, 'Demonstrationen gegen den Schah: Wischnewski übt Kritik', 2 June 1967.

91. Bibliothek des Abgeordnetenhauses Berlin, Stenographische Berichte des Abgeordnetenhauses, 5. Wahlperiode/12. Sitzung (1. Band), 'Antrag der Fraktion der FDP über Einsetzung eines Untersuchungsausschusses zu den Ereignissen des 2. Juni', Berlin (West), 22 September 1967.

92. Best demonstrated in the barely controlled debate at the *Bundestag* which followed a question and answer session on the impact of the Shah's visit. B.K., B 141, Nr. 26028, *Iran/Schahbesuch*, Re.: 'Bericht über mündliche Anfrage des Abgeordneten Borm über Demonstrationen beim Schahbesuch', Bonn, 8 November 1967. Ironically this was mostly a debate between members of different wings of the SPD. Good examples of conservative press coverage are the articles on the Shah riots in the Axel Springer owned newspaper *Die Welt* between June and October. Particularly an article by Günter Zehm: *D.W.*, 'Studentische Lust am politischen Rabatz – Die Radikalen tarnen sich als "Gute Demokraten"', 7 June 1967.

93. Gilcher-Holtey, *Die 68er Bewegung*, 66–67.

94. Again the June issue of *Die Zeit* along with a variety of articles in the *Frankfurter Rundschau* and *Süddeutsche Zeitung* illustrate this tendency. This emphasis on continuities is perhaps best encapsulated in a book written on the events of the late 1960s by the *Die Zeit* commentator Kai Herrmann, *Die Revolte der Studenten*.

95. *Die Zeit*, 'Studenten und die Obrigkeit – Sie sind keine Messerstecher', 16 June 1967, German original: 'In diesen Vorgängen ist ihnen (die Studenten) der Begriff einer unkontrollierten Gewalt deutlich geworden, die des Menschen Würde und Freiheit aus Lust an der Brutalität, aus dem Vergnügen an der Vernichtung zu zerstören versucht. Sie empfinden das als "faschistisch", und sie haben Angst: vor dem Knüppel – und vor der Zukunft.'

96. Bay. HstA. Mun., Pol. Dir. Nr. 9582/2, *Bericht KA III an Bayer. Staatsministerium des Innern*, Re.: 'Besetzung und Räumung des Kaiserlich Iranischen Generalkonsulats am 4. 8. 1970', Munich, 11 August 1970.

97. Bay. HstA. Mun., Pol. Dir. Nr. 9582/2, *Brief des Oberbürgermeisters Dr. Vogel an das Polizeipräsidium*, Re.: 'Angebliche Aushändigung einer Namensliste an den persischen Geheimdienst', Munich, 8 February 1971.

98. Amiri, 'Die Iranische Minderheit', 214.

99. W. Kraushaar. 2000. *Die Protest Chronik 1949–1959: Volume 3*, Hamburg: Rogner und Bernhard, 1953–54.

100. *F.A.Z.*, 'Schärfere Ausländerkontrolle zu spät gekommen?', 7 September 1972.

101. *D.S.*, 'Tiefe Finsternis: Chomeini-Anhänger schlagen unter Allah-rufen Chomeini-Gegner zusammen', 3 May 1982.

102. Heldmann, *Verwaltung versus Verfassung*, 97.

Conclusion

NATION AND FRAGMENTATION

MANAGING DIVERSITY

In the first three decades after the foundation of the Federal Republic, the actions of the immigrant movements examined in this book repeatedly forced West German governments to grapple with the consequences of ethnic diversity. While many politicians and state officials continued to assert that Germany was 'not a country of immigration' until the late 1990s, in the preceding decades day-to-day contact with groups as diverse as Croatian and Ukrainian nationalists, Spanish anti-Franco activists, Algerian FLN supporters or radical Iranian students meant that for all levels of government immigrants were a political force to be reckoned with. How West German political parties, state institutions or nongovernmental organizations coped with the specific political cultures of each emerging immigrant community would therefore be as significant as new naturalization laws or levels of prosperity when it came to the eventual integration of guest workers and émigrés.

West Germany was not the only country in which state institutions and political parties were forced to deal with the social consequences of immigration. Between the end of the Second World War and the oil crisis of the mid 1970s, mass immigration helped to transform the face of Western Europe and North America. Gianni Toniolo has described these thirty years as 'Europe's Golden Age', a period in which unprecedented levels of economic growth helped an entire continent recover from economic depression and war.[1] In Western Europe, North America and Japan, the increased prosperity and political stability of the late 1950s and early 1960s fostered gradual democratization of state institutions, the introduction of a consensual relationship between unions and employers as well shifts in cultural attitudes when it came to such issues as women's rights and the environment. In countries such as Britain, France or the United States, the activity of homeland-oriented immigrant movements became intertwined with the political impact of these and other cultural or economic trends.

In Britain, MI5 and Special Branch have monitored developments in the Irish community since the Irish Republican Army re-emerged in 1968. Moreover, by the late 1970s, the growth of Sikh and Muslim extremist organizations among ethnic groups from the Indian subcontinent began to become an area of concern for the British security services as well.[2] In France, many different African and Arab communities, which came into being in Paris and other major cities during the decolonization process, became equally prone to internal strife and intervention from the French state because of developments in their homelands.[3] At the same time, British and French trade union federations actively cultivated members of immigrant movements close to their own working-class support base in much the same way that the DGB engaged with Algerian or Spanish guest workers.[4] In the United States and Canada, the sheer size of such enfranchised ethnic minorities as the Ukrainians, Jews or Irish meant that politicians had to pay heed to the political demands of their community organizations. As a result, the power of such ethnic lobbies has often played a role in shaping the foreign policy of North American governments.[5] In each of these countries, mass immigration during the Cold War has blurred the line between domestic politics and foreign policy, since political developments in states exporting political refugees or economic migrants had a direct impact upon immigrant communities in Western Europe and North America.

The nature of such immigrant political activity was affected by the approach each national government took towards administering and integrating their immigrant populations. Both Canada and the United States usually tried to ensure the political allegiance of their new citizens by naturalizing and enfranchising them as quickly as possible. Over time this tended to dampen the commitment of ethnic communities to diaspora politics, as their politically active members found an equally profitable field for their endeavours in the city councils, regional assemblies and national parliaments of their new countries. Yet considerable differences still existed between Canada and the USA when it came to the political integration of immigrants. Despite the fact that ethnic lobbies continue to exert a strong hold on politicians in Washington, the enfranchisement of immigrants has meant that homeland politics has had a decreasing impact upon the daily lives of ethnic minorities. In Canada, however, the implementation of the doctrine of multiculturalism by the Canadian state after 1968 in order to minimize tension between French and English-speaking provinces meant that successive governments strengthened the cohesion of immigrant groups by providing financial and moral support to their community institutions.[6]

Though West European countries have had to cope with the same challenges, states such as Britain, France, Belgium or the Netherlands could look back to an imperial tradition of contact and rule over the regions from which they drew immigrant labour. By contrast, the countries from which most immigrants to the Federal Republic originated had at most been ruled directly by Germany for a short, and very brutal, period during the Second World War. For all the conflict caused by legacies of empire, the colonial background linking the French state with immigrants from Africa or Britain with immigrants from the Indian subcontinent meant that a common political language existed between immigrants and the indigenous population. As a result, both the British and French states were at least prepared to accept the possibility of immigrant participation in their political systems through the acquisition of citizenship.[7] While this approach has only been partially successful, the existence of an open path into the political establishment for some first or second generation immigrants as well as the emergence of immigrant electoral blocs have enabled immigrant communities in Britain and France to take a direct part in the political process.

As we have seen in the course of this study, without the tradition of integration and multiculturalism that had shaped public discourse in the United States and Canada or the shared legacy of empire to be found in so many European countries, the relationship between immigrants and Germans was shaped by two factors that were intertwined in a fashion specific to the Federal Republic. The impact the historical legacy of the Nazi regime had on the societies of both the homeland states and the Federal Republic meant that controversies involving the recent past often had a major impact on German political life. At the same time, the common language of Cold War conflict cut across national and religious differences and provided a means with which immigrant movements could position themselves in the political framework of the Federal Republic.

Cold War conflict was the more significant of these two factors. The relevance of the Second World War for an immigrant political movement depended on the extent to which its homeland state had been involved in the conflicts of the 1930s and 1940s. While the historical legacy of the Nazi regime was central to the political experience of the Ukrainian, Greek or Spanish communities, it was more peripheral to that of groups such as the Iranians, Turks or Kurds. By contrast, the political divisions fostered by the Cold War were of equal importance to every immigrant community. Ideological polarization mirroring the rivalry between the American and Soviet blocs, which took its most extreme form in the division of Germany into two rival Eastern and Western states, could be found in every state exporting labour to the Federal Republic. Whatever other national agendas an immigrant movement may have had, the key factor determining the kind of partners it would find in Germany was its attitude towards Soviet communism in general, and East Germany in particular. Each chapter of this book has shown the different ways in which these factors combined to affect the internal development of immigrant communities.

The relationship of Ukrainian political groups examined in the first chapter with West German politicians and state officials was complicated by the historical legacy of the national socialist regime in Eastern Europe. After 1945, Ukrainian émigrés initially benefited from long-standing contact with members of the West German political establishment. By contrast the work of Polish activists was obstructed by conservative German bureaucrats and politicians, though they couched their hostility towards Poland and all forms of Polish nationalism in rather more conciliatory rhetoric than that of the Nazi or Weimar governments. Yet the way this historical legacy affected the further development of these two émigré communities was determined by the shifting nature of the Cold War. It was common interest in the demise of the USSR and the boundaries determined by the Yalta Accords that drew Ukrainian émigrés and West German conservatives together. In this context, however strong their anti-communist credentials, other groups such as Polish or Czech émigré organizations unwilling to accept a revision of the post-1945 settlement were never going to be able to overcome a more powerful ethnic German expellee lobby. Thus, during the Adenauer era the reasons for the relative success of Ukrainian nationalists were exactly the same ones ensuring the failure of other East European émigré groups.

Yet the support the Ukrainian community enjoyed from the West German political establishment was of a fragile nature. Having tied themselves so closely to their old contacts in the CSU and the more conservative elements of the security services, an ageing Ukrainian émigré community was caught out when the centre-left gained power. The growing influence of the SPD over policy making at the federal level after 1966, which led to the *Ostpolitik* initiatives of the Brandt government, meant that anti-communist émigrés like the Ukrainian nationalists lost the support of government agencies on which they had become so heavily dependent. This shift did not help other émigré groups either since, as Timothy Garton Ash has pointed out, the SPD's desire to come to a final status agreement over the Oder/Neisse boundary with the Polish and Soviet governments made the Brandt/Scheel coalition unwilling to upset the status quo in Eastern Europe.[8] While the ideological outlook of East European émigré organizations remained constant throughout this period, it was the underlying political consensus of the Federal Republic that had changed fundamentally.

The political position of Croatian nationalist organizations examined in the second chapter was undermined by a similar policy shift. The Croatian community was unique in that it was made up of both émigrés that had fled from Yugoslavia in the late 1940s and a much greater number of economic migrants that had arrived as a result of the guest worker programme. As we have seen, Croatian nationalist groups could take advantage of a large reservoir of potential supporters who could move back and forth between West Germany and their homeland in a fashion that would have been unthinkable for other East Europeans in the FRG. Yet this also created pressure on established émigrés to attain and keep the support of radical guest worker compatriots. These internal tensions led many community leaders to condone or even take part in acts of violence committed by more extreme Croatian activists that were bound to alienate politically moderate Germans from the Croatian nationalist cause.

Moreover, Croatian nationalists found themselves in a weaker position than other East European émigré groups because of the complex relationship that existed between the Federal Republic and the Yugoslav state. The alliance between the *Ustascha* predecessors of the Croatian nationalist movement and the Nazi regime encouraged many within the West German centre-right to distance themselves from groups that might act as a reminder of the German occupation of Yugoslavia during the Second World War. These pressures became more acute once the SPD took power in Bonn, since social democrats openly tried to develop closer relations with the Tito regime. Nevertheless, as the aftermath of the Mehlem attack indicated, the impact that memories of the *Ustascha*'s alliance with the Nazi regime had on West German attitudes towards Croatian nationalism was shaped by the ambiguous strategic position of Cold War Yugoslavia. West German governments considered Yugoslavia, a communist yet anti-Soviet state, to be a potential strategic partner, making it almost impossible for Croatian nationalists to gain West German support. The historical legacy of the Second World War did not prevent the Adenauer government from trying to build an anti-Soviet partnership with the Tito regime, which never ceased to demand the suppression of Croatian nationalist organizations in the Federal Republic. Moreover, it increased the centre-left's distrust of a Croatian nationalist movement whose violent rhetoric and tactics threatened a key aspect of *Ostpolitik*.

The relationships that Spanish and Algerian immigrants developed with the SPD and the West German state, explored in Chapter 3, were heavily influenced by the interest the German Left took in their homelands and the ideological orientation of their own dominant community organizations. Spaniards opposed to Franco and Algerians who supported the FLN were able to build strategic alliances with those elements of the West German Left with which they had a certain level of ideological compatibility. In the case of the Spanish community, the toleration of anti-Franco activity became an important component of wider strategy developed by the SPD in the 1970s, designed to rebuild the Spanish Socialist Party and its unions through aid provided by the DGB and the *Friedrich Ebert Stiftung*.[9] Whether in government or opposition, leading social democrats were in a position to make sure that state institutions exercised flexibility when it came to determining whether the activity of Spanish political groups conformed to the constitutional order of the Federal Republic.

In the case of the Algerians, though individual SPD functionaries openly backed the Algerian nationalist movement, the party and the trade unions avoided any direct or formal cooperation with the FLN. The limited nature of the German centre-left's support for Algerian nationalism in the late 1950s and early 1960s demonstrates how sympathy for an immigrant cause among prominent social democrats did not automatically lead to full institutional support from the SPD or trade unions. The way politicized Algerian immigrants were treated by the security services and the SPD also demonstrates how postwar political change, in this case the shift from hostility to friendship in relations between France and Germany, could impose limits on the extent to which both the German Left and the German Right could work together with certain immigrant political movements. While the legacy of history improved the position of left-wing Spanish guest workers, it neither helped nor hindered the FLN from achieving its goals in the Federal Republic. Moreover, both cases illustrate how the ideological context of the Cold War shaped the manner in which prewar links with homeland states affected the relationship between West German political milieus and immigrant movements. Yet where Cold War conflict brought West German conservatives and émigré anti-communists together, it complicated the SPD's relationship with left-wing immigrants.

The West German security services' contradictory approach towards the conflicts within the Greek community analysed in the fourth chapter, confirms that rather than any specific law and order concerns, the ideological tensions of the Cold War shaped the response of state institutions to immigrant political violence. Until the late 1960s, support for the Greek Communist Party among Greek guest workers and students heightened worries within the centre-right and the security services that the guest worker programme might help pro-Soviet agitators to infiltrate West German factories.[10] The Grand Coalition between the CDU/CSU and SPD transformed this situation. After 1966 the presence of social democrats in government meant that security services and other state institutions dealing with immigrant affairs were encouraged by their political masters to treat the immigrant Left in a more flexible fashion.

In the Greek case however, a major political shift in the homeland had a particular impact on community organizations and their relationship with the West German political establishment. While in the early 1960s West German security services and the *Auswärtiges Amt* had been convinced that Greek democracy was threatened by the communists, it was ultimately undermined by an anti-communist military coup.[11] Attempts by Greek diplomats and intelligence agents to provide support for right-wing Greek guest workers only provoked the moderate West German Left, whose senior leaders believed that this kind of intervention by a homeland regime was a direct attack on the democratic order of the Federal Republic rather than just an internal Greek issue. As long as most of their activists remained close to the SPD and DGB Greek left-wing organizations were able to operate freely even when individual members or splinter groups used violent tactics. Thus, this effort by German social democrats to channel politicized guest workers away from pro-communist groups protected those political groups opposed to the government of a fellow member of NATO. By intervening in such conflicts between guest worker and émigré organizations, West German political parties, nongovernmental organizations and state institutions became direct participants in the internal battles of immigrant communities.

As the two main political parties in the FRG developed increasingly divergent approaches towards relations with the East German regime, immigrant political movements had more space to develop their own specific policy stance when it came to the 'German Question'. Yet the experience of the Iranian community demonstrates that the shift in West German foreign policy from the *Hallstein* doctrine of the 1950s to Willy Brandt's *Ostpolitik* of the 1970s did not benefit all left-wing immigrant organizations. The events explored in the fifth chapter indicate that the gradual rejection of the aims of émigré and expellee groups by SPD governments did not improve the position of immigrants who expressed sympathy with East German communism. Since their most successful homeland organizations were too closely associated with orthodox communism or more fashionable forms of neo-Marxism to be able to gain any wider support in the SPD, Iranians fighting to topple the Shah regime were therefore only able to find allies within the extra-parliamentary New Left.

In this context, allusions to the Nazi regime were used by left-wing supporters of the Iranian opposition as a means with which to attack the West German establishment as well as criticize the Shah regime. Conversely, centre-right media commentators and politicians who considered both German and immigrant members of the New Left to represent a threat to democracy equated the actions of anti-Shah activists with those of the Nazi and communist street thugs of the 1930s. As in the case of the Greek and Croatian communities, historical analogies with the Nazi era became a rhetorical weapon used by supporters and opponents of a homeland regime that played a key strategic role in the Cold War.

Yet the manner in which Cold War conflict and historical memory influenced relations between immigrant political movements and West German political parties or state institutions depended on the internal development of each guest worker or émigré group. The fact that ideological tensions caused by the Cold War had such a considerable impact on these communities demonstrates the extent to which homeland-oriented political activism can affect the integration of immigrants into a host society. While this study has illustrated how the Cold War and, to a lesser extent, the legacy of the Nazi regime affected each immigrant community in the Federal Republic, it has also shown how other factors such as ideological diversity within communities, changes in the homeland states, demography and socio-economic structure could push them into very different social and political directions.

Demographic development could have a particularly stark effect on the political behaviour of immigrant communities. In the late 1940s the relative youth of East European émigré groups that hoped to overturn the Potsdam settlement helped trigger a wave of anti-Soviet activity. Similarly, the large number of younger workers and students within the expanding Iranian, Greek and Spanish communities of the 1960s fuelled a surge in homeland-oriented political activity. In both cases, the assumption that a return to their home countries was imminent helped motivate rank and file immigrant activists. As émigrés aged and their numbers decreased the stabilization of the Cold War order led to a decline in political activity. Thus, it was relatively easy for the Brandt government to cut financial aid to East European émigrés since such miniscule and ageing communities were unlikely to cause much trouble. The great exception to this rule was the Croatian community, whose sudden expansion through the guest worker programme enabled violent nationalist factions to recruit impressionable young Croatian migrants, leading to a further deterioration of relations between Croatian nationalists and the West German government. Conversely, the fact that the Spanish and Greek communities were expanding quickly made it easier for senior social democrats and trade unionists to foster friendly political organizations within these two groups. For all the protection friendly political parties or security services could provide certain guest worker or émigré organizations, demographic change could still push the political development of immigrant groups in directions that were difficult for both West German politicians and community leaders to predict.

Political diversity within an immigrant community, usually reflecting political patterns in the homeland state, could also have a significant impact on how its members responded to their new social environment. The Greeks were most heavily affected by such internal conflict, as rival political groups who either supported or opposed the military regime in Athens threatened to tear their community apart. In such a fraught environment, West German security services and political parties decided to take sides, as conflicts in Greece became inextricably linked with domestic ideological rifts in the Federal Republic through the actions of Greek diplomats and Greek trade unionists in Germany. In a similar fashion, Croatian nationalists or Algerian members of the FLN also used violence to intimidate compatriots who did not support their goals.[12] As has been explored at several points in this study, West German bureaucrats and politicians confronted with such divided communities also had to deal with émigrés and guest workers who used the political language of the Cold War and the legacy of the Nazi regime as rhetorical weapons in the battle against opponents within their own communities.

Major political changes in immigrant homelands as well as relations between their governments and the West German state were also crucial. In the Croatian case, an immigrant political movement that was initially tolerated by the security services was left out in the cold once West German policy makers tried to improve relations with the Yugoslav government. This weakened the position of activists within the Croatian nationalist movement who supported peaceful lobbying and strengthened those who believed in the need for radical action. The hostility of the SPD or CDU/CSU towards a homeland regime could also help immigrant political movements. Spanish socialists opposed to the Franco regime and East European émigrés fighting the Soviet Union even enjoyed some measure of covert government support. Yet in both cases immigrant political movements were seen more as a means to an end rather than as equal political partners. While help for anti-Franco activists was designed to curb communist influence in Spain, the security services saw Ukrainian émigrés as expendable pawns in the battle against the communist bloc. By contrast, the impact of the Athens military coup on a Greek community, which was already beset by heavy tensions between Left and Right, demonstrated how a major political event in a homeland state could suddenly create a new set of domestic problems for a West German government. In each of these cases the division of Europe into two rival ideological camps shaped the political framework in which state institutions and immigrant movements interacted with one another.

What is also striking when one compares these communities is the extent of the social and religious differences between and at times even within them. While the Spanish and Greek communities were mostly made up of guest workers brought in by the labour importation programme, Iranians in the Federal Republic tended to be students and university trained professionals whose parents belonged to the rural and urban middle classes. Émigré groups consisted of POWs and slave labourers who came from all social classes as well as university trained activists who remained for political reasons. Made up of a disparate combination of postwar political refugees, students and guest workers, the Croatians do not fit into any preconceived notions of immigrant communities in West Germany either. The linguistic difficulties of many guest workers from rural or working-class backgrounds strengthened the position of community leaders, who could help vulnerable new arrivals in their dealings with the German bureaucracy through parish church associations, trade unions or such community organizations as the *Kroatischer Sozialdienst*.[13] The feelings of obligation this kind of help could engender can be seen in the influence community notables such as Father Medic-Skoko in 1950s Dortmund or Greek trade union leaders in 1970s Hanover were able to exert over younger guest workers.

By contrast, the middle-class Christian democratic circles with which most senior émigrés were associated or the student movement that supported left-wing immigrant causes were very different from the industrial working-class environment in which economic migrants lived and worked. With a better educational and financial base, Iranians and émigré intellectuals in West Germany were far less dependent upon community leaders than their guest worker counterparts.[14] Moreover, Iranian students arrived in Germany at a point when very few Iranians lived in the Federal Republic, forcing them to construct their own political organizations rather than slotting into any pre-existing structures controlled by compatriots who had other political or class backgrounds. Equally significant was the fact that East European émigrés and Iranians already spoke German or learned it quite quickly in order to be able to work with other colleagues or students. These German language skills and a university education usually helped them to maintain a middle-class lifestyle, encouraging further integration into West German society. As a result, the Iranian community had one of the highest rates of immigrant naturalization before 1989.[15]

Along with their socio-economic structure, the religious tradition of these communities was also important. The large number of Catholics in the Spanish and Croatian communities enabled both to build on established cultural ties with those German regions where Catholic traditions dominated public life. Yet there were still considerable differences in how the Catholic Church affected the position of Spanish and Croatian immigrants. While the success of left-wing unions in recruiting Spanish guest workers limited the influence of the Church, the crucial role played by Catholicism in the Croatian nationalist tradition helped make the Croatian Catholic Mission one of the central elements of community life for Croatians in the Federal Republic. The Catholic Church therefore played a much greater role in shaping the political alliances forged between West Germans and Croatian activists than it did when it came to the local partners chosen by Spanish guest workers.

Intriguingly, the dominant political groups in communities with a Muslim majority had greater similarities with their Spanish counterparts than Croatian organizations when it came to the role of religion in community life. The development of the Iranian, Kurdish and Turkish communities tended to be dominated by secular political groups that caused West German security services much deeper concern than any religious networks until the mid 1970s. The organizations that worried the *Verfassungsschutz* or BKA the most usually espoused extreme leftist ideology such as the neo-Marxism of the Iranian Tudeh Party, or had an extreme ethnic nationalist agenda, like the Turkish 'Grey Wolves'. In fact, conservative Muslim or Islamic fundamentalist organizations only began to grow after the termination of the guest worker programme in 1973, as immigrants who brought their wives and children to the FRG became more focused on maintaining their own cultural traditions within a hostile social environment.[16]

Such massive structural change within groups such as the Turkish or Greek communities meant that in many cases greater affluence and stability did not necessarily lead to greater integration. As Ertekin Özcan has pointed out, disillusioned by a widespread unwillingness among Germans to accept them as social equals, many better educated middle-class Turks in the Federal Republic of the 1970s and 1980s became involved in extreme nationalist or religious groups that isolated them from mainstream German society, a pattern that in different ways was replicated in some of the communities examined in this study.[17] Yet even in the late 1970s, state officials and security services at the municipal and regional level openly stated that together with social democratic or nonviolent nationalist groups, Islamic religious institutions could help to prevent Muslim guest workers from getting involved in networks considered to be too close to Soviet communism or the New Left.[18] The considerable differences between these various communities show how each new ethnic minority created its own specific political culture, formed by a combination of the ideological context of the homeland state and the manner in which its members ultimately settled in the Federal Republic. Rather than primarily being the result of broad national peculiarities determined by some form of vaguely defined 'East European', 'Balkan' or 'Islamic' culture, the relationship between immigrant communities and their host society was strongly affected by the direct sociopolitical context in which their members were operating.

Between 1945 and 1975, immigrants creating such different and often rival community infrastructures transformed the patterns of daily life across the Federal Republic. Only with the rampant growth of an abundant, open and fractious immigrant presence in the course of the 1950s and 1960s did the urban and social spaces of the Federal Republic recognizably become what they are today. One of the few factors shared by such a remarkably diverse set of immigrant groups was the high level of political engagement to be found across these communities. With homeland-oriented activism at the core of this process of community building, adaptation and, paradoxically, integration, the ideological debates that dominated political discourse in homelands and the host society at the height of this migration process formed the social framework in which these immigrant political movements interacted with their German counterparts. The ideological conflicts of the Cold War and related debates over the legacy of the Hitler regime therefore played a fundamental part in shaping the long-term relationship of immigrant communities with Germans and the West German state.

The underlying impact of Cold War conflict on immigrant life in Germany has wider implications for the study of mass immigration as a whole. Each of the last five chapters has examined three factors, political violence involving immigrants, the attitude of state organizations and officials towards migrants and the integration of ethnic minorities into the cultural and political institutions of a host society, which have become key areas of focus in the fields of migration studies and immigration history.[19] The way in which the ideological framework of the Cold War helped to determine the fate of both violent and nonviolent immigrant activists in the Federal Republic can therefore also provide some insights into how political conflict and change in homelands and host societies shaped the immigrant experience throughout Europe and North America after the Second World War.

For all the demographic, religious and social differences between them, the internal development of every one of the immigrant communities examined in this study was determined by three key factors: the political culture of their homelands, how and why their members moved to a new host society, and the sociopolitical conflicts and debates that dominated public discourse in their new country of settlement. The importance of homeland-oriented movements in West Germany undermines the assumption, made by Ulrich Herbert, among others, that immigrant populations react to state policy in uniform fashion, and also dents the hypothesis that transnational diasporas manage to transcend the differences between the societies in which they settle put forward by migration scholars such as Yasemin Soysal. This second approach has underestimated the importance of relationships between immigrant political movements and their West German allies. The ability of indigenous partners to help homeland-oriented organizations despite the scepticism or even outright hostility of state institutions demonstrated the limits on the West German state's capacity to control immigrant life. Moreover, within their own community infrastructure immigrant groups produce their own hierarchies and leaders that any state institution or political party ignores at its peril. When it comes to managing integration, a willingness to engage with these kinds of structures and develop a better awareness of whether such community leaders really do have widespread support in their own communities could enable governments to avoid some of the problems and pitfalls encountered by the West German state.

The response of West German security officials, politicians and diplomats to immigrant political violence is of great significance in this respect. Despite ritualistic denunciations of acts of violence committed by guest workers or DPs by members of the West German political establishment, the divergent treatment of the Spanish, Croatian, Greek and Iranian communities by the security services demonstrated that 'terrorism' did not in itself decide the fate of an immigrant political movement. Though each of these communities contained groups who were prepared to use violent tactics, the extent to which these incidents led to retaliatory action against a wider community by the West German state was entirely dependent upon the ideological stance of its dominant political movement. This selective approach effectively undermines the claim, made by the West German political establishment throughout the Cold War, that each new minority would be treated equally by the state.

This kind of ideologically driven state approach may have fostered a political phenomenon known as 'blowback'. A term coined by CIA operatives working in Afghanistan, 'blowback' was originally used to describe the process by which anti-Soviet guerrilla movements supported by the United States turned on their backers after 1989. The most famous example of 'blowback' is the Wahhabi Islamist organizations that worked together with the CIA in Afghanistan and then went on to identify the United States as their main opponent after the collapse of the USSR.[20] The militancy and isolation that have increased in a variety of immigrant communities in Germany and elsewhere in Europe over the last twenty years could be the result of a particularly European form of 'blowback'. This book has shown that when it came to immigrant groups such as the Turkish or Iranian communities, the West German state tried to suppress immigrant political movements that the security services believed to be ideologically unreliable. Yet many of these organizations were secular, fighting for ideologies, which, for all their profound problems, at least promoted the idea of a universal brotherhood of man. By crushing movements with a Marxist background, European states created a space that was filled by fundamentalist and extreme nationalist groups which possessed appropriate anti-communist credentials. Seen from this angle one could argue that the self-imposed isolation and political extremism of some immigrant communities has proven to be one of the major legacies of the Cold War.

Such judgements over the ideological reliability of ethnic minorities were made by government officials who, as members of the German upper middle class, had little direct contact with the guest workers or DPs they were trying to manage. The politicians and party functionaries who were the other key players when it came to immigration policy had strategic political agendas that did not necessarily provide a sound basis for the long-term integration of immigrants either. When it came to the CDU and East European émigrés, social democrats and the Greek and Spanish opposition, or the New Left and Iranian students,

German political milieus treated immigrant political activists as a means to the end of fostering change in their respective homelands, rather than treating the further integration of their communities into West German society as an end in itself. The tendency of regional and federal officials to focus on their German intermediaries at the expense of direct contact with immigrant leaders meant that the involvement of the SPD or the CDU/CSU in DP and guest worker politics did not ultimately lead to a wider or longer term state strategy to deal with the consequences of mass immigration. These attitudes made it more difficult for even the savviest of first generation immigrant activists to shake off their belief in the possibility of an eventual return to their homeland. Only in the late 1980s, when both immigrants and Germans slowly accepted the fact that the immigrant communities were there to stay, could a different approach come to the fore.

In 1960s and 1970s West Germany however, initiatives designed to foster the long-term integration of immigrants were few and far between. Throughout the history of the Bonn Republic, official policy was always dominated by the initial claim that Germany was not a country of immigration and that guest workers were only a transient presence, there merely to ameliorate a temporary labour shortage. Most guest workers were themselves happy to buy into this illusion, preoccupied as they were with earning enough money to afford a permanent return to their countries of origin.[21] Only when many among their children and grandchildren began to build alliances with or even became an integral part of the kinds of sociocultural milieus that provided the basis of the Green Party of the mid 1980s, such as the squatting scene or the anti-fascist movements, did the political life of immigrant communities focus increasingly on the politics of the Federal Republic without reference to developments in the homeland states. Yet at the same time, within this eponymous second generation, milieus also began to emerge that instead sought to become part of transnational political movements such as Islamic revolutionary networks that intrinsically tied conflict in homeland states and the Federal Republic with a global Manichean struggle between rival civilizations.

Paradoxically, the experience of the Iranian, Greek and Spanish communities shows how homeland-oriented movements could even inadvertently help to integrate their members into the social structures of a host society. Though they often worked to strengthen the 'myth of return', the fact that immigrant organizations and activists had to adapt to a different political system, forge alliances with sympathetic members of the local population and actively engage in public debate in order to further their homeland agenda helped to draw those involved in such movements into the political and cultural discourse of their new country. Whether this process helped to eventually integrate immigrants, as was the case with many Ukrainian, Spanish or Iranian activists, or failed to overcome the fixation with events in the homeland on which most immigrant organizations were founded, as in many parts of the Turkish,

Kurdish, Algerian or Croatian communities, largely depended on the social pressures they experienced in their country or city of settlement. Many immigrants point to their rejection in 1983 of the Kohl government's scheme to lower immigrant numbers by providing grants to those who moved back to their homeland, as the moment when they were finally willing to postpone their planned return indefinitely. The fall of the Berlin Wall in 1989 was of equal significance, since one of its consequences was a new influx of economic migrants and asylum seekers in the early 1990s. In the following years established guest worker communities, whose members had only just accepted that their future lay in Germany, felt as challenged by these newcomers as the indigenous German population. For their part, the old DP organizations were overwhelmed by the arrival of much younger compatriots that were not prepared to defer to elderly émigré leaders, many of whom had not realized how much their homelands had changed since the Second World War.[22] To those who belonged to this third wave of mass migration, both DPs and guest workers, along with their businesses, places of worship and political institutions had become an established part of the society in which these newcomers were trying to find a niche of their own.

Notes

1. G. Toniolo. 1998. 'Europe's Golden Age, 1950–1973: Speculations From a Long-run Perspective', *Economic History Review* LI(2), 252–67.
2. T.O. Lloyd. 1993. *Empire, Welfare State and Europe: English History 1906–1992*, 4th ed., Oxford: Oxford University Press, 519–20; and R. Foster. 1998. *Modern Ireland 1600–1972*, London: Penguin, 589–92.
3. A. Horne. 2002. *A Savage War of Peace: Algeria 1954–1962*, London: Pan Books, 183–207.
4. G. Freeman. 1978. 'Immigrant Labor and Working-Class Politics: the French and British Experience', *Comparative Politics* 11(1), 24–51.
5. C. Sypnowich. 2000. 'The Culture of Citizenship', *Politics & Society* 28(4), 531–55.
6. W.H. Katerberg. 1995. 'The Irony of Identity: an Essay on Nativism, Liberal Democracy, and Parochial Identities in Canada and the United States', *American Quarterly* 47(3), 493–524.
7. R. Brubaker. 2001. 'The Return of Assimilation? Changing Perspectives on Immigration and its Sequels in France, Germany and the United States', *Ethnic and Racial Studies* 24(4), 535–39.
8. T. Garton Ash. 1999. *The Polish Revolution: Solidarity*, 2nd ed., London: Penguin, 329–38.
9. P. Mueller M. and Müller. 2002. *Gegen Freund und Feind – Der BND: Geheime Politik und Schmutzige Geschäfte*, Hamburg: Rowohlt Verl., 472–81.
10. Bay. HstA, Staatsarchiv Munich, Polizei Direktion München, Nr. 9381, *Bericht vom Bundeskriminalamt – Sicherungsgruppe 1Bad Godesberg*: 'Auswertungsbericht zu dem im Ermittlungsverfahren 2 BJ.s 22/65 des Herrn Generalbundesanwalts sichergestellten Beweismaterial – Tätigkeit des KOUNALAKIS für die ENIAA DIMOKRATIKI ARISTERA (EDA)', Bad Godesberg, 31 October 1965.
11. C. von Braunmühl. 1973. *Kalter Krieg und Friedliche Koexistenz: Die Außenpolitik der SPD in der Großen Koalition*, Frankfurt, a.M.: Suhrkamp Verl., 41.
12. *D.S.*, 'Fünfter Dan', 22 March 1981.

13. D. Belosevic. 1995. 'Die Minderheiten aus den ehemaligen Jugoslawien', in C. Schmalz-Jacobsen (ed.), *Ethnische Minderheiten in der Bundesrepublik Deutschland*, Munich: C.H. Beck, 278–85.

14. M. Ghaseminia. 1996. *Zur Lebensituation und Integration Iranischer Staatsangehöriger in Niedersachsen*, Hanover: Universität Hannover, 209–21.

15. K. Amiri. 1995. 'Die Iranische Minderheit', in C. Schmalz-Jacobsen (ed.), *Ethnische Minderheiten in der Bundesrepublik Deutschland*, Munich: C.H. Beck, 207–9.

16. C. Wilpert. 1977. 'Children of Foreign Workers in the Federal Republic of Germany', *International Migration Review* 11(4), 481–83.

17. E. Özcan. 1989. *Türkische Immigrantenorganisationen in der Bundesrepublik Deutschland*, Berlin: Hitit Verl, 171–74.

18. *D.S.*, 'Graue Wölfe: " Jede Mark ist eine Kugel"', 14 June 1980.

19. For example see C. Strikwerda. 1999. 'Tides of Migration, Currents of History: the State, Economy, and the Transatlantic Movement of Labor in the Nineteenth and Twentieth Centuries', *International Review of Social History* 44, 367–94.

20. G. O' Tuathail. 2000. 'The Postmodern Geopolitical Condition', *Annals of the Association of American Geographers* 90(1), 175.

21. U. Herbert and K. Hunn. 2001. 'Guest Workers and Policy on Guest Workers in the Federal Republic', in H. Schissler (ed.), *The Miracle Years: a Cultural History of West Germany 1949–1968*, Princeton: Princeton University Press, 187–98.

22. Özcan, *Türkische Immigrantenorganisationen*, 313–15.

BIBLIOGRAPHY

Primary Sources

Bundesarchiv Koblenz (B.K.)

B 106, Nr. 26030, *Bericht Bundesministerium der Justiz (Referent MR Götz) weitergereicht am Auswärtigen Amt*, Re.: 'Beleidigung des Schah', Bonn, 29 September 1971.

B 106, Nr. 28187, *Bericht des Bundesamt für Verfassungsschutz*, Re.: 'Die Ostemigration in der Bundesrepublik', Cologne, 11 March 1963.

B 106, Nr. 28187, *Dr. Hans Neuwirth (Vorstandsmitglied der Union der Vertriebenen in der CSU) an persönlicher Referent des Bundesinnenministers Dr. Fröhlich*: Re.: 'Verfehlte Behandlung des Ukrainerproblems', Munich, 12 July 1962.

B 106, Nr. 28187, *Bundesministerium des Innern – Vermerk an Ministerialrat Dr. Wolfrum*, Re.: 'Unterredung zwischen Rechtsanwalt Becher und MR Dr. Wolfrum', Bonn, 8 July 1970.

B 106, Nr. 28187, *Katholisches Büro (Bonn) an Bundesministerium für Inneres*, Re.: 'Schreiben des Kommissariats der Deutschen Bischöfe', Bonn, 8 July 1970.

B 106, Nr. 28191, *Bundesministerium des Innern – Bericht*, Re.: 'Ukrainischer Schulverein "Ridna Schkola"', Bonn, 27 February 1970.

B 106, Nr. 28217, *Brief Branimir Jelic an Bundesminister Kai Uwe von Hassel*, Re.: 'Hrvatski Narodni Odbor', Bonn, 14 June 1964.

B 106, Nr. 28217, *Bericht Ministerialrat Dr. Wolfrum*, 'Re.: Kroatisches Nationalkomitee', Bonn, 19 March 1970.

B 106, Nr. 28217, *Bundesamt für Verfassungsschutz – Bericht am Bundesinnenministerium*, Re.: 'Emigration – Kroatische Emigration u.A.', Bonn, 25 May 1970.

B 106, Nr. 28217, *Brief Dr. Wolfrum (Bundesministerium des Innern) an den Bundesrechnungshof*, Re.: 'Zuwendungen an das Kroatische Nationalkomitee im Lichte der bevorstehenden Zusammenlegungen', 6 July 1970.

B 106, Nr. 28191, *Brief Bundesministerium für Flüchtlinge und Vertriebene an das Bundespräsidialamt*, Re.: 'Empfang seiner Exzellenz des Kardinals Slipyi durch Herrn Bundespräsidenten', Bonn, 25 August 1969.

B 106, Nr. 31347, *Bundesministerium des Innern*, Re.: 'Maßnahmen gegen Französische Rechtsextremisten 1961–1967', Bonn, 1968.

B 106, Nr. 63084, *Loseblattsammlung Bundesministerium des Innern*, Re.: 'Vorwort', Bonn 1960.

B 106, Nr. 63084, *Loseblattsammlung des BMI zur Ostemigration*, Re.: 'Jugoslawien', Bonn, 1 April 1960.

B 106, Nr. 63084, *Loseblattsammlung Bundesministerium des Inneren zur Ostemigration*, Re.: 'Die Polen', Bonn, 1960.

B 106, Nr. 63084, *Sammlung des Bundesministeriums des Inneren zur Ostemigration*: 'Kroatische Nationalkomitee und andere Kroatische Organizationen', Bonn, 1961.

B 106, Nr. 63085, *Brief OUN-B Bundesministerium des Inneren*, Re.: 'Stellungsnahme zu der Unrichtigen Beurteilung des Politische Charakters der Organisation Ukrainischer Nationalisten (OUN)', Munich, 16 May 1962.

B 106, Nr. 63088, *Berichte – Bundesnachrichtendienst*, Re.: 'Aufstellung über die in der Bundesrepublik vorhandenen Organisationen heimatloser Ausländer', Pullach, 1960.

B 106, Nr. 63088, *Dossier des Bundesministerium für Inneres*, Re.:'Dokumente des Verfassungsschutzes Kroatischer Organisationen in der BRD betreffend', Bonn, 24 November 1960.

B 106, Nr. 63088, *Bericht des Bundesamtes für Verfassungsschutz am Bundesministerium des Innern*, Re.: 'Agitation und Terrorakte des Sowjetischen Geheimdienstes gegen die Ostemigration in der Bundesrepublik', Köln, 21 November 1961.

B 106, Nr. 63088, *Bundesamt für Verfassungsschutz Bericht*, Re.: 'Die Ostemigration in der BRD', Cologne, 11 March 1963.

B 106, Nr. 63985, *Loseblattsammlung des BMI zur Ostemigration*, Re.: 'Ungarn', Bonn, 1960.

B 136, Nr. 3799, *Bundeskanzleramt Bericht*, Re.: 'Politische Tätigkeit von Gastarbeitern', Bonn, 15 October 1965.

B 136, Nr. 3799, *Bericht – Bundesamt für Verfassungsschutz*, Re.: 'Infiltration ausländischer Gastarbeiter in der Bundesrepublik Deutschland', Cologne, September 1965.

B 141, Nr. 26028, *Generalstaatsanwalt Berlin an Bundesminister der Justiz*, Re.: 'Ermittlungsverfahren wegen Beleidigung des Schahs', Berlin (West), 19 June 1967.

B 141, Nr. 26028, *Iran/Schahbesuch*, Re.: 'Ermittlungsverfahren wegen Beleidigung des Schahs', Generalstaatsanwalt Berlin, 19 June 1967.

B 141, Nr. 26028, *Legationsrat Bach an das Auswärtige Amt Bonn*, Re.: 'Bericht über Deutsch – Iranische Beziehungen nach dem Schahbesuch', Teheran, 10 August 1967.

B 141, Nr. 26028, *Brief des Deutschen Botschafters an das Auswärtige Amt*, Re.: 'Besuch des Bundesinnenministers in Iran vom 9.–14. September 1967', Teheran, 13 September 1967.

B 141, Nr. 26028, *Schahdemonstrationen*, Re.: 'Bericht der Deutschen Botschaft Teheran über Besuch des Innenministers Lücke', Teheran, 13 September 1967.

B 141, Nr. 26028, *Iran/Schahbesuch, Deutsche Botschaft Teheran (Botschaftsrat Bach) an Bundesinnenministerium (Abteilungsleiter Winnefeld)*, Re.: 'Bericht der Deutschen Botschaft in Teheran über Besuch des Deutschen Innenministers den Schahdemonstrationen betreffend', 13 September 1967.

B 141, Nr. 26028, *Bundesministerium der Justiz – Hintergrundberichte über Iranische Studenten*, Re.: 'Teilnehmer an Demonstrationen beim Schahbesuch', Bonn, 19 October 1967.

B 141, Nr. 26028, *Interne Mitteilungen Bundesministerium Justiz*, Re.: 'VDS und Massali', Bonn, October 1967.

B 141, Nr. 26028, *Iran/Schahbesuch*, Re.: 'Bericht über mündliche Anfrage des Abgeordneten Borm über Demonstrationen beim Schahbesuch', 8 November 1967.

B 141, Nr. 26030, *Bayerische Staatsministerium des Inneren am Bundesministerium des Inneren*, Re.: 'Bericht über Aktionen und Demonstrationen Iranischer Studenten', Bonn, 2 November 1971.

B 141, Nr. 30834, *Berichte Bundesministeriums für Vertriebene*, Re.: 'Schnellbrief des Bundesministeriums für Vertriebene an Bundesministerium der Justiz', Bonn, 4 December 1962.

B 141, Nr. 30834, *Antwort des Justizminister Nordrhein-Westfalens bzw. Dr. Heimeshoff (Kanzlei des Landes NRW) an Anfrage des Herrn Bundesminister der Justiz bzw. Herrn Ministerialdirigenten Dr. Dreher*, Re.: 'Ermittlungen gegen Franjo Percic in Dortmund und Andere', Düsseldorf, 5 December 1962.

B 141, Nr. 30834, *Zusammenfassungen Politika 2–9 Dezember 1962 and Borba 3–8 Dezember vom Forschungsdienst Osteuropa*, Re.: 'Stellungnahmen der jugoslawischen Regierung und der jugoslawischen Presse zum Godesberger Vorfall vom 29. November 1962', Düsseldorf, 11 December 1962.

B 141, Nr. 30834, *Auszüge aus Sitzungen des Bundestages Jugoslawien betreffend – Bundesministerium des Inneren*, Re.: 'Auszug aus der 76. Sitzung des 4. Deutschen Bundestages 15. Mai 1963', Bonn, May–July 1963.

B 141, Nr. 30836, *Staatsanwaltschaft Bonn*, Re.: 'Strafsache gegen Franjo Percic u.A. wegen Sprengstoffverbrechens, Mordes, Geheimbündelei: Lebenslauf und persönliche Verhältnisse der Angeklagten', Bonn, 25 June 1964.

B 141, Nr. 30837, *Kommentar des Nordrhein-Westfälischen Innenministers zum Rundfunksender RIAS 'Zeitfunk'*: 'Zum Verbot der sog. Kroatischen Kreuzerbruderschaft', Düsseldorf, 12 March 1963.

B 141, Nr. 30837, *Interner Bericht*, Re.: 'Kroatische Emigrantenzeitungen: Eine Analyse', Bonn, 19 June 1964.

B 141, Nr. 30844, *Untersuchungsprotokolle*, Re.: 'Informationen der Staatsanwaltschaft Bonn über Angeklagter Pastor Rafael Medic-Skoko', 4 June 1963.

B 141, Nr. 258524, *MdB Peter Blachstein (SPD) and Bundesminister der Justiz*, Re.: 'Anti-Franco Flugblatt', Hamburg, 26 December 1963.

B 141, Nr. 258524, *Vorbereitung des Bundesministers des Innern – Fragestunde im Bundestag am 17., 18. und 19. Februar 1965*, Re.: 'Mündliche Anfrage des Abgeordneten Hans Matthöfer (SPD)', Bonn, 16 February 1965.

B 166, Nr. 1173, *Briefe des Auswärtigen Amtes am Verband Deutscher Studentenschaften und Bericht eines VDS Vertreters über Lage Im Iran*, Re.: 'Mitteilung Ungern-Stermberg an Dr. Gehlhoff', Bonn, 18 January 1964.

B 166, Nr. 1173, *Brief der Föderation der Iranischen Studenten an Verband Deutscher Studenstschaften*, Re.: 'Schikanen gegen Iranischen Studenten', Bonn, 4 June 1964.

Politisches Archiv des Auswärtigen Amtes Berlin (Pol. A.A.Ber.)

B 12, Nr. 450, *Referat 508 – Aufzeichnung des DG 31 an MD Freiherr von Welck*, Re.: 'Die Problematik der aus dem Machtbereich der Sowjetunion stammenden Emigration', Bonn, 18 December 1956.

B 12, Nr. 451, *Bericht – Ostlektorat*, Re.: 'Bandera, Stepan – ukrainischer Emigrant und Politiker', Bonn, 19 October 1959.

B 12, Nr. 451, *Bericht LR Ruete an Referat 991*, Re.: 'Erklärung des ZK des ABN im Zusammenhang mit dem Tode von Stefan Bandera', Bonn, 29 January 1960.

B 12, Nr. 451, *Bericht des Bayerischen Landesamts für Verfassungsschutz*, Re.: 'Die nationalistischen Organisationen der Ostemigranten (Jugoslawische Emigration – Stand: 15. Januar 1963)', Munich, 28 March 1963.

B 12, Nr. 455, *Bericht Ref. LR. Scholl/LR. von Staden*, Re.: 'Die Emigration aus der Sowjetunion und den von ihr beherrschten Gebieten', Bonn, 19 November 1956.

B 12, Nr. 455, *Bericht des Auswärtiges Amtes*, Re.: 'Die Emigration aus der Sowjetunion und den von ihr beherrschten Gebieten', Bonn, 19 November 1956.

B 12, Nr. 562, *Brief Dr. Cramer – Verband der Landsmannschaften an Auswärtiges Amt*, Re.: 'Bericht zur jugoslawischen Emigration von 1914 bis zur Gegenwart', Bonn, 1 June 1956.

B 12, Nr. 562, *Bericht Auswärtiges Amt an Bayerische Staatskanzlei*, Re.: 'Tatigkeit jugoslawischer Emigrantenorganisationen in der Bundesrepublik', Bonn, 25 March 1957.

B 12, Nr. 562, *Bericht des Forschungsdienstes Osteuropa am Auswärtigen Amt*, Re.: 'Kroatisch-Katholischer Klerus', Bonn, 11 June 1956.

B 25, Nr. 2, *Auswärtiges Amt – Aufzeichnung (gez. Leg. Janne)*, Re.: 'Unterredung mit SPD Abgeordnete Wischnewski', Bonn, 15 May 1961.

B 25, Nr. 9, *Bericht vom Bundesministerium des Innern (Algerierfrage)*, Re.: 'Vorbeugende Maßnahmen gegen politische Attentate in der Bundesrepublik', Bonn, 16 July 1959.

B 25, Nr. 9, *Aufzeichnung eines Gespräches mit MdB. Wischnewski (Leg. Dr. Weinhold)*, Re.: 'Algerienfrage und die BRD', Bonn, 15 May 1961.

B 25, Nr. 10, *Aufzeichnung einer Sitzung des Bundesministeriums des Innern*, Re.: 'Algerische Umtriebe in der BRD', Bonn, 12 October 1958.

B 25, Nr. 10, *Bericht – Bundeskriminalamt Sicherungsgruppe*, Re.: 'Erkenntnisse über eine französische Untergrundorganisation und über deren geplante Attentate gegen Waffenhändler unde andere mit den algerischen Aufständischen sympathisierenden Personen in der Bundesrepublik Deutschland', Bad Godesberg, 24 June 1959.

B 25, Nr. 13, *Bericht Politische Abteilung*, Re.: 'Attentat auf Ait Ahcéne', Bonn, 6 November 1958.

B 25, Nr. 13, *Abschrift eines Berichtes über Ermittlungen des Generalstaatsanwaltes bei dem Hanseatischen Oberlandsgericht an den Senat der Freien und Hansestadt Hamburg (Landesjustizverwaltung) und dem Auswärtigen Amt*, Re.: 'Ermittlungsverfahren wegen der Sprengstoffattentate auf den Waffenhändler Schlüter und auf den Dampfer "Atlas"', Hamburg', 20 May 1959.

B 25, Nr. 13, *Bundeskriminalamt (Bericht der Sicherungsgruppe am Auswärtigen Amt)*, Re.: 'Erkenntnisse über eine französische Untergrundorganisation (CATENA) und deren geplante Attentate gegen Waffenhändler und andere mit den algerischen Aufständischen sympathisierenden Personen in der Bundesrepublik Deutschland', Bad Godesberg, 24 June 1959.

B 25, Nr. 13, *Brief des Landesgeschäftsführers der CDU Landesverband Saar André am Legationsrat Dr. Frank (politische Abteilung des Auswärtiges Amtes)*, Re.: 'Gründung eines Hilfskomitees für algerische Flüchtlinge in Saarland', Saarbrücken, 6 February 1960.

B 25, Nr. 13, *Antwort an Herrn André (Landesgeschäftsführer der CDU Landesverband Saar)*, Re.: 'Gründung eines Hilfskomitees für algerische Flüchtlinge im Saarland, Bonn', 15 February 1960.

B 25, Nr. 13, *Schnellbrief des Bundesministeriums des Innern*, Re.: 'Gründung eines Vereines für ein freies Algerien in Saarbrücken', Bonn, 12 October 1961.

B 26, Nr. 134, *Bericht Legationsrat Walters an der Zentrale Rechtsschutzstelle*, Re.: 'Mertens', Bonn, 23 April 1959.

B 26, Nr. 161, *Bericht des Bundesamtes für Verfassungsschutz*, Re.: 'Kommunistische Infiltrationsversuche unter spanischen Arbeitern im Bundesgebiet', Köln, 16 April 1962.

B 26, Nr. 161, *Drahtbericht an der Deutschen Botschaft Madrid*, Re.: 'Sympathiekundgebungen spanischer Arbeiter', Bonn, 29 May 1962.

B 26, Nr. 161, *Aufzeichnung Auswärtiges Amt*, Re.: 'Sympathiekundgebungen spanischer Gastarbeiter in Köln am Sonntag, den 3. Juni 1962', Bonn, 2 June 1962.

B 26, Nr. 161, *Aufzeichnung – Besprechung Auswärtiges Amt mit Bundesarbeitsministerium und Bundesministerium des Innern*, Re.: 'Demonstration spanischer Gastarbeiter im Bundesgebiet', Bonn, 7 June 1962.

B 26, Nr. 161, *Aufzeichnung – Politische Abteilung*, Re.: 'Besprechungspunkte für das Gespräch für Herrn Erler', Bonn, 13 June 1962.

B 26, Nr. 161, *Auszug*, Re.: 'Spanische Stellungnahme zum Renger-Bericht', Bonn, 13 June 1962.

B 26, Nr. 161, *Bericht Botschaft Madrid an Auswärtiges Amt Bonn*, Re.: 'Spanische Innenpolitik – Treffen der Opposition in München und Gegenmassnahmen des Franco-Regimes', Madrid, 16 June 1962.

B 26, Nr. 161, *Aufzeichnung*, Re.: 'Spanische Teilnahme am IV. Kongreß der Europäischen Bewegung', Bonn, 18 June 1962.

B 26, Nr. 161, *Aufzeichnung*, Re.: 'Treffen der Opposition in München und Gegenmaßnahmen der Francoregierung', Bonn, 18 June 1962.

B 26, Nr. 161, *Vermerk*, Re.: 'Einstellung der SPD zum Spanien-Problem', Bonn, 18 June 1962.

B 26, Nr. 161, *Bericht des Bundesministerium des Innern*, Re.: 'Kommunistische Infiltrationsversuche unter spanischen Arbeitern im Bundesgebiet', Bonn, 3 July 1962.

B 26, Nr. 181, *Aufzeichnung*, Re.: 'Betreuung Spanischer Gastarbeiter in der Bundesrepublik – Kommunistische Infiltration und Deutsche Abwehrmaßnahmen', Bonn, 11 July 1962.

B 26, Nr. 206, *Diplomgerma Madrid (Drahtbericht)*: 'Bericht über Kundgebungen Spanischer Arbeiter', Bonn, 29 May 1962.

B 26, Nr. 256, *Brief des Bayerischen Staatsministeriums des Innern an Herrn Andreas Borakos*, Re.: 'Tätigkeit des "Koordinationskomitee für Cypernfragen" (SEKA) in München', München, 19 October 1964.

B 26, Nr. 256, *Bericht des Bayerischen Staatsministeriums für Bundesangelegenheiten*, Re.: 'Politische Betätigung griechischer Arbeiter und Studenten in München', Munich, 2 November 1964.

B 26, Nr. 420, *Brief Bayer. Staatsministerium des Innern an den Bundesminister Herrn Dr. Ernst Benda*, Re.: 'Politische Betätigung von Exilgriechen in der Bundesrepublik Deutschland', Munich, 5 October 1968.

B 26, Nr. 420, *Bericht des Bayer. Staatsministerium des Innern*, Re.: 'Politische Betätigung von Exilgriechen in der Bundesrepublik Deutschland', Munich, 5 November 1968.

B 26, Nr. 420, *Bericht Bayer. Staatsministerium des Innern am Auswärtigen Amt*, 'Re.: Politische Betätigung von Exilgriechen in der Bundesrepublik Deutschland', Munich, 22 November 1968.

B 26, Nr. 420, *Bericht Auswärtiges Amt Referat V3*, Re.: 'Politische und terroristische Betätigung von Ausländern und Emigrantenorganisationen in der Bundesrepublik Deutschland', Bonn, 10 September 1969.

B 26, Nr. 432, *Bericht der Botschaft Athen*, Re.: 'Freilassung von Mangakis', Athens, 18 March 1972.

B 26, Nr. 437, *Bericht Botschaft Athen,* Re.: 'Günther Grass – Besuch und Vortrag', Athens, 18 June 1971.

B 26, Nr. 437, *Bericht (der Botschaft Athen),* Re.: 'Kongress der Vereinigung der Griechen in Westdeutschland (in Saloniki)', Athens, 17 December 1971.

B 26, Nr. 437, *Berichte: Deutsches Generalkonsulat Thessaloniki,* Re.: 'Kongress der "Vereinigung der Griechen in Westdeutschland" in Saloniki', Thessaloniki, 30 August 1971 and 17 December 1971.

B 26, Nr. 438, *Berichte des BKA zur illegalen Tätigkeit griechischer Gruppen,* Re.: 'Zusammenarbeit mit SDS u.a.', Bonn, 31 January 1970 to 20 February 1971.

B 26, Nr. 438, *Bericht Deutsche Botschaft Athen an Auswärtiges Amt Bonn,* Re.: 'Festnahme eines dt. Ehepaares, das 15 Plastikbomben nach Griechenland einführen wollte', Athens, 18 December 1971.

B 26, Nr. 450, *Brief des Leiters des Katholischen Büros Bonn (Prälat Wilhelm Wöste) an dem Bundesminister des Auswärtigen (Walter Scheel),* Re.: 'Fragen der ausländischen Arbeitnehmer in der Bundesrepublik', Bonn, 18 June 1971.

B 26, Nr. 450, *Bericht – Politische Abteilung,* Re.: 'Verhaftung des spanischen Staatsangehörigen Carlos Pardo in Madrid', Bonn, 28 June 1971.

B 26, Nr. 450, *Bericht Auswärtiges Amt an die Deutsche Botschaft Madrid,* Re.: 'Illegale Tätigkeit spanischer Gruppen', Bonn, 6 August 1971.

B 26, Nr. 450, *Bericht Deutsche Botschaft and das Auswärtige Amt,* Re.: 'XI. Kongress der UGT in Toulose vom 2.–8.8.1971', Madrid, 14 September 1971.

B 26, Nr. 450, *Besprechung der beamteten Staatssekretäre im Bundeskanzleramt am 10. April,* Re.: 'Großveranstaltung der Kommunistischen Partei Spaniens in Frankfurt und anderen Orten des Bundesgebietes', Bonn, 30 April 1972.

B 26, Nr. 450, *Bericht des BfV,* Re.: 'Großveranstaltung der PCE in Frankfurt am 30. April 1972', Köln, 8 May 1972.

B 26, Nr. 450, *Auszug aus dem Kurzprotokell der 109. Kabinettsitzung der Bundesregierung am 3 und 5. Mai 1972,* Re.: 'Illegaler Aufenthalt des spanischen Kommunistenführers Santiago Carillo in der Bundesrepublik', Bonn, 9 May 1972.

B 26, Nr. 452, *Sekretariat des Außenministers,* Re.: 'Auszug aus dem Kurzprotokoll der 109. Kabinettsitzung der Bundesregierung am 3. und 5. Mai 1972: Bundesinnenminister Genscher zum illegalen Aufenthalt des spanischen Kommunistenführers Santiago Carillo in der BRD", Bonn, 9 May 1972.

B 26, Nr. 452, *Bericht der Politische Abteilung an der Deutschen Botschaft Madrid,* Re.: 'Deutsches Komitee zur Hilfe für demokratische Flüchtlinge e.V.' and Re.: 'Illegale Tätigkeit Spanischer Gruppen', Bonn, 6 August 1971 and 6 December 1971.

B 26, Nr. 452, *Aufzeichnung der politischen Abteilung des Auswärtigen Amtes,* Re.: 'Vorbereitung für Besprechung der beamteten Staatssekretäre im Bundeskanzleramtes – Großveranstaltung der Kommunistischen Partei Spaniens n Frankfurt und anderen Orten des Bundesgebietes am 30. April 1972', Bonn, 7 April 1972.

B 36, Nr. 40, *Aufzeichnung des Bundespräsidialamtes,* Re.: 'Informationsaufzeichnung für den Staatsbesuch des Herrn Bundespräsidenten in Iran', Teheran, 3 September 1963.

B 36, Nr. 40, *Botschaft Teheran/Bundespräsident Lübke,* Re.: 'Aufenthalt in Teheran', Teheran, 13 September 1963.

B 36, Nr. 40, *Botschaftsangelegenheiten,* Re.: 'Verbalnoten der Iranischen Botschaft', March 1962–September 1967.

B 36, Nr. 40, *VLR Dr. Meyer Lindenberg an den Stellvertetenden Chef des Protokolls von Borries*, Re.: 'Bericht über Demonstrationen von ausländischen Studenten im Raum Bonn', Bonn, 30 October 1963.

B 36, Nr. 41, *Interner Bericht des Auswärtigen Amtes*, Re.: 'Kommunistische Elemente unter iranischen Studenten', Bonn, 7 October 1963.

B 36, Nr. 107, *Dr. Ungern-Stermberg (Botschaft der BRD Teheran) an das Auswärtige Amt Bonn*, Re.: 'Politische Betätigung iranischer Studenten in der Bundesrepublik Deutschland', Teheran, 30 April 1964.

B 36, Nr. 107, *Berichte zu Beziehungen mit dem Iran*, Re.: 'Ermittlungsverfahren gegen persische Studenten: Berichte des Bundesamt für Verfassungsschutzes', Bonn, 1963–1967.

B 36, Nr. 108, *Berichte zu Beziehungen mit dem Iran*, Re.: 'Ermittlungsverfahren gegen persische Studenten: Berichte des Bundesamt für Verfassungsschutzes', Bonn, 1963–1967.

B 36, Nr. 108, *Bundesamt für Verfassungsschutz – Abteilung Schleswig-Holstein*, Re.: 'Vermerk über Tätigkeit des Iranischen Staatsangehörigen Massali', Kiel, 1 April 1964.

B 36, Nr. 294, *Botschaftsangelegenheiten*, Re.: 'Besuche des iranischen Botschafters', March–May 1967.

B 36, Nr. 294, *Vermerk, Botschaftsangelegenheiten*, Re.: 'Vorsprache des iranischen Botschafters', Bonn, 14 July 1967.

B 36, Nr. 294, *Bericht – Botschaft der Bundesrepublik Deutschland in Teheran and Auswärtiges Amt Bonn*, Re.: 'Deutsch-iranische Beziehungen', Teheran, 30 September 1967.

B 36, Nr. 294, *Mitteilung – Botschaft der Bundesrepublik Deutschland in Teheran an Auswärtiges Amt Bonn*, Re.: 'Beziehungen des Irans zur sowjetischen Besatzungszone', Teheran, 28 November 1967.

B 36, Nr. 294, *Bericht Abteilung I des Auswärtigen Amtes (VLR I Dr. Gehlhoff) an den Herrn Staatssekretär (i.V. Caspari)*, Re.: 'Hintergrund der Opposition iranischer Studenten gegen den Schah', Bonn, 3 September 1968.

B 36, Nr. 323, *Bericht Auswärtiges Amt Bonn an die Deutsche Botschaft Teheran*, Re.: 'Ausländerrechtliche Maßnahmen (Ausweisung) gegen iranische Staatsangehörige in Berlin', Bonn, 10 January 1967.

B 40, Nr. 37, *Mitteilung – Botschaft der Bundesrepublik Deutschland in Washington DC an Auswärtiges Amt Bonn*, Re.: Besuch – Ehemaliger ukrainischer Premierminister Yaroslav Stetzko', Washington, 7 March 1963.

B 40, Nr. 37, *Forschungsdienst Osteuropa – Bericht an das Auswärtige Amt-Legationsrat Dr. Dirnecker*, Re.: 'Bevorstehender Prozeß gegen die Ukrainer Staschinskyj/Aussage des MdL (CSU-Bayern) Herbert Prochazka u.a. an der Jahresversammlung der Deutsch-Slowakischen Gesellschaft', Düsseldorf, 27 April 1962.

B 40, Nr. 111, *Bundespresseamt*, Re.: 'Sonderdienst – Mord auf Befehl: Der Hintergrund des Prozesses gegen den politischen Doppelmörder Bogdan N. Staschynskij', Bonn, October 1962.

B 40, Nr. 111, *Aufzeichnung LR Pallasch*, Re.: 'Interministerielle Besprechung im Bundesministerium für Vertriebene über Förderungsmassnahmen für osteuropäische Emigranten, am 12. Dezember 1962', Bonn, 14 December 1962.

B 40, Nr. 111, *Ministerkonferenz – Bundesministerium für Vertriebene*, Re.: 'Förderungsmaßnahmen für osteuropäische Emigranten', Bonn, 14 December 1962.

B 40, Nr. 111, *Interner Bericht Auswärtiges Amt*, Re.: 'Emigrantenzuwendungen', Bonn, 28 July 1965.

B 42, Nr. 294, *Berichte über Iranische Angelegenheiten*, Re.: 'Majlis/Wahlen', Teheran, 25 October 1967.

B 42, Nr. 294, *Bericht Abteilung I des Auswärtigen Amtes (VLR I Dr. Gehlhoff) an den Herrn Staatssekretär (i.V. Caspari)*, Re.: 'Hintergrund der Opposition iranischer Studenten gegen den Schah', Bonn, 3 September 1968.

B 42, Nr. 435, *Griechenland – Innere Angelegenheiten*, Re.: 'Teilnahme von Theodorakis an einer Veranstaltung in Bonn', Bonn, 1 June 1972.

B 42, Nr. 568, *Emigrantenpolitik: Bericht des Innenministeriums Baden Württemberg am Auswärtigen Amt*, Re.: 'Beschädigung der jugoslawischen Flagge in Friedrichshafen', Stuttgart, 5 June 1962.

B 42, Nr. 568, *Fernschreiberbericht: Deutsche Botschaft Belgrad am Auswärtigen Amt Bonn*, Re.: 'Vorfälle Friedrichshafen – Grundsatzartikel Borba', Belgrade, 8 June 1962.

B 42, Nr. 568, *Aufzeichnung*, Re.: 'Verunglimpfung der jugoslawischen Flagge auf der internationalen Bodenseemesse in Friedrichshafen am 27.5. und 2. 6. 1962 – hier: Jugoslawischer Protest', Bonn, 22 July 1962.

B 42, Nr. 569, *Bericht Studiengruppe Südost München an das Auswärtige Amt Bonn*, Re. 'Die Kroatische Exil-Ustaschen', Munich, 1 December 1962.

B 42, Nr. 569, *Bericht Studiengruppe Südost an Auswärtiges Amt*, Re.: 'Die Kroatischen Exil-Ustaschen', Munich, 7 December 1961.

B 42, Nr. 569, *Prof. Dr. v. Mende – Forschungsdienst Osteuropa*, Re.: 'Darstellung der jugoslawischen Exilorganisationen in der Bundesrepublik', Düsseldorf, 10 December 1962.

B 42, Nr. 570, *Brief Geschäftsführender Präsidialmiglied vom Rat der Südostdeutschen, Dr. Josef Trischler, an das Auswärtiges Amt*, Re.: 'Entschließung der Bundesdelegierten tagung der Landsmannschaft der Deutschen aus Jugoslawien e.V.'

B 42, Nr. 570, *Bericht Forschungsdienst Osteuropa Düsseldorf*, Re.: 'Übersicht über die Organisationen der Emigranten aus Jugoslawien in der Bundesrepublik Deutschland', 31 December 1962.

B 42, Nr. 571, *Bericht Kriminalpolizei München an Auswärtiges Amt Bonn*: 'Abschrift eines Plakats', Munich, 16 July 1963.

B 42, Nr. 981A, *Bericht des Bundesministeriums für Flüchtlinge und Vertriebene*, Re.: 'Förderung von Osteuropäischen Exilorganisationen seit 1948', Bonn, 6 March 1968.

B 42, Nr. 1000A, *Polizeipräsidium Düsseldorf an Regierungspräsidium Düsseldorf*, Re.: 'Kroatische Emigrantenorganisationen – Mordversuch an 4 Exilkroaten', Düsseldorf, 18 August 1965.

B 42, Nr. 1000A, *Innenministerium des Landes Nordrhein Westfalen an Bundesministerium des Innern*, : 'Kroatische Emigranten – Mordversuch an 4 prominenten Exilkroaten in Düsseldorf am 30.6.1965', Düsseldorf, 8 September 1965.

B 42, Nr. 1000A, *Bericht Auswärtiges Amt Bonn Abteilung IIA5 and Referat V4*, Re.: 'Strafverfahren gegen Stanko Kardum wegen versuchten Totschlags/Attentat auf den jugoslawischen Konsul Klaric in Meersburg am 8. Juni 1965', Bonn, 1 December 1966.

B 42, Nr. 1000A, *Interne Anfrage des Auswärtigen Amtes an das Referat V4*, Re.: 'Strafverfahren gegen Stanko Kardum', 1 December 1966.

B 42, Nr. 1000A, *Bericht Französische Botschaft/Schutzmachtvertretung für deutsche Interessen Belgrad*, Re.: 'Prozess gegen den Exilkroaten Franjo Goreta vor dem Stuttgarter Schwurgericht', Belgrade, 5 May 1967.

B 42, Nr. 1000A, *Aide Memoire Abteilung II des Auswärtigen Amtes*, Re.: 'Tätigkeit Jugoslawischer Emigranten', Bonn, 31 October 1968.

B 42, Nr. 1007, *Konsularische Angelegenheiten*, Re.: 'Berichte des Konsulates Zagreb über Arbeitnehmer aus Jugoslawien, Gastarbeiter und Studiengruppen', 23 September 1963–8 February 1968.

B 42, Nr. 1324, *Bericht – Bundesinnenministerium des Innern*, Re.: 'Attentate, Brandstiftung u.A.', Bonn, 6 May 1969.

B 42, Nr. 1341, *Schreiben Bundeskriminalamt an Auswärtiges Amt*, Re.: 'Zusammenstellung von Erkenntnissen über jugoslawische Emigranten und Gastarbeiter, die in sicherheitsgefährdender Weise in Erscheinung getreten sind', Bad Godesberg, 5 August 1969.

Verhandlungen des Deutschen Bundestages

Anlagen zu den Stenographischen Berichten: Bd. 82–4. Wahlperiode, 7 December 1962 to 11 January 1963.

Drucksachen: Band 82, Bericht über 76. Sitzung des 4. Deutschen Bundestages, 15 May 1963.

Landesarchiv Berlin (L.B.)

B Rep. 015, Nr. 317, *Berichte über Verfassungsfeindliche Veranstaltungen*, Re.: 'Bericht über die auf der "Internationalen Vietnam-Konferenz" gehaltenen Reden, Berlin (West)', 17 February 1968.

B Rep. 015, Nr. 317, *Bericht über die Internationalen Vietnam-Konferenz am 17. Februar 1968 in West Berlin*, Re.: 'Gehaltenen Reden', West Berlin, 21 February 1968.

B Rep. 042, Nr. 27159, *Vereinsakte: Ukrainische Nationale Vereinigung*, Re.: 'Protokoll der Jahresversammlung der Mitglieder der Ukrainischen Nationalen Vereinigung e.V. vom 20. November 1937', Berlin, 23 November 1937.

B Rep. 042, Nr. 27159, *Bericht Ukrainische Nationale Vereinigung an Amtsgericht Berlin*, Re.: 'Vereinsakte 'Ukrainische Nationale Vereinigung', Berlin, 23 January 1940.

Bayerisches Hauptstaatsarchiv Munich (Bay. HstA. Mun.)

Findbuch OMGBY (Amerikanische Militärregierung Bayern): *Nr. 10/109–1/10, Reports/ German Staff*, Re.: 'DP Camps and Security: Report by Alfred Kiss, German Investigator ICD Augsburg', Augsburg, 25 November 1947.

Findbuch OMGBY (Amerikanische Militärregierung Bayern): *Nr. 10/89–1/33, CIC Reports/Intelligence Staff*, Re.: 'Ukrainian DP Meeting and Demonstration in Munich on 10 April 1949', Munich, 11 April 1949.

Landesflüchtlingsverwaltung: Nr. 702, *Bericht an das Bayer. Staatsm. d. Innern Abteilung I C 2*, Re.:' Propagandamaterial östlicher Herkunft', Munich, 24 October 1950.

Nr. 2242, *Niederschrift*, Re.: 'Über die gemeinsame Sitzung des Stiftungsrates und des Kuratoriums des Ost-Europa-Instituts in München am 12.11.1951', Munich, 13 November 1951.

Nr. 2242, *Brief Prof. Dr. März and Staatssekretät Prof. Dr. Oberländer*, Re.: 'Ostinstitut und die Zukunft von Dr. Hans Koch', Munich, 11 June 1962.

Nr. 2242, *Niederschrift des Bildungsministeriums*, Re.: 'Niederschrift über die gemeinsame Sitzung des Stiftungsrates und des Kuratoriums des Ost-Europa-Institutes am 12.11.1951', Munich, 13 November 1962.

Präsidium der Bereitschaftspolizei: Nr. 9/1, *Staatsbesuche*, Re.:'Staatsbesuch des Persischen Kaiserpaares: vorbeugende Maßnahmen', Munich, 23 May 1967.

Präsidium der Bereitschaftspolizei: Nr. 9/1, *Staatsbesuche*, Re.: 'Staatsbesuch des Persischen Kaiserpaares', Ansbach, 26 May 1967.

Nr. 127, *Bericht vom Bayerischen Landesamt für Verfassungsschutz*, Re.: 'Die Politische Struktur der Ostemigration', Munich, 1 April 1960.

Staatskanzlei: Nr. 13173, *Bayerischer Landtag, 7. Wahlperiode, Stenographischer Bericht,* 20. Sitzung: Fragestunde, Munich, 24 November 1971.

Staatskanzlei: Nr. 13173, *Brief Erwin Lauerbach (Staatssekretär im Bayer. Staarsministerium f. Unterricht u. Kultus) an Dr. hc. F.-J. Strauß a.D. MdB.*, Re.: 'Unterredung mit Griech. Ministerpräsident', Munich, 23 April 1972.

Staatskanzlei: Nr. 13173, *Deutsch-Griechische Beziehungen*, Re.: 'Griechische Vereine und Arbeiterkommissionen', April 1972.

Nr. 13316, *Iranisches Generalkonsulat 1953–1964, Berichte über Studentenunruhen*, Re.: 'Iranischen Studenten im Sitzstreik – vom Überfallkommando (der Polizei) aus dem Konsulat gewiesen', Munich, 11 July 1961.

Nr. 13324, *Auszug aus dem Stenographischen Bericht der 104. Sitzung des Bayerischen Landtags vom 29. März 1961*, Re.: 'Fall Vracaric', Munich, 30 November 1961.

Nr. 13324, *Auszug*: 'Auszug aus dem Stenographischen Bericht der 104. Sitzung des Bayerischen Landtags vom 29. November 1961 über die Ausführungen des Herrn Abgeordneten Dr. Wüllner zum Haushaltsplan des Staatsministeriums der Justiz (Epl. 04)', Munich, 30 November 1961.

Nr. 13324, *Bericht Polizeipräsidium München (Kriminalabteilung III) an das Bayer. Staatsministerium des Innern*, Re.: 'Sprengstoffanschlag auf das jugoslawische Generalkonsulat', Munich, 31 July 1972.

Nr. 13613, *Lageberichte zur Inneren Sicherheit 1969*, Re.: 'Gedenkfeier zum Tode Stepan Banderas', Munich, 11 October 1969.

Nr. 13616, *Lageberichte Innere Sicherheit 1968–1972*, Re.: 'Fernschreiberbericht – Exil-Ukrainische Kundgebung anlässlich des Besuches einer sowjetischen Delegation am KZ. Dachau', Munich, 3 September 1972.

Nr. 16164, *Handelsbeziehungen*, Re.: 'Zusammenarbeit mit Slowenische und Serbische Kommissionen', 1962–1971.

Nr. 16187, *Beziehungen zu Iran*, Re.: 'Feier des 2500 jährigen Bestehens der Persischen Monarchie in München', Munich, October 1973.

Nr. 16656, *Berichte über Innere Angelegenheiten*, Re.: 'Fall Mertens', Munich, April 1961.

Nr. 91890, *Ministerium des Innern, Clipping from Bild*, 'Bomben-Attentat bei Frankfurt –Auf Geheimsender der Exilrussen', Munich, 27 June 1957.

Präs. D. Bayer. Landpolizei: Nr. 3, *Bericht des Bayerischen Staatsministerium des Innern*, Re.: 'Abdruck einer Übersicht der im Bundesgebiet hauptsächlich verbreiteten Agitations und Propagandaschriften', Munich, 23 February 1967.

Nr. 111, *Brief – Bayer. Staatsministerium des Inneren to Bayer. Staatskanzlei*, Re.: 'Nationalfeiertage der Ostemigranten und der kommunistischen Ostblockstaaten', Munich, 4 February 1963.

Polizei Direktion München: Nr. 9280, *ABN – Propagandamaterial*, Re.: 'Freiheit den Menschen, Unabhängigkeit den Völkern – Die Sowjetrussische Ausstellung – Eine Provokation', Munich, 18 January 1968.

Polizei Direktion München: Nr. 9280, *Bericht KK III über eine öffentliche Veranstaltung*, Re.: 'Veranstaltung – Zentralvertretung der Ukrainischen Emigration in Deutschland e.V.', Munich, 11 January 1968.

Nr. 9374, *Bericht Kriminalabteilung III*, Re.: 'Veranstaltungen griechischer Vereinigungen', Munich, 11 August 1968.

Nr. 9374, *Bericht Abteilung KK III*, Re.: 'Veranstaltungsbericht – Nationalfeier 28.10.1940 am 3.11.1968 im Hackerkeller', Munich, 13 January 1969.

Nr. 9374, *Bericht KK III vom 13.4. 1970*: 'Übersetzung', Munich, 13 April 1970.

Nr. 9374, 'Dokumentation – Gefahr für griechische Demokraten in der Bundesrepublik Deutschland – Herausgeber IG Metall, Ortsverwaltung Hannover, H. Menius', Hannover, 7 June, 1970.

Nr. 9374, *Bericht – Polizeipräsidium Hannover an Regierungspräsident München*, Re.: 'Gewalttätige Ausseinandersetzungen zwischen Griechen am 11. und 12.4.1970 in Neustadt/Rbge.', Hanover, 26 June 1970.

Nr. 9377, *Bericht KK III*, Re.: 'Veranstaltungsbericht – Protest gegen die Militärjunta in Griechenland und die Wahlen am 29.9.1968', Munich, 26 September 1968.

Nr. 9381, *Bericht vom Bundeskriminalamt – Sicherungsgruppe 1Bad Godesberg*, Re.: 'Auswertungsbericht zu dem im Ermittlungsverfahren 2 BJ.s 22/65 des Herrn Generalbundesanwalts sichergestellten Beweismaterial – Tätigkeit des KOUNALAKIS für die "ENIAA DIMOKRATIKI ARISTERA (EDA)"', Bad Godesberg, 31 October 1965.

Nr. 9389, *Bericht Abteilung KK III*, Re.: 'Veranstaltungsbericht – Kundgebung gegen den Faschismus des PAE (Gesamtgriechische antidiktatorische Union=GAU)', Munich, 21 April 1968.

Nr. 9389, *Bericht Kriminalpolizei München Bay. Landesamt für Verfassungsschutz*, Re.: 'Kongreß der Antidiktatorischen Komitees in der Bundesrepublik', Munich, 3 April 1969.

Nr. 9394, *Rundschreiben des Polizeipräsidiums am BKA und sämtliche Landeskriminalämter*, Re.: 'Griechische Zentrumsunion, Parteiorganisation in der Bundesrepublik Deutschland', Bonn, 29 January 1968.

Nr. 9394, *Rundschreiben des BKA an das Bay. Landeskriminalamt usw.*, Re.: 'Griechische Zentrumsunion, Parteiorganisation in der Bundesrepublik Deutschland', Munich, 5 February 1968.

Nr. 9394, *Bericht Abteilung KK III*, Re.: 'Veranstaltungsbericht – Protestversammlung aus Anlaß des Jahrestages der Machtübernahme in Griechenland – 21. April 1968', Munich, 25 April 1968.

Nr. 9582/2, *Bericht KA III an Bayer. Staatsministerium des Innern*, Re.: 'Besetzung und Räumung des Kaiserlich Iranischen Generalkonsulats am 4. 8. 1970', Munich, 11 August 1970.

Nr. 9582/2, *Brief des Oberbürgermeisters Dr. Vogel an das Polizeipräsidium*, Re.: 'Angebliche Aushändigung einer Namensliste an den persischen Geheimdienst', Munich, 8 February 1971.

Nr. 17234, *Bericht Direktion der Schutzpolizei an der Kriminalpolizei München*, Re.: 'Schutzvorkehrungen anläßlich des kroatischen Nationalfeiertages', Munich, 10 April 1970.

Nr. 17234, *Bericht Heinz Thurnhofer (POM 26. Polizeirevier) an die Direktion der Schutzpolizei*, Re.: 'Ansammlung einer größeren Menschenmenge vor dem Südausgang des Hauptbahnhofes in der Bayerstraße', Munich, 12 April 1970.

Nr. 17234, *Bericht Heinz Thurnhofer (POM 26. Polizeirevier) an die Direktion der Schutzpolizei*, Re.: 'Ansammlung einer größeren Menschenmenge vor dem Südausgang des Hauptbahnhofes in der Bayerstraße', Munich, 12 April 1970.

Niedersächsisches Hauptstaatsarchiv Hannover (NHstA. Hann.)

NHstA. Hann., Nds. 100: Nr. 6, *Berichte zu Studentenunruhen*, Re.: 'Aktion Roter Punkt', May 1969–October 1969.

Nr. 9, *Berichte über Studentendemonstrationen*, Re.: 'Griechen', Hanover, November 1969.

Nr. 48, *Landeskriminalpolizeiamt Niedersachsachsen*, Re.: 'Ausländische Arbeitnehmer', Hanover, 8 September 1966.

Nr. 148, *Erfahrungsbericht des Landeskriminalamtes Saarland*, Re.: 'Die Aktivität der algerischen Aufständischen im Saarland', Saarbrücken, 19 September 1958.

Nr. 148, *Bericht des Landeskriminalamtes Niedersachsen*, Re.: 'Ausländerpolizeiliche Behandlung von Algerier', Hanover, 2 November 1959.

Nr. 148, *Vortragsvermerk für den Niedersächsischen Landesminister des Innern*, Re.: 'Ausländerpolizeiliche Behandlung der Algerier', Hanover, 2 November 1959.

Nr. 148, *Innenministerium – Ausländerangelegenheiten 1969-1979*, 'Re.: Vorbeugende Bekämpfung terroristischer Aktionen von Ausländern: Hintergründe', Hanover, 6 May 1967.

Nr. 148, *Bundes- und Landeskriminalämter*, Re.: 'Bericht der Unterkommision "Vorbeugende Bekämpfung terroristischer Aktionen von Ausländern"', Bad Godesberg, 7 May 1969.

Nr. 148, *Vermerk LKA*, Re.: 'Ausländer in Niedersachsen', Hanover, 23 February 1970.

Nr. 758, *Fernschreiberbericht Polizeidirektion Hannover an LKA Niedersachsen und LfV Niedersachsen*, Re.: 'Verfahren wegen Verdachts verräterische Beziehungen – spanischer Gastarbeiter', Hanover, 5 March 1963.

Nds. 120 Lün.: Nr. 37, *Aufzeichnungen Niedersächsisches Ministerium des Inneren zu Probleme nichtdeutscher Flüchtlinge*, Re.: 'Bericht über eine Tagung des Evangelischen Hilfswerks in der Ostdeutschen Akademie Lüneburg vom 3. Bis 5. April 1957', Hanover, 8 March 1957.

Nds. 147: Nr. 133, *Fallbericht des Niedersächsischen Landeskriminalamtes*, Re.: 'Fall Matuzic', Hanover, 19 June 1974.

Nr. 225, *Ermittlungsakte zu Sprengstoffanschlag am Griechischen Konsulat*, Re.: 'Beschwerden wegen Übersetzungspersonal', 7 September 1970.

Nr. 225, *Akten des Landeskriminalamtes zu Politische Bedrohungen/Anschläge 1960-1975*, Re.: 'Gewaltfälle – Griechen I 1965-1967', Hanover, June 1976.

Nr. 386, *Landeskriminalamt/Fremdenlegion*, Re.: 'Schematische Befragungen und Erlebnisberichte', Hanover, December 1957–July 1961.

Nr. 386, *Berichte zu Gewerkschaftsangelegenheiten*, Re.: 'Ermittlungsverfahren gegen griechischen Beamten wegen Erpressung griechischer Gastarbeiter um Austritt aus der Gewerkschaft zu erzwingen', Hanover, 24 August, 1970.

Nr. 386, *Untersuchung*, Re.: 'Staatsanwaltschaft Hannover – Ermittlungsverfahren gegen griechischen Beamten, u.a. wegen Erpressung griechischer Gastarbeiter (um Austritt aus der Gewerkschaft zu erzwingen) August 1970 – Juli 1971', Hanover, 24 August 197 and 18 July 1971.

Nr. 794, *Berichte des Landeskriminalamtes/Werbung für Fremden Wehrdienst 1952–1961*, Re.: 'Fremdenlegion 1956–1959', Hanover 1952–1961.

Nr. 1031, *Landeskriminalamt – Bericht*, Re.: 'Ausländische Organisationen – Spanier', Hanover, September 1974.

Nds. 721: Nr. 86, *Staatsanwaltschaft Hannover*, Re.: 'Strafsache wegen Körperverletzung 24. November 1968', Hanover, 12 August 1969.

Nr. 201, *Staatsanwaltschaft Hannover*, Re.: 'Ermittlungssache gegen Horacio Fernandez-Montez und Enrique Alonso Iglesias wegen Landfriedensbruch im spanischen Konsulat', Hanover, 16 December 1971.

Hauptstaatsarchiv Nordrhein Westfalen (HstA. NRW)

NW 308, Nr. 195, *Polizeipräsidium Bonn an Innenministerium des Landes NW*: 'Sprengstoffanschlag am 29.11.62 auf das Gebäude der Schwedischen Botschaft – Jugosl. Abt. – in Mehlem, hier: Vernehmungsprotokolle', Bonn, 22 February 1963.

NW 308, Nr. 195, *Auszüge aus Vernehmungsniederschriften*, Re.: 'Ermittlungsverfahren Percic u.a. wegen Sprengstoffverbrechens', Bonn, 26 February 1963.

NW 308, Nr. 195, *Vernehmungsniederschriften*, Re.: 'Auszüge aus Vernehmungsniederschriften zum Ermittlungsverfahren Percic u.a.', 135–204, 26 February 1963.

NW 308, Nr. 195, *Staatsanwaltschaft NRW*, Re.: 'Auflösungsverfügung gegen die "Kroatische Kreuzerbruderschaft e.v."', Düsseldorf, 8 March 1963.

NW 308, Nr. 195, *Verbotsverfügung – Bundesministerium des Innern*, Re.: 'Verbotsverfügung gegen der Kroatische Demokratische Ausschuß – Hrvatski Demokratski Odbor (HDO) – mit Sitz in Münster', Bonn, 7 September 1967.

Nr. 196, *Staatsanwaltschaft Bonn*, Re.: 'Auszüge aus Vernehmungsniederschriften zum Ermittlungsverfahren gegen Percic und Andere wegen Sprengstoffverbrechens', 7 January 1963.

Nr. 196, *Rundschreiben – Landesamt für Verfassungsschutz*, Re.: 'Kreuzerbruderschaft u. A.: Polizeiliche Überwachungsmaßnahmen', Cologne, 8 March 1963.

Nr. 196, *Justiz – Kroaten*, Re.: 'Verwaltungsrechtsache Kroatische Kreuzerbruderschaft Köln', 27 October 1965.

Nr. 196, *Akten des Nordrhein Westfälischen Innenministerium*, Re.: 'Verwaltungsrechtsstreit wegen Auflösung einer Vereinigung: Kroatische Kreuzerbruderschaft', 25 April 1966.

Nr. 197, *Willhelm Schöttler an NRW Innenminister Minister Willi Weyer*, Re.: 'Vorschläge zur Eindämmung kommunistisch-jugoslawische Umtriebe', Recklinghausen, 11 August 1965. *Süddeutsche Zeitung (S.Z.)*, 'Spendenlisten geben Aufschluß', 19 May 1964.

Nr. 197, *Korrespondenzen*, Re.: 'Brief NRW Innenminister an Wilhelm Schöttler', Düsseldorf, 11 August 1965.

Hauptstaatsarchiv Hessen Wiesbaden (HstA. H.W.)

Abt. 503, Nr. 1192, *Abschrift des Hessischen Landeskriminalamtes,* Re.: 'Erfahrungen über das Verhalten von Ausländern in der BRD – ENO (Europäische Neuordnung)', Frankfurt, 13 April 1962.

Nr. 3312, *Landesverfassungsschutz Hessen,* Re.: 'Verfassungsfeindliche Organisationen und Versammlungen 1950–1972', Wiesbaden , December 1973.

Bundesbeauftragte für Staatsicherheitsunterlagen (BStU) Berlin

Aktenreihe 000053/Ohnesorg: 'Schriftmaterial: "Folter und Terror", A. Hamann', Berlin, 1 June 1967.

Bibliothek des Abgeordnetenhauses Berlin

Stenographische Berichte des Abgeordnetenhauses: 5. Wahlperiode/12. Sitzung (1. Band).

Press Sources

Abendzeitung, 'Ein Augenzeugenbericht der Münchener Demonstrationen', 11 April 1949.

Abendzeitung, 'Was die Kommunisten Sagen', 11 April 1949.

Augsburger Allgemeine, 'Konsul Grabovac verließ Bunderepublik – Polizeieskorte brachte jugoslawischen Diplomaten zur österreichischen Grenze', Augsburg, 9 December 1961.

Bild Zeitung (Bild), 'Farah wird zweimal verzaubert', 27 May 1967.

Bild Zeitung (Bild), 'Buh-Rufe: Maskierte Männer an der Straße', 29 May 1967.

Bonner Rundschau (B.R.), 'Kroaten an der Grenze gefaßt', 3 December 1962.

Bonner Rundschau (B.R.), 'Propagandalawine erwarted die Urlauber des VW-Werks in Wolfsburg – Abstimungsergebnis der italienischen VW-Arbeiter mit Spannung erwartet', 16 December 1962.

Bonner Rundschau (B.R.), 'Gastarbeiterkinder sollen deutsche Sprache lernen – Kardinal Frings: Wohnungen für Ausländer bauen!', 2 May 1962.

Bonner Rundschau (B.R.), 'Trick mit Fremdarbeitern', 2 December 1963.

Bonner Rundschau (B.R.), 'Attentat ohne Vorbesprechung? Haupttäter Percic: "Ich trage die Verantwortung"', 17 March 1964.

Bonner Rundschau (B.R.), 'Schatzmeister der Kroaten fühlt sich von Jugoslawen bedroht', 2 April 1964.

Bonner Rundschau (B.R.), 'Tür als corpus delicti', 17 April 1964.

Bonner Rundschau (B.R.), 'Eid des Schweigens',14 April 1964.

Bonner Rundschau (B.R.), 'War kein Geheimbund', 15 April 1964.

Bonner Rundschau (B.R.), 'Persische Ärzte sollen KPD unterstützt haben: Gefängnis gefordert – Verteidiger: Die Angeklagten verdienen Respekt', 28 May 1964.

Bonner Rundschau (B.R.), 'Mildere Bestimmungen – Exil-Kroaten profitieren von Mauer-Anschlägen', 2 June 1964.

Bonner Rundschau (B.R.), 'Nach den Verteidiger-Plädoyers: Urteilsverkündung im Kroatenprozeß am Donnerstag', 19 June 1964.

Bonner Rundschau (B.R.), 'Tumult der Exilkroaten', 19 June 1964.

Bonner Generalanzeiger (B.G.), 'Deutsche Köche riefen "Viva España!" – Spanische Gastarbeiter demonstrierten – Polizei: Keine Zwischenfälle', 29 May 1962.

Bonner Generalanzeiger (B.G.), 'Bombenanschlag auf Jugoslawische Handelsmission', 30 November 1962.

Bonner Generalanzeiger (B.G.), 'Ordnungsstrafe für Kroaten wegen Beleidigung Titos', 23 May 1964.

Bonner Generalanzeiger (B.G.), 'Exilkroaten keine kriminellen Gewaltverbrecher', 12 June 1964.

Frankfurter Allgemeine Zeitung (F.A.Z.), 'München: das Dorado der Emigranten', 4 March 1963.

Frankfurter Allgemeine Zeitung (F.A.Z.), 'Bei den Kaiserlichen Majestäten aus Persien – Über den Gala-Empfang im Brühler Schloß Augustusburg', 29 May 1967.

Frankfurter Allgemeine Zeitung (F.A.Z.), 'Demonstrationen gegen den Schah: Wischnewski übt Kritik', 2 June 1967.

Frankfurter Allgemeine Zeitung (F.A.Z.), 'Eine Zumutung', 21 July 1967.

Frankfurter Allgemeine Zeitung (F.A.Z.), 'Kritik an der persischen Note', 28 July 1967.

Frankfurter Allgemeine Zeitung (F.A.Z.), 'Dementi aus der persischen Botschaft', 8 August 1967.

Frankfurter Allgemeine Zeitung (F.A.Z.), 'Verfahren wegen Beleidigung des Schahs: Anklage nur in Einzelfällen/Kein persisches Berichtigungsverlangen', 9 August 1967.

Frankfurter Allgemeine Zeitung (F.A.Z.), 'Für Persien Tragbar', 17 August 1967.

Frankfurter Allgemeine Zeitung (F.A.Z.), 'Schärfere Ausländerkontrolle zu spät gekommen?', 7 September 1972.

Frankfurter Rundschau (F.R.), 'Auch der zweite Start mißglückte – Hassan Ait Ahcene will nach Tunis zurück/Das unaufgeklärte Attentat', 8 December 1958.

Frankfurter Rundschau (F.R.), 'Belgrad schützt Botschaftsgebäude', 14 December 1962.

Frankfurter Rundschau (F.R.), 'Im Sonnigen Belgrad Reagierte man Besonnen', 17 December 1962.

Frankfurter Rundschau (F.R.), 'Persische Pervesion', 28 July 1967.

Frankfurter Rundschau (F.R.), Bernhard Schütze, 'Ich nenne den Schah einen Mörder und bitte um Strafe', 2 August 1967.

Frankfurter Rundschau (F.R.), '2000 erstatteten Selbastanzeige: Lauterkeitskampagne der "Schah-Beleidiger"', 10 August 1967.

Göttinger Tageblatt, 'Griechische Arbeiter Erpresst?', 25 February 1968.

Hannoversche Neue Presse (H.P.), 'Griechen-Spitzel im Arbeitsamt?', Hanover, 4 March 1969.

Hannoversche Neue Presse (H.P.), 'Griechische Botschaft: Wir Brauchen Keine Schläger', 21 April 1970.

Hannoversche Allgemeine Zeitung (H.A.Z.), 'Hannover ist nicht Athen', 16 April 1970.

Konkret, 'Messer, Knüppel, Eisenstange', 21 May 1970.

Münchener Merkur, 'Ukrainische Demonstration am Herkomerplatz', 11 April 1949.

Neue Revue, 'Ein Tag im Leben der Shahbanu Farah', 28 May 1967.

Neues Deutschland, 'Empörung und Erbitterung in der Studentenschaft', 4 June 1967.

Der Spiegel (D.S.), 'Nach Hause: Dafür sind wir Polen', 10 April 1948.

Der Spiegel (D.S.), 'Oberländer: Drittes Reich im Kleinen', 2 December 1959.

Der Spiegel (D.S.), 'Gastarbeiter: Lieber Piano', 10 April 1967.

Der Spiegel (D.S.), 'Griechische Gastarbeiter: Lieber Piano', 28 April 1967.

Der Spiegel (D.S.), 'Knüppel Frei', 9 June 1967.

Der Spiegel (D.S.), 'SAVAK: Spur in den 4. Stock', 12 October 1967.

Der Spiegel (D.S.), 'Griechen: Schwarze Krallen', 14 April 1969.

Der Spiegel (D.S.), '"Aus Unsere Seele": *Spiegel*-Interview mit dem Stellvertretenden Vorsitzenden des Berliner "Freundschaftskreises der CSU" Branko Jelic', 16 February 1970.

Der Spiegel (D.S.), 'Verbrechen: Griechen-Terror – Arm der Obristen', 27 April 1970.

Der Spiegel (D.S.), 'Griechenland Regime-Werbung: Reise Gratis', 8 June 1970.

Der Spiegel (D.S.), 'Liebesgrüße aus Belgrad', 17 May 1971.

Der Spiegel (D.S.), 'Terrorismus: Hals über Kopf', 19 July 1976.

Der Spiegel (D.S.), 'Ausländer: Graue Wölfe', 23 August 1976.

Der Spiegel (D.S.), 'Auf eigene Faust', 23 July 1979.

Der Spiegel (D.S.), Dieter Wild, 'Chomeini soll Leben', 23 November 1979.

Der Spiegel (D.S.), 'Graue Wölfe: "Jede Mark ist eine Kugel"', 14 June 1980.

Der Spiegel (D.S.), 'Fünfter Dan', 22 March 1981.

Der Spiegel (D.S.), 'Mußt du Schießen', 3 August 1981.

Der Spiegel (D.S.), '"Das ganze sieht nach Hinrichtung aus" Massaker an Albanern: Wie der jugoslawische Geheimdienst Killeraufträge in der Bundesrepublik besorgt', 25 January 1982.

Der Spiegel (D.S.), 'Tiefe Finsternis: Chomeini-Anhänger schlagen under Allah-rufen Chomeini-Gegner zusammen', 3 May 1982.

Süddeutsche Zeitung (S.Z.), 'Schwere Zusammenstöße in München', 11 April 1949.

Süddeutsche Zeitung (S.Z.), 'Grabovac verläßt München – Sicherheit des Konsuls nicht mehr garantiert, sagt das jugoslawische Generalkonsulat', 8 December 1961.

Süddeutsche Zeitung (S.Z.), 'Die Meisten distanzieren sich vom Terror', 13 December 1962.

Süddeutsche Zeitung (S.Z.), 'Vier Ausländer in der Bundesrepublik: Lob und Tadel im deutschen Gästebuch', 24/25/26 December 1962.

Süddeutsche Zeitung (S.Z.), 'Ein Strauß vom persische Paradestudenten: umfangreiche Sicherheitsvorkehrungen beim Schah-Besuch behindern einen herzlichen Empfang des Kaiserpaars durch die Bevölkerung', 29 May 1967.

Süddeutsche Zeitung (S.Z.), 'Perseraustausch Zum Schahbesuch – 107 müssen die Stadt verlassen/Kaisertreue Ersatzgruppe', 30 May 1967.

Süddeutsche Zeitung (S.Z.), '"Die hat ja gar keine Krone auf": Schah Reza und Farah wurden von Prominenten begrüßt, von Polizisten abgeschirmt und vom FC Bayern besiegt', 2 June 1967.

Süddeutsche Zeitung (S.Z.), 'Der Todesschuß fiel während der Zauberflöte', 5 June 1967.

Süddeutsche Zeitung (S.Z.), 'Offene Fragen im Fall Ohnesorg', 7 June 1967.

Süddeutsche Zeitung (S.Z.), 'Gedenkfeier am Grab Banderas', 13 October 1969.

Süddeutsche Zeitung (S.Z.), 'Griechische Botschaft in Bonn attackiert Greulich', 23 April 1970.

Süddeutsche Zeitung (S.Z.), 'In Kurze: Sowjetische Delegation in Dachau', 4 September 1972.

Die Welt (D.W.), 'Pablos Freunde ließen nicht locker – Das rote Netz der Dolores Ibarruri – Kommunistische Agenten beeinflussen spanische Gastarbeiter', 8 July 1962.

Die Welt (D.W.), 'Das rote Netz der Dolores Ibarruri – Kommunistische Agenten beeinflussen spanische Gastarbeiter', 12 July 1962.

Die Welt (D.W.), 'Scharfe Worte gegen Franco auf dem SPD Parteitag', 27 May 1962.

Die Welt (D.W.), 'Weichmann zog Bilanz des Schah-Besuchs – Dank an Hamburger – Trotzdem: "Schwarzer Tag für das Tor zur Welt"', 5 June 1967.

Die Welt (D.W.), Günter Zehm, 'Studentische Lust am politischen Rabatz – Die Radikalen tarnen sich als "Gute Demokraten"', 7 June 1967.

Die Welt (D.W.), 'Zeitlose Idealisten im Außendienst für Bayerns Idol', 13 March 1970.

Die Zeit, 'Studenten und die Obrigkeit – Sie sind keine Messerstecher', 16 June 1967.

Die Zeit, Heinz Grossmann, 'Die Jubelperser – Neue Methoden, Meinungen zu behindern, werden offenbar', 30 June 1967.

Recordings

Moesser, P. and L. Olias. 1958. *Der Legionär (Hundert Mann und ein Befehl)*, sung by Freddy Quinn, Copyright Polydor Records.

Books and Articles

Abrahamian, E. 1982. *Iran: Between Two Revolutions*, Princeton: Princeton University Press.

Aden, H. 1999. 'Das Bundeskriminalamt: Intelligence-Zentrale oder Schaltstelle des bundesdeutschen Polizeisystems?', *Bürgerrechte & Polizei/CILIP* 62(January), 6–17.

Adineh, D. and M. Schuckar. 1992. 'Iraner in Deutschland', in Berliner Institut für Vergleichende Sozialforschung (ed.), *Ethnische Minderheiten in Deutschland: Arbeitsmigranten, Asylbewerber, Ausländer, Flüchtlinge, regional und religiöse Minderheiten, Vertriebene, Zwangsarbeiter*, Berlin: Parabolis Verlag, 54–61.

Ahmad, F. 1993. *The Making of Modern Turkey*, London: Routledge.

Amiri, K. 1995. 'Die Iranische Minderheit', in C. Schmalz-Jacobsen (ed.), *Ethnische Minderheiten in der Bundesrepublik Deutschland*, Munich: C.H. Beck, 203–207.

Anaya, P.O. 2002. *European Socialists and Spain: the Transition to Democracy 1959–1977*, Basingstoke: Palgrave.

Angenendt, S. 1992. *Ausländerforschung in Frankreich und der Bundesrepublik Deutschland. Gesellschaftliche Rahmenbedingungen und inhaltliche Entwicklung eines aktuellen Forschungsberichtes*, Frankfurt a. M.: Campus.

Anweiler, O. 1977. '25 Jahre Osteuropaforschung – Wissenschaft und Zeitgeschichte', *Osteuropa* 27, 791–798.

Armstrong, J.A. 1990. *Ukrainian Nationalism*, 3rd ed., Englewood: Ukrainian Academic Press.

Aschmann, B. 1999. *'Treue Freunde...'?: Westdeutschland und Spanien 1945–1963*, Stuttgart: Franz Steiner Verlag (Historische Mitteilungen Nr. 34).

Bade, K.J. 1984. 'Die Ausländerbeschäftigung in der Bundesrepublik zwischen Arbeitswanderung und Einwanderung', in Klaus J. Bade (ed.), *Auswanderer – Wanderarbeiter – Gastarbeiter*, Ostfieldern: Scripta Mercaturae Verlag, 9–72.

Bade, K.J. 1994. *Ausländer, Aussiedler, Asyl: Eine Bestandsaufnahme*, Munich: Beck'sche Reihe.

Balfour, M. 1982. *West Germany: a Contemporary History*, London: Croom Helm.

Bark, D.L. and D.R. Gress. 1993. *A History of West Germany (Part 2): Democracy and its Discontents 1963–1991*, Oxford: Blackwell.

Becker, J. 1978. *Hitler's Children, the Story of the Baader-Meinhof Gang*, London: Granada.

Behrooz, M. 2000. *Rebels with a Cause: the Failure of the Left in Iran*, New York: I.B. Tauris.

Belosevic, D. 1995. 'Die Minderheiten aus den ehemaligen Jugoslawien', in C. Schmalz-Jacobsen (ed.), *Ethnische Minderheiten in der Bundesrepublik Deutschland*, Munich: C.H. Beck, 84–89.

Bender, P. 1986. *Neue Ostpolitik: Vom Mauerbau bis zum Moskauer Vertrag*, Munich: Deutscher Taschenbuch Verlag.

Bernitt, M. 1981. *Die Rückwanderung spanischer Gastarbeiter: Der Fall Andalusien*, Königstein: Hanstein Verl. (Materialien zur Arbeitsmigration und Ausländerbeschäftigung, Bd.7).

Beste, H. 2000. 'Feindbildkonstruktionen und Bedrohungsszenarien – Die Kurden', in H. Beste (ed.), *Morphologie der Macht*, Opladen: Lesle und Budrich, 373–402.

Bethlehem, S. 1982. *Heimatvertreibung, DDR-Flucht, Gastarbeiterzuwanderung (Geschichte und Gesellschaft, Bochumer historische Studien, Bd. 26)*, Stuttgart: Klett-Cotta.

von Beyme, K. 1976. *German Political Systems: Theory and Practice in the Two Germanies*, London: SAGE Publications (German Political Studies Volume 2).

Biess, F. 2001. 'Survivors of Totalitarianism', in H. Schissler (ed.), *The Miracle Years: a Cultural History of West Germany 1949–1968*, Princeton: Princeton University Press, 57–82.

Bingen, D. 1998. *Die Polenpolitik der Bonner Republik von Adenauer bis Kohl 1949–1991*, Köln: Nomos.

Blaschke, J. 1991. 'International Migration and East-West Migration. Political and Economic Paradoxes', *Migration* 11(12), 29–46.

Bogs-Maciejewski, H. 1988. *Was Jeder vom Verfassungsschutz Wissen Sollte*, Heidelberg: Becker c.f. Müller Verl.

Böke, K., M. Jung and T. Niehr. 2000. *Ausländer und Migranten im Spiegel der Presse – Ein diskurshistorisches Wörterbuch zur Einwanderung seit 1945*, Wiesbaden: Westdeutscher Verlag.

Bommes, M. 2001. 'Bundesrepublik Deutschland: Die Normalisierung der Migrationserfahrung', in K.J. Bade (ed.), *Einwanderungskontinent Europa*, Osnabrück: Universitäts Verl.

Boshyk, Y. (ed.). 1986. *Ukraine during World War II: History and its Aftermath*, Edmonton Canadian Institute of Ukrainian Studies.

Botsiou, K. 1998. *Griechenlands Weg nach Europa: von der Truman-Doktrin bis zur Assoziierung mit der Europäischen Wirtschaftsgemeinschaft 1947–1960*, Frankfurt a.M.: Peter Lang Verl. (Moderne Geschichte und Politik Nr. 14).

Brady, J.S., B. Crawford And S.E. Wiliarty (eds). 1999. *The Postwar Transformation of Germany: Democracy, Prosperity and Nationhood*, Ann Arbor: University of Michigan Press.

Brandt, W. 1982. *Links und Frei – Mein Weg 1930–1950*, Hamburg: Fischer Verlag.

von Braunmühl, C. 1973. *Kalter Krieg und Friedliche Koexistenz: Die Außenpolitik der SPD in der Großen Koalition*, Frankfurt, a.M.: Suhrkamp Verl.

Braunthal, G. 1996. *Parties and Politics in Modern Germany*, Amherst: Westview Press.

Brehm, T. 1989. *SPD und Katholizismus – 1957 bis 1966*, Frankfurt a.M.: Peter Lang Verl. (Erlanger Historische Studien Nr. 14).

Brodeur, J.-P., P. Gill and D. Töllborg. 2003. *Democracy, Law and Security: Internal Security Services in contemporary Europe*, Aldershot: Ashgate.

Broszat, M. 1972. *Zweihundert Jahre Deutsche Polenpolitik*, 2nd ed., Frankfurt a.M.: Suhrkamp.

Broszat, M. and L. Hory (eds). 1964. *Der Kroatische Ustascha Staat*, Stuttgart: Deutsche Verlagsanstalt.

Brown, J.F. 1991. *Surge to Freedom: the End of Communist Rule in Eastern Europe*, Twickenham: Adamantine.

Brubaker, R. 2001. 'The Return of Assimilation? Changing Perspectives on Immigration and its Sequels in France, Germany and the United States', *Ethnic and Racial Studies* 24(4), 531–548.

Bundesamt für Verfassungsschutz (ed.). 2000. *Bundesamt für Verfassungsschutz: 50 Jahre im Dienst der inneren Sicherheit*, Köln: Carl Heymanns Verl.

Burleigh, M. 2002. *Germany Turns Eastwards – a Study of Ostforschung in the Third Reich*, London: Pan.

Caglar, A. 1991. 'Das Kultur-Konzept als Zwangsjacke in Studien zur Arbeitsmigration', *Zeitschrift für Türkeistudien*, Nr. 31, 93–105.

Carr, R. 1982. *Spain 1808–1975*, 2nd ed., Oxford: Clarendon Press.

Carr, R. and J.P. Fusi 1981. *Spain: Dictatorship to Democracy*, 2nd ed., London: George Allen and Unwin.

Castles, S. 1998. *The Age of Migration: International Population Movements in the Modern World*, London: Macmillan.

Castles, S. 2000. *Ethnicity and Globalisation*, London: SAGE Publications.

Close, D.H. 2000. *Greece since 1945: Politics, Economy and Society*, London: Pearson Education.

Colosio, G. 1986. *Ausländische Arbeitsmigranten: Analyse und Bewertung ihrer Situation aus Theologischer und Ethnologischer Sicht*, Inauguraldissertation an der Katholisch-Theologischen Fakultät der Universität Tübingen, Tübingen.

Conföderation Iranischer Studenten (CISNU) (ed.). 1976. *Iran Report Extra: Ausverkauf eines unterentwickelt gehaltenen Landes – am Beispiel der wirtschaftlich-politischen Beziehung der BRD zum Iran*, Frankfurt a.M.: CISNU.

Connor, I. 2000. 'German Refugees and the Bonn Government's Resettlement Program: the Role of the Trek Association in Schleswig-Holstein 1951–3', *German History* 18(3), 337–361.

Conquest, R. 1986. *The Harvest of Sorrow: Soviet Collectivization and the Terror-Famine*, London: Hutchinson.

Conradt, D.P. 2001. *The German Polity*, 7th ed., New York: Longman Press.

Czerwick, E. 1981. *Oppositionstheorien und Außenpolitik: Eine Analyse sozialdemokratischer Deutschlandpolitik 1955-1966*, Königstein: Anton Hain (Studium zum politischen System der Bundesrepublik Deutschland Nr. 27).

Davies, N. 1991. *God's Playground: a History of Poland – Volume II 1795 to the Present*, 2nd ed. Oxford: Clarendon Press.

Diederichs, O. 1993. 'Die "Arbeitsgruppe Ausländer" der Berliner Polizei – eine Sondereinheit mit Doppelfunktion', *CILIP/Bürgerrechte und Polizei*, 45.

Dietz, B. 1997. *Jugendliche Aussiedler: Ausreise, Aufnahme, Integration*, Berlin: Spitz.

Dohse, K. 1981. *Ausländische Arbeitnehmer und bürgerlicher Staat*, Königstein: Hain.

Eccarius-Kelly, V. 2008. 'The Kurdish Conundrum in Europe: Political Opportunities and Transnational Activism', in W. Pojmann (ed.), *Migration and Activism in Europe since 1945*, New York: Palgrave Macmillan, 57–80.

Eryilmaz, A. and M. Jasmin. 1998. *Fremde Heimat*, Essen: Ruhr.

Esser, H. 1980. *Aspekte der Wanderungssoziologie: Eine Handlungstheoretische Analyse*, Darmstadt: Luchterhand.

Esser, H. 1983. 'Gastarbeiter', in W. Benz (ed.), *Die Bundesrepublik Deutschland: Band 2 – Gesellschaft*, Frankfurt a.M.: Fischer Verlag, 126–153.

Esser, H. 1990. *Generation und Identität: theoretische und empirische Beiträge zur Migrationssoziologie*, Opladen: Westdeutscher Verlag.

Esser, H. 1996. 'Die Mobilisierung ethnischer Konflikte', in K.J. Bade (ed.), *Migration, Ethnizität, Konflikt*, Osnabrück: Rasch, 63–87.

Evans, R.J. 1996. *Rituals of Retribution: Capital Punishment in Germany 1600-1987*, Oxford: Penguin.

Faist, T. 1994. 'How to Define a Foreigner? The Symbolic Politics of Immigration in German Partisan Discourse 1978–1992', in M. Baldwin-Edwards and M. Schain (eds), *The Politics of Immigration in Western Europe*, Newbury-Portland: Frank Cass, 50–71.

Falk, S. 1998. *Dimensionen Kurdischer Ethnizität und Politisierung: Eine Fallstudie Ethnischer Gruppenbildung in der Bundesrepublik Deutschland*, Baden-Baden: Nomos.

Farmer, K.C. 1980. *Ukrainian Nationalism in the Post-Stalin Era: Myths, Symbols and Ideologies in Soviet Nationalities Policy*, Boston: Martinus Nijhoff Publishers.

Fazel, R. 1985. 'Tribes and State in Iran: From Pahlavi to Islamic Republic', in H. Afshar (ed.), *Iran: A Revolution in Turmoil*, London: Macmillan, 80–98.

Featherstone, K. and D. Katsoudas. 1987. *Political Change in Greece: Before and After the Colonels*, New York: St. Martin's Press.

Fedyshyn, O.S. 1971. *Germany's Drive to the East and the Ukrainian Revolution 1917-1918*, New Brunswick: Rutgers University Press.

Fels, G. 1998. *Der Aufruhr der 68er – zu den geistigen Grundlagen der Studentenbewegung und der RAF*, Bonn: Bouvier Verl.

Finkel, A. and N. Sirhan (eds). 1990. *Turkish State, Turkish Society*, London: Routledge.

Foster, R. 1998. *Modern Ireland 1600-1972*, London: Penguin.

Freeman, G. 1978. 'Immigrant Labor and Working-Class Politics: the French and British Experience', *Comparative Politics* 11(1), 24–51.

Fulbrook, M. 1991. *Germany 1918-1990: the Divided Nation*, London: Fontana Press.

Fulbrook, M. 1995. *Anatomy of a Dictatorship: Inside the GDR 1949-1989*, Oxford: Oxford University Press.

Funk, A. 1991. "'Innere Sicherheit": Symbolische Politik und exekutive Praxis', in B. Blanke and H. Wollman (eds), *Die alte Bundesrepublik: Kontinuität und Wandel,* Opladen: Westdeutscher Verl, 367–388.

Funk, A. and W.-D. Narr. 1984. *Verrechtlichung und Verdrängung: Die Bürokratie und Ihre Klientel,* Opladen: Westdeutscher Verl.

Garton Ash, T. 1999. *The Polish Revolution: Solidarity,* 2nd ed., London: Penguin.

Gasiorowski, M.J. 1990. 'Security Relations between the United States and Iran, 1953–1978', in N.R. Keddie and M.J. Gasiorowski (eds), *Neither East Nor West: Iran, The Soviet Union, And The United States,* New Haven: Yale University Press, 145–165.

Gehrmacher, E. and E. Kubat. 1978. *Ausländerpolitik in Konflikt,* Bonn: Universitäts Verl.

Ghaseminia, M. 1996. *Zur Lebensituation und Integration Iranischer Staatsangehöriger in Niedersachsen,* Hanover: Universität Hannover.

Gilcher-Holtey, I. 2001. *Die 68er Bewegung,* Munich: C.H. Beck.

Gilmour, D. 1985. *The Transformation of Spain: From Franco to the Constitutional Monarchy,* New York: Quartet Books.

Glees, A. 1996. *Reinventing Germany: German Political Development since 1945,* Oxford: Berg.

Goebel, O. 1997. 'Gladio in der Bundesrepublik', in J. Mecklenburg (ed.), *GLADIO: Die Geheime Terrororganisation der NATO,* Berlin: Elefanten Press, 48–89.

Graaf, J. De and A.P. Schmid. 1982. *Violence as Communication,* London: SAGE Publications.

Grebing, H. 1990. *Flüchtlinge und Parteien in Niedersachsen – Eine Untersuchung der politischen Meinungs- und Willensbildungsprozesse während der ersten Nachkriegszeit 1945-1952/53,* Hanover: Hahnsche Buchhandlung Hannover.

Green, S. 2004. *The Politics of Exclusion: Institutions and Immigration Policy in Contemporary Germany,* Manchester: Manchester University Press.

Gröpl, C. 1993. *Die Nachrichtendienste im Regelwerk der deutschen Sicherheitsverwaltung – Legitimation, Organisation und Abgrenzungsfragen,* Berlin: Duncker und Humblot (Schriften zum Öffentlichen Recht, Band 646).

Grothusen, K.-D. 1977. 'Südosteuropa und Südosteuropaforschung. Zur Lage der Südosteuropaforschung in der BRD', in P. Nitsche, E. Oberländer and H. Lemberg (eds), *Osteuropa in Geschichte und Gegenwart,* Bohlau: Cologne, 408–426.

Grugel, J. and T. Rees. 1997. *Franco's Spain,* London: Arnold (Hodder Headline Group).

Hale, W. 1990. 'The Turkish Army in Politics 1960-1973', in A. Finkel and N. Sirman (eds), *Turkish State, Turkish Society,* Routledge: London, 53–78.

Hanrieder, W.F. and G.P. Auton. 1980. *The Foreign Policies of West Germany, France, and Britain,* New Jersey: Prentice-Hall Inc.

Hartung, K. 1987. *Der Blinde Fleck: Die Linke, der RAF und der Staat,* Frankfurt a.M.: Neue Kritik.

Heckmann, F. 1980. 'Einwanderung als Prozess', in J. Blaschke (ed.), *Dritte Welt in Europa,* Frankfurt a. M.: Syndikat.

Heckmann, F. 1981. *Die Bundesrepublik Ein Einwanderungsland?: Zur Soziologie der Gastarbeiterbevölkerung als Einwanderer-Minorität,* Stuttgart: Klett-Cotta.

Heldmann, H.-H. 1972. 'Araber-Hatz in der BRD: Schlimme Neuigkeiten aus unserer Fremdenrechtspraxis', *Vorgänge* 10(11), 298–303.

Heldmann, H.-H. 1989. *Verwaltung Versus Verfassung: Ausländerrecht 1965-1988, Europäische Hochschulschriften* Vol. 882, Frankfurt a.M.: Peter Lang Verl.

Heper, M. and J. Landau. 1991. *Political Parties and Democracy in Turkey,* London: I.B. Tauris.

Herbert, U. 1986. *Geschichte der Ausländerbeschäftigung in Deutschland: 1880–1980,* Berlin: J.H.W. Dietz.

Herbert, U. and K. Hunn. 2001. 'Guest Workers and Policy on Guest Workers in the Federal Republic', in H. Schissler (ed.), *The Miracle Years: a Cultural History of West Germany 1949–1968,* Princeton: Princeton University Press, 187–218.

Hermann, K. 1967. *Die Revolte der Studenten,* Hamburg: Christian Wegener Verl.

Hirsch, K. 1979. *Die Heimatlose Rechte: Die Konservativen und Franz Josef Strauß,* Munich: Wilhelm Goldmann Verl.

Hirschmann, K. 2001. 'Terrorismus in neuen Dimensionen: Hintergründe und Schlussfolgerungen', *Aus Politik und Zeitgeschichte* 51, 7–15.

Holmes, L. 1988. *Politics in the Communist World,* 2nd ed., Oxford: Clarendon Press.

Hooper, J. 1995. *The New Spaniards,* 2nd ed., London: Penguin.

Horchen, H.-J. 1988. *Die Verlorene Revolution: Terrorismus in Deutschland,* Herford: Busse Seewald Verl.

Horn, M. 1982. *Sozialpsychologie des Terrorismus,* Frankfurt a.M.: Campus.

Horne, A. 2002. *A Savage War of Peace: Algeria 1954–1962,* London: Pan Books.

Irvine, J.A. 1993. *The Croat Question: Partisan Politics in the Formation of the Yugoslav Socialist State,* San Francisco: Westview.

Irving, R. 2002. *Adenauer: Profiles in Power,* London: Longman.

Jacobmeyer, W. 1985. *Vom Zwangsarbeiter zum Heimatlosen Ausländer: Die Displaced Persons in Westdeutschland 1945–1951,* Göttingen: Vandenhoeck & Ruprecht.

Janssen, H. and M. Schubert. (eds). 1990. *Staatssicherheit: Die Bekämpfung des politischen Feindes im Inneren,* Bielefeld: AJZ Verl.

Junco, J. A. and A. Schubert. 2000. *Spanish History since 1808,* London: Arnold (Hodder Headline Group).

Katerberg, W.H. 1995. 'The Irony of Identity: an Essay on Nativism, Liberal Democracy, and Parochial Identities in Canada and the United States', *American Quarterly* 47(3), 493–524.

Katzenstein, P.J. 1987. *Policy and Politics in West Germany: the Growth of a Semisovereign State,* Philadelphia: Temple University Press.

Katzenstein, P.J. 1990. *West Germany's Internal Security Policy: State and Violence in the 1970s and 1980s,* Cornell: Western Societies Program (Cornell Centre for International Studies nr. 28).

Keddie, N.R. 1981. *Roots of Revolution: an Interpretative History of Modern Iran,* New Haven: Yale University Press.

Kersten, K. 1991. *The Establishment of Communist Rule in Poland 1943–1948,* Berkeley: University of California Press.

Kettenacker, L. 1997. *Germany since 1945,* Oxford: Opus.

Kevenhorster, P. 1974. *Ausländische Arbeitnehmer im politischen System der BRD,* Opladen: Westdeutscher Verl.

Kilcullen, D. 2005. 'Countering Global Insurgency', *Journal of Strategic Studies* 28(4), 597–617.

Klaric, Father J. (ed.). 2003. *Hrvatska Dijaspora u Crkvi i Domovini,* Frankfurt a.M.: Spengler's Druckwerkstatt.

Knipping, F. and K.-J. Müller. (eds). 1995. *Aus der Ohnmacht zur Bündnismacht – Das Machtproblem in der Bundesrepublik Deutschland 1945–1960,* Paderborn: Schöningh.

Koehl, R. 1957. *RKDV: German Resettlement and Population Policy – a History of the Reich Commission for the strengthening of Germandom*, Cambridge: Harvard University Press.

Korte, H. 1981. 'Entwicklung und Bedeutung von Arbeitsmigranten und Ausländerbeschäftigung in der Bundesrepublik Deutschland zwischen 1950 und 1979', in H. Mommsen (ed.), *Vom Elend der Handarbeit: Probleme historischer Unterschichtenforschung*, Konstanz: Hartung-Korre.

Korte, H. 1984. *Die etablierten Deutschen und ihre ausländischen Aussenseiter – Macht undZivilisation (Materialien zu Norbert Elias' Zivilizationstheorie 2)*, Frankfurt a.m.: Suhrkamp.

Kourvetaris, G. 1999. *Studies on Modern Greek Society and Politics (East European Monographs Nr. 534)*, New York: Boulder Press.

Kraushaar, W. 2000. *Die Protest Chronik 1949–1959: Volume 3*, Hamburg: Rogner und Bernhard.

Krippendorff, E. and V. Rittberger (eds). 1980. *The Foreign Policy of West Germany: Formation and Contents (German Political Studies – Vol. 4)*, London: SAGE Publications.

Krohn, C.-D. and L. Winckler (eds). 1991. *Exilforschung: Ein Internationales Handbuch – Exil und Remigration*, 9th ed., Munich: Edition text + kritik.

Kulyk, V. 2003. 'The Role of Discourse in the Construction of an Émigré Community: Ukrainian Displaced Persons in Germany and Austria after the Second World War', in R. Ohliger and K. Schönwälder (eds), *European Encounters: Migrants, Migration and European Societies since 1945*, Aldershot: Ashgate, 211–235.

Lampe, J.R. 1997. *Yugoslavia as History: Twice There Was a Country*, Cambridge: Cambridge University Press.

Laqueur, W. 1987. *The Age of Terrorism*, London: Weidenfeld and Nicolson.

Laqueur, W. 2001. *A History of Terrorism*, New Jersey: Transaction Publ.

Laqueur, W. 2003. *No End to War: Terrorism in the Twenty-First Century*, New York: Continuum.

Leggewie, C. 1990. *Multikulti. Spielregeln für die Vielvölkerrepublik*, Berlin: Rotbuch.

Lehmann, J. 1988. *Ausländische Arbeiter unter dem Deutschen Imperialismus: 1900–1985*, Dietz: Berlin.

Lehmann, J. 1988. 'Die Hypothek der Vergangenheit: Das Verhältnis der Bundesrepublik zu Spanien', *Hispanorama* 50, 78–82.

Leitner, H. 1983. *Gastarbeiter in der städtischen Gesellschaft: Segregation, Integration und Assimilation von Arbeitsmigranten am Beispiel jugoslawischer Gastarbeiter*, rankfurt a. M.: Campus.

Leitz, C. 1996. *Economic Relations between Nazi Germany and Franco's Spain 1936–1945*, Oxford: Clarendon Press.

Livingston, M.H. 1978. *International Terrorism in the Contemporary World*, Westport: Greenwood Press.

Lloyd, T.O. 1993. *Empire, Welfare State and Europe: English History 1906–1992*, 4th ed., Oxford: Oxford University Press.

Lohmann, R. 1974. 'Politische Auswirkungen auf die Bundesrepublik Deutschland', in R. Lohmann and K. Manfrass (eds), *Ausländerbeschäftigung und Internationale Politik*, Munich: Oldenbourg, 127–141.

Löw, K. (ed.). 1994. *Terror und Extremismus in Deutschland*, Berlin: Duncker u. Humboldt Verl.

Luciuk, L. 2000. *Searching for Place: Ukrainian Displaced Persons, Canada and the Migration of Memory*, Toronto: University of Toronto Press.

Luettinger, P. 1986. 'Der Mythos der schnellen Integration. Eine empirische Untersuchung zur Integration der Vertriebenen und Flüchtlinge in der Bundesrepublik Deutschland bis 1971', *Zeitschrift für Soziologie* 1, 20–36.

Mahrad, A. 1985. *Die Außenpolitik Irans von 1950 bis 1954 und die Aufnahme der Beziehungen zwischen Iran und der Bundesrepublik Deutschland (Sozialwissenschaftliche Studien zu internationalen Problemen Nr. 103)*, Saarbrücken: Breitenbach Verl.

Mandel, R. 1989. 'Turkish Headscarves and the "Foreigner Problem": Constructing Difference through Emblems of Identity', *New German Critique* 46, 27–46.

Markus, V. 1992. 'Political Parties in the DP Camps', in W.I. Wsewolod (ed.), *The Refugee Experience: Ukrainian Displaced Persons after World War II*, Edmonton: Canadian Institute of Ukrainian Studies Press, 111–124.

Marshall, B. 2000. *The New Germany and Migration in Europe*, Manchester: Manchester University Press.

Maruniak, W. 1994. 'Ukrainians in the Federal Republic of Germany', in A.L. Pawliczko (ed.), *Ukrainians throughout the World*, Toronto: University of Toronto Press.

Marvall, J. 1982. *The Transition to Democracy in Spain*, London: Croom Helm.

Meister, D.M. 1997. *Zwischenwelten der Migration: biographische Übergänge jugendlicher Aussiedler aus Polen*, Weinheim: Juventa-Verl.

Mensolff, A. 1996. *Krieg gegen die Öffentlichkeit: Terrorismus und Politischer Sprachgebrauch*, Opladen: Westdeutscher Verl.

Merseburger, P. 2002. *Willy Brandt: Visionär und Realist 1912–1992*, Stuttgart: Deutsche Verlags-Anstalt.

Merten, K. 1987. 'Das bild der Ausländer in der deutschen Presse', in G. Dallinger and D. Schmidt-Sinus (eds), *Ausländer und Massenmedien: Bestandsaufnahme und Perspektiven*, Bonn: Franz Spiegel Gmbh, 69–84.

Michaelis, L.O. 1999. *Politische Parteien unter der Beobachtung des Verfassungsschutzes – Die Streitbare zwischen Toleranz und Abwehrbereitschaft*, Baden Baden: Nomos Verlag. (Schriften zum Parteinrecht Nr. 26).

Milani, M.M. 1994. *The Making of Iran's Islamic Revolution: From Monarchy to Islamic Republic*, Boulder: Westview Press.

Miller, M.J. 1981. *Foreign Workers in Western Europe: an Emerging Socio-political Force*, New York: Praeger.

Milne, S. 2004. *The Enemy Within: The Secret War Against the Miners*, 2nd ed., London: Verso.

Ministerium für Arbeit, Gesundheit und Soziales (ed.). 1992. *Ausländer, Aussiedler und Einheimische als Nachbarn. Ermittlung von Konfliktpotenzialen und exemplarischen Konfliktlösungen*, Wuppertal: Ministerium für Arbeit, Gesundheit und Soziales des Landes Nordrhein-Westfalen.

Moeller, R.G. 2001. 'Remembering the War in a Nation of Victims: West German Pasts in the 1950s', in H. Schissler (ed.), *The Miracle Years: a Cultural History of West Germany 1949–1968*, Princeton: Princeton University Press, 83–109.

Moeller, R.G. 2001. *War Stories: the Search for a Usable Past in the Federal Republic of Germany*, Berkeley: University of California Press.

Morokvasic, M. 1993. *Krieg, Flucht und Vertreibung im ehemaligen Jugoslawien*, Berlin: Demographie Aktuell 2 (Humboldt-Universität).

Mueller M., and P.F. Müller. 2002. *Gegen Freund und Feind – Der BND: Geheime Politik und Schmutzige Geschäfte*, Hamburg: Rowohlt Verl.

Münz, R., *Zuwanderung nach Deutschland. Strukturen, Wirkungen, Perspektiven*, Frankfurt a.m.: Campus.

Naftali, T. 2004. 'Berlin to Baghdad: the Perils of Hiring Enemy Intelligence', *Foreign Affairs* 83(4), 126–129.

Nahaylo, B. 1999. *The Ukrainian Resurgence*, London: Hurst & Company.

Narr W.-D. 2001. 'Die arme Verfassung: Verfassungsschutz, V-Leute und NPD-Verbot', *Bürgerrechte und Polizei/CILIP*, 71.

Neumann, P.R. 2009. *Old and New Terrorism*, London: Polity Press.

Nicholls, A.J. 1997. *The Bonn Republic: West German Democracy 1945–1990*, London: Longman.

Nirumand, B. 1967. *Persien: Modell eines Entwicklungslandes – Oder: Die Diktatur der Freien Welt*, Frankfurt a. M.: RoRoRo aktuell.

Ohliger, R., K. Schönwälder and T. Triadafilopoulos. 2003. *European Encounters: Migrants, Migration and European Societies since 1945*, Aldershot: Ashgate.

Okey, R. 2001. *The Habsburg Monarchy 1765–1918*, London: Macmillan.

Østergaard-Nielsen, E.K. 1998. *Diaspora Politics: the Case of Immigrants and Refugees from Turkey Residing in Germany since 1980*, Thesis (D.Phil.), Oxford: University of Oxford.

O' Tuathail, G. 2000. 'The Postmodern Geopolitical Condition', *Annals of the Association of American Geographers* 90(1), 166–178.

Overmans, R. 1999. *Deutsche Militärische Verluste im Zweiten Weltkrieg*, Munich: R. Oldenbourg Verl. (Beiträge zur Militärgeschichte Bd. 46).

Özcan, E. 1989. *Türkische Immigrantenorganisationen in der Bundesrepublik Deutschland*, Berlin: Hitit Verl.

Padgett, S. and T. Burkett. 1986. *Political Parties and Elections in West Germany: the Search for a New Stability*, 2nd ed., London: St. Martin's Press.

Pagenstecher, C. 1994. *Ausländerpolitik und Immigrantenidentität zur Geschichte der 'Gastarbeit' in der Bundesrepublik*, Berlin: Dietz Bertz Verl.

Panayi, P. 2000. *Ethnic Minorities in Nineteenth and Twentieth Century Germany: Jews, Gypsies, Poles, Turks and Others: Themes in Modern German History*, Harlow: Longman.

Paterson, W.E. and Southern, D. 1992. *Governing Germany*, Oxford: Blackwell.

Pau, P. and Schubert, K. 1999. 'Bundesgrenzschutz: Eine omnipräsente und omnipotente Bundespolizei?', *Bürgerrechte & Polizei/CILIP* 62, 21–31.

Pedahzur, A. and L. Weinberg. 2003. *Political Parties and Terrorist Groups*, London: Routledge (Routledge Studies in Extremism and Democracy Nr. 2).

Pesaran, M.H. 1985. 'Economic Development and Revolutionary Upheavals in Iran', in H. Afshar (ed.), *Iran: a Revolution in Turmoil*, London: Macmillan, 15–50.

Pimlott, J. (ed.). 1997. *International Encyclopaedia of Terrorism*, London: Fitzroy Dearborn publ.

Pitsela, A. 1986. *Straffälligkeit und Viktimisierung ausländischer Minderheiten – Dargestellt am Beispiel der Griechischen Volksgruppe*, Freiburg: Max-Planck Institut für Strafrecht.

Pope, H. and N. Pope. 1997. *Turkey Unveiled: Atatürk and After*, London: John Murray Ltd.

Prantl, H. 2002. *Verdächtig: Der starke Staat und die Politik der inneren Unsicherheit*, Hamburg: Europa Verl.

Prokoptschuk, G. 1963. *Deutsch-Ukrainische Gesellschaft 1918–1963*, Munich: Deutsch-Ukrainische Ges. Verl.

Pulzer, P. 1995. *German Politics: 1945–1995*, Oxford: Oxford University Press.

Rabert, B. 1995. *Links- und Rechtsterrorismus in der Bundesrepublik Deutschland von 1970 bis Heute*, Berlin: Bernard & Graefe Verl.

Raschhofer, H. 1964. *Political Assassination: the Legal Background of the Oberländer and Staschinsky Cases*, Tübingen: Fritz Schlichtumage Verl.

Reid, A. 1997. *Borderland: a Journey through the History of the Ukraine*, London: Phoenix.

Reynolds, D. 2001. *One World Divisible: a Global History since 1945*, London: Penguin.

von Riekhoff, H. 1971. *German-Polish Relations 1918–1933*, Baltimore: Johns Hopkins University Press.

Rist, R.C. 1978. *Guestworkers in Germany: the Prospects for Pluralism*, Toronto: Toronto University Press.

Rohrbach, P. 1918. 'Ukrainische Eindrücke', *Deutsche Politik* 3, 53–56.

Rosati, D. 1998. 'Von den Baracken zur Kommunalwahl: Die Arbeit des ACLI', in R. Alborino and K. Pölzl (eds), *Italiener in Deutschland – Teilhabe oder Ausgrenzung?*, Freiburg im Breisgau: Lambertus, 83–93.

Roseman, M. 1997. 'The Federal Republic of Germany', in M. Fulbrook (ed.), *German History since 1800*, London: Arnold, 177–203.

Ross, C. 2002. *The East German Dictatorship: Problems and Perspectives in the Interpretation of the GDR*, London: Arnold.

Rothschild, J. 1993. *Return to Diversity: a Political History of East Central Europe since World War II*, Oxford: Oxford University Press.

Rudolph, H. 1996. 'Die Dynamik der Einwanderung im Nichteinwanderungsland Deutschland', in H. Fassman and R. Münz (eds), *Migration in Europa. Historische Entwicklung, aktuelle Trends, politische Reaktionen*, Frankfurt a. M.: Campus, 161–182.

Rydel, J. 2003. *Die polnische Besatzung im Emsland 1945–1948*, Osnabrück: Fibre Verl.

Sala, R. 2005. '"Gastarbeitersendungen" und "Gastarbeiterzeitschriften" in der Bundesrepublik (1960–1975) – ein Spiegel internationaler Spannungen', *Zeithistorische Forschungen* 3, 366–387.

Sampson, A. 1988. *The Arms Bazaar*, London: Cornet (Hodder and Stoughton).

Scharko, B. 1988. *Na Hromadsky Nivy*, Munich: Zentralverwaltung der Ukrainer in der Bundesrepublik Deutschland.

Scheffler, T. 1995. *Die SPD und der Algerienkrieg 1954–1962*, Berlin: Verlag das Arabische Buch (Forschungsschwerpunkt Moderner Orient Nr. 7).

Schenk, D. 2003. *Die Braunen Wurzeln des BKA*, Frankfurt a.M.: Fischer Verl.

Schmitter, B.E. 1980. 'Immigrants and Associations', *International Migration Review* 14, 179–192.

Schöneberg, U. 1985. 'Participation in Ethnic Associations: the Case of Immigrants in West Germany', *International Migration Review* 19(3), 426–31.

Schöneberg, U. 1992. *Gestern Gastarbeiter, Morgen Minderheit: Zur sozialen Integration von Einwanderern in einem 'unerklärten' Einwanderungsland*, Frankfurt a.M.: Peter Lang Verl. (Europäische Hochschulschriften 169).

Schönwälder, K. 2001. *Einwanderung und Ethnische Pluralität: Politische Entscheidungen und öffentliche Debatten in Großbritannien und der Bundesrepublik von den 1950er bis zu den 1970er Jahren,* Essen: Klartext.

Schultz, H.-E. 1990. 'Politische Justiz gegen eine "Auslandsvereinigung" und die Rolle des "Kronzeugen" als zentrales Beweismittel in schauprozeßartigen Mammutverfahren: Der PKK-Prozeß in Düsseldorf', in H. Janssen and M. Schubert (eds), *Staatssicherheit: Die Bekämpfung des politischen Feindes im Inneren,* Bielefeld: AJZ Verlag, 151–169.

Seidel, C.C. 2001. *Angst vor dem 'Vierten Reich': Die Alliierten und die Ausschaltung des deutschen Einflusses in Spanien 1944–1958,* Munich: Schöningh.

Sen, F. 1994. *Ausländer in der BRD: Ein Handbuch,* Opladen: Lesle und Budrich.

Sen, F. and H. Aydi. 2002. *Islam in Deutschland,* Munich: Beck'sche Reihe.

Silber, L. and A. Little. 1996. *The Death of Yugoslavia,* London: Penguin.

Singleton, F. 1993. *A Short History of the Yugoslav Peoples,* Cambridge: Cambridge University Press.

Smith, G., W.E. Paterson, P.H. Merkl And S. Padgett. (eds). 1992. *Developments in German Politics,* Basingstoke: Macmillan.

Smith, G., W.E. Paterson and S. Padgett. 1996. *Developments in German Politics 2,* Basingstoke: Macmillan.

Sobel, L. A. 1975. *Political Terrorism (Vol. 1),* Oxford: Clio Press.

Sobel, L. A. 1978. *Political Terrorism (Vol. 2),* Oxford: Clio Press.

Sökefeld, M. 2008. *Struggling for Recognition: the Alevi Movement in Germany and in Transnational Space,* Oxford: Berghahn Books.

Soysal, Y. 2000. 'Citizenship and Identity: Living in Diasporas in Postwar Europe?', *Ethnic and Racial Studies* 23(1), 1–15.

Spengler, B. 1995. *Systemwandel in Griechenland und Spanien: Ein Vergleich,* Saarbrücken: Peter Lang Verl. (Saarbrücker Politikwissenschaft Nr. 20).

Spiliotis, S.-S. 1997. '"An Affair of Politics, Not Justice": the Mertens Trial (1957–1959) and Greek-German Relations', in M. Mazower (ed.), *After the War Was Over: Reconstructing the Family Nation and State in Greece 1943–1960,* Princeton: Princeton University Press, 293–313.

Stefanski, V.-M. 1984. *Zum Prozeß der Emanzipation und Integration von Außenseitern: Polnische Arbeitsmigranten im Ruhrgebiet,* Dortmund: Forschungsstelle Ostmitteleuropa (Schriften des Deutsch-Polnischen Länderkreises der Rheinisch-Westfälischen Auslandsgesellschaft Nr. 6).

Stein, G. 1994. *Endkampf um Kurdistan?: Die PKK, die Türkei und Deutschland,* Munich: Aktuell.

Steinert, J.-D. 1995. *Migration und Politik: Westdeutschland-Europa-Übersee 1945–1961,* Osnabrück: secolo Verl.

Straßner, A. 2004. 'Terrorismus und Generalisierung – Gibt es einen Lebenslauf Terroristischer Gruppierungen?', *Zeitschrift für Politik* 4(51), 359–383.

Strikwerda, C. 1999. 'Tides of Migration, Currents of History: the State, Economy, and the Transatlantic Movement of Labor in the Nineteenth and Twentieth Centuries', *International Review of Social History* 44, 367–94.

Subtelny, O. 1989. *Ukraine: A History,* Toronto: University of Toronto Press.

Sypnowich, C. 2000. 'The Culture of Citizenship', *Politics & Society* 28(4), 531–55.

Szporluk, R. 2000. *Russia, Ukraine and the Breakup of the Soviet Union,* Stanford: Hoover Institution Press.

Tanner, M. 2001. *Croatia: a Nation Forged in War,* New Haven: Yale University Press.

Theobald, V. and M. Huppert (eds). 1998. *Kriminalitätsimport,* Berlin: Arno Spitz Verl.

Thomas, N. 2003. *Protest Movements in 1960s West Germany,* Oxford: Berg.

Toniolo, G. 1998. 'Europe's Golden Age, 1950–1973: Speculations From a Long-run Perspective', *Economic History Review* LI(2), 252–67.

Troche, A. 2001. *'Berlin Wird Am Mekong Verteidigt' – Die Ostasienpolitik Der Bundesrepublik un China, Taiwam Und Süd-Vietnam 1954–1966,* Düsseldorf: Droste (Forschungen und Quellen zur Zeitgeschichte, Band 37).

Ukrainische Freie Universität. 1962. *Satzung der Arbeits und Förderungsgemeinschaft der Ukrainischen Wissenschaften e.V.,* Munich: Ukrainische Freie Universität.

Ulfottke, U. 1998. *Verschlußsache BND,* Munich: Heyne Sachbuch.

Ulrich, R. 1994. 'Foreigners and the Social Insurance System in Germany', in G. Steinmann and R. Ulrich (eds), *The Economic Consequences of Immigration to Germany,* Heidelberg: Physica-Springer, 61–80.

Veremis, T. 1997. *The Military in Greek Politics – From Independence to Democracy,* London: Hurst & Company.

Wallraff, G. and A. Lengas. 1982. '"eine Vielzahl gemeinsamer Interessen"', in G. Wallraff and E. Spoo (eds), *Unser Faschismus nebenan: Erfahrungen bei NATO-Partnern,* Hamburg: Kiepenheuer und Witsch, 93–101.

Wallraff, G. and E. Spoo (eds), *Unser Faschismus nebenan: Erfahrungen bei NATO-Partnern,* Hamburg: Kiepenheuer und Witsch.

Weinhauer, K. 1998. *Schutzpolizei in der Bundesrepublik – Zwischen Bürgerkrieg und Innerer Sicherheit: Die Turbulenten sechziger Jahre,* Paderborn: Schöningh.

Weitz, E.D. 'The Ever-Present Other: Communism in the Making of West Germany', in H. Schissler (ed.), *The Miracle Years: a Cultural History of West Germany 1949–1968,* Princeton: Princeton University Press, 219–232.

Wierling, D. 2001. 'Mission to Happiness: the Cohort of 1949 and the Making of East and West Germans', in H. Schissler (ed.), *The Miracle Years: a Cultural History of West Germany 1949–1968,* Princeton: Princeton University Press, 110–126.

Wilpert, C. 1977. 'Children of Foreign Workers in the Federal Republic of Germany', *International Migration Review* 11(4), 473–485.

Winkler, B. 1994. *Was Heißt denn Hier Fremd?: Thema Ausländerfeindlichkeit und Verantwortung,* Munich: Humboldt Verl.

Winter, M. 1998. *Politikum Polizei – Macht und Funktion der Polizei in der Bundesrepublik Deutschland,* Münster: LIT (Politische Soziologie, Band 10).

Wölker, U. 1987. *Zur Freiheit und Grenzen der politischen Betätigung von Ausländern,* Berlin: Springer Verl.

Woodhouse, C.M. 1985. *The Rise and Fall of the Greek Colonels,* London: Granada.

Wsewolod, W.I. (ed.). 1992. *The Refugee Experience: Ukrainian Displaced Persons after World War II,* Edmonton: Canadian Institute of Ukrainian Studies Press.

Yurkevich, M. 1992. 'Ukrainian Nationalists and DP Politics', in W.I. Wsewolod (ed.), *The Refugee Experience: Ukrainian Displaced Persons after World War II,* Edmonton: Canadian Institute of Ukrainian Studies Press, 125–143.

Zonis, M. 1991. *Majestic Failure: the Fall of the Shah,* Chicago: University of Chicago Press.

INDEX